THE EMPLOYEE RIGHTS HANDBOOK

Effective Legal Strategies to Protect Your Job From Interview to Pink Slip

Steven Mitchell Sack
The Employee's Lawyer®

Revised and Enlarged Third Edition

Legal
Strategies
PUBLICATIONS
Merrick, New York

THE EMPLOYEE RIGHTS HANDBOOK
Effective Legal Strategies to Protect Your Job
From Interview to Pink Slip

By Steven Mitchell Sack
Attorney at Law

ISBN: 978-0-9636306-7-4
Library of Congress Control Number: 2010926886
Third Edition, Printed in the United States of America
0 9 8 7 6 5 4 3 2 1

DISCLAIMER

This publication is designed to provide accurate and authoritative information in regard to the subject matter covered. It is sold with the understanding that the publisher is not engaged in rendering legal, accounting, or other professional services. If legal advice or other expert assistance is required, the services of a competent professional person should be sought. *From a Declaration of Principals jointly adopted by a Committee of the American Bar Association.*

Cover and Page Design by One-On-One Book Production, West Hills, California.

To Bernard Sack,
my father of blessed memory,
who taught me that knowledge is power

To abused and mistreated workers everywhere

Also by Steven Mitchell Sack

The Salesperson's Legal Guide

Don't Get Taken: How To Avoid Everyday Consumer Rip-Offs

*The Complete Legal Guide to Marriage, Divorce,
Custody and Living Together*

The Hiring & Firing Book

*From Hiring to Firing: The Legal Survival Guide
For Employers in the 90's*

The Complete Collection of Legal Forms for Employers

The Lifetime Family Legal Guide

*Sales Rep Strategies For Dealing With Principals
Successfully*

The Working Woman's Legal Survival Guide

Lawyer on Call

Getting Fired

Acknowledgments

■ ■ ■ ■ ■ ■ ■ ■ ■

I would like to thank many individuals for assisting me in the preparation of this book.

Gratitude is extended to Diane Burak for her editing skills and diligence working with me while the manuscript was taking shape. I also appreciate the efforts and support of Larry Burak whose several years of enthusiasm for the project and my work never wavered.

Kudos are also given to Carolyn Porter and Alan Gadney of One-On-One Book Production for their assistance in the production and marketing of this book, Hillary Herskowitz of Blink Marketing Group for her publicity efforts, Jeremy Goldsmith and Steve Lillo at PlanetLink for creating my website, and Norma Jean Keefer for managing the website.

I also thank attorney Scott Lucas for his assistance in reviewing portions of the manuscript for accuracy and including numerous comments and additional valuable material throughout the work.

Fellow attorneys Scott Lucas, Stanley Spiegler, Michael Berger, Peter Hillman, Michael Mirotznik, Eric Stern, my brother Jonathan Sack, and others with whom I interact regularly must also be mentioned for their wisdom and guidance.

My literary agent Alex Hoyt, Laurence Alexander, and former publicists Donna Gould and Rick Frishman also played an important role in my literary career.

Special thanks are also extended to my wife Gwen and sons Andrew and David. Also, Dr. Subhi Gulati, Philip Sassower and family, my mother Judith, and my extended family and friends deserve praise for their encouragement.

As always, I wish to express my appreciation and gratitude to Bernard Sack, my father of blessed memory, whose insights and dreams helped make this book a reality.

Finally, special thanks must be given to all the legislators, lawyers, judges, and others who have enacted and enforce legislation to protect employees in the workplace.

Contents

■ ■ ■ ■ ■ ■ ■ ■ ■ ■

AGREEMENTS, FORMS, SAMPLE LETTERS, AND COMPREHENSIVE CHECKLISTS INCLUDED IN THIS BOOK

Author's Note

■   ■   ■   ■   ■   ■   ■   ■   ■

The information in this book is the author's attempt to reduce complex and confusing law to practical general legal strategies. These strategies are meant to serve as helpful guidelines and concepts to think about in all legal decisions affecting your job. They are not intended as legal advice per se, because laws vary considerably throughout the 50 states and federal system and the law can be interpreted differently depending on the particular facts of each case. Thus, please consider this author's note as a disclaimer or warning reminding you that it's critical to consult experienced counsel regarding the applicability of any strategy or point of information contained herein.

Every effort has been made to make this book as complete and accurate as possible. However, there may be mistakes, both typographical and in content. Therefore, this text should be used only as a general guide and not as the ultimate source of information. Furthermore, the book contains information that is current only up to the publishing date.

Additionally, the book is sold with the understanding that the publisher is not engaged in rendering legal, accounting, or other professional service. If legal advice or other professional assistance is required, the services of a competent professional must be sought. The author and publisher shall have neither liability nor responsibility to any person or entity with respect to any loss or damage caused, or alleged to be caused, directly or indirectly, by the information or use of the information contained in this book.

If you do not wish to be bound by the above, you may return this book to the publisher in reasonably good condition for a full refund.

Finally, fictitious names have been used throughout the work and any similarity to actual persons, places, or events is purely coincidental.

Introduction

■ ■ ■ ■ ■ ■ ■ ■ ■

Why You Need This Book

This book was written to save you money and aggravation.

I often compare a job to a romance. Companies woo applicants with promises of security, fulfillment, and riches. Then, when the honeymoon is over, even qualified people often find themselves being treated unfairly. Many employees are not promoted, despite doing good work, often because they are women, over forty, or belong to a minority. Many others are fired for no justifiable reason. Still others fail to receive anticipated financial benefits, including accrued vacation pay, overtime, commissions, earned bonuses, promised raises, or expenses.

You have the power to change that by reading this book. Years ago, when I became a lawyer in 1980, the law favored employers when it came to resolving employment disputes. It used to be that employers could fire workers with little fear of legal reprisal. But this kind of exploitation may be a thing of the past. More and more terminated workers are successfully arguing and proving that company promises made at the time of the hiring interview are binding on the employer. Terminated employees in the distant past would merely bow their heads and shuffle out the door after hearing they had been fired. Now most terminated workers are questioning those decisions and regularly negotiating better severance packages and other post-termination benefits.

The growing trend to protect workers is probably due to the fact that the law has finally grasped the concept that a job is an integral part of a person's life. Even the tens of thousands of independent sales reps and agents in this country who derive compensation in the form of commissions have received a boost from laws passed in more than 36 states. These laws guarantee prompt payment of commissions upon termination or resignation and award up to triple damages, plus reasonable attorney fees and costs of litigation, from companies who fail to pay reps in a timely fashion or who fail to comply with the appropriate state law.

From a lawyer's perspective, the creation of these and numerous other "pro-employee" laws such as the Age Discrimination in Employment Act, the Older Workers Benefit Protection Act, the Civil Rights Act of 1991, the Americans With Disabilities Act, the Family and Medical Leave Act, and the Worker Adjustment and Retraining Notification Act, to name just a few, was unthinkable when I started practicing law 30 years ago.

The idea for writing *The Employee Rights Handbook* began in the fall of 1984 when I was interviewed by the *Wall Street Journal* for an article about the rights of terminated executives. Individuals who read the article consulted with me to determine if they had any legal options after being fired. I began negotiating post-termination benefits for a large number of clients and was pleased when cash settlements and other perks were often obtained, demonstrating that a majority of private employers desire to explore amicable solutions to avoid legal expenses and costs, adverse publicity, and potential damages that sometimes arise after a firing.

The Employee Rights Handbook was first published by Facts on File, Inc. in 1991 and I received many positive letters and comments from readers. I began appearing on radio and television shows throughout the country talking about employee rights and gave interviews on the subject in national and regional newspapers and magazines. This led to my hosting a weekly live three hour radio talk show from 1999 through 2004 called "Steven Sack, the Employee's Lawyer" on the i.e. america radio network. A second edition of the book was published by Warner Books in 2000.

This third revised and enlarged edition takes off where the other works ended. I have added many new sections and updated information where the law changed over the past decade. New case decisions, trends, and developments have been incorporated into the text wherever possible. The result, I believe, is an even more valuable and timely body of work on employee rights for your use.

People should be able to benefit from the book regardless of their background, education, age, job experience, or work skills. *The Employee Rights Handbook* offers practical advice and hundreds of preventive steps to take to help you avoid many common problems. The tips and comments may prove to be invaluable. For example, you will learn how to be properly hired to reduce the chances of exploitation later. You will understand your on-the-job rights and how companies are obligated to deal fairly and in good faith with longtime workers. In many cases this prohibits employers from terminating workers merely to deny them an economic benefit, such as a pension, commission, bonus, or enhanced medical benefits, that has been earned or is about to become due.

The book will also instruct you on how to resign properly so you do not forfeit valuable benefits. Additionally, you will learn the correct steps to take when you are fired to protect your rights and increase the chances of obtaining severance compensation and other post-termination benefits. The material can reduce the odds of your being fired unfairly and give you ammunition to maximize claims if you are fired. For example, you will learn how to increase the odds of winning an unemployment or workers' compensation case.

Although the book was not meant to replace a lawyer, it will help you initially determine whether your problem requires a lawyer's assistance. If you currently have a lawyer, the information will help you make that lawyer work more effectively on your behalf, and it will enable you to make more intelligent choices and avoid being pressured into making decisions you may regret.

You will certainly become more aware of the legal consequences of your boss's actions. If litigation becomes necessary, the chances of success and the value of a claim may increase substantially by recognizing potential exploitation and knowing what to do about it. The book contains suggested courses of action to take before consulting a lawyer. Such advice may prove invaluable to your lawyer once he or she has been retained. But you will also discover that many of the strategies and suggestions can be followed without the help of a lawyer.

A goal in writing this book was to give you the practical information clients receive at a fraction of the cost. As my father of blessed memory used to say, "Knowledge is power," so I suggest you read the applicable sections before making a decision or when you have a problem. That is what "preventive law" is all about.

The Employee Rights Handbook addresses key topics where clients typically seek guidance to make it relevant and useful. Whatever your compensation level or the industry you work in, the sample letters to send, checklists to consult, and actual agreements in the book will help you learn the proper steps to take on your own and the right moves to make before contacting a lawyer if one is needed.

The Employee Rights Handbook covers areas where people are commonly exploited and misinformed, such as:

- Employees entering the job market for the first time who need to know what negotiating points to discuss, what to ask for, and how to protect themselves before being hired

- Seasoned workers experiencing on-the-job sexual harassment, pregnancy discrimination, invasion of privacy, defamation, and other problems

- Part-time workers not receiving proper overtime compensation, tips, or benefits

- Longtime workers suddenly fired for no apparent reason

- Employees denied expected benefits and compensation

- Individuals recently fired and denied reasonable severance, favorable job references, or unemployment benefits

- Female, minority, and older employees who wish to learn how to protect their jobs and earnings

- Union employees and people generally interested in knowing all of their rights before working, while on the job, and after their employment relationship has ended

The glossary at the end of the book will help you understand the meaning of many legal terms and concepts and apply them properly.

The benefits of applying this information can be significant. An employee worked a full year and was expecting a bonus of $22,500 to be paid on February 15 of the following year. The company had a policy of requiring workers to be employed on the date of payment in order to receive the bonus. The employee was fired on February 10 for alleged misconduct due to an unauthorized absence taken the day before. The employer refused to pay the bonus or severance and the client consulted me for guidance.

I advised that the company's actions were unfair and told him what to say. He immediately scheduled an appointment with a personnel director and explained that he had a valid excuse for missing work. He told the employer that he properly and timely reported the absence, and that he had met with an experienced employment attorney who advised that the company's policy of paying earned bonus only for people still employed the following year was unfair and perhaps discriminatory. Although the gentleman was unable to get his job back, he did manage to negotiate a generous severance package, which included a favorable letter of reference, unemployment insurance benefits, and the expected bonus.

The client later told me that workers at the company told him "to forget about it" before seeking my advice. That is the kind of assistance you will hopefully derive from *The Employee Rights Handbook*.

No one should take a job expecting the worst. However, this book can help you recover money for your efforts when you have been wronged. Every page of this revised and enlarged third edition of *The Employee Rights Handbook* was written to help you protect and enforce your rights. Deliberate effort was made to reduce complicated court rulings, regulations, and labor laws into effective legal strategies you can understand and follow.

For the millions of employees who think they have no rights in the working world, think again—you are about to learn that knowledge is power and that you have more rights in the workplace than you think!

Steven Mitchell Sack, Esq.
New York City, New York

PART I
■ ■ ■ ■ ■ ■ ■ ■ ■
How to Be Hired Properly

People are exploited in many ways when they look for a job. Some are victimized by discriminatory advertisements and brochures during job recruitment. Others are asked illegal questions during the job interview. Still others rely on phony promises or are subjected to various forms of job misrepresentation.

Chapter 1 covers problems sometimes encountered before hiring and suggests steps that can be taken to avoid such problems. The information will assist you in discovering how to reduce the chances of being misled by a job offer or being abused during the hiring interview. For example, you will learn when it is illegal for a potential employer to ask you to submit to a lie detector or drug test. You will understand just how far a potential employer can go in obtaining private credit and background information to verify your job qualifications. Additionally, you will learn answers to such questions as: Can you rely on statements of job security and other promises before you begin working? Are such promises binding? What effect, if any, do disclaimers have in employment applications, job descriptions, and letter offers?

This chapter also offers strategies to help you properly investigate an employer before accepting a job. Many individuals rush too quickly into jobs they know nothing about, often after resigning from a good job. They then discover that the new job is not what they expected in terms of remuneration or job duties.

Chapter 2 discusses how to be hired properly. The hiring phase is an important part of the employment relationship. During this phase you can increase your job security, acquire additional compensation and benefits, reduce misunderstandings, and protect your rights. Unfortunately, most workers do not understand or know how to accomplish this. They accept work without clearly defining the terms of their employment or negotiating for additional terms. Others forget to ask for a written contract; they shake hands with the new employer and assume that everything will go smoothly. Later when problems develop, they learn that their failure to negotiate properly has placed them at a serious legal disadvantage.

In this second chapter you will gain valuable information on how to negotiate for a job. You will discover why it is best to obtain a written contract and how to protect yourself when you don't receive one. The chapter contains a detailed checklist of key negotiating points to ask and insist upon, whatever job you are seeking. You will also learn how to clarify confusing points regarding bonuses, advances, and other compensation terms.

The chapter also contains points to avoid in any agreement, such as restrictive covenants (also known as covenants not to compete) and other onerous contract provisions. Finally, the chapter stresses the right questions to ask and correct steps to take before accepting any job.

■　■　■　■　■　■　■　■　■

Avoiding Pre-hiring Abuses

Most employers train and advise staff in charge of hiring applicants to correctly design advertisements and brochures, screen people carefully, avoid misrepresenting any job, fill a vacancy, and conduct the hiring interview legally to avoid charges of discrimination and breach of contract. Staff members are also taught how to properly investigate a candidate's references and statements on the employment application to avoid charges of defamation and invasion of privacy. Unfortunately, however, some employers do not follow the law.

Illegal Advertisements and Brochures

The prospective employee's first exposure to a company sometimes begins after reading an advertisement or brochure. Applicants should be concerned with two potential forms of exploitation in this area.

First, employers may use descriptions in ads and brochures implying that the job is secure. Words often used include "long-term growth," "permanent," "secure," and "career path." Such words may create an inference that the employer is offering a job that cannot be terminated except for notice or cause. However, most employers have no intention of giving workers additional job security despite such words in ads and brochures. (You will learn in the next chapter that the issue of job security is a point that should be negotiated and confirmed at the hiring interview so you know what kind of job protection, if any, you will be receiving.) Second, employers often draft advertisements and brochures that fail to comply with various federal and state discrimination laws. For example, employers are prohibited from publishing advertisements indicating any preference, limitation, specification, or discrimination based on age. Help-wanted notices containing phrases such as "age 25 to 35 preferred," "recent college graduate," "sales trainee, any recent degree," "sales executive, 2-4 yrs. out of college," and others of a similar nature may illegally discriminate against the employment of older persons when used in relation to a specific job.

Such laws apply equally to help-wanted advertisements that favor men over women, whites over blacks, or any other class of people to the detriment of protected minorities.

Proper advertisements list the job title and division in which the position is available, hours of work, salary and benefits, job duties and responsibilities, qualifications, and the deadline for applying. Typically, such ads contain the manner of a reply (i.e., by telephone, in person, through the mail, or e-mail). They also usually contain an EEO statement so that all applicants are notified that the employer does not discriminate on the basis of race, color, creed, or age.

STRATEGY: *If you read such an ad and believe it discriminates by denying you access to any job interview, contact your nearest Department of Consumer Affairs office, Equal Employment Opportunity Commission office, division of human rights office, or the state attorney general's office. You may be able to file charges and obtain damages or force the employer to rewrite the ad as a result.*

Employment Applications and Applicant Screening

Proper screening procedures begin with an accurate, detailed job description so that applicants know what type of job is being offered. Generally, candidates are requested to complete a formal application form pertaining to the candidate's educational background, work experience, references, and other pertinent information.

Many employers require candidates to sign lengthy employment applications. Be aware that most employment applications are used to undercut job security, reduce an employer's exposure to invasion of privacy lawsuits when investigating your past employment and credit information, and give the employer added grounds for immediate termination when false statements contained in the application are discovered.

The following language was taken from an employment application reviewed for a client:

> I acknowledge that I have given (name of company) the right to make a thorough investigation of my past employment, education, and activities without liability, and understand that any false answer, statement, or implication made by me in my employment application or at any job interview shall be considered grounds for my immediate discharge.
>
> If hired, I agree to conform to the rules and regulations of (name of company) in all respects. I understand that my employment with and compensation from (name of company) can be terminated at any time without notice or cause at the option of either of us. I also acknowledge that no representations or promises regarding continued employment for any specified period of time have been made to me during job discussions.
>
> Just as I am free to resign any time without notice, so may (name of company) terminate me at any time with or without cause and with or without notice. Upon my resignation or termination, I agree to return all company property in my possession or under my control at the company's request.

Most employment applications typically contain a space for the applicant's signature and date, particularly when disclaimers similar to the above are included. Be aware that if you do not allow the potential employer to investigate your background and work experience or if you refuse to sign such an application, you will probably not be considered for the job. Employers can insist on this requirement, and it is legal in most situations.

However, always review employment applications before signing them. Question ambiguous or misleading language. Some employers discriminate against certain applicants when only they, and not others, are required to fill out formal applications. And, just as some employers are guilty of asking illegal hiring questions at the formal interview, many employment applications contain illegal inquiries in personal areas involving your age, citizenship, disabilities, credit and garnishment history, arrest records, and other private matters. The following section will familiarize you with the kinds of questions that are illegal and must never be asked of you either directly at an interview or on a job application form.

Recognize that particular clauses in the application can and may be used against you at a later date. That is why you should request a copy of the employment application after you have signed it. This can minimize a frequent problem that arises when the application becomes a part of a job dispute or firing but you cannot locate (and the employer won't give you) the application in question.

Finally, be careful not to embellish your past work experience and qualifications. Most employers thoroughly investigate all statements made on job applications these days. Material misstatements are usually dealt with by immediate discharge when discovered, no matter how long or successfully the person has worked for the company.

Illegal Questions at the Hiring Interview

In the past, employers could ask almost any question they wanted of an applicant or employee. Questions could be asked about marital status, past arrests, alcohol and drug use, credit history, childbearing plans, or age. Now such questions are illegal.

The law has taken great strides to protect female applicants in this area. Questions pertaining to child care, marital status (for example, Who will look after your child if you are hired? Do you have children? What form of birth control, if any, do you use? If you became pregnant while working, would you continue to work? Are you married? Does your husband support your decision to work?), and related matters are illegal.

Generally, employers may ask questions to learn about a candidate's motivation and personality. Such questions can relate to former job responsibilities and outside interests. However, inquiries into an applicant's race, color, age, gender, religion, and national origin that further discriminatory purposes are illegal under Title VII of the Civil Rights Act of 1964, as amended. This law applies to private employers, employment agencies, labor organizations, and training programs.

Additionally, each state has its own discrimination laws, which often go even further in protecting the rights of applicants during job interviews. Companies must conduct pre-employment interviews properly to avoid liability, since innocent questions can often cause employers to face costly and time-consuming charges of discrimination filed with the federal Equal Employment Opportunity Commission and with various other human rights agencies, the Civil Liberties Union, and the state attorney general's office. If discrimination is found, an applicant may be awarded significant damages, including a job offer, attorney costs, and other benefits. Following enactment of the Civil Rights Act of 1991, successful claimants may also demand jury trials and receive compensatory damages (i.e., money paid for emotional pain and suffering) of up to $300,000, depending on the employer's size, and punitive damages, plus legal fees and money for expert witnesses who testify at the trial.

The following chart gives you a better understanding of the kinds of questions that are illegal under federal Equal Employment Opportunity Commission guidelines and state regulations. This chart should be used only as a guide, since some questions that are indicated as being illegal can be asked in certain situations (for example, where the applicant is applying for a security-sensitive job). Thus, the potential illegality of such questions must always be examined in the context in which they are asked.

Interview Questions and the Law

SUBJECT	LEGAL	ILLEGAL
Name	What is your full name? Have you ever worked under a different name? If so, what name? What is the name of your parent or guardian? (but only in the case of a minor job applicant) What is your maiden name? (but only to check prior employment or education)	Have you ever changed your name by court order or other means?
Residence	What is your address? How long have you been a resident of this state? of this city? What is your phone number?	Do you rent or own your home? How long have you lived in the United States? Do you live with someone? If so, what is your relationship with that person? Do you live in a foreign country?
Color		What is your skin coloring?
National origin		What is your ancestry? place of birth? What is your mother's native language? What is your spouse's nationality? What is your maiden name?
Citizenship	Are you a citizen of the U.S.? If not, do you intend to become one? Do you have a legal right to be employed in this country? Are you a native-born citizen?	Of what country are you a citizen? Are your parents or spouse naturalized or native-born citizens? When did they acquire citizenship?
Age	Are you old enough to work? Are you between 18 and 65 years of age? If not, state your age.	How old are you? What is your date of birth? Why did you decide to seek employment at your age?
Religion		What is your religion? Are you available to work on the Sabbath? What religious holidays do you observe? What church do you attend?

SUBJECT	LEGAL	ILLEGAL
Marital status	What is your marital status?	Are you dating anyone? Are you married, single, divorced, separated, engaged, or widowed? Which is more important to you, a family or a career? If you are single, are you living with anyone? If you have children, what are their ages? What would you do if your spouse was required to transfer out of state? Would you take time off under the Family and Medical Leave Act? Do you feel capable of supervising men? Where does your spouse work? What does your spouse do? When do you plan to marry? Do you plan on having children? Who will care for the children while you work? What is your spouse's health insurance coverage? How much does your spouse earn? What is your view on ERA? Are you a feminist? Do you advocate the use of birth control or family planning? Are you the head of the household? Are you the principal wage earner? Should we call you Mr., Mrs., Miss, or Ms.?

SUBJECT	LEGAL	ILLEGAL
Disability	Do you currently use illegal drugs? Have you ever been convicted for driving under the influence? Would you submit to a company-paid physical or provide a doctor's certificate of health after being offered the job?	What medications are you currently taking? Have you ever been treated for drug use? How often did you use drugs in the past? Are you an alcoholic? How much and how frequently do you drink? Do you have a disability that would interfere with your ability to perform the job? Have you ever filed for workers' compensation benefits? Have you ever been injured on the job? Do you have AIDS? Do you have cancer? Have you ever been treated for mental health problems? Have you ever been unable to handle work-related stress? How many sick days were you out last year? Why were you sick so often? Have you ever been compensated for injuries?
Job require-ments	Can you lift heavy objects with or without reasonable accommodations? (but only if the job directly requires this)	
Credit	If hired, would you allow us to order a credit report to confirm statements made on your employment application (provided you receive a copy)?	Do you have any credit problems? Have you recently filed for personal bankruptcy? Is your salary presently subject to legal attachment or wage garnishment?
Arrest record	Have you ever been convicted of a felony within the past seven years? Do you have a valid driver's license?	Have you ever been arrested? Have you ever pled guilty to a crime? Have you ever been in trouble with the law?

SUBJECT	LEGAL	ILLEGAL
Child-care responsi-bilities	Is there any reason that you will not be able to come to work every day, on time? (only if asked of all applicants)	Do you have any young children at home? Do you have a baby-sitter? How old are your children?
Language	Do you speak a foreign language? If so, which one?	What is your native tongue? How did you acquire the ability to read, write, and speak a foreign language?
Relatives	Names of relatives already employed by this company.	Names, addresses, age, and other pertinent information concerning your spouse, children, or relatives not employed by the company. What type of work does your mother/father do?
Organiza-tions	List all organizations in which your membership is relevant to this job.	List all clubs, societies, and lodges to which you belong.

The table demonstrates just how often job applicants are exploited in this area (since many illegal questions are typically regarded as routine).

You should also be aware that illegality sometimes arises when employers:

- Ask applicants for photographs before hiring
- Ask applicants for references from clergy before hiring
- Ask questions of females that are not asked of males
- Ask questions about the applicant's military service in countries other than the United States
- Ask questions about the applicant's military record or type of discharge

According to the Older Workers Benefit Protection Act, employers are forbidden from discussing or asking any questions pertaining to a person's age. Thus, if you are an older (i.e., over 40) job applicant and are told that you "lack formal education credits," "are overqualified," "are overspecialized," or that the company is "looking to hire someone with a more recent college degree," speak to an employment attorney if you are denied a job. It may be illegal for a company to refuse to hire an older applicant by arguing that being overqualified for a position means that the applicant is unqualified for the position. (Simply showing that a younger individual was hired over a qualified older applicant does not prove age discrimination if the employer can show that the decision was based on an honest evaluation of the candidate's qualifications; e.g., that the prospective employee would be bored or likely to leave upon finding a better job, or both.)

Employers are not permitted to ask questions about past arrests, since these often end in acquittal, dismissal, withdrawal of charges, or overturning of the conviction.

Be aware that employers sometimes design medical history forms that contain discriminatory questions. If you are asked discriminatory questions on a medical form or during a physical exam, you have the right to refuse to answer such questions. Thus, be sure to review all employment applications and forms to determine whether they contain discriminatory questions and be aware of improper questions during the interview. If you feel that a question is discriminatory, point this out to the interviewer. Be tactful. Explain that you believe the question is illegal and that you decline to answer it for that reason.

Some employers will appreciate your candor and may be impressed by your knowledge of the law. Others may feel you are a threat and may decline to offer you the job. However, if you feel you were denied a job based on a refusal to answer discriminatory questions, contact an appropriate agency to protect your rights. This includes a regional office of the division of human rights in your state, a local chapter of the Civil Liberties Union, or a regional office of the Equal Employment Opportunity Commission. If you work for a company with fewer than 15 employees, you should probably first contact a state or local antidiscrimination agency, since federal law generally applies to companies with 15 or more employees.

If you believe you were victimized, document your complaint by writing a letter similar to the one on page 14. Follow up the letter by contacting the agency to confirm that action is being taken to protect your rights. Speak to a lawyer to determine your options if you are not satisfied with the progress of the investigation. You should also consider filing a formal discrimination lawsuit through a private attorney (after an investigation by a state agency or the EEOC) if you were denied a job by refusing to answer discriminatory questions or furnishing answers to illegal questions. Sometimes it is not necessary to hire a lawyer because a state agency or EEOC will sue on your behalf.

STRATEGY: *Some applicants innocently provide illegal information. Employers are trained to circumvent the law at an interview by asking the applicant a general question such as "Tell us about yourself." The applicant then volunteers personal information the employer has no right to hear, such as "Well, I'm married to a teacher, we have two young children, and I desire a position with your firm because I'm bored of being a housewife and want to wait several years before having more children." Try to limit what you say and avoid volunteering personal information at an interview where possible.*

Recognize that discriminatory questions are often asked after the formal interview has concluded (for example, during lunch after the interview but before the decision to hire has been made). Answers to such questions may not be considered in the hiring process, and the ramifications of asking illegal questions in such informal settings are just as serious as when they are asked during a formal interview.

Sample Letter
to Protest Illegal Interview Questions

Your Name
Address
Telephone Number
Date

Name of Official
Title
Name of Agency
Address

Dear (Name of Official),

This letter is a formal protest against certain hiring practices of (name of employer), which I believe are illegal.

On (date) I was interviewed by (name and title of employee) for the position of (specify). The interview took place at (specify). During the interview, (name of employee) asked the following questions, which I believe were illegal under federal and state law: (specify).

I explained to the interviewer that such questions were improper and refused to answer them. The interviewer told me such questions were routinely asked of all job candidates and that the interview would be terminated immediately if I chose not to answer them.

The interviewer then told me I had "an attitude problem" and that the position was no longer available. Based on this, I believe I have been victimized by discrimination, since I am highly qualified for the job in question and was never given an adequate opportunity to display my qualifications.

I authorize you to investigate this matter on my behalf if it is determined that my charges have merit. You may also institute legal proceedings if appropriate. I am available to meet with you at your office at a mutually convenient date to furnish you with additional details and can be reached at (home address and telephone number). Thank you for your cooperation and attention in this matter.

Very truly yours,
Your Name

Sent certified mail, return receipt requested.

Unfair Job Requirements

Are you a member of a protected minority (for example, a person of color, female, person over forty) who has been barred from applying for a job on the basis of your education or skills? If so, is the education or skills requirement specified in the ad, recruiting brochure, or employment opportunity notice really necessary to do the job properly? If not, you may have a valid discrimination claim.

When employers set a higher requirement than is needed for a job just to attract a different kind of applicant, they sometimes inadvertently discriminate against a particular class of applicant; this is illegal.

For example, in the case of *United States v. Georgia Power Company*, the requirements of a high school diploma and aptitude test scores by the employer raised a question as to whether such requirements were really related to successful job performance. The diploma requirement was found to be unlawful, since it did not measure an individual's ability to do the job. In fact, the court determined that since blacks, as opposed to whites, were more likely not to have completed high school in Georgia in the late 1960s and early 1970s, such a requirement essentially excluded them from working for the company.

Thus, if you are a member of a protected minority and believe you are being unfairly excluded from applying for employment due to unfair job requirements, you may wish to speak to a representative from a regional office of the federal Equal Employment Opportunity Commission or state division of human rights.

Disabled Applicants

Due to the enactment of the Americans with Disabilities Act (ADA), employers must be certain that recruitment and job application procedures do not discriminate against qualified job applicants based on their disabilities. Many knowledgeable companies have written their ads so that the following (or similar) words are present: "Our company is an Equal Opportunity Employer and does not discriminate on the basis of a physical or mental handicap."

Employers are required to take reasonable steps to accommodate the needs of handicapped workers under federal and state law. Persons with disabilities cannot be disqualified from applying because of the inability to perform nonessential or marginal functions of the job; proper language in job advertisements can demonstrate a company's desire to comply with the law and not initially exclude qualified but disabled applicants from the potential job pool.

Under the ADA, an employer may deny a job to an individual with a disability if the individual fails to meet a selected criterion under the act. However, a disabled applicant can only be rejected if the person cannot perform essential job functions, even with reasonable accommodation. You cannot be disqualified because of an inability to perform nonessential or marginal functions of the job.

The following is a good summary of rules to remember in this area:

1. Employers must avoid disability-related questions in interviews or questions about your ability to perform specific job-related tasks or requirements.

2. Employers cannot inquire what kind of accommodation the person needs in order to perform the job properly if hired.

3. A medical exam can only be requested after hiring and provided it is a condition of employment for all entering employees in that position.

Immigration Checks

The Immigration Reform and Control Act of 1986 (IRCA) states that employers should hire only U.S. citizens and aliens who are authorized to work in the United States. The law requires every employer to verify the employment eligibility of every worker hired to avoid civil fines and criminal penalties for failure to comply with the law's record-keeping requirements. Companies must follow fixed guidelines regardless of company size or the number of employees being hired. The Immigration and Naturalization Service (INS) has developed a form (I-9) that employers must complete and retain in order to verify employment eligibility for all employees.

Essentially, employers have five verification obligations:

1. Employees must be instructed to fill out their portion of Form I-9 when they begin work.

2. Employers must check documents establishing employees' identity and eligibility to work.

3. Employers must properly complete the remaining portion of Form I-9.

4. Employers must retain the form for at least three years or until one year after a person leaves employment, whichever is later.

5. Employers must present the form for inspection to INS or Department of Labor officials upon request after three days' advance notice.

All companies must verify the identity and work authorization of every person hired. Evidence must be examined, collected, and saved by the employer to refute charges that it knew it was hiring an unauthorized alien.

Form I-9 must be completed and attested to by the new employee at the time of hiring; the company must review all documentation and submit the form within three business days of the hiring. The applicant has 21 additional business days to furnish documents that are lost or not yet processed. Copies of the INS form may be obtained from any district INS office and photocopied for future use by other applicants.

All completed I-9 forms must be saved for at least three years after the hiring, or for one year after the person is terminated, whichever occurs later; these rules apply to temporary workers and independent contractors as well. However, companies are not obligated to verify employment eligibility for people working as employees for such independent contractors.

Employers failing to follow the law are currently liable for fines ranging from $250 to $2,000 for each unauthorized alien hiring for a first offense; $2,000 to $5,000 for each unauthorized alien for a second offense; and $3,000 to $10,000 for each unauthorized alien for subsequent offenses. The law also imposes criminal penalties against companies and their principal officers up to $3,000 for each unauthorized alien with respect to whom a violation occurs, or imprisonment for not more than six months, or both.

STRATEGY: *Speak to an employment attorney or contact a regional office of the EEOC or state discrimination agency if you believe that, although you are a U.S. citizen, you were denied a job because of a foreign accent, are foreign born, or were required to take a fluency exam or other tests not given to native-born applicants. Although the company may be acting properly pursuant to IRCA, it may nonetheless be violating your Title VII discrimination rights pursuant to the Civil Rights Act of 1964, as amended.*

Background Checks

Background checks often provide employers with helpful information about a job applicant, especially to discover if false or misleading information was provided in an employment application (e.g., an overstatement of educational degrees). Certain jobs, such as those dealing with children, the elderly, or disabled require screening under federal and state laws. Companies in the financial and banking industries conduct background checks to determine the creditworthiness of potential employees who will handle money or engage in financial transactions. Other employers, to avoid claims of negligent hiring and retention, are particularly interested in learning more about an individual's criminal history and arrest record before hiring. Background checks can range from verification of an applicant's Social Security number to a detailed account of the potential employee's history and acquaintances. Some employers even search social networking Websites for the profiles of applicants.

However, various federal and state laws prohibit employers from violating an applicant's rights of privacy, especially concerning their medical information, credit history, school records, or military service.

The following information will highlight the law in this area and advise applicants of the steps to take if information is misused.

1.   ARREST RECORDS AND CRIMINAL HISTORY. The law involving arrest records is favorable to the rights of individuals in most states. Although arrest record information is public record, employers are not permitted to ask questions verbally or in writing about past arrests since these often end in acquittal, dismissal, withdrawal of charges, or overturning of the conviction. Most states do not allow employers to take adverse action against an applicant based on an arrest or criminal accusation that is not pending or resulted in the applicant's favor. Some states, including California, prohibit employers from seeking the arrest record of a potential candidate from any source unless the person is out of jail but pending trial. Additionally, an employer may violate federal and state discrimination laws when it inquires into an applicant's past arrest or criminal history without justification.

Criminal convictions are treated differently under various state laws. In New York, for example, an employer may only inquire about a criminal conviction of a misdemeanor or felony (not a lesser offense, like a traffic conviction), and cannot deny employment based on a criminal conviction unless there is a direct relationship between the conviction and the job sought (e.g., such as for a public utility, law enforcement, security guard firm, or child care facility), or employment of the applicant poses an unreasonable risk to property or safety. In many states, criminal histories or "rap sheets" compiled by law enforcement agencies are not public record and aren't accurate.

Because the law varies so in this area, it's a good idea to research and understand your state's law when applying for a job if you've been arrested or possess a criminal conviction record. Speak to a knowledgeable employment attorney for advice and guidance where applicable. If you are an African American or Latino, recognize your rights and ability to file a charge of discrimination with the EEOC and sue the potential employer for race, color or national origin discrimination when you are not offered a job as a result of a distant criminal conviction or arrest not leading to a conviction. Practice how you will respond to an illegal verbal or written inquiry by a prospective employer. Challenge all company action in the checking of your arrest records or criminal convictions or being denied employment since the recent policy of most states is to encourage the employment of former offenders

2.   INVESTIGATION OF BANKRUPTCY RECORDS. According to the federal Bankruptcy Code, no private employer may terminate the employment of, or discriminate with respect to employment against, an individual who is or has been a debtor or bankrupt under the Bankruptcy Act, or an individual associated with such debtor or bankrupt, solely because such debtor or bankrupt is or has been a debtor or bankrupt under the Bankruptcy Act, has been insolvent before the grant or denial of a discharge, or has not paid a debt that is dischargeable in a case under the Bankruptcy Act.

When considering minority candidates, case law and the EEOC advise against refusing to hire based on a poor credit rating, because minorities often have more difficulty paying their bills and such a policy effectively excludes a class of applicant from the job market.

3.   CREDIT INFORMATION. The federal Fair Credit Reporting Act places certain restrictions on the use of credit reports and investigative consumer reports by employers. Under this law, employers are forbidden to use credit reports (defined as summaries of a person's credit history) for hiring or employment decisions. The same is true for investigative consumer reports (defined as descriptions of a person's creditworthiness and general reputation in her community based on interviews with co-workers, friends, and neighbors.)

Employers cannot obtain any report without written permission. If your consent is obtained and a report is made, you have the right to receive a copy, including the name and address of the credit agency supplying it, together with a written description of your rights under the law.

When any adverse action is taken, such as your not being hired, you are entitled to receive notice of such adverse action, the name, address, telephone number of the consumer reporting agency that provided the report to the employer, and a written statement by the employer indicating that such information was not used in any way in the adverse action.

STRATEGY: *As a result of the law's requirements, speak to a knowledgeable employment attorney immediately if you believe your rights have been violated in this area.*

In the majority of states and under the federal Consumer Credit Protections Act, it is illegal for a company to fire a person being sued for the nonpayment of a debt or when the company is instructed to cooperate in the collection of a portion of the person's wages through garnishment proceedings for any one indebtedness. Many states have strict laws on the books in this area so always check your state's law.

4. PRE-EMPLOYMENT DRUG AND ALCOHOL TESTING. Drug screening tests are on the rise, particularly in high-technology and security-conscious industries. They generally have been upheld as legal, particularly with respect to job applicants (as opposed to employees who are asked to submit to random tests as a requisite for continued employment). Applicants have fewer rights to protest such tests than employees. The reason is that drug tests are generally not viewed as violating people's privacy rights, since applicants are told in advance that they must take and pass the test to get the job and that all applicants must submit to such tests even to be considered for employment.

However, the right to test does not give potential employers the right to handle test results carelessly. Unwarranted disclosure of this information can result in huge damages, so be aware that you have rights in this area. You may also have rights in the event you are refused a job because you allegedly failed a test and it is determined later that there was a mistake in the test results (in other words, that the test results were really negative). Speak to a lawyer immediately if you are denied employment for allegedly failing a drug test when you know this cannot be so, if you are fired shortly after accepting employment for allegedly failing a test, or if the results of a failed test are conveyed to nonessential third parties, causing you humiliation and embarrassment. (Chapter 4 in Part II, dealing with on-the-job rights of employees, covers the legality and strategies of drug and alcohol tests for workers in more detail.)

Drug and alcohol tests of job applicants are neither encouraged nor prohibited by the ADA, and the results of such tests may be used as a basis for disciplinary action. The reason is that an employer does not have to hire an applicant who poses a direct threat to the health or safety of himself/herself or others. In determining whether an individual poses such a threat, the nature and severity of the potential harm, duration of the risk, and the likelihood and immediacy that potential harm will occur are all factors to consider.

An employee or applicant who is currently engaging in illegal drug use is not protected under federal ADA law. Nor is a current alcoholic whose employment presents a threat to the safety of others.

5.   LIE-DETECTOR AND OTHER PRE-EMPLOYMENT TESTS.
The federal Polygraph Protection Act of 1988 forbids employers to give any job applicant a lie-detector test or agree to submit to such a test in order to be hired. This law also forbids the use of such tests in all states that previously allowed them and prohibits the use of lie detectors in all pre-employment screening.

Many states have enacted strong laws protecting job applicants from stress tests, psychological evaluator tests, and other honesty tests.

In other states the trend is to eliminate or strongly discourage the use of such tests. To be safe in this area, you are strongly advised to speak to a knowledgeable attorney who can advise you on the current status of such laws in your state. Additionally, all tests presently being used should be carefully reviewed, since such tests must comply with existing federal and state law.

STRATEGY: *If you are asked to submit to such a test as a condition of being offered a job and believe that the test is unfair, harmful, or distasteful, it may be a good idea to investigate the particular law in your state before acting in this area. Even if such tests are legal, they may be discriminatory by causing a different effect, positive or negative, on any race, gender, or ethnic group when compared with another group. Any tests that cannot work as well with minorities as with other groups are illegal under EEOC guidelines. Thus, investigate whether inherent discrimination problems exist with such tests so that all tests given do not contain hidden bias or unfairly penalize one group over another.*

---

6. INVESTIGATION OF SOCIAL NETWORK SITES. Many employers are now using social network websites as a tool to investigate a candidate's background and frequently reject applicants after learning the person is an alcohol or drug user or parties excessively.

While no law prohibits employers from searching online social network sites to conduct background checks of job applicants, some states, including New York, have laws prohibiting companies from refusing to hire workers as a result of legally permissible recreational activities (such as the use of alcohol or cigarettes) before or after the work day. More discussion about this is contained in Chapter 4.

Be aware that if you are denied a job because you post negative comments about an employer's labor practices, this may violate the National Labor Relations Act. You may also have a viable lawsuit resulting from a breach of your privacy rights in this area.

7. MEDICAL RECORDS. The ADA prohibits employers from requesting an applicant's medical records before hiring. The law does permit employers to inquire about an applicant's ability to perform specific job duties.

8.   SCHOOL RECORDS. Under the Family Educational Rights and Privacy Act and similar state laws, educational records such as transcripts, recommendations and financial information are generally confidential and may not be released by the school without a student's written consent.

9.   MILITARY SERVICE. Military service records may be released only under limited circumstances, and consent is generally required. The military may, however, disclose name, rank, salary, duty assignments, awards, and duty status without the member's consent.

10. WORKERS' COMPENSATION RECORDS. Workers' compensation appeals are part of the public record. Information from a workers' compensation appeal may be used in a hiring decision if the employer can show the applicant's injury might interfere with his ability to perform required duties.

Applicant References

When companies fail to investigate an applicant's background and they hire a person unfit for the position who causes harm or injury to another, they are sometimes liable under a legal theory referred to as negligent hiring and retention.

Under this negligent-hiring doctrine in most jurisdictions, employers have a duty of reasonable care in hiring individuals who, because of employment, may pose a threat of injury to fellow employees and members of the public. Negligent-hiring claims have been made against employers for murders, rapes, sexual assaults, physical assaults, personal injuries, and property losses allegedly committed or caused by an unfit employee. In one case a McDonald's worker in Colorado, while on the job, sexually assaulted a three-year-old boy. The fast-food restaurant had hired the man without a complete background check, which would have shown a history of sexually assaulting children. The family sued and a jury reportedly awarded the victim $210,000.

However, liability may not be found under the negligent-hiring theory in cases where the employee's acts are not foreseeable and where the pre-employment investigation of an employee's qualifications did not give rise to actual or constructive knowledge of a potential problem. For example, a union was held not liable for recommending the hiring of a cruise ship employee who committed a sexual assault upon another seaman while both men were vacationing onshore after working together on the cruise ship, because evidence of a propensity for aggressive behavior did not show up in the union's standard pre-employment investigation of the perpetrator.

Employers may be liable to the applicant and employee under legal claims (including defamation, intentional infliction of emotional distress, and violations of the implied covenant of good faith and fair dealing) when references are not investigated properly or are leaked to nonessential third parties.

For example, in one case a man terminated from an insurance company discovered that his former boss, in reference checks, had called him "untrustworthy, disruptive, paranoid, hostile, irrational, a classic sociopath." He sued and a jury decided those characterizations were out of line, a mistake that cost the company $1.9 million.

Such cases typify the legal dilemma employers face with reference checks. When hiring, if they miss a potential problem, some courts find them negligent. But when giving references, if they say too much, they may be liable for defaming former workers. Thus, employers must be familiar with local, state, and federal laws in this area.

Be aware that you may have rights in the event that harmful confidential information (for example, credit references) is communicated to nonessential third parties to your detriment. For more information and strategies on this subject, consult the section in Chapter 8 that discusses defamatory job references.

Job Misrepresentation and Phony Employment Schemes

People are often exposed to phony advertisements and employment schemes promising large income for part-time work or offering jobs with unlimited earning potential. The following is an example of a typical ad.

OVER $1000 PER WEEK possible by working at home. Manage your own time--no prior experience necessary.

Newspapers are filled with ads for such jobs. However, the vast majority of these ads are misleading. Applicants sometimes travel great distances (at their own expense) to apply. They then learn that a large amount of some product (for example, $10,000 worth) must be purchased in order to sell for the company and be hired!

As a general rule, be skeptical of work-at-home employment ads. Many ads turn out to be envelope-stuffing pyramid schemes requiring people to purchase introductory mailing lists. These lists actually cost you more than you can possibly earn from work-at-home activities.

Always beware of companies you can't communicate with by telephone, especially those that only list a post office box address. This is because there may be no one to reach when you have questions about the work or have not received agreed-upon payments.

It is also a good idea to understand how much money and time you will be required to expend to get started and whether the job requires special training or skills. Inquire about refund policies.

Most important, never commence work at home until you understand the amount of compensation and how often you will be paid. Avoid working for long periods of time without being paid; demand to receive payment on a regular basis (never less than once a month). That way you can cut your losses if the company misses a payment.

Finally, if you are buying a work-at-home franchise, demand to review all the written documents concerning the venture, including the prospectus, before you invest. Speak to your lawyer, accountant, and similar franchise owners for advice whenever possible.

Job offers that require people to buy a product before working are not the only common illegal employment scheme. Applicants are sometimes misled by interviewers who oversell by making exaggerated guaranteed-earnings claims. For example, applicants are told, "If you come to work for us, you will make $100,000 in commission this year, based on what our other salespeople make." People then accept the job based on such representations, not realizing that the statements may be illegal. This is because, according to the Federal Trade Commission, a promise of earnings that exceed the average net earnings of other employees or sales reps is an unfair and deceptive trade practice.

STRATEGY: *Always be on the alert when a potential employer makes claims regarding guaranteed earnings. You have the right to see copies of the wage statements (for example, W-2s or 1099s) of other employees of the company to confirm such claims. If the employer tells you such information is confidential, tell him or her to remove the names of the employees. If the employer refuses to do this or cannot provide ample factual information to support such claims, think twice before accepting the job.*

To avoid misleading potential employees, prudent employers hedge by using the following types of phrases when advising applicants of potential earnings. "It is possible you may make $100,000 this year, since three out of eight sales reps achieved that figure last year," or "Although not typical, we have had employees who earned as much as $100,000 in a given year."

Some employers also misrepresent the amount and quality of assistance to be rendered. The law is violated when false promises of support are made or when other material terms (for example, exclusive sales territories) are offered that do not exist.

STRATEGY: *To protect yourself in this area, always speak directly to the people who will supposedly assist you. Find out what their functions and duties are and how long they have worked for the employer. Talking to people directly will help you form a "gut" opinion and make it easier to determine when false claims have been made.*

If you believe you have been victimized by an employment scheme or a work-at-home advertisement, you have many options. Obviously, you can contact a lawyer to protect your rights and take action on your behalf. Such action could include filing a private lawsuit based on fraud and misrepresentation. Some lawsuits even allow you to sue the officers of an employer in their individual capacities.

You can also contact the nearest regional office of the Federal Trade Commission, the Better Business Bureau, or the U.S. Postal Service. Numerous federal and state laws have been enacted, including the Uniform Deceptive Trade Practices Act, the Racketeer Influenced and Corrupt Organizations Act (RICO), and other labor statutes, to prevent employers from engaging in a variety of phony employment schemes or using the mails to further such schemes. The Federal Trade Commission has the authority to investigate claims and impose cease and desist orders prohibiting the continuation of illegal activity by phony employers. Each state's attorney general's office maintains a division for labor fraud and other related deceptive employment practices. In certain cases the U.S. Postal Service can issue a court order preventing employers from using the mails or receiving mail.

STRATEGY: *Whenever you are in doubt about a particular employer or an individual representing the employer, contact your local Better Business Bureau. Most Better Business Bureaus maintain lists of employers and individuals accused of engaging in phony employment-related practices. Obtaining such information before accepting employment or participating in a dubious venture can save you a great deal of aggravation and expense down the road.*

Also, try to recognize phony employment schemes and advertisements before problems develop, and take immediate action when appropriate.

Abuses by Employment Agencies, Search Firms, or Career Counselors

In your anxiousness to find a job, you may risk being exploited by unscrupulous persons or organizations promising to help you find employment. The required placement fee may be exorbitant, you may pay nonrefundable fees for so-called leads that do not lead to employment, you may be asked illegal discriminatory questions at the initial interview, or you may be told that you must register in prescribed training for which the agency gets a fee.

How can you avoid such skullduggery? Here are a few of the ways you can protect yourself from unethical or illegal employment practices.

1. **KNOW WITH WHOM YOU ARE DEALING.** The main purpose of an employment agency is to find a job for you. Career counselors and search firms offer additional services such as resume and letter preparation and training in interview techniques, as well as providing job-opening leads. Career counselors do not, however, obtain jobs for applicants.

2. **UNDERSTAND THE TERMS OF THE ARRANGEMENT.** Ask the following questions before you agree to be represented by an employment agency, search firm, or career counselor:

■ Is the firm licensed? (In some states, employment agencies are licensed and regulated by the Department of Consumer Affairs. To obtain a license, the agency must fill out a detailed application, post a performance bond, maintain accurate financial records, and avoid engaging in illegal acts. Career counselors and search firms generally are not required to be licensed to conduct business.)

- What are the precise services the firm or individual will render?

- What is required of the job applicant (prepare a resume, buy interviewing attire, etc.)?

- When will the firm or individual earn its fee: when you are offered a job by an acceptable employer, when you accept the job, or when you have worked a minimum amount of time?

- What is the maximum fee to be charged?

- Who will pay for the fee, you or the employer? When is it payable?

- What happens if you decide not to accept a job that is offered?

- Is a deposit required once a job is accepted?

- Will you receive a detailed description of each potential employer before you go on an interview, including the name, address, kind of work to be performed, title, amount of wages or compensation, hours, and whether the work is temporary or permanent?

- Will the agency investigate whether the potential employer has defaulted in the payment of salaries to others during the past five years?

- What happens to the fee if you resign or are fired within a short period of time?

- Will the agency help you obtain another job if you are terminated?

- Does the agency have the right to represent you on an exclusive basis?

- What happens to the fee if you become disabled and cannot work?

3. CONFIRM EVERYTHING IN WRITING. Since oral contracts are often difficult to prove, try to reduce the arrangement to writing. If you have questions, don't sign a contract until you understand what it will mean to you. If the contract is long and complicated, you may need the advice of a lawyer before signing.

4. DON'T PAY MONEY IN ADVANCE OF RESULTS. While it is illegal for employment agencies to charge fees before they have found a job for you, career counselors and search firms are allowed to charge up-front fees. Resist such requests, because promised services are sometimes not received.

5. KNOW IN ADVANCE WHAT IS PROHIBITED. Check with your local library, bar association, or Better Business Bureau for a description of what employment agencies, career counselors, and search firms are allowed to do and what prohibitions exist. For example, under the laws in many states, it is illegal for an employment agency to:

- Induce you to terminate your job so the agency can obtain new employment for you
- Publish false or misleading ads
- Advertise in newspapers without providing the name and address of the agency
- Send you to an employer without obtaining a job order from the employer
- Require you to subscribe to publications, pay for advertising or mailing costs, enroll in special courses, or pay for additional services
- Charge a placement fee when the agency represents that it was a fee-paid job
- Discriminate on the basis of gender, age, or race
- Require you to complete application forms that obtain different information from male and female applicants
- Make false representations or promises

6. SEEK IMMEDIATE RELIEF IF YOU HAVE BEEN EX-PLOITED. Don't procrastinate if an employment agency or career service takes advantage of you. The longer you wait, the harder it may be to prove your case and collect damages. If you believe you have been exploited, send a letter to the firm to document your protest. The letter should state the reasons for your dissatisfaction and the manner in which you would like the problem resolved. The letter below illustrates this. If the financial exploitation is significant, contact a lawyer immediately. In any event, if your problem is not resolved amicably, contact your local Department of Consumer Affairs or Better Business Bureau, outlining your complaint in writing, as shown in the example beginning on this page. In many states these agencies have the power to investigate charges and take action, including revoking licenses, when wrongdoing is proved. If you are still dissatisfied with the outcome, you can consider suing in small-claims court or through formal litigation.

Sample Complaint Letter to Job-Search Firm

Your Name
Address
Telephone Number
Date

Name of Officer
Name of Firm
Address

Dear (Name of Officer),

On (date) I responded to an advertisement your firm ran in (name of newspaper or magazine). The ad specifically promised that your firm could find a job for me as a salesperson in the cosmetics industry. The ad stated that a ($X) advance was fully refundable in the event I could not obtain a job paying more than $37,000 per year.

Per your request, and after several telephone conversations, I sent you a check for ($X), which was cashed. That was four months ago.

Since that time I have received one letter from you dated (specify), which states you are reviewing my employment history.

In view of the fact that you have not obtained full-time employment on my behalf, I hereby demand the return of ($X), per our agreement.

If I do not receive the money within 14 days from the date of this letter, be assured that I shall contact the Department of Consumer Affairs, Better Business Bureau, the frauds division of the attorney general's office, and my lawyer to commence a formal investigation.

Hopefully this can be avoided and I thank you for your immediate cooperation in this matter.

Very truly yours,
Your Name

Sent certified mail, return receipt requested.

Follow-up Letter to Department of Consumer Affairs (or appropriate agency)

Your Name
Address
Telephone Number
Date

Commissioner
Department of Consumer Affairs
Address

Re: Formal complaint against ABC Employment Agency, license #XXXXX

Dear Commissioner,

I hereby make a formal complaint against (name of firm). I believe the firm has committed the following illegal acts: (specify).

The facts on which I base my allegations are as follows: (state the facts in detail).

On (date) I sent the agency a formal demand letter requesting the return of my deposit. This letter was sent by certified mail, was received by the firm, yet I have received no response. I enclose a copy of the letter for your review together with all pertinent documentation from my files.

I request that you convene a formal investigation regarding this matter. Feel free to contact me at the above address if you need further assistance or information.

Thank you for your cooperation and attention.

Very truly yours,
Your Name

Sent certified mail, return receipt requested.
cc: the employment agency, your lawyer, Better Business Bureau, and the frauds division of the state attorney general's office

Tips to Avoid Being Hired by a Deceitful Employer

No matter what type of job you are considering, always investigate the potential employer even if you desperately need the job. Typical information you would like to learn are facts regarding the employer's business reputation, credit rating, financial status, rate of employee turnover, morale problems with workers, whether the company has been involved in any employee-related lawsuits recently (and if so, did the employee win or lose?), and commitments to the community in which the company is located.

For example, if you are being hired to replace someone in an important position, try to obtain the name of the person you might be replacing and find out why the individual is no longer there. Better still, by speaking to that person you could learn valuable information to influence your decision. Many applicants who follow this advice discover that the individual decided to resign because he or she was being harassed on the job by a supervisor, the job was long and tedious, or promised commissions, bonuses, raises, and promotions were not given.

It is particularly important to do your homework when you are being offered an important position that includes long-term employment, stock options, profit sharing, and other valuable financial benefits. Such an investigation should be made to assess the chances that the employer has sufficient assets to pay these benefits or that the employer will still be in business when you retire.

Most lawyers and accountants who represent successful business clients obtain the following kinds of financial information from credit reporting agencies and the banks with whom the company does its business. The following list of questions is a good starting point in this area:

1. WHAT IS THE LEGAL FORM OF THE EMPLOYER? Is it a corporation, an S corporation, a limited liability corporation, a partnership, or a sole proprietorship? (You should know the legal distinctions among these terms for additional protection.)

2. WHAT ARE THE NAMES OF THE PRINCIPAL SHARE-HOLDERS OR PARTNERS?

3. WHAT IS THE FINANCIAL HISTORY OF THE EMPLOYER? Is it a recently established business, or has it been in existence for a while? (Many new businesses fail within the first few years, hurting employees in the process by firing them suddenly and not paying adequate severance benefits. I always instruct clients wishing to join non-established employers to proceed with caution.)

4. WITH WHOM DOES THE EMPLOYER MAINTAIN BANK-ING RELATIONS? For how long has it done so? What is the average balance on deposit? Does the employer have a line of credit? If so, for how much?

5. HOW MANY PEOPLE WORK FOR THE COMPANY? Do any of them belong to a union? Is the employer opposed to union participation? Could you join a union? What additional benefits would you receive if you joined a union? Has the employer recently been involved in any litigation with any of its employees? What was the lawsuit about? Did the employer win? What was the effect on employee morale? What is the rate of employee turnover?

6. DOES THE EMPLOYER OFFER GENEROUS BENEFITS? These include such items as liberal sick day and vacation policies, paid maternity and paternity leaves, etc., and will be discussed in greater detail in the next chapter.

7.   HAS THE EMPLOYER FILED A RECENT FINANCIAL STATE-MENT? Was it a certified statement? (Certified financial statements are usually more accurate and verifiable than regular financial statements.) What are the company's assets and liabilities? Does it have an unusually high late-paying accounts receivables problem? (This might indicate a cash flow problem and potential bankruptcy situation if the receivables aren't paid.)

8.   WHAT ARE THE EMPLOYER'S ASSETS? Does it own real estate, patents, inventions, licenses, and other tangible assets?

9.   WHAT DOES THE LATEST BALANCE SHEET REVEAL? This is an important document. It shows the employer's financial status on the last date of the reported fiscal year. For example, you can learn what the employer owns in terms of cash, marketable securities, accounts receivable, inventory, and property and equipment. The balance sheet will also indicate money owed for unpaid bills and taxes, loan repayments to banks, bondholders, and other lenders. You may also be able to determine the amount of the employer's working capital, costs of doing business, and other pertinent information. If you are being hired for an important position and are given stock or stock options, be sure that you obtain copies of such documents for the current year and several past years of the employer's operations.

10. WHAT ARE THE LIABILITIES OF THE EMPLOYER? Are there any outstanding encumbrances, judgments, or liens?

11. HAS THE BUSINESS BEEN SOLD RECENTLY? Did the new owners assume the liabilities or just purchase the assets? This is important. Suppose you are owed bonuses which the old employer refuses to pay. The new owners may be able to step away from this obligation if they only purchased the company's assets and not its liabilities.

12. WHO ADMINISTERS THE EMPLOYER'S PENSION PLAN?
Is it a reliable company?

You should never accept a new job blindly, particularly when a high salary and other substantial benefits are offered. Negotiating a job is a two-way street. The employer spends much time and expense verifying the personal background, job qualifications, and prior references of job applicants. You should try to gather as much information as possible on the employer's history, management style, and financial stability as well. In certain instances, what you learn may give you second thoughts--you may come to suspect that you will not be promoted properly or even that the company may not be around in the future.

Thus, try to gather as much information as possible before making your decision. Talk to fellow workers; listen to what they say. Many are accessible and honest and will give you a true picture of the way the employer really runs its business (as opposed to what you're told at the interview).

Better still, speak to friends and business associates in the industry to learn more about the employer's business reputation. For example, if you learn names of customers, suppliers, or distributors of the employer, it may be a good idea to inquire discreetly to learn their opinions about the company. What you learn may surprise you. The same is true for reputable employment agencies who have dealt with the employer in the past and can tell you about the company's reputation and business methods. Finally, if you are about to work for a large company, you may be able to locate written information in the business press or Internet.

Remember, ask questions and do your homework. You may learn information that will save you money and aggravation in the future.

2

Negotiating the Job

S mart applicants never accept employment until they have carefully discussed and clarified all key terms, conditions, and responsibilities of the job up front, no matter what type of job is being offered. You risk being exploited when you fail to do so. When key terms (including the compensation arrangement and benefits package) are not agreed on before the hiring, the law will not generally impute such rights and you cannot force an employer to give valuable benefits not promised before the start date after you begin working.

Never be afraid to negotiate. Remember that a successful job negotiation is one of give and take. Obviously, the more points you insist on, the more benefits and protections you will obtain. Be aware, however, that certain employer policies may not be negotiable. While salary, title, duties, authority, and such are fair game for negotiation, fringe benefit, profit-sharing, and pension programs are usually fixed and not open to negotiation. Reviewing your prospective employer's employee handbook or personnel manual will give you a good idea of where the flexibilities and inflexibilities are. Types of negotiations and strategies you can use are discussed in the following pages.

Most well-run companies respect applicants who thoroughly negotiate their jobs. Thus, use the following checklist of negotiating points wisely. Even if you cannot negotiate many of the points cited below, you can minimize disappointment and confusion by knowing what to expect after you begin working. Thorough negotiations can also reduce potential litigation claims arising from breach of contract, wrongful discharge, and other legal problems that frequently arise during and after the employment relationship has ended.

Finally, do not expect to get everything you request. However, by understanding the nature of successful job negotiations and the many options that are available, you can receive additional benefits and protection merely by recognizing what to ask for.

Checklist of Key Negotiating Points to Cover During the Hiring Interview

The following checklist is divided into three main sections: The Job; Job Security; and Salary and Benefits. Where appropriate, detailed "strategies" have been inserted into the checklist for further information.

The Job

1. Job description. (Understand the nature of the job being offered.)

2. What is your title?

3. What will be your job functions? Will you report to a superior? If so, who?

4. When are you expected to begin working (start date)?

5. What is your employment status?

   a. Are you considered a regular full-time employee eligible for all employer-provided fringe benefits (as opposed to a part-time or exempt employee paid on an hourly basis with limited fringe benefits) ?

   b. Are you considered an employee or an independent contractor? (As an independent contractor, you may be required to pay all federal, state, and local withholding taxes, Social Security, and other taxes. However, there are certain advantages to being hired as an independent contractor which will be discussed later in this chapter.)

    c. Are you being hired as a consultant? If so, can you work for other companies, have outside work and sidelines, etc.? This, too, will be discussed later in the chapter.

Job Security

1. Will you be given job security (as opposed to merely being "hired at will," which gives the employer the right to fire you at any time with or without notice and with or without cause)?

2. If so, what kind of job security is being offered?

STRATEGY 1: *Your objective in negotiating for job security is to avoid being fired suddenly at the employer's discretion.*

The best job security to obtain is to be employed for a definite term—for example, two years. This means that the employer cannot fire you prior to the expiration of that term except for a compelling reason—that is, for cause. (Most employers are reluctant to hire people for a definite term because it reduces their ability to fire employees at any time.) Thus, always ask for a definite term when being hired. Use your discretion as to the amount of job security you request. Your request can range from six months to several years. Tell the employer you want an X-year contract; the employer will know what you mean.

STRATEGY 2: *If the employer refuses to hire you for a definite term, ask for a guarantee that you cannot be fired except for cause or as long as you achieve certain goals (for example, a minimum sales quota if you are being hired as a salesperson). This request can give you needed protection without locking the employer into a time frame.*

STRATEGY 3: *If this request is refused, ask to be guaranteed a written warning within a definite period of time (for example, 30 days to cure alleged deficient performance) before being fired. This will protect you from a sudden firing, and some employers will accept this. Or you can ask for a written notice of termination (for example, 30 days before the contract will end) before the effective termination date so that you can plan ahead and look for other employment while still collecting a paycheck.*

STRATEGY 4: *If the employer refuses #3, request pay in lieu of notice in the event you are fired without warning; for example, ask to receive two weeks' additional pay at your current salary level in the event you are fired suddenly. (This is in addition to severance pay, more fully discussed below.)*

STRATEGY 5: *Be sure you understand if you are being hired for a probationary period. Some employers establish a probationary period (for example, the first 90 days of employment) ranging from 30 to 120 days to evaluate an employee's performance. If you are hired for a probationary period but are fired before the end of the period, you may be entitled to receive salary and other benefits until the end of the probationary period in certain situations.*

Salary and Benefits

1. What is your base salary, and when is it payable? Understand all deductions from your paycheck.

2. When does the pay period start and end?

3. If payday falls on a holiday, when are paychecks distributed?

4. Is overtime offered? If so, at what rate? Is there a seniority basis for offering overtime (e.g., a policy that overtime is first offered to longtime workers)? Most states, in addition to federal law, require that overtime must be paid whenever a part-time or hourly employee works in excess of 40 hours per week. Special employees working in

government contracting or subcontracting work may also be required to be paid overtime if they work more than eight hours on any given day. Discuss this if relevant.

5. Will you be required to outlay expenses? If so, are expenses reimbursable? Be sure you know the kind and amount of expenses that are. Be sure you understand the kind of documentation to be supplied to the employer for reimbursement and how long you must wait before reimbursement.

6. Are you entitled to commissions? If so, understand how commissions are earned, the commission rate, and when commissions are paid.

7. Are you to receive a bonus? If so, how is it calculated, and when is it paid? Is the bonus gratuitous (in other words, merely paid at the employer's whim and discretion in an amount determined solely by the employer), or is it enforceable by contract with a verifiable sum linked to some specific formula (profits, revenue, output, etc.)?

Many people fail to understand their rights regarding bonuses and are later disappointed or exploited. For example, while some people work a full year counting on a bonus and don't receive it, others receive bonuses that are not even closely related to what they were expecting. But that is not the worst problem that frequently arises. Employers sometimes fire individuals after the bonus has technically been earned (at the end of the year) but before it is distributed (on February 15 of the following year). They then tell the ex-employee that he or she must be working for the company at the time the bonus is paid in order to collect!

These common abuses can be avoided by understanding and negotiating the following strategies.

STRATEGY 1: *Request a verifiable bonus that is not subject to the employer's discretion. Specify the amount, when it will be paid, and that there are to be no strings or conditions attached. In other words,* *treat the bonus as part of your salary package; this will increase your legal rights in the event you are not paid.*

STRATEGY 2: *Request a pro rata bonus in the event you resign or are fired prior to the bonus being paid. For example, if the bonus is computed on sales volume and you work a full year and resign or are fired on December 1 of that year, you should be able to receive eleven-twelfths of the expected bonus. Many employers will accept this provided you give ample notice before the resignation and you are not fired for misconduct (that is, for cause).*

STRATEGY 3: *Avoid allowing the employer the right to arbitrarily determine when and if a bonus will be paid and in what amount. This arrangement is considered a gratuitous bonus, which may not be enforceable by contract. When an employer controls the timing, amount, and whether or not to pay a bonus at all, or states that the money is paid in appreciation for continuous, efficient, or satisfactory service, employees have a weaker chance to recover an expected bonus from the employer when they are not paid.*

STRATEGY 4: *Resist arrangements that require you to be on the job after a bonus is earned in order to receive it. If the employer insists on this condition, negotiate the right to receive a bonus if you are fired due to a business reorganization, layoff, or any reason other than gross misconduct.*

STRATEGY 5: *Get it in writing. Verbal promises to pay bonuses are not always enforceable. Confirm your understanding in writing for additional protection. (You will learn how to do this effectively later in this chapter.)*

STRATEGY 6: *Are additional services required in order to earn the bonus? If so, promises to pay a bonus for work, labor, or services already completed at the time the promise is made may not be valid.*

STRATEGY 7: *Try to link the bonus to some verifiable formula (for example, gross profits or sales volume). Such an arrangement can give you extra legal protection; in the event you are not paid a correct amount, you would be able to verify the bonus from the company's books and records. In fact, if a bonus-enforceable-by-contract arrangement could be proved in court, you would have the right to inspect the employer's books and records in a lawsuit.*

Many employers are reluctant to base bonuses on verifiable components because they are aware of the vulnerability to exposure in a lawsuit. However, you should leave nothing up to chance when negotiating a bonus. You want to know precisely how the bonus is to be earned and steps to take (for example, the right to be given company records for review) in the event you are not paid what you believe you are owed. Insist on nothing less.

8. What fringe benefits will you receive? Most employees fail to properly negotiate extra compensation in the form of fringe benefits. Many forms of fringe benefits are even more valuable than salary because they are nontaxable. Don't forget to ask for fringe benefits during the negotiating process.

The following detailed summary of fringe benefits will be helpful in this area.

INSURANCE BENEFITS. These include basic group term life insurance, basic accidental death and dismemberment coverage, optional group term life insurance, dependent term life insurance, optional accidental death and dismemberment insurance, business travel accident insurance, weekly income accident and sickness plans, illness payment plans, short and long-term disability insurance plans, medical benefit plans, dental benefit plans and legal benefit plans.

This list is not meant to be all-inclusive. Rather, it gives you an idea about the kinds of benefits that are available. However, most insurance benefits are not negotiable, since employers must offer them to all employees so as not to be liable for charges of discrimination.

OTHER BENEFITS. These can include the use of an automobile, free parking, car insurance, gasoline allowance, death benefits, prepaid legal services, credit cards, and loans at reduced rates of interest with favorable repayment schedules. Be sure you know all the elements of your benefit package, and don't be afraid to negotiate extra benefits when appropriate.

PENSIONS AND PROFIT-SHARING PLANS. Are you entitled to additional compensation in the form of defined benefit, profit-sharing, money purchase, and pension plans? Other benefits you should be aware of are Social Security benefits, Individual Retirement Accounts (IRAs), 401(k) plans, thrift plans, stock bonus plans, and employee stock ownership plans (ESOPs).

All of these plans are extra financial perks to help you accumulate additional revenue for financial security and your retirement. Be sure you understand what benefits the employer offers in this area and what contributions will be made on your behalf. Other questions to ask:

- Are you required to contribute matching sums of money? If so, how much will this cost you? Can you increase or decrease matching contributions at your discretion? If so, is notice required and how much?
- Does the investment accumulate tax-free?
- Can the money be taken prior to your retirement? If so, is there a penalty?
- What happens if you resign or are fired for cause? Is the money forfeited?
- What happens if the company is sold or goes bankrupt? Is the money protected?
- Who administers the plan benefits? How can you be sure that there are no funding liabilities—in other words, how can you

be sure that monies will be set aside as promised? Are the plan benefits invested in such a manner as to preclude large losses?

■ If as a result of an acquisition through the purchase of the company you are laid off, how will COBRA and ERISA laws apply? ERISA (Employee Retirement Income Security Act) as modified by COBRA (Consolidated Omnibus Budget Reconciliation Act of 1986) is a federal law designed to protect you and your beneficiaries' pension and other benefit rights when you are laid off. Note that ERISA does not apply to employment by churches or federal, state, or local governments, or by companies with 20 or fewer employees, and may not apply if it can be proved that your termination was for gross misconduct. However, in most situations, these laws ensure that money previously set aside on your behalf will be given to you, regardless of internal changes or organizational restructuring in your company.

All of these points and many more should be explored and explained to your satisfaction. Since these financial benefits can account for a large part of additional compensation, never overlook their importance. Always negotiate to receive the maximum amount of benefits available.

RAISES AND JOB ADVANCEMENT. Are periodic raises given? What is the procedure for merit raises and job advancement?

STRATEGY: *Employees are sometimes disappointed by the size of annual or periodic merit increases or the speed of job advancement. To avoid problems in this area, be sure you know if such increases are determined by one person's subjective decision. If they are, request the right to appeal this person's decision and discuss how this may be accomplished.*

RELOCATION EXPENSES. This is money often paid to employees who are required to relocate. Points to discuss and negotiate include questions like these: How much relocation pay will be given? When is it payable, and who will pay for it? Are taxes taken out of the payments?

Be sure to determine whether you need to furnish supporting documentation (copies of bills for legal fees incurred in a house closing, etc.) in order to receive reimbursement. Also, ask what arrangements will be made if you resign or are terminated within a short period of time.

STRATEGY: *Do not allow the employer to unilaterally cancel relocation expenses if the job doesn't work out, because you may have relocated yourself and your family thousands of miles at great expense with no protection. If you are planning to relocate to a distant location, always receive assurances in writing that relocation expenses will be paid regardless of how long you work for the company.*

SEVERANCE PAY. Does the employer have a definite stated policy regarding severance (e.g., two weeks of severance for each year of employment)?

Inquire whether severance is paid if you resign as opposed to being fired. Some companies do not pay severance upon resignation and do not pay severance when the termination is for cause.

VACATION PAY. How much vacation pay you get often depends on your salary grade, type of job offered, and how well you negotiate. Be sure you understand how vacation pay is computed and other important matters regarding the granting of vacation time. Consider the following as starting points:

- Must vacation days be used in the year they are granted, or can they be carried over to the next year? If they can't, can a prorated share (e.g., one-half the days) be carried over?
- How long must you work in order to be qualified?
- Does the amount of vacation time increase depending on the number of years with the company (e.g., two weeks of vacation pay for the first five years, increasing to three weeks of paid vacation from years six to ten)?
- Must vacation days be taken all at once, or can they be staggered? If so, how?

■ How much notice are you required to give before you can take vacations?

■ Are there times during peak seasonal demands when requests will not be granted?

■ If you leave or are terminated, will you be paid for all unused vacation time?

This last point should be considered carefully. Employees frequently leave their jobs expecting to receive large payments for unused vacation (carried over for several years) but are denied payment in this regard. Some states require companies to pay accrued vacation pay in all circumstances, even when the employee is fired for cause. Thus, check with the Department of Labor in your state or speak to competent legal counsel.

PERSONAL DAYS. Personal days give you a chance to attend to personal business, religious observances, or special occasions. Some companies add them to vacation time with pay. Others only allow personal days without pay. In addition, inquire about absences due to medical and dental appointments, bereavement pay, military leave, paternity leave, appearance in court, and jury duty.

PERSONAL LEAVES. Employers are not required by law to allow employees paid personal leaves of absence, but must apply such practices consistently to all employees if they do. If you are considering taking an extended leave, what about the continuation of medical benefits during this period? Ask whether medical and other benefits terminate at the end of the month when the leave becomes effective. Can you keep those benefits in effect during the absence period by continuing to pay your payroll deductions?

Be aware that federal law prohibits companies from requiring employees to work an extended period of time (such as 12 months) before being allowed to take unpaid personal leaves. The Equal Employment Opportunity Commission has ruled that not allowing unpaid leave has a disparate impact on women who desire to nurse their newborn children and may violate the federal Family and Medical Leave Act (FMLA).

DISABILITY LEAVE. If you will be a full-time employee, you may be entitled to disability leave should you become unable to work due to a nonoccupational illness.

Note: A company cannot treat pregnancy-related disability or maternity leave differently than it treats other forms of disability leaves of absence. This is explained in greater detail in Chapter 5.

DISABILITY. What happens in the event you are disabled? Can you receive salary and other benefits for a predetermined period of time? If so, how much and for how long? Understand the meanings of temporary disability and permanent disability and know what ramifications will ensue in the event of such disability.

Other Matters of Concern

In addition to financial benefits, job security, and duties, there are many other matters to discuss at the hiring interview. The following checklist will cover concerns often enunciated by the employer (which may or may not be relevant depending upon your particular situation).

1. Are you required to protect confidential information and trade secrets acquired while working for the company? If so, agree how this can be accomplished.

2. Can you have side ventures in a noncompeting business, or must you work exclusively for the company on a full-time basis?

3. Who owns inventions and processes created by you during employment?

4. Will disputes be resolved by litigation or binding arbitration? Can the prevailing party recover attorney fees and court costs from the losing party?

5. To perform your job better and reduce misunderstandings, it is also wise to receive information regarding the following policies:

- Time clock regulations
- Rest periods
- Absences
- Safety and accident prevention
- Authorized use of telephones
- Reporting complaints
- Making suggestions
- Resolving disputes
- Personal appearance rules
- Solicitation rules
- Conflict of interest and code of ethic rules

6. Does the company require you to sign a contract containing a restrictive covenant prohibiting you from working for a competitor or calling on customers previously solicited during your employ? If so, does the company require all new employees to sign similar contracts?

Restrictive covenants are provisions in employment agreements that prohibit a person from directly competing or working for a competitor after leaving his or her employer. The effect of such clauses varies greatly. For example, they can:

- Restrict an employee from working for a competitor of the former employer
- Restrict an employee from starting a business or forming a venture with others that competes against the former employer

- Restrict an employee from contacting or soliciting former or current customers or employees of the employer

- Restrict an employee from using confidential knowledge, trade secrets, and other privileged information learned while working for the former employer

- Restrict an employee from any of the above in both geographic and time limitations

The above points are illustrated by the following clauses taken from employment agreements:

For a period of one (1) year following the termination of your employment for any reason, it is agreed that you will not contact or solicit any person, firm, association, or corporation to which you sold products of the Company during the year preceding the termination of your employment.

Upon termination of the Doctor's employment under this Agreement for any reason, the Doctor shall not engage in the practice of neurology or open his own office for the practice of neurology or associate himself with other physicians within a five (5) mile radius of the office of the Corporation or a five mile radius of any hospital for which the Doctor has worked on behalf of the Corporation for a period of one (1) year after the effective date of termination.

In consideration of compensation paid to me as an employee, I hereby recognize as the exclusive property of the employer and agree to assign, transfer and convey to the employer, every invention, discovery, concept, idea, process, method and technique which I become acquainted with as a result or consequence of my employment and agree to execute all documents requested by the employer to evidence its ownership thereof.

You may be surprised to learn, however, that such clauses are not always enforceable. Although every case is different, judges have been taking dimmer views of such attempts to restrict an employee's livelihood. Consult Chapter 8 for more information about the weight such clauses can carry once you are fired or resign.

Whether or not such covenants are legal, however, defending lawsuits involving restrictive covenants is time-consuming and expensive, so you should avoid signing such agreements in the first place. Many employers have a tendency to "hang" such a clause over individuals by threatening to institute legal action after a person's resignation or termination. This can discourage you from contacting prospective employers and customers in your industry and trade or establishing your own business. Thus, consider the following strategies for help in this area.

STRATEGY 1: *Carefully review and resist signing contracts containing restrictive covenants. An employee who works without an employment contract and who leaves without taking any trade secrets has total freedom to work elsewhere in the same industry. This generally includes the right to solicit the ex-employer's customers. However, you may be subjecting yourself to a lawsuit (even when no valid grounds exist) by signing an agreement containing such a clause.*

Always read your employment contract carefully before signing it. What does the restrictive covenant say? For example, does it prohibit you from working for a competitor or calling on customers you previously sold for the company for an excessive period (e.g., two years) ? If so, make the employer aware of this. Negotiate to reduce the covenant to a reasonable period you can live with (e.g., three months) and insist on the right to receive continued salary and other benefits while the restrictive covenant is in effect. Remember, everything is negotiable before you sign on the bottom line. Once the agreement is signed, however, you may be bound by its terms.

STRATEGY 2: *Always obtain a copy of the agreement after it is signed. Many people forget to do this. After they resign or are discharged and receive a formal demand requesting them to refrain from certain acts (usually in the form of a written cease and desist letter), they cannot locate the agreement containing the restrictive provision. This places them at a disadvantage. For example, they may be unable to obtain an accurate opinion from a lawyer if he or she cannot review the contract or may be forced to spend unnecessary legal fees trying to obtain a copy from the employer. Thus, request a copy of all documents that you sign, and store them in a safe place for later review.*

Confirming These Points in Writing

Once you and the company have agreed to key terms, it is essential to confirm the deal in writing. Legal disputes often arise when people are hired on a handshake. A handshake, or oral agreement, indicates only that the parties came to some form of agreement; it does not say what the agreement was. Failure to spell out important terms often leads to misunderstandings and disputes. Even when key terms are discussed, the same spoken words that are agreed upon have different meanings from the employee's and company's perspective. Written words limit this sort of misunderstanding.

Although a written contract cannot guarantee you will be satisfied with the company's performance, it can provide additional remedies in the event of the employer's nonperformance. Once the agreement is signed, the law presumes that the parties incorporated their intentions into the contract. The instrument "speaks for itself," and courts will not hear testimony about understandings or discussions before the contract was signed unless the information is necessary to interpret ambiguous terms or establish particular trade customs.

Additionally, be aware that clauses in written contracts can give you negotiating strength. For example, some employment contracts state that terms cannot be changed without the written consent of both parties. If such a clause was included in your contract and an employer attempted to reduce your salary or other benefits, this could not be done without your written approval.

Written contracts also protect employees who are fired in a manner prohibited by the contract. The following is an example of a situation that could occur.

Andrew received a one-year contract to work as an advertising executive. The contract stated that it would be automatically renewed for an additional year if notice of termination was not received at least 90 days prior to the expiration of the first year. Andrew's company gave him notice that the contract would not be renewed one week prior to the start of the next year. Andrew sued for damages; the court ruled that he was entitled to additional compensation because the employer failed to abide by the terms of the agreement.

Working on a handshake for an indefinite period of time is risky. In most states the law says that if you are hired without a written contract and for a nonspecific period of time, you are "hired at will." This means that, subject to various exceptions outlined in later chapters of this book, your employer can fire you at any time without notice and without cause.

Due to the unfairness of the at-will doctrine, which affects tens of millions of employees, many more people are no longer accepting being hired on a handshake. Instead, they are recognizing that they can be better protected by including favorable clauses in clearly drafted contracts and are insisting on receiving written agreements whenever they accept a job.

A good employment contract should describe in specific detail all important aspects of your employment, such as term of the contract, duties, authority and responsibility, job description and title, compensation and reimbursement, benefits, termination, and methods for resolving disputes, such as arbitration, mediation, and more.

There are three purposes for every written contract. First, the act of writing helps ensure that both parties to the contract understand and agree to its terms. Second, the written word provides a reminder to both parties of the terms of the agreement. Third, the written, signed, and witnessed contract can serve as evidence if legal action is required to enforce the terms. Each employment contract must be drafted to meet specific situations, needs, and understandings for both the employee and the employer.

Everything in the contract should be very specific. Anything that is vague or open for later negotiation creates a potential misunderstanding and may fail to carry weight in a court of law. So be sure to cover everything that is important to you, and be sure that all understandings based on your discussions and negotiations are included in the written words of the contract.

Consider, for example:

- Compensation: salary, salary increases, bonus program and requirements, profit sharing, etc.

- Job description: statement of job duties, authorities, responsibilities, title, etc.

- Terms of employment: contract period and provision for renewal, at-will, etc.

- Fringe benefits: pension plan (and when vested), life and health insurance, savings plan, company contribution, etc.

- Vacation time: number of days, when earned, carryover, etc.

- Sick leave: number of days, conditions for allowance, salary and benefits continuance during extended health-based absences, etc.

- Arbitration: provision for arbitration or mediation in the event of unreconcilable disagreements affecting the basis of a term in the employment agreement.

- Termination/resignation: terms leading to employment termination or allowing no-fault resignation, with terms for payment and continuation of benefits upon leaving the company's employment, etc.

- Special provisions: office facilities, parking space, dining room rights, recreational facilities, health maintenance programs, medical examinations, company car or equivalent, etc.

Don't stop with the above mentioned points. Consider all of the things that are important to you related to the job, its benefits, its responsibilities, and its expectations, both positive and potentially negative. Consider what will happen if the economic fortunes of the company fade. What if your job or department is abolished? What if the firm is taken over by another firm? Will you, as the newest employee, be the first to be laid off? Or do you have employment protection? If not, are there protections for termination payments if you are asked or invited to leave?

Whenever you obtain an employment contract or any business document, read it carefully. Question all ambiguous and confusing language. Consult a lawyer if you do not understand the meaning of any terms. Remember that contracts prepared by employers usually contain clauses that work to your disadvantage. Thus, you should review the agreement thoroughly before signing.

When written agreements are used, be sure that all changes, strike-outs, and erasures are initialed by both parties and that all blanks are filled in. If additions are necessary, include them in a space provided or attach them to the contract itself. Then note on the contract that addenda have been added and accepted by both parties. This prevents questions from arising if addenda are lost or separated, because it is difficult to prove there were any without mention in the body of the contract.

Also be sure that the contract is signed by a bona fide officer who has the legal authority to bind the employer to important terms. Finally, always obtain a signed copy of the executed agreement for your files and keep it in a safe place where you store other valuable documents.

Turning an Oral Contract Into a Written Document

A formal agreement is not always required to serve your purposes; in some cases an oral contract confirmed in writing can be an acceptable substitute. Before I describe how this may be accomplished, a few words about oral contracts are appropriate. An oral contract is a verbal agreement between the employee and the company defining their working relationship. Such contacts may be binding when the duties, compensation, and terms of employment are agreed to by both parties.

There are certain types of contracts that must be in writing to be legally binding. The rule requiring this is called the statute of frauds. While there are a number of items covered in the statute of frauds, the one of direct interest to you regarding employment states that any contract agreement that will require more than a year to complete must be in writing.

Each state has its own version of the statute of frauds, and various courts interpret its provisions differently. However, remember that most courts do not support indefinite employment agreements based on an oral contract, because employment could be terminated at any time prior to the elapse of a year. Thus, to ensure enforceability of a working arrangement in excess of one year, you must include such an arrangement in writing.

Many workers have oral agreements simply because their companies refuse to give them a written contract. In fact, companies like to operate under oral agreements because there is no written evidence to indicate what terms were discussed and accepted by both parties when they entered into the employment arrangement. If disputes arise, it is more difficult for the employee to prove that the company failed to abide by the terms of the agreement. For example, if a bonus totaling $10,000 to be paid was accepted orally, a dishonest employer could deny this by stating that a gratuitous bonus arrangement had been accepted that was substantially less than $10,000. The employee would then have to prove that both parties had agreed upon the higher bonus figure.

When a legal dispute arises concerning the terms of an oral contract, a court will resolve the problem by examining all the evidence that the employee and company offer and weighing the testimony to determine who is telling the truth. Thus, to avoid problems, all employees should try to obtain a written contract to clarify their rights. However, if your company refuses to sign a written agreement, there are ways to protect yourself if you have an oral contract. Your chief concern should be directed toward obtaining written evidence that indicates the accepted terms, including information that defines your compensation, additional benefits, job security concerns, notice of termination requirements, and other considerations.

If your company refuses to sign a written agreement, it is advisable to write a letter whenever you reach an oral agreement relating to your job. Whatever deal is agreed upon, a letter should be drafted similar to the following.

Sample Letter
Confirming an Oral Agreement

Your Name
Address
Telephone Number
Date

Name of Corporate Officer
Title
Name of Employer
Address

Dear (Name of Officer),

I enjoyed meeting you on (date). This letter confirms that I agree to be employed by (name of company) as a (specify job title or position) for an initial term of one (1) year commencing on February 10, 2011, and terminating on February 9, 2012.

As compensation for my services, I agree to accept an annual salary of $40,000 payable in equal weekly installments in the sum of (specify). Additionally, I shall receive this reimbursement by a separate check within two (2) weeks of my presentation of appropriate vouchers and records.

This agreement cannot be shortened or modified without the express written consent of both parties. Additionally, in the event notice of termination is not received no later than one (1) month prior to the expiration of the original term, this agreement shall be automatically renewed, under the same terms and conditions, for an additional one (1) year period.

Upon termination of this agreement for any reason, I shall be entitled to receive my bonus and salary for the remaining period of the quarter in which my termination occurs.

If any terms of this letter are ambiguous or incorrect, please reply within (specify) days from your receipt hereof. Otherwise, this letter shall set forth our entire understanding in this matter.

I look forward to working for (name of company).

Very truly yours,
Name of Employee

Sent certified mail, return receipt requested.

After being hired, always write a letter similar to the above confirming the points you and the company agreed upon if you cannot obtain a written contract. Be aware that in many instances the letter you write to the company can serve in place of a formal employment contract. You may find that your letter holds you to your stated understanding of the employment terms, so be very careful, specific, and accurate in your wording. If the company replies in agreement, particularly if it replies in writing, or does not argue with your stated understanding, a court may rule that these terms are also binding on the company. Another way that a company may be bound to certain terms of employment is through statements published in their employee handbook or personnel manual. This aspect is discussed in detail in Chapter 6.

Write the letter with precision, since ambiguous terms are resolved against the letter writer. Be sure to keep a copy of the letter for your own records and save the certified mail receipt. If at a later date the terms of the oral agreement are changed (for instance, additional compensation is paid to you or your duties are expanded), write another letter specifying the new arrangement that has been reached. Keep a copy of this letter and all correspondence sent to and received from your company for your protection. This may also include a series of e-mails sent back and forth between the parties.

PART II
■ ■ ■ ■ ■ ■ ■ ■ ■
How to Protect Your On-the-Job Rights

Most employees are unaware of the numerous rights that exist in the workplace. These rights are frequently violated and the law allows people to recover damages when employees, agents, and their companies act improperly.

This section of the book covers your rights on the job. Chapter 3 is devoted to employee benefits. It discusses a variety of subjects including overtime, equal pay, and union rights of employees. Chapter 4 discusses privacy and other basic freedoms of employees. This includes searches, interrogations, wiretapping, eavesdropping, and other forms of surveillance that are often perpetrated on employees. It also discusses such diverse subjects as a person's right to work in a smoke-free environment, federal legislation dealing with the right to be warned of a mass layoff prior to a plant closing, and whether employees can have access to their personnel records.

You will also learn about your rights regarding lie-detector and other tests, and whether or not you can lawfully refuse to submit to such tests while working. AIDS, drug, and alcohol testing will also be discussed so you will know your rights in this area.

Finally, you will learn how workers are protected under the Occupational Safety and Health Act (OSHA), a law that requires all employers to provide a safe and healthful workplace.

Chapter 5 is devoted to how workers can protect themselves from discrimination. In this chapter you will learn what constitutes age, gender, pregnancy, race, handicap, and religious discrimination and how to enforce your rights and protect yourself if you are a victim in this area. For example, if you are being forced to work in a hostile and offensive environment (if, for example, you are the victim of sexual harassment), you will learn how to prove your claim by sending letters to document such exploitation.

You will also learn how to file a formal complaint with the Equal Employment Opportunity Commission or other appropriate agency to start the ball rolling. Additionally, the chapter provides strategies to help you win your case. More than 100,000 charges of on-the-job discrimination are filed with various agencies each year; the chapter will help you know when you are being victimized, how to fight back, and how to successfully prove your case and collect damages when you are being treated unfairly.

3

■ ■ ■ ■ ■ ■ ■ ■ ■

Employee Benefits

Being properly hired is only the first step in the employment relationship. It is also important to know your rights in the event that problems develop on the job.

The first section in this chapter discusses union rights of employees. Although much of the information and strategies discussed in the book pertain to nonunion employees, a brief explanation of the genesis of your on-the-job rights as a union member are included here.

▍Union Rights of Employees

To understand your rights under modern labor law, it helps to understand the source of the laws and regulations that serve to protect workers who belong to unions. Labor law as we know it today began in 1935 with the Wagner Act, created by Congress to protect union members from the excesses of employers. The three main objectives of the Wagner Act were to end labor conflict (including conflict among labor unions themselves), to create a system for fair collective bargaining, and to create a concept to identify unfair labor practices. The National Labor Relations Board (NLRB) was created to interpret and enforce the Wagner Act.

The NLRB acts as a court, hearing disputes related to labor law. It oversees labor-union representation elections and union representation, and it determines or defines appropriate bargaining units. By definition, the NLRB enters the picture when employees seek to protect themselves by "concerted action" for "mutual aid and protection."

In 1947 the Taft-Hartley Act was passed by Congress to protect employers from the excesses of unions. The act outlawed the closed shop, in which an employer would agree to hire only union members, but allowed what is called an agency shop. In an agency shop a person coming to work for a unionized shop does not have to join the union but must within a certain time start paying union dues. While federal law allows the agency shop, state right-to-work laws can outlaw them.

The Taft-Hartley Act added to labor law prohibitions against union coercion, unreasonable union dues, and featherbedding. It also allowed the president of the United States to stop a strike that endangered health or safety. The 80-day cooling-off period was another result of the Taft-Hartley Act.

The next step in labor law was the Landrum-Griffin Act of 1959, which was enacted for the purpose of protecting union members from the unions themselves. Most notable in the act was what is known as a Bill of Rights for union members. Elements of this act guaranteed union members that they would receive equal treatment, could criticize the union (free speech and assembly), and could sue the union. It provided for fair union discipline hearings, fair and open elections, review of union financial information, and fair representation.

A labor union is an organization of working people who collectively negotiate (or attempt to negotiate) benefits, better working conditions, grievances, and employment contracts for its members. The federal Taft-Hartley Act allows certain classes of workers to band together, form, and join unions. Supervisors, managers, executives, and some government employees cannot be union members because "blue-collar" (nonmanagement) working-class status is often required for membership.

If you belong to a union, much of your protection as a union member derives from the powers and actions of the National Labor Relations Board together with the U.S. Department of Labor and state law. For example, if you believe that your union is not zealously representing your interests, or has engaged in an unfair or illegal labor practice, it may be necessary to file a grievance against your union through a local office of the NLRB. Federal law is more powerful than state law with regard to minimum legal requirements. States, however, can have even more restrictive laws.

Under the federal National Labor Relations Act and state laws, employers are forbidden from penalizing workers who decide collectively to discuss common grievances and form and participate in a labor union. Workers cannot be disciplined, demoted, reassigned, fired, threatened, or treated poorly as a result of union involvement. Neither can employers offer nonunion workers more benefits or better working conditions than union workers. Speak to a labor lawyer to protect your rights if this is the case.

In certain situations, such as when an employer has entered into a comprehensive collective bargaining agreement with a union permitting the union to act as spokesperson for all workers of the company, you may be forced to belong to a union even if you do not want to participate in union activities. This means that union dues may be automatically deducted from your paycheck, and there is little you can legally do about it. However, in some states, people are permitted to work at companies without being required to participate in union activities or be affiliated with a union.

There are several advantages and disadvantages in belonging to a union. For example, employers are bound to follow rules concerning discharge procedures in collective bargaining agreements previously negotiated and ratified by a union. In such agreements employers are sometimes forbidden from terminating union workers except in situations involving worker misconduct or serious offenses. If a union worker is fired wrongly or under circumstances suggesting that the employer acted improperly, the union should schedule an arbitration proceeding or grievance procedure without delay so that an impartial arbitrator can hear the case and hopefully reinstate the terminated worker (and order back pay and other lost benefits in appropriate circumstances).

STRATEGY: *If you are a union member and are treated unfairly while working, denied expected benefits, or fired from a job, immediately speak to a union delegate and/or lawyer hired by the union or a private lawyer to discuss your rights. The specifics of your work relationship are spelled out in the collective bargaining agreement. Most agreements allow you to discuss a problem with a designated union representative, who will then communicate the matter to union officials. If the union determines that your grievance is sound, the union should guide you through the complaint process.*

Most collective bargaining agreements provide little or no severance pay and other post-termination benefits for terminated union workers. This differs from nonunion employees, who may be able to receive larger severance packages after having worked for an employer for many years and been discharged through no fault of their own, such as for a job elimination or company reorganization.

When a union is organizing a strike, an employer may be able to keep workers off the premises legally (known as a lockout) in an attempt to force the union to back down. Union workers may not receive any pay during a lockout, and sometimes the employer does not have to rehire workers if they were permanently replaced while on strike. Some unions provide short-term strike funds to workers who are forced to go out on strike. Under federal law, the obligation to rehire union workers who were replaced often depends on whether the employer acted properly before the strike. For example, if the employer engaged in an unfair labor practice that caused the strike (e.g., failing to provide a safe work environment), the employer may be legally required to rehire its original union workers. Rules concerning the circumstances permitting union workers to legally strike (e.g., to protest unsafe working conditions) are spelled out in the National Labor Relations Act.

Remember, if your complaint involves an employer, your relief will come from the NLRB. Unfortunately, if you have a complaint against a small company, the NLRB will not act. And the law does not apply to state or local government jobs. However, if your complaint is against your union, it must go through the NLRB or the Department of Labor, but a safety complaint would be filed with OSHA (Occupational Safety and Health Administration).

Most actions against unions allege a violation of the statutory duty of fair representation derived from section 9(a) of the National Labor Relations Act. This law provides individual employees with recourse when a union fails to grieve a member's firing in a hearing, fails to take a bona fide case to arbitration under the rules of an existing collective bargaining agreement, or allows the statute of limitations to expire before taking timely action in a grievance on behalf of a member. Union members can also bring suit against the union and the employer in a hybrid duty of fair representation claim under Section 301 of the Labor Management Relations Act (LMRA) if the claim alleges a failure to follow the collective bargaining agreement (CBA) between the union and employer or the reasonable interpretation of the CBA.

A union breaches the duty of fair representation when its conduct toward a member is arbitrary, discriminatory, or in bad faith. Although a union may not arbitrarily ignore a meritorious grievance or process it in a perfunctory fashion, members do not have an absolute right to have their grievances taken to arbitration. A union is allowed to exercise reasonable discretion as to how it can best satisfy the interests of the collective unit. In firing cases, it is essential to prove that your discharge was contrary to the union contract and that the union's acts or omissions seriously undermined the arbitral process. This is often a difficult burden to meet and most actions against unions in this area are not successful.

STRATEGY: *The author is sometimes consulted by disgruntled union members seeking redress when their union fails to properly protect their interests, usually after a firing. Case decisions at the NLRB grant wide latitude to a union's right to exercise discretion as a way of justifying its actions. That doesn't mean though that you can't win a case in compelling circumstances. Consult an experienced employment attorney to discuss your rights and options when you have proof that your union failed to enforce your rights in a timely fashion which led to your discharge, failed to request* *reasonable accommodations or prevent you from suffering sexual harassment, or handled your grievances with discriminatory intent.*

Regardless of your union or nonunion status you can appeal to the EEOC under Title VII of the Civil Rights Act of 1964 if you are being discriminated against because of your race, color, religion, gender, or national origin. Strategies to prove and win discrimination cases are discussed in Chapter 5.

The body of employment law governing the rights of unions and union members is changing rapidly, often depending on which administration is in power. Experts state that in the coming years a union's right to financial information from an employer alleging financial hardship will expand, an employer's right to ban employees' use of its e-mail system may be eliminated, and many pro-business decisions implemented during the President Bush era will be reversed. Also if the Employee Free Choice Act (EFCA) is passed, this will make it easier for people to form unions and obtain collective bargaining agreements.

STRATEGY: *In light of such potential shifts, monitor all changes and proposed changes of the law for maximum advantage.*

Part-Time Employees

Part-time workers must typically comply with the same company rules, policies, and procedures as full-time employees, including working regular stated hours. Most states define part-time workers as those who are employed on jobs with fewer than 30 hours per week. Part-time workers are usually paid on an hourly basis and are not entitled to company benefits, such as extended vacations, company pension and profit-sharing plans, health insurance, and other benefits. Some states grant coverage to employees who work more than a stated number of hours (e.g., 25) per week. Under federal ERISA law, employees who generally work one thousand hours in a pension plan year must be included in all appropriate company pension plans that are offered to other similar workers.

STRATEGY: *Contact the nearest office of your state's Department of Labor to learn about all benefits that must be offered to you as a part-time worker. In some states part-time workers must have paid overtime, vacations, lunch breaks, and coffee breaks like regular workers. Be certain you understand what benefits are or are not available before accepting a job to be sure the company complies with all appropriate benefits laws. If, for example, you do not qualify for medical benefits, inquire how much extra it would cost to be included in such coverage. You may also learn that the company will offer prorated fringe benefits, including shorter paid vacations, sick leave, and life insurance, just by asking. Point out to the prospective employer that by offering you and similar part-timers prorated benefits, the company may qualify for cheaper group HMO and medical insurance rates.*

Under the federal Equal Pay Act, part-time workers and temporary employees are not subject to strict rules that men and women doing the same job must be paid equally. And many companies not wishing to offer benefits required to be offered to employees under the federal Family and Medical Leave Act (FMLA) are exempt from that law when they employ a sufficient number of temporary, contract employees or part-time workers (defined in the act as those who work 25 or fewer hours a week) to reduce the number of full-time employees to fewer than 50. However, when companies use temporaries to supple- ment full-time personnel, the practice has been successfully attacked by unions on the grounds that bargaining-unit employees are deprived of job opportunities and overtime.

As a part-time worker, you may be terminated for poor performance and are subject to the company's work rules and requirements like other workers. Your paycheck will reflect payroll deductions and taxes. All legal obligations owed by the company to its workforce, such as complying with safety (OSHA) rules and regulations, not making promises it does not intend to keep, and avoiding discriminatory acts, apply to you as well.

STRATEGY: *Negotiate the right to convert into a full-time position if your work skills are satisfactory or if the employer's needs or your needs change. Don't forget to discuss this with management where appropriate. Additionally, inquire if the employer will allow you and someone else to share a job that requires 40 or more hours of work per week. Some companies are offering job shares where circumstances warrant. The advantage of a job share is that these employees often obtain prorated shares of benefits normally available only to full-time workers. They also work flexible hours and have the opportunity to take time off during the workweek to meet family obligations, such as child care, or pursue other interests. Inquire if the employer has a job-share plan in effect.*

Leased and Temporary Employees

Leased and temporary employees work for the service firm supplying workers to the client company. Although they report directly to an employer, they receive their paychecks and benefits from the company leasing their services. Leased employees typically do not work at one job site for more than a fixed period (e.g., one year). Once a particular job is finished, they are then assigned to work at another company.

Most temps earn an average 40 percent less per hour than full-time workers and do not have health benefits, pensions, and life insurance. This has caused some commentators to point out that when you are a temp you are treated at a lower status despite the advantages of a flexible work schedule.

Although leased employees are obligated to conduct themselves in accordance with the work rules and regulations stipulated by the company for which services are being provided, they must ultimately answer to the leasing company hiring them. When a dispute arises, such as whether unemployment insurance is available after a layoff or firing, the issue may depend on the rights and remedies available against the leasing company and not the client.

All applicants applying for work as leased employees should know the ramifications of their status before accepting employment. At a minimum, get answers to the following questions:

- Which company will pay me?
- Can I collect overtime for my efforts? If so, how do I go about this?
- To whom do I look for instructions about when, where, and how work is to be performed?
- Who controls my work schedule?
- Under what circumstances may I be dismissed?
- Who furnishes the tools and equipment used by me for the job?
- How do we resolve problems I may have with the client?
- Am I prohibited from working directly for the client company (such as being required to sign a restrictive covenant in an employment contract) if they like my skills and work performance?
- Do I have a say in my assignments?
- How often do I have to report back to the leasing company?
- What are my benefits, and who pays for these benefits?

Although employee leasing is being used more these days, critics contend that employees suffer by not receiving commensurate benefits from the company leasing their services. Thus, it is critical to negotiate a fair hourly rate or weekly salary as well as obtain equivalent benefits that would be available if you worked for a company as a regular employee.

The relationship of a leased or temporary worker to an employer has unique ramifications with respect to workers' compensation, unemployment insurance benefits, and tax matters. In some states a person who is employed by a leasing company is also considered to be in the special employ of the client company despite the fact that the leasing employer is responsible for the payment of wages, has the power to hire and fire, has an interest in the work performed by the employee, maintains workers' compensation for the employee, and provides some of the employee's equipment. This means, for example, that if you are injured while working for the client company, you may be covered under workers' compensation and cannot institute a private negligence lawsuit.

However, if the client company approved your hiring and possessed the right of control, an employer/employee relationship might be found, making the client responsible for any discriminatory acts (including sexual harassment) perpetrated against you on the job site. The same is true if you desire to take time off to care for a newborn or an adopted child, an elderly parent, or a sick spouse under the federal Family and Medical Leave Act (FMLA).

Under what conditions will companies using temporary labor be required to comply with the FMLA? Generally, where two or more businesses exercise some control over the work or working conditions of the employee, a joint relationship may be found to exist. Once this occurs, the client as the secondary employer may have the obligation to comply with the FMLA and cannot discriminate against you if you seek to exercise your rights under this law.

STRATEGY: *If you are a leased or a temporary employee, speak to a lawyer immediately if you believe your rights are being violated. This may include, for example, being a victim of gender, race, age, or disability discrimination, or being denied unemployment insurance benefits or workers' compensation coverage after an accident.*

Statutory Employees

Many people who work at home or who are paid on a commission basis (such as life insurance agents or salespeople) are classified by the IRS as statutory employees. The fact that you may work out of your home with little or no direction or control from an employer and are paid commissions for services rendered does not matter for tax purposes. If you are a statutory employee, your commissions or pay will be subject to the same tax withholding requirements as other employees. Speak to your accountant or professional adviser for more information on this subject, such as to determine if you are a statutory nonemployee not subject to withholding requirements. (Some licensed real estate agents and direct sellers such as door-to-door salespeople are considered statutory non-employees.)

Employee Versus Independent Contractor Status

There is a growing effort by federal and state agencies to investigate and audit companies who misclassify employees and annually cheat the government out of hundreds of millions of dollars of unpaid taxes and wages. Independent contractors are less costly than salaried workers because an employer is not responsible to pay for or withhold their payroll taxes, fund the employer-matching portion of the Federal Insurance Contributions Act (FICA), or provide benefits. Workers classified as employees have more rights under federal and state labor laws, such as being protected against discrimination, minimum wage and overtime pay abuses, workers' compensation coverage, actions from labor organizations seeking to enforce safety, and pension and employee benefit considerations, among other considerations. As an example, employers are generally liable for the negligent acts of their employers but not for their independent contractor workers.

A widely reported case in this area involved a ruling against Microsoft. A group of freelance programmers who were paid higher hourly rates than comparable employees commenced a lawsuit demanding various savings and stock-option benefits. After the U.S. Court of Appeals for the 9th Circuit ruled that Microsoft exercised sufficient control over these workers, they were deemed to be employees and entitled to such benefits.

The IRS generally opposes independent status because companies who retain independents don't have to withhold income or employment taxes. Since a contractor can manipulate earnings by claiming all business-related expenses on Schedule C (where expenses offset gross business income), the IRS believes that many dollars of compensation go unreported. Additionally, if you are an independent contractor who is injured while working, you are not bound to collecting workers' compensation damages for your injuries. This is advantageous, since the awards are typically larger for claimants who commence private lawsuits for injuries than for those who receive workers' compensation benefits.

As an independent contractor, however, you are not permitted to file for unemployment benefits after a job has ended or you are terminated unless it is determined at the unemployment hearing that you are legally an employee. You probably cannot avail yourself of employer-provided disability and health insurance plans and may have to establish your own retirement and pension plans. Since you will receive an IRS Form 1099 and not a W-2 form with deductions withheld, you are responsible to pay all applicable Social Security, unemployment insurance, state and local income taxes, and workers' compensation insurance benefits for any people you employ. Under the laws of many states, you will probably have a more difficult time asserting discrimination claims. Furthermore, you cannot assert claims for overtime, since wage and hour laws apply only to employees.

No precise legal definition of an independent contractor exists, and each state has its own laws to determine whether an individual is an employee or an independent contractor. When the courts attempt to determine the difference, they analyze the facts of each particular case.

Significant factors courts look for when making this distinction are:

1. The company's right of control over the worker.

2. Whether the individual works exclusively for the company or is permitted to work for others at the same time.

3. Whether the parties have a written agreement that defines the status of the worker and states she is not considered an employee for the purposes of the Federal Contributions Act and the Federal Unemployment Tax Act and that the

individual must pay all self-employment and federal income tax.

4. Whether the individual controls her own work schedule and the number of working hours.

5. Whether the individual operates from her own place of business (or pays rent if an office is provided) and supplies her own stationery and business cards not at the company's expense.

Typically, employees undertake to achieve an agreed result and to accept an employer's directions as to the manner in which the result is accomplished, while independent contractors agree to achieve a certain result but are not subject to the orders of the employer as to the means that were used. In each case, the court looks at the specific facts in making its determination. For instructive purposes, the company's right of control is best explained by the use of examples.

Courts have found workers to be employees if companies:

- Have the right to supervise details of the operation
- Require salespeople to collect accounts on its behalf
- Provide workers with an office, company equipment, company car, and/or reimbursement for some or all expenses
- Require workers to call on particular customers
- Deduct income and FICA taxes from their wages or salary
- Provide workers with insurance and workers' compensation benefits
- Restrict their ability to work for other companies or jobs and require full-time efforts

This list is not meant to be all-inclusive, but rather to help you determine what classification you fall under. Since the law is quite unsettled, the IRS follows a summary of rules used to determine proper status. According to the IRS, an employer-employee relationship for tax purposes exists when the person for whom the services are performed has the right to control and direct the individual who performs the services, not only as to the result to be accomplished by the work but also as to the details and means by which the result is accomplished. In this connection it is not necessary that the employer actually direct or control the manner in which services are performed; it is sufficient if the firm had the right to do so. The designation or description of the relationship of the parties in a written agreement other than that of an employer and employee is immaterial if such a relationship exists, and the IRS will disregard other designations (such as being called a partner, agent, consultant, or independent contractor) in the agreement.

STRATEGY: *The odds of finding employee status become lower when you form a corporation and receive compensation from your corporation. The IRS is also impressed when you or your corporation works for several companies and not just one.*

When an initial determination is made by the IRS finding employee status, costly damages, penalties, and interest can ensue to you and the company hiring you. In misclassification cases the company will be required to pay all back withholding taxes plus interest, even if the misclassified independent contractors have already paid their taxes. The IRS and other agencies might also levy huge fines and press criminal charges against company officials.

Independent contractors are responsible to provide their own workers' compensation insurance under most state worker compensation laws. However, a company is obligated to provide workers' compensation insurance on the independent contractor's behalf (and employees of a subcontractor) when the independent contractor fails to provide his own.

Speak to a competent lawyer or accountant immediately upon receiving an initial IRS or state taxing authority notice of determination or request for facts. Competent tax advice and guidance are crucial in this area.

If you are not a statutory or common law employee (which includes leased employees, part-time workers, and temporaries), you are legally considered to be an independent contractor. This is so even if you call yourself a consultant or subcontractor. As an independent contractor, it is crucial to discuss all the terms and conditions of your working relationship with a company or individual. This must be done before commencing work, no matter what your trade or profession. All key terms of the relationship, including the services to be rendered, payment, stages of payment, whether expenses are to be reimbursed (and to what extent), and the length (also known as the term) of the arrangement, should be understood and agreed upon to reduce misunderstandings.

Summary of IRS Rules to Determine Employee Versus Independent Contractor Status

Many of these rules are followed by the IRS when determining employee or independent contractor status. Speak to an accountant or other professional for more advice.

1. **INSTRUCTIONS.** Employees generally follow instructions about when, where, and how work is to be performed; contractors establish their own hours and have no instructions regarding how the job should be completed.

2. **TRAINING.** Employees typically receive training via classes and meetings regarding how services are to be performed; contractors generally establish their own procedures and receive no training.

3. **SERVICES PERFORMED PERSONALLY.** Services are typically performed personally by the employee; contractors may utilize others to perform job tasks and duties.

4. **SUPERVISION.** Most employees are supervised by a foreman or representative of the employer; contractors generally are not.

5.   SET HOURS OF WORK. An employee's hours and days are set by the employer; contractors dictate their own time and are often retained to complete one particular job.

6.   FULL TIME REQUIRED. An employee typically works for only one employer; contractors may have several jobs or work for others at the same time.

7.   WORK ON PREMISES. Employees work on the premises of an employer or on a route or site designated by the employer; contractors typically work from their own premises and pay rent for their own premises.

8.   MANNER OF PAYMENT. Employees are generally paid in regular amounts at stated intervals; contractors are paid upon the completion of the job or project, in a lump sum or other arrangement (such as on a commission basis).

9.   FURNISHING OF TOOLS AND MATERIALS. Employees are usually furnished tools and materials by employers; contractors typically furnish and pay for their own tools, materials, and expenses.

10. PROFIT. Employees generally receive no direct profit or loss from work performed, while contractors do.

11. JOB SECURITY. Employees may be discharged or quit at any time without incurring liability; contractors are typically discharged after a job is completed and are legally obligated to complete a particular job to avoid liability.

Determining proper classification status ultimately boils down to the unique facts of each case. No single act or event is typically paramount. A problem is that the IRS, state taxing agencies, and the Department of Labor sometimes use different rules when deciding a case. The IRS recently revised its 20-factor test and now looks at three general categories when evaluating the degree of control over the worker. The broad categories focus on behavioral control, financial control, and the type of relationship between the parties. Be sure you understand, review, and discuss these IRS changes with your financial advisor where applicable.

Consultants

A consultant is deemed to be an independent contractor by the IRS. Thus, it is important to operate legally as an independent regardless of the kind of sales promotion, marketing, engineering, or other professional services you may provide. The first step is to utilize a written agreement whenever you contract to provide services. Among other items, always confirm:

- A description of the services to be rendered
- The amount of time to be provided for such services (e.g., "no more or less than x hours per week")
- The method of compensation, whether a per diem rate, hourly rate or fixed price for the entire job. If you are to receive a flat fee, negotiate to be paid in installments with as much up-front payment as possible and never at the end of the job.
- A commission, royalty, or incentive (such as a cost reduction or savings) from your efforts
- Reimbursement for travel and incidental expenses
- Manner of invoice and payment
- Term of the agreement
- Provisions for resolving disputes, such as binding arbitration

(Note: Information about arbitration, mediation, other forms of litigation and working with a lawyer effectively are discussed in Chapters 9 and 10.)

Statutory Non-Employees

A statutory non-employee is treated the same as an independent contractor. As such, statutory non-employees are generally excluded from the protections of most workplace laws and are treated as self-employed for federal income tax, employment tax, disability, and social security benefits purposes.

Examples of statutory non-employees include licensed real estate agents and direct sellers. The IRS defines a direct seller as a person who sells goods to an end-user consumer (such as selling cosmetics door-to-door). The IRS considers direct sellers to be statutory non-employees when their compensation is a direct result of sales output, when they use a written employment agreement that specifies that they are not employees, when they control their own work schedule and are not required to report to an employer, and when their selling is done outside an established retail store or showroom.

STRATEGY: *The distinction as to whether you are legally deemed a statutory non-employee or a statutory employee is not clear-cut. For example, many delivery drivers, life insurance agents, home workers, and salespeople who might not appear to be typical employees are treated as such by state laws and the IRS. If you are a statutory employee, you are covered by wage and hour laws, overtime, and tax withholding requirements imposed on employers.*

Comparable Worth

Comparable worth is the concept of paying women equally for "comparable jobs" in the same organization. It describes the notion that sex-segregated jobs should be analyzed to determine their worth to an employer and should not be confused with equal pay for equal work. In the public sector, some states and localities have compared jobs and found that some fit the definition when the value of the work and the amount of effort and independent judgment involved are equal. As a result, some women's wages have been raised. Comparable-worth cases are not presently recognized under the Equal Pay Act (EPA), although a few female claimants are suing private employers in this area under federal and state discrimination laws. Experts suggest that passage of the proposed Paycheck Fairness Act may provide economic relief in this area for mistreated workers.

Failure to Pay Appropriate Compensation

A recent survey published by the U.S. Department of Labor concluded that employers in all industries continue to deny or underpay workers' wages, benefits, and related compensation. Common areas of exploitation include paying less than the minimum wage; not paying time and a half for overtime; misclassifying workers as exempt from overtime; not paying tipped workers their fair share of tips or the tipped-worker minimum wage; not allowing a meal break; and illegally retaliating against workers who attempt to unionize or complain about wages issues. Disputes also arise when employers violate state laws by failing to pay wages on time; not reimbursing workers for legitimate business expenses; making improper wage deductions; and failing to make overtime payments for legitimate work that wasn't approved by a supervisor.

Rules governing hourly jobs, such as the minimum wage that can be paid, overtime, and restrictions on child labor, are primarily based on the Fair Labor Standards Act (FLSA), also known as the federal Wage and Hour Law. Some states have passed more stringent laws. For example, every state has wage and hour laws that regulate when and how employees are paid. Certain states require that employees receive a meal period a few hours after beginning work; other states require breakfast periods as well. Rules concerning the amount of paid time employers are required to extend for coffee and lunch breaks vary from state to state, and employers must typically pay accrued wages no less than twice per month. (Note, however, that some states require that employees be paid at least once a week.)

Like the EPA, the FLSA generally requires that male and female workers receive equal pay for work that requires equal skill, effort and responsibility. It also defines when employers may give compensatory time (time given off from work instead of cash payments). For part-time workers, employers may not be required to provide any benefits other than those covered under state and federal law, including Social Security, unemployment insurance and workers' compensation insurance. Speak to a representative at your state's Department of Labor regional office to get the facts.

This section will examine common problem areas and give you a better understanding of your rights to receive appropriate wages, tips, overtime, and related compensation.

Tips

Millions of people are paid on an hourly plus tips basis. If you earn more than $30 in tips, your employer can pay you less than the minimum wage (up to 50 percent less in certain instances) provided the total amount of wages and tips reaches the federally guaranteed minimum wage. However, employers are generally forbidden from taking tips away from you. Rules governing the sharing of tips, withholding requirements, and deductions from your salary or tips due to cash shortages, breakage, uniforms or use of tools and equipment are governed by state law. Check with a local Department of Labor office to determine how much minimum pay you must receive if you get additional tips in your job.

In addition, and totally aside from the minimum wage "tip credit" issue, employees who serve as waiters, busboys, bartenders or in other jobs that are customarily "tipped" should know that several states have laws prohibiting employers from taking "tips" that are left for employees. Other states (including New York) also require that "service charges" or other percentage-based "gratuities" added to the customers' bill must be paid over to the wait staff.

The author once represented a group of waiters who claimed their employer illegally kept the automatic gratuity charges it collected from guests. The waiters alleged the employer added a 20% service charge at banquets in place of the tip, but failed to distribute it to the wait staff. A New York State Court of Appeals decision ruled that clubs, restaurants, and banquet halls could not legally take a cut of tips and service charges customers leave unless they clearly understood that the mandatory service charges would not be paid to the workers as tips.

In tip pooling cases, all tip earnings are pooled together and then redistributed among service employees. Disputes arise when employers demand that assistant managers, maitre d's, kitchen staff and other agents of the employer (i.e., management) receive a portion of the tips, which may be illegal. This area of the law is evolving under state and federal law so consult an experienced employment attorney for advice and guidance where applicable.

Overtime Pay

The federal FLSA mandates that most employees receive one and one-half times their regular rate of pay for hours worked in excess of 40 per week. While this may sound straightforward, overtime law can actually be quite complex.

Employees in certain industries are not entitled to overtime pay regardless of the number of hours they work. The following are among the categories of employees who are generally not entitled to overtime pay: certain salespersons; certain mechanics; certain transportation workers; certain computer systems analysts; computer programmers and similarly skilled employees; teachers; fishing industry employees; certain agricultural employees; certain commission employees of retail and service establishments; certain outside salespersons; employees of certain amusement or recreational establishments; organized camps, or religious or non-profit educational centers; seamen; babysitters and companionship service employees; certain criminal investigators; announcers, news editors and chief engineers of certain TV and radio stations; certain domestic service employees; certain foster care employees; certain lumber industry employees and motion picture theater employees. I have prefaced some of these categories by the word "certain" because the FLSA contains conditions that must be met for workers in these categories to be considered exempt.

In addition to these specific categories of exempt employees, overtime is generally not available for workers who are paid on a salary basis and work in administrative, executive, or professional jobs. If you are an hourly employee, these three broad exemptions (administrative, executive and professional) do not apply. Of these three exemptions, the administrative exemption is the broadest. An employee is an exempt administrative employee and therefore generally not entitled to overtime pay if (1) he is paid on a salary basis (i.e., is not an hourly or commission employee), (2) his primary duty consists of office and non-manual work directly related to management policies or general business operations of the employer's customers, and (3) his work requires the exercise of discretion and independent judgment. Department of Labor regulations note that exempt administrative work includes work performed by so-called white collar employees engaged in advising management, planning, negotiating, representing the company, purchasing, promoting sales, and business research and control.

Despite this guidance, it is not always easy to know whether an employee is entitled to overtime pay for work in excess of 40 hours per week. Thus, one must conduct a highly detailed analysis of the employee's day-to-day level of discretion and authority to determine if he is exempt or not.

Even if an employee is an otherwise exempt administrative, executive or professional employee, he may still be entitled to overtime pay if an employer docks part of his weekly pay for lateness, partial day absences or similar reasons because such actions by the employer can convert a salaried employee into a de facto hourly employee. Be aware of this.

If you worked more than 40 hours per week without receiving overtime pay, and do not believe you had enough authority and discretion to be considered an exempt administrative, executive or professional employee, contact a knowledgeable employment attorney or a representative of your state's Department of Labor or the Wage and

Hour Division of the U.S. Department of Labor for help if the ex-employer fails to respond to your complaints (preferably in writing).

Employers who fail to pay required overtime are liable for any unpaid overtime compensation and an equal amount as liquidated damages, plus attorney fees and costs. For willful violations, damages sometimes include earned overtime up to three years back, plus punitive damages.

Since the purpose of the FLSA is to ensure that employees are paid their full wages, employers may not make any deals to settle wage-hour claims for less than the full amount (even when a release is signed by the employee to defeat the rights of the worker). While courts are usually pleased when prospective litigants compromise their differences, no such compromise is accepted under FLSA.

If you are an hourly worker, you may be entitled to overtime pay under the following conditions:

■ If you arrive to work earlier than your starting time and do light work at the request of the employer

■ If you typically work through lunch breaks at the employer's request

■ If you take work home with the knowledge and permission of the employer

■ If at home you are required to be "on call" and ready to report to work within an hour

■ If you work several hours of overtime on a Friday and the employer states that you can leave work several hours early the following week

■ If the job requires you to stay overnight for out-of-state assignments or travel extensively while on company business (but not for normal commuting travel to and from your home)

STRATEGY: *Speak to an employment attorney if you are required to do extensive traveling on company business and are not paid for your*

time. The author represented a television reporter-producer who was encouraged to spend hundreds of hours each month traveling around the world to obtain provocative news stories. A settlement representing overtime pay was effectuated even though the reporter was paid a salary and was considered exempt by the employer.

Confer with counsel if you are unsure whether or not you are truly considered an exempt worker. Be sure that the company fairly rotates overtime between men and women. Discrimination often ensues when supervisors fail to equalize overtime (e.g., they offer substantially more overtime to males than females or minority workers).

The Wage and Hour Law is complex, and matters are often subject to detailed investigations. However, employers are generally required to give nonexempt workers as much advance notice as possible when they are expected to stay late. They should also rotate overtime, maintain a roster recording each worker's overtime, and establish rules as to how the roster system will work. Federal law requires employers who offer overtime to post signs outlining the federal minimum wage and overtime regulations conspicuously in places where workers enter and exit.

Additional rules concerning overtime:

1. Generally, employers cannot force workers to waive their entitlement to overtime.

2. If the company has no knowledge that an employee is working overtime and has established a rule or policy, conspicuously posted, that prohibits overtime work, an employee may not be entitled to overtime pay after making a claim.

3. The FLSA does not protect employees who deliberately over report their overtime hours. The employer may terminate an employee who falsifies overtime hours and may not be subject to claims of retaliation or unfair treatment.

4. Generally, employees cannot refuse to work overtime unless they have a valid reason (e.g., taking care of a sick child). If the refusal to work overtime is not for good cause and the employer suffers undue hardship, this may be grounds for a valid termination and denial of unemployment benefits, even for union workers protected by collective bargaining agreements. However, if you believe you were fired unjustifiably, speak to a lawyer immediately.

5. If you are requested to participate in a company-sponsored program after hours, such as a mercy session (e.g., a company-sponsored blood drive), and are an hourly worker, you may be entitled to overtime compensation.

Question all attempts by your employer to dock you for time taken to attend jury duty, to vote, and to handle medical emergencies. Most states do not allow employers to do this. If you are in doubt about a company's action in this area, call your local U.S. Labor Department Wage and Hour Division office for further details.

Wages

Vacation pay, sick pay, and severance pay are not legal obligations covered by federal law, but privileges your employer may offer. But once these policies are established and promised to employees, employers are obligated to follow through and offer them to everyone. You are not legally entitled to cost-of-living pay raises or merit raises unless they are part of an established employer policy or a written, implied, or union agreement. Your employer is not required to pay you overtime for working on holidays unless this is covered under a union agreement or other contract stipulating overtime. Ask your lawyer what benefits are covered solely by a provable verbal or written contract between you and your employer, and which are governed by state or federal law.

You should also bear in mind that meal period, rest breaks, and rest periods are covered by state law and violations are subject to state action and fines. However, the fact that your state mandates meal and break periods does not necessarily mean that you can file a civil action against your employer for failing to provide such meal periods or breaks. In many states, the employee's only recourse is to complain to the state's Labor Department and hope that the Labor Department officials take action against the employer.

Many state labor laws require employers to give at least a 30 minute meal break to employees who work more than six hours a day. Hourly employees are not generally entitled to compensation while taking a meal break. However, if you are given work duties, such as being required to accept deliveries or keep an eye on machinery during a meal break, you are probably entitled to compensation.

Each state has its own laws governing rest periods and coffee breaks. While such breaks may increase employee morale and worker efficiency, being entitled to take them, and for how long, vary from state to state.

Hourly workers must be paid for the time it takes to change into a uniform (like a nurse's garb) if that is required for the job.

It is illegal to be retaliated against for asserting an overtime or benefits claim and state laws protect employees who file wage and hour complaints. Seek relief if you are demoted, transferred, or fired as a result of asserting your rights. Get legal advice to understand all of your options, including filing a small claims action without the expense of hiring a lawyer when the amount of owed benefits is relatively small (e.g., less than $4,000).

Understand what you must assert to prove a valid claim. You must identify the person or business that damaged or caused you harm, calculate the amount of damages you suffered with provable evidence, determine there is some basis in law to have a court award you damages, and be sure you were not the main cause of your own harm (e.g., haven't waited too long to start the action subjecting yourself to a statute of limitations defense, or did not sign a written release.) All of this information should be understood after receiving a comprehensive opinion from an experienced employment attorney.

STRATEGY: *If you are a salaried exempt professional, question all company policies that impose partial or full-day unpaid leaves. If you are an hourly employee, recognize that most compensatory plans (also called comp plans) allowing workers time off without pay in the work period following the week they worked excessive hours, or allowing them to work more than 40 hours one week to make up for working fewer than 40 hours in a previous week, may be illegal. Each workweek must be considered separately in determining overtime hours, regardless of the length of the pay period, except for certain occupations (e.g., police officers and firefighters); employers giving time off must compute the value of such benefits at one and a half times the regular rate of pay.*

Salary

Obtaining owed salary begins when you are hired. Clarify your base salary, when it is payable, and understand all deductions from your paycheck. When does the pay period start and end? If payday falls on a holiday, when are paychecks distributed? It is important to compute what you are owed when you resign or are fired. For instance, if you are fired on a Tuesday morning, most states require that you be paid for the entire day, and possibly for the entire week.

Additionally, most state and federal record-keeping laws require employers to provide employees with a wage statement each payday. The pay stub must disclose the number of hours worked, the gross wages, deductions, and net wages. Check your state's requirements if you are being denied a regular detailed statement of your wages.

Many states have laws which impose strict time limits on employers regarding final paychecks. Such laws generally require companies to pay earned salary and wages within several days of a termination or when you quit. In New York, for example, the failure to pay owed salary and wages within a week allows litigants to sue and recover the amount owed plus a 25 percent penalty if the violation was "willful," plus legal fees, interest, and costs of the suit. Some states impose even greater penalties, such as double or triple the amount of money owed, plus attorney fees to collect the money.

Always send the employer a letter specifying the amount due and demanding immediate payment if you are not paid what is owed. Do this promptly before you decide to consult with or hire a lawyer to document a claim. Send the letter by certified mail, return receipt requested, to prove delivery, and save a copy for your records. An example of such a demand letter is found in Chapter 9.

If the employer fails to pay after receiving your letter, send another final letter requesting payment. Your letters may evidence the employer's willful refusal to pay what is owed. Judges, juries and labor departments dislike employers who fail to pay wages, and such letters are helpful in documenting a claim. Often the sending of a letter will do the trick, because the employer will know you are serious about protecting your rights, and that you know the law.

Contact a lawyer or regional office of your state's Department of Labor for assistance if you still have trouble recovering the money. Examples of such letters begin on page 549. Such letters can be used by anyone without the expense of hiring a lawyer. Simply fill in the blanks with the appropriate information, draft it neatly (preferably in type), and send the letter by certified mail, return receipt requested, to prove delivery. Always make and save a copy of the letter and the return receipt for your records.

Vacation Pay

Most states require employers to pay accrued vacation pay in all circumstances, even after resignations by employees or terminations for cause. Although each company is free to implement its own rules governing vacation pay, employers must apply such policies consistently to avoid charges of discrimination and breach of contract. To reduce problems, be sure you understand how long you must first work to qualify, whether vacation days must be taken in a given year, whether they can be carried over to the next year, and whether you can be paid in cash for unused, earned vacation days. How much notice is required before being allowed to take vacation time? Does the amount of vacation time increase depending on the number of years with the company (e.g., two weeks of vacation pay for the first five years, increasing to three weeks of paid vacation for years six to ten)?

Additionally, employers with at least 50 workers can require employees who take FMLA leave to first use up their vacation days.

At the exit interview, make sure you'll be paid for unused vacation and comp time and get an accounting in writing. If the ex-employer owes you money and fails to respond to your initial letter (see example on pages 553 and 554) and even a second, final request, contact an employment attorney or your state's Department of Labor for assistance.

Bonus

Some employers fire workers right before they are scheduled to receive a bonus and deny such bonuses by stating a person must be employed on the day bonus checks are issued as a condition of payment. If this happens to you, or you are denied a bonus for any reason, send a letter similar to the one on page 552 to protect your rights. Argue that you would have received the bonus but for the firing. Demand that you are entitled to receive a pro rata share of the bonus if you are fired close to but before the end of the year. For example, if you are fired on December 1, negotiate to receive eleven-twelfths of the bonus you were expecting.

Many people fail to understand their rights regarding bonuses and are later disappointed or exploited. Depending on the facts, employers may have no legal obligation to pay an annual bonus if you're fired or quit, unless you can prove a bonus was agreed upon. Try to link the bonus to some verifiable formula such as profits of your division, company revenue or output. Such an arrangement can give you extra legal protection; in the event you aren't paid a correct amount, you would be able to verify the bonus from the company's books and records. In fact, if a bonus-enforceable-by-contract arrangement could be proved in court, you could have the right to inspect the employer's books and records in a lawsuit.

STRATEGY: *The key to claiming you are entitled to a bonus is to overcome an employer's standard defense that bonus policies are discretionary, gratuitous, and paid at the employer's whim and discretion in an amount determined solely by the employer. Request a verifiable bonus that is not subject to the employer's discretion when negotiating a job to avoid this possibility. Specify the amount, when it will be paid, and that there are no strings or conditions attached. Treat the bonus as part of your salary package; this will increase your legal rights in a breach of contract lawsuit in the event you aren't paid.*

It also helps if you regularly received bonuses to demonstrate it was an integral part of your total compensation package. Document all promises made to you concerning a bonus. For example, if a senior vice president tells you on September 15 that you can expect a minimum bonus for the year totaling $X, make an entry in a diary of the words spoken including the date, time, location, and whether others overheard the conversation. Proving an oral offer to pay a minimum bonus may help you win a breach of contract lawsuit. However, it's best to confirm your understanding in writing to prove such an arrangement.

The best way to assert a valid legal claim for an earned raise or bonus is after you receive a concrete promise from the company in a contract, policy manual, or other writing which grants a pay increase upon the happening of a certain event (such as reaching profitability in your department) and that objective occurs. Be aware, however, that if the employer reserves the right not to pay the raise or bonus for any reason in its sole discretion, you are probably out of luck.

Commissions

Most states require that salespeople receive earned commissions immediately after a firing or resignation. Often these laws provide independent contractor representatives up to three times additional damages in excess of the commission, plus attorney fees, costs and interest when monies are not promptly paid. Determine if you are entitled to commissions. If so, have you promptly computed how much money is due? This is done by understanding how commissions are paid (e.g., when your orders are accepted by the company, shipped by the company, or paid by the customer) and being able to prove such an arrangement from documents or other evidence, such as checks received from the company with notations indicating the commission rate paid on previous transactions.

Some dishonest employers fire salespeople right before they are supposed to receive or earn commissions. For example, it is not unusual for an employee to solicit and procure a large order but be fired just before the company fulfills the contract or the customer finalizes the deal. Don't let this happen to you. Speak to an employment attorney immediately to enforce your rights. Always send a detailed written demand for unpaid commissions. This should be done by certified mail, return receipt requested, to document your claim and prove delivery. Such a demand will "start the clock" for the purpose of determining the number of days that commissions remain unpaid and put the employer on notice that additional damages and penalties may be owed if money is not received immediately. A written demand is essential in enforcing your rights and may get the employer to contact you and resolve the matter amicably out of court. An example of such a letter is included in Chapter 9 on page 551.

Health Benefits

Some states require employers to provide workers with health care insurance. However, when health insurance coverage is voluntarily provided, employers may not discriminate; they must offer the same coverage to all employees regardless of gender, age, or disability. For example, if health insurance benefits are provided to the spouses of male workers, the same coverage must be provided to the spouses of female workers, and the extent of the coverage provided for dependents must be equal.

The law demands equality in health coverage for pregnant workers. Most state laws say that disabilities caused or contributed to by pregnancy, miscarriage, abortion, or childbirth and subsequent recovery are temporary disabilities and should be treated as such under any health or temporary disability insurance or sick leave plan available in connection with employment. This position is affirmed by federal law under the Pregnancy Discrimination Act of 1978 (PDA). Although companies are not required to provide any health care benefits, when they do, pregnancy must be treated the same way as any other medical condition; voluntary health care benefits must include coverage for pregnancy and pregnancy-related conditions and for those who are statistically more likely to incur high medical costs. (The PDA does not require employers to pay health insurance benefits for abortion except where the life of the mother would be endangered if the fetus were carried to term or where medical complications have arisen from an abortion.)

An employer cannot base employment decisions on the fact that a worker is pregnant, since employers must treat pregnancy the same as they would treat any other employee medical condition. If company health care is provided, maternity care must be included and coverage must be the same for spouses of males and females. Limitations on maternity coverage for preexisting conditions must be similar to limits on other conditions. If extended benefits (such as paid sick leave and benefits) are given for other disabilities, so, too, must extended benefits be given for pregnancies occurring during a covered period of the plan.

Once health insurance is provided, the employer is bound under federal law, including the Consolidated Omnibus Budget Recon-ciliation Act (COBRA) and the Employee Retirement Income Security Act (ERISA), to follow through on its promises unless the company reserved the right, in company handbooks and memos distributed to its workforce, to alter or amend promises of benefits at any time, with or without notice.

Many insurance policies have preexisting-condition clauses that disallow certain kinds of coverage for medical conditions that existed prior to the employee accepting employment. This was legal, as were benefits that are capped (i.e., no more than $X of reimbursement for a particular condition per year) until the recent passage of the Health Care and Education Reconciliation Act of 2010.

The complexity of the employee benefits law is well established. New cases are constantly being decided and statutory developments implemented that have an impact on particular plans and practices. It is critical for you to constantly update and evaluate the effect of these legal developments on your own health and benefit plans. One area in particular — retirement health care benefits and successor benefits (when a person leaves a company to work in a new job) — has raised numerous problems. An employer's obligation to provide post-termination or retiree health benefits largely turns on whether those benefits are actually vested at the time of leaving. Claims for employee benefits are typically covered under federal ERISA law; speak to a qualified benefits or employment attorney for more details.

Many companies are cutting back on the amount of health coverage provided, and some companies are currently offering several plans at great expense. Often, after it is too late, employees learn that their health coverage is inadequate.

Always understand the minimum coverage you are receiving and what you must pay on your own for additional basic protection. Answers to the following questions can help you in this area.

- How much is your monthly premium? Is this taken directly out of your paycheck? Are you allowed to pay more on your own to get better coverage or shift your money to a more cost-effective plan?

- Does the company have a summary plan of benefits? If so, read the summary to get a better idea of the basic benefits offered. (It may still be necessary to read the entire plan to get more specific information and check the fine print.)

- What are the plan's exclusions and limitations? What mental and physical conditions does the plan not cover?

- Does the plan cover preexisting conditions?

■ How much is your annual deductible (the amount you must pay before your insurance kicks in)?

■ What is the process for filing claims? Do you have to pay and submit proof of payment before reimbursement, or can you submit claims directly from your physician? How long must you wait before reimbursement?

■ Can you appeal a negative decision not to be reimbursed? If so, what is the process for filing an appeal?

■ Is your family also covered?

■ Does the plan pay for second opinions and preventive tests such as mammograms and Pap smears?

■ If you are close to retirement age, what impact will Medicaid and Medicare coverage have on your benefits?

■ If you are close to retirement, what guarantees regarding continued retiree health benefits will you receive?

■ Does medical, dental, and hospitalization coverage stop the day you are fired or resign, or is there a grace period (e.g., through the end of the month)?

■ Can you extend coverage beyond the grace period?

■ Can you assume any group health policy (sometimes referred to as a conversion policy)?

STRATEGY: *The federal Health Insurance Portability and Accountability Act of 1996 (HIPAA) benefits workers in several ways. It provides greater portability to employees with respect to their medical insurance when they change employment. It also places limitations on when an employer may impose preexisting-condition clauses for new employees under an employer-sponsored medical plan. This reduces the chances of being excluded from a health plan or coverage due to a preexisting medical condition or illness upon being hired or while working. The law also limits the employer group medical plan from discriminating against individual employees based on health status. For example, underwriting by excluding injuries from medical plan coverage resulting from* *high-risk activities such as motorcycling, skiing, or bungee jumping may not be permitted.*

Enactment of the landmark health care legislation recently signed into law by President Obama is certain to reduce abuses concerning pre-existing illness exclusions.

Under the HIPAA, a group health plan generally may not apply a preexisting-condition exclusion to an employee or dependent unless the exclusion relates to a condition for which medical advice, care, or treatment was recommended or received within the six-month period before the employee's hire date. Additionally, the maximum period that a preexisting-condition exclusion may be enforced is limited to 12 months for someone who enrolled when first eligible and 18 months for a late enrollee.

Talk to an employment attorney whenever you believe you are unfairly denied or being excluded from your employer's medical coverage or when your COBRA coverage ceases. The HIPAA may augment COBRA coverage under certain circumstances. Be aware that as a result of the HIPAA, the chances of your medical coverage being denied has decreased, especially if you had similar coverage under a prior employer's plan.

AIDS and Medical Coverage

The EEOC has ruled that companies may not exclude AIDS coverage from their medical plans altogether because such an exclusion violates the ADA. Some smaller companies that established self-insured plans were excluding coverage for preexisting conditions for a period of time (typically up to a year) after a person became employed. As a result, companies must proceed with caution and seek competent legal advice before implementing any self-insured plan that seeks to preclude coverage for HIV and AIDS sufferers. Additionally, any plan previously established that excludes persons with AIDS may now have to be modified, especially due to the passage of the new health care law.

COBRA Health Benefits

Federal COBRA law requires most private employers to continue to make existing group health insurance available to workers who are discharged or resign from employment. All employees who are discharged as a result of voluntary or involuntary termination, such as for poor performance, negligence, or inefficiency (with the exception of those who are fired for gross misconduct), may elect to continue plan benefits currently in effect at their own cost, provided the employee or beneficiary makes an initial payment within 30 days of notification and is not covered under Medicare or any other group health plan. The law also applies to qualified beneficiaries who were covered by the employer's group health plan the day before the discharge. Thus, for example, if the employee chooses not to continue such coverage, her spouse and dependent children may elect continued coverage at their own expense.

The extended coverage period is 18 months upon termination of the covered employee; upon the death, divorce, or legal separation of the covered employee, the benefit coverage period is 36 months to spouses and dependents.

The law requires that employers or plan administrators separately notify all employees and covered spouses and dependents of their rights to continued coverage. After receiving such notification, the individual has 60 days to elect to continue coverage. Additionally, employees and dependents whose insurance is protected under COBRA must be provided with any conversion privilege otherwise available in the plan (if such coverage exists) within a six-month period preceding the date on which coverage would terminate at the end of the continuation period.

Some employers run afoul of the law in failing to follow rules regarding notification requirements, conversion privileges, excluded individuals, and time restrictions. In the event the employer fails to offer such coverage, the law imposes penalties ranging from $100 to

$200 per day for each day the employee is not covered and other damages.

STRATEGY: *Know your COBRA rights before accepting any job and in the event you resign or are fired. This is especially true if you or a spouse or dependent is sick and needs the insurance benefits to pay necessary medical bills. You are entitled to such protection even if you have worked for the employer for a short period of time. Most short-term employees can generally enjoy COBRA protection for periods exceeding the length of their employment. The only requirement is that you must have been included in the employer's group plan at the time of the firing and that the employer was large enough (i.e., employed 20 or more workers, including part-timers, independent contractors, and agents, during the preceding year) under federal law to qualify.*

Under federal law, employers with less than 20 employees are not required to provide COBRA coverage. However, many states impose equivalent (or better) COBRA benefits and continuation coverage after the COBRA period lapses to employees and their dependents who work for small companies. This is typically done through the use of state-mandated HMO group health insurance policies and contracts rather than direct coverage by an employer (as is generally the case for COBRA). The extent of medical coverage, continuation, and conversion privileges usually begins when you are hired and is set forth in employee handbooks or company benefit booklets; employers can be liable for failing to provide adequate notice of such rights. Speak to a benefits counselor at your company or an experienced employment attorney for more details where applicable.

You cannot obtain benefits if you are fired for gross misconduct. This term is relatively ambiguous; the burden of proof is on the employer to prove that the discharge was for a compelling reason (such as starting a fight or stealing).

If an employer reduces your working hours to a point that makes you ineligible for group health coverage, or fails to notify you of the existence of such benefits, contact the personnel office immediately to protect your rights.

Other points to remember:

- A company's hands may not be tied in the event that a group health plan is modified or eliminated; an employer may be permitted to change or eliminate a current plan provided all qualifying beneficiaries and covered employees are allowed to participate similarly under new plans, if any

- Coverage for adopted children, children born out of wedlock, and other dependents has been expanded under federal law and recent court decisions

- Speak to a lawyer if you or a dependent is excluded from COBRA protection because of the existence of a secondary health plan or other factors, such as because of an alleged discharge for gross misconduct

- Never waive your COBRA rights when accepting severance payments or signing a release after a discharge

- Be sure the company notifies you in a timely fashion so you can make the election properly before the short period of employer-provided coverage expires

- Workers who don't return from disability leave are entitled to COBRA benefits as being "involuntarily terminated"

Under the American Recovery and Reinvestment Act of 2009 (ARRA), the federal government will subsidize 65% of COBRA premiums for eligible workers for up to 15 months who were fired after September 1, 2008 through February 28, 2010. Employees earning more than $145,000 will not receive this benefit. You are only required to pay 35% of the COBRA premium if you qualify and were laid off during this period and can save many hundreds of dollars per month with this subsidy. Speak to a benefits counselor at your company or an experienced employment attorney for more details where applicable.

ERISA Benefits

Employer-sponsored health, pension, and profit-sharing plans are governed by the federal Employee Retirement Income Security Act of 1974 (ERISA). ERISA sets minimum standards for benefit plans, the vesting of benefits, and communication to plan participants and their beneficiaries. This includes all plans, funds, or programs that provide medical, surgical, or hospital care benefits; retirement income or the deferral of income after retirement or termination (such as severance); or deferred compensation plans such as stock bonus and money purchase pension plans. The act covers six basic areas:

- Communications: what must be disclosed to employees, how it must be disclosed, and what reports must be filed with the federal government
- Eligibility: which employees may participate in a benefit plan
- Vesting: rules regarding when and to what extent benefits must be paid
- Funding: what employers must pay into a plan to meet its normal costs and to amortize past service liabilities
- Fiduciary responsibilities: how the investment of funds must be handled and the responsibilities of the plan administrators to oversee the plan and plan benefits
- Plan termination insurance: the availability of insurance to protect the payment of vested benefits

The law does not require employers to establish pension or profit-sharing plans. Once they do, however, virtually all private employers are regulated by ERISA in one form or another.

The first step to understanding and enforcing your ERISA rights is to ask for details regarding the nature of your benefits when you are hired. You are entitled to an accurate, written description of all benefits under federal law. Be aware of all plans, funds, and programs that will be established on your behalf. These may include the following:

Defined contribution plans. These include profit-sharing plans, thrift plans, money purchase pension plans, and cash or deferred profit-sharing plans. All these plans are characterized by the fact that each participant has an individual bookkeeping account under the plan which records the participant's total interest in the plan assets. Monies are contributed or credited in accordance with the rules of the plan contained in the plan document.

Defined benefit plans. These are characterized as pension plans that base the benefits payable to participants on a formula contained in the plan. Such plans are not funded individually as are defined contribution plans. Rather, they are typically funded on a group basis.

Employee welfare benefit plans. These are often funded through insurance and typically provide participants with medical, health, accident, disability, death, unemployment, or vacation benefits.

ERISA plans. These may not be as definite as the plans above. Rather, if the employer communicates that certain benefits are available, who the intended beneficiaries are, and how the plan is funded, the employer may be liable to pay such benefits even in the absence of a formal, written plan.

An investigation by the U.S. Department of Labor uncovered hundreds of companies misusing and diverting 401(k) employee pension programs. In 401(k) plans, workers save and invest their own money for retirement through automatic savings programs set up by their employers. When the plans are operated correctly, workers determine how much they contribute, the employer withholds the stipulated amount from employee paychecks, and the company forwards the money to a plan administrator, who invests worker contributions in a manner selected by the worker. The Department of

Labor discovered that many small and mid-size companies violated plan rules and federal law by delaying payment to plan administrators, diverted funds to pay other corporate expenses, or stole the money outright and never reported the contributions.

The best way to avoid such problems is to monitor and regularly scrutinize reports given to you by the employer concerning your current benefits. If your returns show constant losses, plan officials may not be investing your money properly. Speak to management about how you want your money invested. If your statements are coming late or at odd intervals, check with your benefits department to find out why. Demand such reports if they are not periodically forthcoming. If your retired friends say they can't get the pension plan to pay them what's due, start checking further. Always request such reports when you believe the company is having financial difficulties, such as when paychecks are not being distributed on time. Most important, keep track of how much you're contributing to the pension and then match your records to the reports you receive from the plan. These statements should indicate the amount you and your employer have contributed, plus the rate of return you've earned on your investments. If the numbers don't match, it is possible (especially with small companies) that the employer is illegally holding or diverting your contributions.

To safeguard benefits, ERISA mandates that assets in a beneficiary's pension be virtually "untouchable." This is accomplished by requiring that plan administrators file numerous reports with the U.S. Department of Labor, the Internal Revenue Service, and the Pension Benefit Guaranty Corporation (a federal agency located in Washington, D.C.), including plan descriptions, summary plan descriptions, material changes in the plan, description of modifications of the terms of the plan, an annual report (Form 550), an annual registration statement listing employees separated from services during the plan year, and numerous other reports for defined benefit plans covered by the termination insurance provisions with the Pension Benefit Guaranty Corporation.

Demand a copy of the employer's pension and/or profit-sharing plans from the plan administrator if the employer refuses to furnish you with accurate details. (You may have to pay for the cost of photocopying said plans when requesting them.) ERISA provides that plan participants are entitled to examine without charge all plan documents filed with the U.S. Department of Labor, including detailed annual reports and plan descriptions. If you request materials and do not receive them within 30 days, you may file suit in federal court. In such a case, the court may require the plan administrator to provide the materials and pay up to $100 a day until you receive them, unless the materials are not sent for reasons beyond the control of the administrator.

STRATEGY: *If you are fired just before the vesting of a pension (e.g., two months before the vesting date), argue that the timing of the firing is suspect and that public policy requires the employer to grant your pension. If the employer refuses, consult an experienced employment attorney immediately.*

Contact the plan administrator immediately to protect your rights if your claim is denied or if you suspect there are problems with your plan. Under federal law, every employee, participant, or beneficiary covered under a benefit plan covered by ERISA has the right to receive written notification stating specific reasons for the denial of a claim. You have the right to a full and fair review by the plan administrator if you are denied benefits.

If you suspect the company has not acted properly with respect to your benefits, inquire about your account with the plan administrator. Determine whether the amount of each payment corresponds with the amount that was deducted from your paycheck and reflects any promised matching contributions. If you are not satisfied with the answers, contact your nearest Department of Labor office to discuss the matter with a representative. Request an investigation on behalf of you and your coworkers where warranted.

If you have a claim for benefits that is denied or ignored in whole or in part after making a request to a plan administrator, speak to a lawyer and consider filing a lawsuit in either state or federal court. If it should happen that plan fiduciaries misuse a plan's money, or if you are retaliated against for asserting your rights (such as being demoted, reassigned, or fired), seek assistance from the U.S. Department of Labor, or file suit in federal court. The court will decide who should pay court costs and legal fees. If you are successful, the court may order the employer or person you have sued to pay these costs and fees.

If your company goes out of business, files for bankruptcy, or has no assets, some states require the owners (i.e., stockholders) and officers to be personally liable to repay pension and other retirement benefits. Thus, all may not be lost if you discover that your benefits were diverted and the company goes out of business. Speak to a lawyer about this point.

The Pension Benefit Guaranty Corporation has created an office to help workers trace their pensions. By law, a pension plan that terminates is required to make only one attempt to get in touch with workers. The Pension Benefit Guaranty Corporation can assist you by making repeated attempts to find the plans of employers that have gone out of business. Contact this agency in Washington, D.C., and supply it with copies of any plan summaries and plan identification numbers, which are often printed on such papers. Permanently save all plan documents and summaries, because you never know when the information will come in handy to document and enforce a claim.

Speak to a benefits lawyer if your company orally modifies any plan benefits, if a summary description does not accurately depict essential elements of the plan, or if a division of the company you are working for is sold and the new company offers far less severance and other benefits than previously promised. When companies merge and workers are laid off or denied promised benefits they previously enjoyed, issues of severance and other post-termination and on-the-job benefits should be scrutinized by a competent lawyer to determine whether ERISA violations have occurred.

Meals, Transportation and Related Benefits

Generally, reimbursement for meals, transportation, and related expenses is includable in an employee's gross income. When such benefits are taxable, the benefits generally must be reported by the employer and are subject to federal income tax, Social Security, and federal unemployment withholding. Nontaxable benefits need not be reported by an employer to the IRS. However, a benefit is excludable from the employee's gross income if the value of the benefit is so small as to make accounting for it administratively impractical (e.g., a company-provided auto for six hours per month). If the company has a computerized accounting system, the burden is on the employer to demonstrate why it is unreasonable to track the benefits provided.

Employer-provided meals, meal money, and local transportation fare provided to employees are excluded if offered on an occasional basis (e.g., one, two, or three times per month) as a result of overtime and to enable the employee to work overtime. So, too, are special "provided meals" paid by the employee with a company charge account or employer-given cash at the time of the meal for the convenience of the employer. (This rule does not apply to actual meal money or cash reimbursements paid to employees.)

Tuition Assistance

Tuition assistance is an effective way of bolstering employee performance and morale while benefiting the company with better skilled workers. When considering a tuition reimbursement program, be aware of:

- Company objectives in offering the program
- Employee eligibility, such as who is qualified for reimbursement
- Limits to the kinds of reimbursable items
- Using company time to attend courses

- Proper reporting, including procedures for turning in receipts and the kinds of receipts required for reimbursement

- Situations when reimbursement is forfeited (e.g., not receiving a C grade or better, being fired for cause, or receiving an unsatisfactory job performance evaluation before the course is completed)

STRATEGY: *Be aware that employers are sometimes legally obligated to pay employees for attending company classes, especially when the employees' participation is mandatory and attendance is a condition of keeping the job or gaining a promotion.*

Working Hours

Some states require coffee breaks, others do not. In addition, certain states require that employees receive a meal period a few hours after beginning work; other states require breakfast periods as well. Thus, check with the Department of Labor in your state for further details.

Must an employee be paid for on-call meal periods? In one case an arbitrator ruled that since the workers were in a state of constant readiness and could not leave the hospital, they were still on duty, even when taking meals, and such status was primarily for the benefit of the hospital.

Requests to eat in company facilities as a part of the job may constitute compensable work time. However, although a company may be liable to pay its workers when they are compelled to lunch at their workplace, there is little doubt that a company has the right to determine the timing of all breaks and how many workers must be present at a particular location at all times, if such a rule is established for a legitimate business reason.

Time Card Procedures

Federal law requires that all companies keep an accurate record of an employee's work. Most companies consider it a serious work infraction, leading to dismissal, for a worker to punch in the time of another or falsify time card records. Never consider doing this for any reason.

■ ■ ■ ■ ■ ■ ■ ■ ■

4

Recognizing Employee On-the-Job Rights and Conduct

Employees possess many on-the-job rights which are sometimes violated by executives, security personnel, private investigators, and fellow workers. The law allows employees to pursue a variety of legal causes of action when their rights have been violated, such as actions for invasion of privacy, intentional infliction of emotional distress, libel, slander, and wrongful discharge. Areas such as personal appearance rules, romantic relationships with coworkers, drug and AIDS testing, legal off-premises behavior, and many other subjects are generally protected by the U.S. Constitution. This chapter will discuss a variety of areas impacting workers and suggest strategies to overcome such problems.

Lie Detector Tests

The federal Polygraph Protection Act of 1988 bans lie-detector tests (including polygraphs, deceptographs, voice-stress analyzers, psychological-stress evaluators, and similar devices) in most situations. For example, employers cannot regularly test employees as a matter of policy or in cases of continuing investigations where no suspects have been found, or use the test as a "fishing expedition" to intimidate or harass individuals or to determine whether an employee has used drugs or alcohol.

The law restricts most companies, regardless of size, from taking action against employees who refuse to submit to such tests. For example, if an employee refuses to take the test, he or she cannot be fired as a result. Although tests can be used in connection with the investigation of workplace thefts, embezzlement, sabotage, check kiting, and money laundering, employers must follow detailed safeguards to avoid the imposition of fines and penalties. Moreover, there must be a reasonable suspicion that the tested employee was involved in the activity being investigated, and the employer must provide the subject with a statement detailing the incident in question and the basis of the suspicion of wrongdoing. Fines and penalties include back pay, job reinstatement and related damages, attorney fees and costs to successful litigants, civil penalties up to $10,000, and injunctive relief for actions brought by the U.S. Secretary of Labor within three years from the wrongful act.

Here is a thumbnail sketch of the relevant portions of the law.

EFFECT ON STATE LAWS. In those states that currently have stronger laws prohibiting lie-detector tests (defined as any mechanical or electrical device used to render a diagnostic opinion regarding honesty), the federal law is of no consequence and state law governs.

PROHIBITED USES. Generally, employers are prohibited from directly or indirectly requiring, requesting, suggesting, or causing an applicant or employee to take any lie-detector test. Tests can be administered in connection with an investigation, but only after reasonable suspicion has been established and many procedural safeguards have been carefully followed. The procedural safeguards are as follows:

1. The individual must be given the opportunity to consult with and obtain legal counsel before each phase of the test.

2. The individual must be provided with at least 48 hours' notice of the time and place of the test.

3. The individual must receive notification of the evidentiary basis for the test (i.e., the specified incident being investigated and the basis for testing).

4. The individual must be advised of the nature and characteristics of the test and instruments involved (e.g., two-way mirrors or recording devices).

5. The individual must be provided an opportunity to review all questions to be asked at the examination.

6. The individual must be given a copy of the law that advises rights and remedies for employees and that gives him or her the right to stop the test at any time.

Additionally, all employers are required to post notices on bulletin boards that advise workers of the existence of this federal law and their rights thereunder.

ACCEPTED USES. Although the federal law restricts the circumstances under which the tests can be given, it does allow for lie-detector use to investigate serious workplace improprieties. However, employees who submit to such a test must be given the test results together with a copy of the questions asked. Additionally, employers are forbidden from administering more than five tests per day, and each test must not run beyond 90 minutes. All persons administering such tests must be qualified by law (i.e., bonded with at least $50,000 of coverage or an equivalent amount of professional liability insurance) and are forbidden from asking questions regarding religious, racial, or political beliefs, matters relating to sexual behavior, affiliations with labor organizations, or any matter not presented in writing to the examinee prior to the actual test. Nor can they recommend action to employers regarding test results.

Since employers must have a reasonable basis for suspicion of wrongdoing to order the test, companies must be sure that such suspicions are well founded lest they face liability. Additionally, all results of the exam and actions taken as a result of the test must be carefully guarded against careless dissemination to nonessential third parties. It is also interesting to note that the federal law forbids companies from allowing nonsuspects to voluntarily take the test to "clear their own name."

Finally, refusal to submit to such a test and the results of the test alone may not serve as a basis for adverse employment action. Employers must possess other evidence, including admissions by the examinee or evidence indicating that the employee was involved in the activity being investigated, to justify a firing or denial of promotion.

If you believe you are being asked to submit to such a test in violation of federal or state law (or a collective bargaining agreement if you are a union member), were fired as a result of taking such a test, or that proper procedural safeguards were not followed, speak with a representative of your local Department of Labor, Civil Liberties Union, attorney general's office, or a private employment attorney immediately to protect your rights. All private employers must be mindful of the law to avoid problems, and workers have many rights in this area.

Lie-detector, voice-stress analyzer, psychological-stress evaluator, and other tests cannot be given as part of a "fishing expedition" to uncover facts. Employers may use the test only as part of an ongoing investigation, must be able to demonstrate the suspected employee's involvement in the matter under investigation, and must be careful to follow all pretest, test, and post-test procedures; the failure to follow any of the above can lead to serious repercussions.

Access to Personnel Records

Each state has its own laws regarding an employee's or ex-employee's right to inspect his or her personnel file. In some states employees or their representatives have the right to review their personnel records pertaining to employment decisions. However, they generally cannot inspect confidential items such as letters of reference, information about other employees, records of investigation, or information about misconduct or crimes that have not been used adversely against them.

Some states have passed laws allowing employees access to their personnel records to correct incomplete or inaccurate information at a reasonable time and place. In such states you are usually not allowed to copy any of the documents in the file except for those you previously signed (such as an employment application or performance review). Such states usually allow you to make notes, however. In other states you generally do not have the right to review your records, so check the law in your state. (The Federal Privacy Act deals mainly with access to employee records. This law forbids federal government employers from disclosing any information contained in employee files without the written consent of the employee in question. Discuss the ramifications of this federal law with your lawyer if applicable.)

Even in states where access to records is not permitted, employers are prohibited from distributing confidential information, such as medical records, to nonessential third parties and prospective employers, and you are generally permitted to inspect all your files containing confidential medical and credit information. Some union employees covered under collective bargaining agreements have the right to examine their own records and to be informed of what information is used in making decisions relevant to their employment.

If you need legal help in your efforts to inspect the personnel file an employer (or past employer) has on you, and you don't have a personal attorney upon whom you can call, your local or state bar association will most likely have a referral service. Ask for an attorney experienced in employment law. Statutes of this sort are constantly changing; only those who specialize in employment law in your state may be up to date on the finer points that may affect you.

STRATEGY: *Since it is often difficult to review the contents of your personnel file, make and save copies of all documents the minute you receive them so you don't have to retrieve them later. In some arbitrations and lawsuits, employers are prohibited from introducing "memos in the file" that were never read or signed by you. Advise your lawyer about this.*

Some states grant workers the automatic right to include a rebuttal statement in their personnel file if incorrect information is discovered. Other states allow employees to do this when the employer will not debate such comments. A few states have laws that require employers to send copies of rebuttal statements to prospective employers or other parties when information pertaining to a worker or her employment history is conveyed. Since each state treats the subject differently, review your state's law.

Some states require employers to seek workers' approval before employee records can be collected, distributed, or destroyed, and it may be illegal to distribute personal information without your consent. Thus, the circulation of confidential memoranda within a company has given rise to lawsuits, particularly where the employer did not take adequate precautions to determine whether derogatory information was accurate.

Some states prohibit employers from gathering and maintaining information regarding an employee's off-premises political, religious, and other nonbusiness activities without the individual's written consent. In these states employees and former employees can inspect their personnel file for the purpose of discovering if any such information exists. If their file contains such information, the employer may be liable for damages, court costs, attorney fees, and fines.

With respect to medical records and investigations, the law generally recognizes that a duty of confidentiality can arise to protect this information and avoid dissemination to nonessential third parties. Under emerging state laws and case decisions, employers who request medical information may be liable for the tort of intrusion and for the tort of public disclosure of private data. Several states have recognized a claim for negligent maintenance of personnel files when files containing inaccurate medical information are made available to third parties. For example, Connecticut enacted a statute requiring employers to maintain medical records separately from personnel files and permitting employees to review all medical and insurance information in their individual files.

STRATEGY. *Always try to review the contents of your personnel file, especially when you believe that the employer is treating you unfairly (for example, denying you a promotion or raise). If damaging or false information is discovered, try to photocopy such information if possible. Don't forget to inquire whether a rebuttal can be included in your file. Finally, if the employer refuses your request, investigate whether the law in your particular state permits you to review the contents of your file.*

Access to Credit Reports and Medical Records

The federal Fair Credit Reporting Act places certain restrictions on the use of credit reports and investigative consumer reports by employers. Under this law, employers are forbidden to use credit reports (defined as summaries of a person's credit history) for hiring or employment decisions. The same is true for investigative consumer reports (defined as descriptions of a person's creditworthiness and general reputation in her community based on interviews with coworkers, friends, and neighbors).

As a result of this law, employers cannot obtain any report without your permission. If your consent is obtained and a report is made, you have the right to receive a copy, including the name and address of the credit agency supplying it, together with a written description of your rights under the act.

When any adverse action is taken, such as your not receiving a promotion, you are entitled to receive notice of such adverse action, the name, address, and telephone number of the consumer reporting agency that provided the report to the employer (which includes an 800 number if one is available), and a written statement by the employer indicating that such information was not used in any way in the adverse action. Information also given with this is a statement that you can obtain a free copy of the report within 60 days of the notice and your right to dispute the accuracy or completeness of the report with the consumer reporting agency. The law also requires that the employer notify the credit reporting agency before receiving the report that it received your permission, provided you with the required notice, will not use the information to violate federal or state discrimination laws, and will not use the information to make any adverse action.

STRATEGY: *As a result of the law's requirements, speak to a knowledgeable employment attorney immediately if you believe your rights have been violated in this area.*

Many states prohibit the unauthorized disclosure of an employee's medical records as well as the unauthorized acquisition of medical information. In a few states, the unauthorized acquisition of medical records or information is punishable as felony theft.

Some states require that an applicant or employee not be charged the cost of an employer-requested physical or that they be given a copy of the results. In other states the physician must obtain the job applicant's or employee's written consent before disclosing examination results to the employer. It is probably permissible for an employer to require you to take a physical as the last part of the screening process to get a job, provided all applicants are requested to participate in this process. However, be aware that some company doctors are not trained properly and ask discriminatory questions during the examination, or request answers to discriminatory questions contained on poorly drafted medical history forms; being denied employment on the basis of answers to such questions is illegal.

Thus, recognize that you may have rights in the event that confidential credit or medical information is conveyed to outsiders by your employer without your consent or knowledge or is used to your detriment. In fact, only relevant, accurate information should be maintained by the employer, and reasonable procedures should be adopted to assure the accuracy, timeliness, and completeness of such information. With respect to medical data, all information regarding an employee's health, diagnosis, and treatment of illnesses or other personal information revealed during medical consultations must be maintained in the strictest confidence to avoid violations of state privacy laws.

STRATEGY: *Employers should give applicants and employees the opportunity to review their records and correct mistakes before inaccurate information is disseminated. In many well-run companies, requests for information from law enforcement agencies, government agencies, unemployment insurance offices, credit agencies, security investigators, and search firms must typically be accompanied by subpoenas or official documents. This ensures the reliability of the identity of the source requesting such information. Additionally, unless prevented by injunction, it is a good idea for employers to advise employees of the source of the subpoena, the date when the information will be given, and an explanation of the person's rights.*

Employee Searches

The law regarding employee searches involves a careful balancing of the employer's right to manage his or her business and the privacy rights of employees. For example, the Fourth Amendment to the United States Constitution provides protection for all persons against unreasonable search and seizure of their persons, homes, and personal property, and this doctrine applies when the employer is the government. However, most private employers are exempt from this doctrine (unless the private employer does extensive business with or is heavily regulated by the government) and are generally permitted to use a variety of techniques when suspecting a worker of misconduct. These include searching the employee's office or locker without his knowledge or consent and requesting the employee to open his briefcase or package upon leaving a company facility.

Although each case is decided on its own merits, the law generally states that office searches are permissible if an employer has a reasonable basis for suspecting the employee of wrongdoing and the search is confined to nonpersonal areas of his or her office. The reason is that the office and documents relevant to company business are the property of the employer and can be searched anytime.

However, clearly visible personal items cannot be searched, and employers cannot conduct a search if there is no reasonable ground for suspicion. Legitimate searches of an employee's briefcase, locker, or packages also depends upon whether the employee had a reasonable expectation of privacy.

The absence or presence of any regulation or policy placing employees on notice that routine searches would be conducted is the primary factor in determining whether or not searches of employees or their work areas or property are legal. For example, when signs are posted throughout a company reminding workers that personal property is subject to search, when memos are distributed stating that surveillance measures will be taken on a regular basis, and when handbooks are disseminated stating that personal property is subject to search in company lockers, case decisions indicate such measures reduce claims of illegal privacy invasions, particularly when such policies explain the necessity for conducting searches, set forth procedures minimizing personal intrusion, and advise employees that their refusal to cooperate may lead to discipline or discharge.

With such policies in place, one court found that packages may be searched. Another court decided that searching vehicles on company property was legal. One court even found a search valid on the basis that an employee had voluntarily accepted and continued employment notwithstanding the fact that the job subjected him to searches on a routine basis. This, the court concluded, demonstrated his willingness and implied consent to be searched (thereby waiving the claim that his privacy rights had been violated).

However, when the employer does not have such policies in place, the lack of published worker rules and regulations may actually encourage an expectation of privacy claim. For example, in one case the employer searched an employee's purse, which was contained in a company locker. The court ruled that this violated the employee's reasonable expectation of privacy because she was permitted to use a private lock on her locker and there was no regulation authorizing searches without employee consent.

You should also recognize that the expectation of privacy is greatest when a pat-down or other personal search of an employee is conducted. Knowledgeable employers are reluctant to conduct personal searches, especially if they are random or done without specific, probable cause with respect to the individual involved.

In one case an employer's security guards detained and searched an auto worker leaving a plant because he was suspected of stealing auto parts. According to testimony at the trial, the guards yelled at the employee in addition to shoving him. Although serious inventory shortages had been reported in the area where the employee was seen wandering shortly before leaving the plant, he was awarded $27,000 in damages after proving he had been singled out and treated unfairly by being subjected to the search and no stolen parts were found on his person during the search.

If you believe you are the victim of an employer's illegal search, ask yourself the following questions:

- Have similar searches been conducted on you or your property before? If so, did you acquiesce in the search?
- Have similar searches been conducted on other employees?
- Were you given a warning that the employer intended to conduct a search?
- Was the object of the search company property?
- Did the search have an offensive impact? Were you grabbed, jostled, struck, or held? Were you coerced, threatened physically, or mentally abused in order to make you cooperate?
- Were you held against your will? Were you so intimidated by the experience that you were afraid to leave?
- Were you chosen at random for a pat-down search with no actual suspicion of wrongdoing?

■ Did the employer search your belongings in an area that was truly private?

■ Were you stigmatized (e.g., fired) by a search when in fact you did nothing wrong?

■ Did the employer search you in front of nonessential third parties, and was your business reputation harmed by such action?

If you answered yes to the last six questions, speak to an employment attorney immediately to discuss your rights. You may have a strong case, especially if you were fired, placed on probation, suspended, or given an official reprimand after the search and you did nothing wrong. The tort actions most frequently alleged as a result of an improper employer search are assault, battery, defamation (in particular, slander), false imprisonment, invasion of privacy, and abusive discharge. For example, if you are detained against your will during the search, you may be able to allege a valid cause of action for false imprisonment.

This happened to a checkout clerk who was accused of failing to ring up merchandise purchases. The employee was searched and interrogated by security personnel and told to accompany them to another location for additional questioning. At the trial the company proved that the woman failed to ring up purchases. However, a jury awarded the employee $25,700 on the grounds of false imprisonment, because the woman was never told she could leave the room where she was being questioned and was forced to remain there for several hours.

Such cases illustrate that you may have rights that are violated during or after a search. For example, you may be able to sue the employer for slander and invasion of privacy if a search is conducted in front of nonessential third parties in a way that is suggestive that you are a thief.

Employee Interrogations

Employers can question workers in an effort to discover illegal acts. However, employees have rights during these interviews. Depending on the particular state where the act occurs, these may include:

- The right to receive an explanation regarding the purpose of the interrogation (e.g., are you a suspect?)
- The right to insist on the presence of a union representative at the interview if the worker is a union member and has reason to suspect it may result in disciplinary action
- The right to limit questions to relevant matters
- The right to refuse to sign any written statements
- The right to remain silent
- The right to speak to a lawyer before speaking
- The right to leave the room at any time

All of the above points must be carefully reviewed if you are wrongly accused or treated improperly in an interrogation. If the employer conducts the interrogation incorrectly, grave legal consequences can ensue. The following true case demonstrates this.

Three company representatives kept a supervisor in a manager's office for several hours until he finally signed a resignation notice and "admitted" his guilt concerning certain money given to him for driving duties. The man sued the company for false imprisonment and won. The court also found that the facts supported the tort of intentional infliction of emotional distress.

All employees should recognize that an employer may be violating your rights during an interrogation in the event you are restrained or confined by force or threat of force, thereby denying your freedom of movement (i.e., false imprisonment). It is no defense if you are detained during working hours; confinement cannot be done for the purpose of extracting a confession.

If you are a union member employee working in the private sector the National Labor Relations Act (NRLA) empowers you under the well established Weingarten rule to insist on having a union delegate or union official attend any interrogation when there is a reasonable belief you will face disciplinary consequences from your conduct. Some state laws grant public sector union employees similar rights. Speak to a union delegate where applicable.

Do not hesitate to assert your rights if you believe you are being treated unfairly; if you are falsely accused of misconduct in front of others or are intimidated into answering questions at an interrogation, you may have a good case for defamation or false imprisonment.

Wiretapping and Eavesdropping

Although technological developments have enhanced surveillance capabilities and employers are increasingly using electronic monitoring devices to keep tabs on employee conduct during the workday (primarily designed to combat employee theft), confidential information about an employee is also sometimes acquired.

Wiretapping and eavesdropping policies are generally regulated and to some degree prohibited by federal and state law. Title III of the Omnibus Crime Control and Safe Streets Act of 1968 prohibits the deliberate interception of oral communications, including telephone conversations. Thus, conversations between employees uttered with the expectation that such communications are private (for example, in a ladies' bathroom) are confidential, and employers are forbidden from eavesdropping under this statute. Employers who fail to comply with this federal law are liable for actual and punitive damages and criminal liability for willful violations.

State law varies with respect to wiretapping, eavesdropping, and surveillance practices. In some states it is legal for individuals and companies to record telephone or in-person conversations with another person without first obtaining the other person's consent (you only need the approval of one of the two parties to tape). In such states the recording may subsequently be used as evidence in a civil or criminal trial under proper circumstances (e.g., that the tape was not tampered with or altered and that the voices on the tape can be identified clearly).

However, other states are not as liberal and forbid the interception of oral or wire communications unless both (or all) parties are advised and give their consent. Such states prohibit employers from operating any electronic surveillance device, including sound recording and closed-circuit television cameras, in employee lounges, rest rooms, and locker rooms (surveillance is permitted in actual work areas) and make it virtually impossible for employers to lawfully engage in surreptitious eavesdropping.

One company placed wiretaps on business telephones in certain stores. The court ruled that this was a violation under federal law and a violation of the employees' privacy rights under Georgia law. In another case a company monitored the calls of one of its sales representatives. A supervisor overheard the sales representative say she was going to accept another employer's offer. The supervisor told the employee what he had learned and tried to dissuade her from leaving. The employee left anyway and sued the company for invasion of privacy. The court ruled that the employer had violated the law by listening to her personal calls, and awarded her damages.

In another case a company president installed wiretapping machines on four business telephone lines. When a vice-president learned about this, he spoke with the company's lawyer and had the machines removed. He was later fired, and he sued the former employer; the court ruled he had a recognizable claim under Title II of the Omnibus Crime and Control Act.

Thus, in order to know your rights in this area, it is essential to know the laws of your particular state (since such laws vary widely).

Employers frequently maintain microphones between counter areas and the boss's office or instruct the office operator to listen in and monitor suspicious or personal telephone calls by employees. This is illegal in many situations. However, if the conversation is in a public area, if one of the parties consents to a taping, or if the employer had a genuine suspicion of wrongdoing and only monitored business calls and not personal calls, the eavesdropping or taping may be legal.

In most states it is illegal for employers to set up cameras in a nonwork area, take photographs, or use video cameras to monitor workers, especially in places where female employees have expectations of privacy (i.e., in rest rooms, locker rooms, bathrooms, and lounges). It is also illegal for employers or their workers to observe you disrobe or change clothes without your knowledge. (Workers generally do not have rights of privacy to stay in rest rooms for extended periods of time, particularly after being warned of such excessive respites and when the rest room visits are not medically related.) Also prohibited, by the National Labor Relations Act, is employer surveillance of employee union activity, discussions about unions, or union meetings. Speak to a lawyer immediately if you think your privacy rights have been violated.

Be aware that in certain instances "extension phone" monitoring (in which microphones are placed near a customer service desk to measure a worker's productivity and communication with the public or detect nonbusiness telephone use) has been upheld as legal. One employer did this and was sued by an employee claiming illegal interception of her conversations. The court ruled in favor of the employer, finding that the monitoring was done "for a legitimate business purpose" with the knowledge of the affected employee. This was proved, since written notification of the monitoring program was given to employees beforehand (who were monitored for training purposes).

In another case the legality of extension phone monitoring was also upheld when a supervisor used an extension phone to listen in on an employee suspected of disclosing confidential information to a competitor. The court found the supervisor's conduct (which was spurred by a customer's tip) to be legal.

Thus, it is best to research appropriate state law or speak to an experienced employment attorney if you believe your rights in this area have been violated. This is because if an electronic surveillance law in your state imposes greater restrictions than federal law, an employer must comply with the requirements of both laws.

You should also know that photographing employees without their knowledge or consent for surveillance purposes may violate federal or state laws regarding invasions of a worker's privacy rights, depending on the facts. If the pictures are released to nonessential third parties and are strongly suggestive of guilt, and such release results in defaming your reputation, you may have a valid cause of action for defamation.

If you discover that your employer has wiretapped your business or home telephone with electronic devices and is eavesdropping on your business or private conversations, speak to a lawyer to determine whether your state permits the employer to listen in on an extension telephone used in the ordinary course of business. This is sometimes allowed (depending on state law) provided you were notified in advance that your business calls would be monitored. However, once you talk about private matters, it is generally illegal for the employer to continue to listen to calls. (You may be legally fired, though, for discussing personal matters while on company time.)

STRATEGY: *In most states you have the right to be told that your phone conversations, interrogations, or interviews may be taped. Even if an employer is allowed under state law to set up a monitoring system, that doesn't give the employer the right to administer it improperly. As a general rule, private conversations should not be taped. And employers should decide, in advance, who will be allowed to review their surveillance tapes, because the dissemination of confidential information to nonessential third parties can be costly.*

E-Mail Messages, Blogging and Related Subjects

Does an employer have the right to monitor e-mail messages or intercept your mail? This often depends on the facts of each case and the law in your state. While you may consider your electronic-mail communications to be confidential, think again, especially when the employer has a written policy in a contract, employee manual or other workplace personnel guide stating that electronic mail be used solely for business purposes and that the company has the right at any time to review, audit, and disclose all materials sent over or stored in its e-mail system. When such monitoring policies state that work e-mail belongs to the employer, employees have diminished privacy rights regardless where the e-mails are written or received.

The law is less clear whether employers may legally access an employee's or former employee's e-mails, which were sent from or received through a personal Gmail, Hotmail or other e-mail account and transacted through a company-issued computer. Although violations of several federal laws are sometimes cited by lawyers for employees, most notably the Stored Communications Act (SCA) and the Electronic Communications Privacy Act (ECPA), cases often hinge on whether an employer has a right to access the computer or e-mails and if the employee was notified and thereby aware of the policy. However, if an employer forensically analyzes a former worker's computer issued by the company and discovers e-mails sent to an attorney from a personal AOL account which did not go through the company's servers, a court may determine it illegally viewed privileged lawyer-client communications, especially when no written personnel policy warning employees that their e-mail and computer use is regularly monitored (creating an expectation of privacy), even if they are sent remotely over a portable device.

With such a written policy, an employer can prohibit non-job-related solicitations on company e-mail and employees can be legally disciplined and/or terminated for violating the policy. Additionally, although the National Labor Relations Act (NRLA) recognizes that employees and unions have the right to communicate with each other in order to organize, solicit and/or bargain effectively, the National Labor Relations Board ruled it was legal for a company to deny a union or employees seeking to solicit or organize from using company e-mail systems as a means to communicate. Experts suggest the recent ruling allows most U. S. employers a basic property right to lawfully control access to their e-mail systems and block usage to anyone attempting to organize its work force. (Note: The ruling also stated it was illegal discriminatory enforcement for the same employer to allow employees' use of its e-mail system as a tool to organize meetings for private clubs or promote private organizations or profit-making ventures.)

STRATEGY: *Avoid sending personal e-mails at work because they cannot be destroyed. The author has represented employees who were fired and/or forced to forfeit large severance payments and other compensation after sending disloyal, defamatory or damaging e-mail statements to co-workers. Such comments were discovered before or during the discovery phase of a lawsuit with devastating financial consequences. In fact, one of the first things a company or its lawyers is sure to examine these days after a firing is all of the departing employee's e-mails to avoid paying severance or use such information as leverage (e.g., a counterclaim to your lawsuit). Thus, avoid sending non-business e-mail communications where possible. Choose the tone and content of your words carefully.*

On the other hand, harassing text messages received from co-workers, managers, supervisors, and others can prove to be potent evidence in sexual harassment cases filed by disgruntled female employees. Text messages leave behind an electronic record and help prove harassment, hostile or bullying environments in the workplace. Experts suggest that textual harassment is on the rise and large verdicts have been obtained by exploited workers whose lawyers use offensive text messages as proof of illegal conduct. Thus, save harmful offensive text messages if you receive them and speak to a knowledgeable employment attorney immediately to consider the best course of action to take. Armed with such information, for example, your lawyer may recommend you first to complain to management before instituting a lawsuit if the matter is not amicably resolved.

Blogging has become quite popular as employees use the medium as a forum for venting their frustrations about their employer and co-workers. Can an employer suspend or terminate a worker who posts defamatory material or confidential salary and pay policies on her personal blog? What about a well-intentioned employee who accidentally creates blog entries that disclose company trade secrets?

In virtually all at-will employment states, companies may discharge workers for any non-discriminatory reason. This means an employer has the legal right to fire any worker who posts a negative blog about the company or reveals confidential or proprietary information, even by mistake. Generally, no expectation of privacy exists when an employer publishes a written policy stating that anyone posting a negative blog about the company, its products, or personnel will not be permitted and will lead to immediate discipline, up to and including discharge.

However, experts suggest it may be illegal for companies to make hiring and firing decisions based on personal information discovered by written blogging or social networking, such as on Facebook. While employers may desire to use blogging and social networking sites for hiring purposes to learn more about an applicant or employee, doing so could violate a host of laws in the areas of privacy, discrimination, and fair financial practices. For example, a Facebook profile may contain private data and information about a person's health, financial condition, and political beliefs, which are generally off-limits to employers; using such information in hiring and employment decisions may be illegal. In fact, some states (notably California and New York) forbid employers from negative employment decisions due to a person's off-premises conduct or lifestyle.

Speak to a knowledgeable employment attorney if you believe or learn a potential or current employer misused private personal information from a personal blog or social networking site to effectuate a negative employment decision. The law is not well settled in this area so consulting a competent attorney to learn more or researching the law in your state is a good idea.

STRATEGY: *While employers may have the right to review e-mail with such a policy in place, they generally cannot open your personal mail, especially mail marked "Personal and Confidential." Speak to a knowledgeable employment attorney immediately if you feel your privacy rights are being violated.*

All forms of employee testing raise significant issues of potential violations of an employee's privacy rights. This includes honesty, psychological, and personality tests, genetic screening, substance abuse tests, and polygraph examinations (previously discussed in this chapter). This section will examine some of the issues involved.

AIDS Testing

Individuals with AIDS, as well as those with HIV, are covered by the Americans with Disabilities Act (ADA). Since AIDS is a protected disability under the law, employers cannot discriminate against an applicant or employee with the disease, and afflicted workers must receive reasonable accommodation as a result of their condition. This may include liberal use of leave time and restructuring of responsibilities on a voluntary basis. Forcing an employee with AIDS to change her work habits may be considered an ADA violation.

However, in order to be regarded as an impairment, the employee's HIV status must be known by the company. For example, one plaintiff was unable to prove that he had been discharged solely because of a perceived disability where the company did not know he was HIV positive.

While there are no federal laws prohibiting mandatory AIDS tests for workers, some states have laws related to the issue. As an example, AIDS testing of employees is required in various localities for food handlers, processors, and waiters, and virtually all states, government agencies, and the military mandate AIDS testing in blood donations. However, since AIDS is a protected illness under the ADA, prehiring and on-the-job AIDS tests are probably illegal in many circumstances and employers can be liable for refusing afflicted workers access to their jobs.

HIV screening should not be required as part of preemployment or routine workplace medical examinations. Companies must also establish education and training programs to reduce potential workplace problems, especially in places such as hospitals where there is a higher risk of HIV exposure.

All companies should develop and follow comprehensive AIDS policies so that people with AIDS or HIV infection receive the same rights and opportunities as workers with other serious illnesses. Such policies must comply with all relevant state and federal laws and regulations and be based on the scientific fact that HIV cannot be transmitted through ordinary workplace contact. All policies should be communicated by supervisors and upper management, but all medical information concerning employees should be screened to maximize confidentiality.

The enactment of the ADA has significantly protected AIDS sufferers' privacy rights, since many preemployment and on-the-job medical investigation practices and procedures that were once considered legal are now prohibited. For example, intrusions into a person's medical background and history are now substantially reduced. Application forms can no longer solicit answers to questions about whether the applicant is an individual with a disability, has a medical condition, or has ever been hospitalized or treated for a mental or emotional problem. Questions such as how many days was the applicant absent from other jobs and whether the applicant is currently taking medication are illegal, and employers are required to establish policies for staff and health providers regarding the disclosure and use of employee medical information.

Employers should review company handbooks and draft statements protecting against the unnecessary dissemination of medical information, and institute policies requiring supervisors and health providers to consult with company lawyers before disclosing any medical information. Related problems that have emerged must be carefully addressed: for example, how can your company be sure that the results of any job-related medical tests will remain confidential so as to avoid charges of slander or libel and other invasions of privacy?

Genetic Testing

The issue of genetic testing was once unsettled and some major corporations regularly tested the relationship of inherited genetic traits to occupational disease to determine if there are certain predisposing risks to employees and job applicants. But state laws determined such activity was illegal and large damages have been awarded to workers who were subjected to mandatory pre-employment examinations which, without their knowledge, tested for conditions including pregnancy, sickle-cell, and syphilis. In one case the EEOC sued a major company alleging unauthorized genetic testing. The employer wished to learn if workers with carpal tunnel syndrome (causing the filing of Workers' Compensation claims) was the result of a genetic defect. It was reported that the company paid an out-of-court settlement of $2.2 million for such wrongful acts.

To eliminate ambiguity in this area, Congress passed the Genetic Information Nondiscrimination Act of 2008 (GINA). The law prohibits employers from discriminating against applicants or employees regarding compensation, terms or conditions of employment on the basis of their genetic predispositions. GNA makes it unlawful for an employer to fail or refuse to hire or fire any employee because of genetic information or limit, segregate, or classify an employee in any way that would deprive or limit her from employment opportunities.

Speak to a knowledgeable employment attorney to understand your rights, obligations, and options in this area where applicable. The lawyer may also advise that state laws, the FMLA and/or the ADA were violated depending on the facts of the case.

Drug and Alcohol Testing

The fight against drug and alcohol abuse in the workplace often results in drug tests of employees. There has been a sharp rise in employer interest in drug and alcohol testing, fueled in part by high-profile drug deaths and publicity surrounding the marketing of drug tests. More employers are resorting to such tests, especially preemployment testing, to identify drug users and reduce the incidence of on-the-job accidents and absences.

Critics argue that indiscriminate testing violates employees' rights of privacy, due process, and freedom from unreasonable search and seizure, and that test results are often incorrect, unreliable, or disseminated to nonessential third parties. Proponents of testing cite its success (e.g., the military's program has dramatically lowered drug use in the armed forces) and the growing confidence in the reliability of current testing methods.

Generally, since private employers are not held to the same constitutional standards as local, state, and federal government employers, private employers may implement and conduct drug and alcohol tests provided certain procedural safeguards are followed to minimize potential offensiveness. This typically includes adopting a comprehensive testing policy and putting it in writing, periodically reminding employees of the stated drug or alcohol testing policy, reducing the incidence of errors, treating test results carefully (i.e., confidentially) to avoid improper dissemination, and following local, state, and federal laws and decisions in this area.

Despite the general legitimacy of such tests, some state and local governments have passed laws prohibiting the testing of employees for drugs or alcohol.

State law varies dramatically. Some states permit employee testing with required procedural safeguards to ensure that the testing is done in a reasonable and reliable manner with concern for an employee's rights of privacy. Other states only permit individual tests where a particular employee is suspected of being under the influence of drugs or alcohol and his impaired state adversely affects job performance.

Case decisions in other states prohibit employee testing in positions that are not safety or security-sensitive as a matter of public policy, particularly programs involving a large number of employees where there is no suspicion of individual wrongdoing.

Since the law differs so dramatically from state to state, is constantly changing, and may be even more stringent than the requirements of the ADA, it is critical that you obtain advice from counsel.

Under federal law, companies represented by unions cannot unilaterally implement a testing program without bargaining with the union over changes and conditions of employment. To do so would violate the National Labor Relations Act. However, the Supreme Court has upheld an employer's right to test employees for drugs and alcohol, rejecting a union's argument that testing is reasonable under the Fourth Amendment only when based upon individualized suspicion that an employee is impaired by drugs or alcohol on the job. In one case affecting railway employees, the Court ruled that the government's policy of testing all employees was important in assuring the safety of the railways and therefore outweighed the privacy rights of nonsuspected workers en masse.

THE DRUG FREE WORKPLACE ACT. The federal Drug Free Workplace Act of 1988 has had a major impact on federal contractors and grantees with federal contracts, requiring them to conduct antidrug awareness programs and require workers to report any drug-related convictions as a condition of receiving federal funds. The law requires company-contractors, ranging from weapons manufacturers to publishing companies, and employee-grantees, ranging from state governments to drug abuse treatment facilities, to publish strict statements prohibiting drugs and educating employees on substance abuse. Employers must also report to the procuring agency any workers convicted of workplace-related drug activities and certify that they will not condone unlawful drug activity during the performance of the contract.

Under the Drug Free Workplace Act, to receive a federal contract for the procurement of any property or service in excess of $25,000 or for any employer or individual receiving any grants, regardless of the dollar amount, from the federal government, an employer must certify that it will provide a drug-free workplace. This includes publishing and distributing a statement advising employees that the unlawful manufacture, distribution, dispensation, possession, or use of any controlled substance (including prescription drugs) is prohibited. The employer must institute a "drug-free awareness program" to inform employees about the dangers of drug abuse in the workplace, the employer's drug-free workplace policy, any drug counseling, rehabilitation, and employee assistance programs that are available, and the penalties (e.g., discharge) that may be imposed upon employees for violations of the antidrug policy.

Each employee working on the contract or grant must be given a copy of this statement. The statement must indicate that the employee will abide by the terms of the statement and that he/she will notify the employer if convicted of a criminal drug statute within five days of conviction (employees must be hired pursuant to written contracts informing them of these requirements). The employer must then notify the contracting agency of such occurrence within ten days of receiving this notice. Contractors and grantees must make a "good faith" effort to continue to maintain a drug-free workplace through implementation of the above.

Each contract awarded by a federal agency is subject to the suspension of payments or termination of the contract if the agency determines that the contractor made a false certification, failed to notify the agency within ten days of an employee's drug conviction, or failed to notify employees of the dangers of drug use.

Although the federal law creates a heightened drug awareness policy, it does not mandate drug testing for company applicants or employees. Nor does the act explicitly sanction such testing as a way for a federal contractor to satisfy the requirements of the act. However, the existence of this law means that companies working for the federal government must conform to its more stringent guidelines rather than follow conflicting state laws.

There is great incentive for companies dealing with the government to comply with the requirements of this law. But the decision to test is still basically an individual one, particularly for private employers that do not deal with the government.

THE AMERICANS WITH DISABILITIES ACT. Perhaps the most significant change affecting drug and alcohol testing involves the ADA. In reality, the ADA provides greater protections for individuals with disabilities than do many state laws.

The ADA specifically excludes from protection any employee or applicant who is currently engaged in the use of drugs. One section states that "employers may discharge or deny employment to persons who illegally use drugs, on the basis of such use, without fear of being held liable for discrimination." Another section allows employers to prohibit alcohol as well as illegal drug use at the workplace, and states that they may require that employees not be under the influence of alcohol or illegal drugs in the workplace, and may hold an employee who uses illegal drugs or is an alcoholic to the same qualification standards for employment or job performance as other employees.

Thus, postemployment drug tests are permitted, and employees who are currently illegal drug users are not protected from adverse action. However, if an individual has successfully completed a supervised drug rehabilitation program or has otherwise been rehabilitated successfully and no longer uses drugs, or is presently participating in a supervised drug rehabilitation program and no longer uses drugs, that person cannot be penalized.

Administration of drug tests is not considered to be a medical examination, so prehiring drug tests by employers do not violate the ADA's prohibition on medical examinations prior to an employment offer. In light of this, many companies are considering administering drug tests earlier in the applicant-screening process to eliminate drug users and save the company the expense of a posthiring medical examination. Additionally, since the act neither prohibits nor encourages drug testing, employers probably have the right to conduct ongoing drug-testing programs with all employees.

STRATEGY: *If you work for a private employer and are not a member of a union, what concerns should you have when advised that the employer intends to test you for drugs and alcohol? First, if the employer has decided to test, you may be entitled to advance notification in work rules, policy manuals, and employment contracts to reduce perceived privacy rights in this area. For example, the manual should outline the steps management would take when it suspected that an employee was impaired on the job, such as immediate testing, with a description of how the test will be administered and the consequences flowing from a positive result, such as immediate discharge with no severance or other benefits. If no such notice was received before the test was administered, you could have a valid claim that your privacy rights were violated, especially when there was no rational reason for asking you to submit to the test (e.g., you were randomly selected) and you were requested to take the test without warning.*

Second, even if your privacy rights are not violated, all tests must be administered in a consistent, evenhanded manner. For example, if you are black or a woman, and employees belonging to your classification of race or gender are being tested and fired as a result of such tests in far greater numbers than other classifications, a charge of race or sex discrimination might be valid under certain circumstances.

Third, test results must be treated in the same manner as other confidential personnel information. Unwarranted disclosure of this information (even within your company) when made with reckless disregard for the truthfulness of the disclosure, or excessive publication, can allow you to sue for damages.

Additionally, a firing based on a positive test finding that later proves inaccurate could lead to a multitude of legal causes of action, including wrongful discharge, slander, and invasion of privacy. Thus, if the employer fails to hire a reputable testing company or the test's results are inaccurate, you can challenge the test on this basis; be aware that six-figure verdicts are sometimes awarded for violations in this area.

The Centers for Disease Control report that the most common test, the EMIT urine test, is plagued by a high degree of false positive results due to human error and inexperienced testing personnel. Other problems with this test are that it does not prove intoxication (i.e., the inability of the employee to perform his or her job duties) at the time the test is taken (which should always be the governing factor in any discharge decision) and may also indicate positive results for employees who have only used legal over-the-counter drug medications.

Thus, recognize that there may be ways to challenge the test results in the event you are fired or treated unfairly. You should speak to an experienced employment attorney immediately if you believe that:

- The test was not administered fairly; i.e., no advance warnings were given or there was inconsistent enforcement
- The penalty for violations was too severe (e.g., an employee was fired for possessing a small amount of marijuana in his locker but proved he did not smoke the drug on company property)
- The reliability of test procedures and/or results is suspect
- The employer cannot prove the identity of the illegal drug allegedly found in the test
- The specimen was not properly identified as belonging to the accused worker
- The test was given randomly with no expectation that an employee had an impairment caused by persistent on-the-job drug or alcohol use (i.e., no observation of disorientation was present)
- No confirmatory tests were made following positive preliminary screening
- The company engaged in discriminatory practices relating to its testing procedures

Federal workers, employees engaged in security-conscious industries (e.g., those who are required to carry firearms), and employees who handle money or engage in transporting members of the public (bus drivers, train engineers, etc.) have fewer legal rights to oppose drug and alcohol tests, because of the nature of their jobs. For example, random drug testing was upheld for horse jockeys. The court ruled that horse racing was one of a special class of industries accustomed to heavy state regulation and that the need for safety and honesty to promote the integrity of the industry outweighed the jockey's significantly diminished expectations of privacy.

However, as stated above, even when testing is legal, employers must follow proper procedures to be sure that results are accurate and are not disseminated carelessly. Additionally, such tests are being challenged all the time, and the law is constantly changing in this area.

The same concerns that apply to drug tests are also applicable to alcohol tests. For example, instead of drawing blood, companies should use accurate breath-testing devices whenever possible to minimize offensiveness. Test procedures should ensure reliable test results. Results should be handled on a strict need-to-know basis inside and outside the company. Employees should be given an opportunity to explain any result, and the test results should be reconfirmed if possible.

Finally, companies that administer preemployment drug tests to applicants who test positive for drug use must be careful not to automatically disqualify them should the applicant apply for another chance of employment within a fixed period of time (such as six months thereafter). The reason is that such an individual may be deemed a "qualified individual with a disability" who may be able to prove successful completion of, or who is in the midst of successfully participating in a rehabilitation program. Companies must avoid inflexible drug policies with a fixed waiting period for future employment and evaluate each case on its own merits and be careful of how they test. One worker filed a lawsuit in Louisiana after he was discharged for testing positive for marijuana. The main thrust of his lawsuit was that he had suffered great emotional distress when a company representative was required to stand by and watch as he urinated to provide a sample. He also alleged invasion of privacy under

Louisiana law, wrongful discharge, intentional infliction of emotional distress, and defamation. The company argued that having a supervisor stand by was the only way to ensure that the test was not faked. However, the worker testified that he was taunted and insulted by the supervisor while taking the test. The jury agreed and awarded him $125,000, which was upheld on appeal, based on the theory of negligent infliction of emotional distress.

ALCOHOL USE AND THE ADA. The act makes a distinction between drug users and alcoholics. Individuals disabled by alcoholism are entitled to ADA protection. This includes applicants who would automatically not be considered for a job in the past as a result of testing positive for alcohol. Now all employers with 15 or more employees must determine if that individual is capable of performing essential functions of the position offered with reasonable accommodation. Some experts have suggested that, in light of the inherent problems associated with preemployment alcohol tests, employers should now consider eliminating such tests altogether.

Until enactment of the ADA the main federal law protecting handicapped individuals against discrimination was the Vocational Rehabilitation Act of 1973, which applied to government contractors and employers who received federal assistance. Today's numerous state and federal antidiscrimination laws, including the ADA, mean that all companies must follow strict procedures to ensure that their treatment of alcoholic employees conforms to the law, since these workers are entitled to reasonable accommodation and protection from discrimination on the basis of their physical handicap of alcoholism. Employers may still prohibit the use of alcohol on the job and require that employees not be under the influence of alcohol when they report to work. Additionally, workers who behave or perform poorly or unsatisfactorily due to alcohol use may, like other workers, be fired or reprimanded. The ADA does not protect workers who drink on the job, or current abusers who cannot perform their jobs properly or who present a direct threat to the property or safety of others.

Reasonable accommodation of an alcoholic often consists of offering the employee rehabilitative assistance and allowing the opportunity to take sick leave for treatment before initiating disciplinary action. To be safe, even if the employee refuses treatment, documentation must show that repeated unsatisfactory performance took place before a termination decision is made.

In one case a company was found liable for not offering leave without pay for a second treatment in a rehabilitation program. The judge commented that one chance is not enough, since relapse is predictable in the treatment of alcoholics. In another case the judge outlined a series of steps an employer must take to avoid violating the law. His guidelines are instructive:

- Offer counseling.
- If the employee refuses, offer a firm choice between treatment and discipline. If the employee chooses treatment, the employer cannot take any detrimental action during a bona fide rehabilitation program.
- In case of relapse, automatic termination is not appropriate, but some discipline short of discharge may be imposed.
- Before termination, determine if retention of the worker would impose an undue hardship on the company. If removal is the only feasible option, the company must still evaluate whether the alcoholic condition caused poor performance; if so, the company should counsel and offer leave with pay first.

Typically, arbitrators consider the following factors when deciding any drug or alcohol-related matter:

1. Whether possession or sale is involved;
2. The type of drug used;
3. If the alcohol or drug-related conduct or sale occurred on company premises;
4. The history of drug or alcohol use;

5. The impact on the reputation of the employer; and

6. The effect on the orderly operation of the employer's business.

After considering test objectives (to screen applicants using drugs, to test employees suspected of using drugs/alcohol, etc.) smart companies adopt a plan and record it in work rules, policy manuals, employment contracts, and/or collective bargaining agreements to reduce perceived privacy rights of employees and document company policy. For example, the manual might outline the steps management will take if they suspect that an employee is impaired on the job, including immediate testing, how the test will be administered, and the consequences flowing from a positive result. Before adopting a formal plan, employers should:

■ Consider education and rehabilitation alternatives as well as all legal obligations

■ Determine the scope of the testing program's coverage, which employees or applicants will be tested, under what conditions, and the selection of testing facilities

■ Inform workers that employees are not permitted to come to work under the influence of alcohol or drugs, even when consumed off the company's premises

■ Develop rules to cover off-premises conduct but be aware that invasion of privacy claims rise when off-premises conduct is monitored

■ Inform employees that testing for substance abuse may be required to avoid OSHA penalties for employer negligence

STRATEGY: *If you do have a drinking problem, consult an employment attorney immediately if you are told to either enter an alcoholic treatment program or be fired. One employee rejected such an ultimatum and was discharged. A federal court ruled that she was fired not because of her violation of company policy (as the company suggested), but ultimately as a result of her disability. She was awarded significant damages as a result.*

The line between reasonable and unreasonable requests to undergo drug and alcohol testing will continue to be more clearly drawn as court decisions and state legislatures articulate specific policies on this issue. There is no doubt that more drug policy and testing cases will reach the courts because of the strong desire in government and political circles to eliminate drug and alcohol abuse in the workplace. However, the information in this section should help you recognize that you may have rights before, during, and after any test is administered to you.

Marijuana Use

A number of states, including Michigan and Colorado, have recently enacted laws legalizing marijuana use for bona fide health reasons. As a result, employers in those states who fire workers testing positive for smoking pot may be liable. These statutes differ from federal law which prohibits marijuana use for any reason. Some employees are also suing companies for violating the ADA by alleging they used marijuana for a legitimate medical purpose but were terminated. Speak to a knowledgeable employment attorney for advice and guidance in this area where applicable.

Smoking in the Workplace

More workers than ever before are demanding the right to work in a smoke-free environment. This right is being upheld with increasing regularity through federal legislation, state laws, city ordinances, and case decisions.

Various federal agencies, including the Merit Board and the Equal Employment Opportunity Commission, have ruled that employers must take reasonable steps to keep smoke away from workers who are sensitive to it, and the Occupational Safety and Health Administration has issued similar requirements to enhance safety in the workplace. All of these developments have caused most employers to reevaluate their smoking policies and implement either formal or voluntary rules, depending upon applicable state and local laws.

Critics contend that such policies violate an individual's right to privacy. However, because of increased public sentiment and awareness in favor of such policies, and since in virtually all states an employer has a common-law duty to provide a reasonably safe workplace for its employees, the enforceability of on-the-job bans is increasingly being upheld throughout the country.

As a result, most employees have successfully eliminated smoking in the office where they work. Others are suing for and receiving unemployment compensation after resigning from their jobs. Still others are seeking disability pay. In one case a woman was awarded $20,000 in disability pay because she developed asthmatic bronchitis after being transferred to an office with several smokers. The court also ruled that unless her employer (a government agency) transferred her to a job in a smoke-free office within 60 days, she would be eligible for disability retirement benefits of $500 per month.

Some employers have even enacted policies denying jobs to applicants who smoke. And companies have become more tolerant and responsive to complaints by nonsmokers and are now more willing to accommodate their needs. It should be noted that such accommodations make sense because employers are fearful of formal litigation, OSHA investigations, union intervention, or EEOC involvement (which is being brought with increasing regularity in this area).

Most employers have put flexible smoking guidelines into place. Such policies have included permitting employees to vote on whether smoking will be permitted in conference rooms and common areas (such as cafeterias and lounges), provided this is permitted by state law. Some companies have even instituted inflexible no-smoking policies for all staff, visitors, and customers in response to recent legal and health trends.

Some manufacturers, prompted by the discovery that materials used in their plants can be hazardous to smokers, are announcing that workers will be discharged unless they stop smoking in warehouses and factories. Such policies are enacted with the approval of OSHA, since management has the right to designate rules pertaining to work assignments to ensure an employee's health and safety.

For example, it was reported that one major U.S. corporation introduced an absolute ban on smoking after the company discovered that mineral fibers used in nine of its acoustical-products plants could have adverse health effects on both smokers and nonsmokers. To date, such a policy has gone unchallenged from workers at its plants.

If you desire to work in a smoke-free environment, the following strategies may help you protect your rights and increase the chances of a successful lawsuit.

STRATEGY 1: *Gather the facts. Document the environmental condition of your work location to support your request. For example, it is important to determine the number of smokers, type of ventilation, physical arrangement of desks, how often people around you smoke, etc.*

STRATEGY 2: *Acquire medical proof. Visit a doctor if you suffer an illness from working in a smoke-filled environment. Note the prescriptions and the amount of time lost from work. It is also a good idea to visit your employer's medical department (if one exists) to document your condition.*

STRATEGY 3: *Speak to management. Present management with a letter from your personal doctor stating your need to work in a smoke-free area. If possible, request a transfer collectively with other workers.*

STRATEGY 4: *Consult a lawyer to determine your rights. The lawyer can assert several options on your behalf. For example, she can assist you in presenting demands directly to the employer or union representative, file an action in court, contact OSHA, or sue the employer under the Equal Employment Opportunity Act. Legal fees are sometimes awarded to successful litigants under these acts. (Although such action may be illegal, be aware that your employer* *may fire or penalize you for enforcing your rights. This possibility should be considered before you decide to hire a lawyer.)*

STRATEGY 5: *Confirm all grievances in writing. After the initial discussion, it is a good idea to document your request by presenting management with a letter similar to the following.*

Sample Letter Requesting a Smoke-Free Environment

Your Name
Address
Telephone Number
Date

Name of Supervisor
Title
Name of Company
Address

Dear (Name of Supervisor):

This will confirm the conversations we have had regarding the need to provide me (us) with a work environment free of tobacco smoke. Enclosed is information to support the request to eliminate smoking in work areas.

Also enclosed is a petition signed by employees in our work location. As my (our) ability to work is constantly undermined by the unhealthy, toxic pollutants to which I (we) am (are) chronically exposed, I (we) will appreciate your giving this request priority and your prompt attention.

Thank you for your cooperation in this matter.

Very truly yours,
Your Name

P.S. If a prompt response is not received, please be advised that I (we) may be forced to contact an OSHA representative for assistance. Hopefully, this will not be necessary.

Sent certified mail, return receipt requested.
cc: your personal physician, union delegate, other management personnel, etc.

(Send a similar version to management whenever you are exposed to any potentially unhealthful working condition.)

Wait a few days after sending such a letter. Then, if a satisfactory response is not made, you may wish to send an additional letter similar to the following.

Sample Follow-up Letter Requesting a Smoke-Free Environment

Your Name
Address
Telephone Number
Date

Name
Title
Department
Company Name
Address

Dear (Name)

As of this date, I (we) have received no reply to my (our) request of (date). [If temporary or interim measures were tried but were unsuccessful, identify them here.]

To protect my (our) health while in your employ, it is vital that the company provide me (us) with a smoke-free work area so as to comply with the laws of this state (specify applicable statute). I (we) have asked organizations that are expert in the area of occupational health to provide you with additional information on my (our) behalf.

I (we) will appreciate your immediate response to this urgent matter.

Sincerely,
Your Name

Send copies to middle management, the president of the company, the medical director of the company, the union representative, and your personal physician.

STRATEGY 6: *Contact an appropriate agency for further information. Your state's Department of Labor, Department of Health, or OSHA office will provide you with more information.*

STRATEGY 7: *Speak to a doctor about workers' compensation. If you incur medical expenses due to a smoke-related on-the-job illness, discuss filing a workers' compensation claim with your doctor.*

Employers risk potential lawsuits based upon invasion of privacy, intentional infliction of emotional distress, and wrongful discharge, among other causes of action, for violations stemming from unlawful interference into an employee's personal relationships and other off-duty conduct. The next section will examine areas such as employers' attempts to regulate free speech, personal appearance, relationships with coworkers, and related subjects typically protected by the U.S. Constitution.

Free Speech

Beginning in the late 1960s, the United States Supreme Court ruled that government employees could not be fired in retaliation for the workers' exercise of free speech. In one leading case a teacher was fired for sending a letter to a local newspaper criticizing the school board. While acknowledging the government's need to conduct business efficiently, the court balanced the perceived harm to both parties and concluded that the basic right of free speech was more important (especially if government business was not disrupted). This and other cases came to allow public sector employees to speak out freely upon matters of public concern without fear of retaliatory dismissal. Later cases made a distinction in situations where government employees spoke out about matters such as office morale, transfer policies within a particular department, and creation of grievance committees, and the Court ruled that the U.S. Constitution does not protect employees from dismissal on the basis of insubordination in these areas.

STRATEGY: *Some companies overcome problems by proving that the reason for a discharge was a result of legitimate business criteria such as poor performance and not bias. They are advised by counsel to avoid enunciating that the reason for discharge or discipline was annoyance with a worker's protest or comments on matters of public concern when they can demonstrate other "traditional" reasons for the action taken. Be aware of this and act accordingly.*

The notion of free speech, privacy, freedom from discharge as a result of whistle-blowing, and related constitutional rights has now been expanded to private employees, particularly in states that have enacted broad civil rights laws. Are there limits on freedom of expression? Can companies restrict employees' political affiliations? When does something stop being a political issue and become a rights issue? In many states a private employer cannot discipline, fail to promote, or fire an employee because the company does not agree with the employee's comments on matters of public concern. Generally, even though the employer has the right to discharge employees at will without cause or notice, the enactment of special civil rights laws in these and other states protects workers who speak out freely when this activity does not substantially or materially interfere with the employee's bona fide job performance or the parties' working relationship. In states having such laws, companies are liable for damages caused by discipline or discharge, including costs of bringing the lawsuit.

On the other hand, decisions made by the courts and the NLRB have made it plain that there is no legal protection for activities that are (1) unrelated to working conditions, (2) flagrantly disloyal, (3) damaging to the employer's property or reputation, or (4) materially disruptive.

English-Only Rules

With more foreign-born employees entering the workforce, a wave of English-only regulations has been spreading among companies throughout the United States. Some of these regulations are very restrictive (only English may be spoken on company premises); others are fairly loose (only English may be spoken when customers are present); and many more are merely the verbal equivalents of informal company policy.

The Equal Employment Opportunity Commission has published strict guidelines relating to English-only rules. Therefore, the commission will presume that such a rule violates Title VII and will closely scrutinize it.

However, depending on the circumstances, it may be permissible to regulate use of a foreign language in cases where groups of employees are performing hazardous tasks and fast and precise communication among all of them is essential. The burden of proving such a compelling business necessity falls to the employer.

Voting Rights

A majority of states have laws that prohibit employers from influencing how their employees vote. In some states private employers may not influence the political activities, affiliations, or beliefs of their employees and employers are prohibited from discharging employees because of their political beliefs. State statutes differ markedly, so research your state's law.

Rights of Due Process

Generally, private employers do not have to give a hearing to employees accused of wrongdoing. However, if such a promise or right is contained in the company's policy handbook, written rules, or procedures, or has been extended to others in the past, a company may have a legal obligation to allow an employee to grieve company action at an internal hearing.

STRATEGY: *The best way employers can overcome liability is to avoid making promises or giving such rights to employees in the first place. If promises have been given, they must be followed accurately and uniformly to avoid charges of breach of contract or discrimination. For example, if a* *male employee was allowed to appeal a firing decision before a committee, the same option must be offered to a fired female worker.*

Asserting Union Rights

The National Labor Relations Act prohibits the firing of an employee because of his or her involvement in any union activity, because the employee bargained collectively, or because the employee filed charges or testified pursuant to the act.

Contact your union, regional office of the National Labor Relations Board, state Department of Labor, or a lawyer if you believe your rights have been violated.

Off-Duty Conduct

Attempts to regulate personal relationships and off-duty conduct of employees may subject employers to legal exposure. Disciplinary action in response to off-duty behavior that has no direct relationship to the workplace should not be administered.

To be successful in this area, employers must:

1. Demonstrate a legitimate business need;

2. Communicate reasonable policies in company handbooks, memos, or other written documents; and

3. Warn employees as to what constitutes objectionable conduct and the penalties for committing violations of stated company policy. Certainly, at a minimum, the regulations or policies enunciated must comply with your state's civil rights laws, must be consistent with other company policies, and cannot violate discrimination statutes in the process.

For off-the-job illegal conduct, a company typically has the right to fire a worker if the illegal conduct harms the employer's reputation or has a negative impact on job performance. A more prudent course of action, however, may be to suspend the worker without pay pending a conviction on the criminal charges, just to be safe.

Some employers fire any worker they suspect of criminal activity. But terminating a worker for erroneous off-the-job reasons or unfounded rumors of moonlighting could be grounds for a wrongful dismissal or defamation lawsuit.

Legal Activities Off-Premises

In some states a private employer cannot discipline, fail to promote, or fire an employee because the company does not agree with the employee's comments on matters of public concern. A majority of states have laws that prohibit employers from influencing how their employees vote. Attempts to regulate off-duty legal conduct is also sanctioned.

Most states have laws making it illegal for companies to fire workers who participate in legally permissible political activities, recreational activities, or the legal use of consumable products before or after working hours. Political activities include running for public office, campaigning for a candidate, and participating in fund-raising activities for a candidate or political party. Those activities may be protected if they are legal and occur on the employee's own time, off company premises, and without the use of employer property or equipment.

Recreational activities are defined as any lawful leisure-time activities for which the employee receives no compensation. The definition of consumable products even protects the rights of people who smoke cigarettes or drink alcohol before and after working hours and off the company's premises.

The right not to be demoted, retaliated against, or fired for engaging in these legally permitted activities generally depends on state law. To date, many states have passed laws making it illegal to be fired from a job because you are a smoker and smoke off-premises; the trend is for more states to follow. For example, in New York, employers cannot discriminate in hiring, promotion, and other terms of employment due to off-duty activities in four specific categories: political activities, use of a consumable product, recreational activities, and union membership or exercise of any rights granted under federal or state law (such as voting).

In the vast majority of states with such laws, it is illegal to refuse to hire smokers. It may also be illegal to discriminate against smokers by charging higher insurance premiums unless the company can demonstrate a valid business reason, such as higher costs. However, employees who smoke off-duty must still comply with existing laws and ordinances prohibiting smoking on-premises, such as only in designated areas. And just because it may be legal to drink alcohol off-premises late into the night does not give you the right to stagger into work drunk the next morning.

Employers who violate state law in this area are generally subject to a lawsuit by their state's attorney general seeking to restrain or enjoin the continuance of the alleged unlawful conduct. Hefty penalties are provided in some of these laws. Additionally, individuals may commence their own lawsuits and recover monetary damages and other forms of relief, including attorney fees, under the laws of many states.

Contact a representative at the American Civil Liberties Union in New York City for advice and guidance if you are being pressured to stop asserting legal political activities, affiliations, or political action. This includes banding together with other workers to protest poor working conditions.

Since some states do not have specific laws protecting employees who engage in political activity and other activities, and the laws vary, always consult with counsel and review applicable state law before engaging in questionable activities or taking action to protect such activities.

Regarding off-duty surveillance, some states prohibit employers from gathering and maintaining information regarding an employee's political, religious, and other nonbusiness activities. In these states employees and former employees can inspect their personnel file for the purpose of discovering whether any such information exists. If their file contains such prohibited information, the employer may be liable for damages, court costs, attorney fees, and fines.

Personal Appearance Rules

Some companies prescribe standards in dress and personal appearance. Although such codes have been attacked at times, they are legal provided the policies do not unfairly impact a group of workers, such as females. If a different rule is imposed for female employees than for male employees, such as requiring women waitresses to wear skimpy clothes while male counterparts wear whatever they wish, the policy may be discriminatory and a violation of Title VII for an adverse (disparate) impact based on gender. A grooming code that severely impacts women (e.g., requiring all female employees to have short haircuts), thus having an adverse impact under Title VII, may also violate the law unless the employer can demonstrate a legitimate business necessity (such as safety considerations) to enforce the rule.

When employers prove that a dress code is reasonable and job-related, it will probably be enforceable, and employers may terminate workers who refuse to follow reasonable rules. In many situations arbitrators and judges will uphold a company's personal appearance policy when it is justifiable. Good-grooming regulations are often imposed in an attempt to reflect a company's image in a highly competitive business environment. Reasonable requirements in furtherance of that policy may be legal if challenged, particularly if the company disseminated written rules advising workers of the consequences flowing from violations of such policies.

However, the law varies by state and depends on each set of facts. In one case, for example, a worker dyed her hair purple. She was given one week to change her hair color. When she rejected the boss's order, she was fired. The company was so incensed that it opposed her claim for unemployment compensation. It stated at a hearing that her job involved dealing with customers, many of whom were revolted by her unconventional hair coloring, and keeping her aboard would have resulted in loss of business. The company also believed it was misconduct and insubordination for the worker to refuse a reasonable request to change her eccentric hairstyle.

The worker defended her position by stating that the company had no right to dictate her personal appearance and that there was no evidence that customers complained about her purple hair. She stated that since several customers had complimented her new appearance, she was unjustifiably terminated in a manner that should not have precluded her from receiving unemployment benefits.

The court found there was no evidence that the color of the worker's hair significantly affected the employer's business or caused customer complaints. Although it stated that the company had the right to fire her as an at-will employee, it was unlawful to deny her unemployment benefits for her actions. It wrote: "We do not question the employer's right to establish a grooming code for its employees, to revise its rules in response to unanticipated situations, and to make its hiring and firing decisions in conformity with this policy. However, it is possible for an employee to have been properly discharged without having acted in a manner as would justify denial of unemployment benefits."

STRATEGY: *While rules requiring employees to wear uniforms may be legal, such rules can violate your rights if the cost of purchasing mandatory uniforms is deducted from your pay. This may be a violation of the Fair Labor Standards Act if your wages then drop below the minimum wage. It may also be a violation of federal and state discrimination laws if female employees are required to purchase uniforms while males are not.*

Office Romances

Does management have the right to actively enforce a non-fraternization rule aimed at curbing interoffice romances? This varies depending on the facts. One supervisor who was fired commenced a lawsuit against a former employer. The supervisor had allegedly given his live-in lover a promotion that placed her above several employees with more seniority, even though the company had an unwritten, traditional rule forbidding social relationships between management and lower-echelon employees. When questioned by the home office, the supervisor admitted that he and the coworker were lovers; citing the nonfraternization rule, the company abruptly terminated him.

The supervisor took the company to court and argued that his employment contract brought with it the company's implied covenant of good faith and fair dealing, which the company violated when he was fired. He also stated that the nonfraternization rule was unfair, unreasonable, and selectively enforced.

The company responded that its nonfraternization rule became reasonable and necessary after the company discovered that attachments between supervisory employees and their subordinates led to accusations of favoritism, which had a negative impact on morale. The company also argued that since the employee had no written contract guaranteeing job security, he could be fired at any time for any or no reason.

The court found that the company was legitimately concerned with appearances of favoritism and employee dissension caused by romantic relationships. Given his actions, the terminated supervisor did not make a strong case that the company failed to act in good faith toward him.

Other courts have similarly upheld the dismissal of employees romantically involved with coworkers. In one case, termination because of marriage to the employee of a competitor was found not to violate public policy, and the worker's lawsuit for unfair discharge was rejected. Other employees have been fired for violating company fraternization rules by having extramarital affairs or taking a girlfriend to an out-of-state convention. However, since the law is unsettled in this area and each case is decided on its own set of facts and circumstances, never assume that a company's actions are legal in this area. Consult an employment attorney for advice.

STRATEGY: *Although it may be legal to forbid employees from fraternization, all employees must be treated similarly to avoid violations. For example, if an employer reprimands a male employee for dating a coworker but fires a female employee for a similar infraction, the employer may be committing illegal sex discrimination.*

Some companies require employees involved in an office romance to execute a consensual social relationship agreement to reduce exposure to sexual harassment and other related claims. Such "love contracts" typically state that neither party was coerced due to a supervisor/subordinate status and that the couple independently and collectively desire to pursue a consensual sexual relationship. The contracts also require the parties not to exhibit excessive public displays of affection and to immediately confer with a human resources counselor when a problem exists so the company can conduct a fact-finding investigation to determine wrongdoing.

Whether such agreements are legal and enforceable is determined on a case-by-case basis according to the facts and applicable federal and state law. Speak to an employment attorney to explore your rights and options before signing a similar document.

For off-the-job illegal conduct, a company typically has the right to fire a worker if the illegal conduct harms the employer's reputation or has a negative impact on job performance. The law is not so clear regarding attempts to regulate legal off-the-job behavior. Some cases have given employers the right to bar employees from cohabiting with persons who work for a competitor. In one such case a court upheld a company's written policy that stated: "The Company will not continue the employment of any person who lives in the immediate household of a person employed by a competitor." But in another case in a different state, an employer's rule prohibiting workers from dating employees of a competitor was found to be illegal.

No Solicitation or Distribution Rules

Many companies prohibit employees from soliciting or distributing literature or other items. Typically, such policies are legal provided the company enunciates the policy in writing and applies it consistently. One company handbook states its policy as follows:

> *To prevent disruptions of Company business and harassment of Company personnel, Employees may not:*
>
> ■ *Engage in soliciting donations or contributions;*
>
> ■ *Sell chances, raffle tickets, services, or merchandise;*
>
> ■ *Distribute merchandise or literature of any kind on company property during working hours. This includes soliciting or distributing literature to non-employees or visitors at any time.*
>
> *Under no circumstances may non-employees be allowed to distribute literature or solicit employees on company premises. Breaking any of these rules is considered serious misconduct and may be grounds for immediate discharge.*

A few companies allow employees to solicit or distribute literature during "nonworking" hours—those periods, such as mealtimes, when they are not engaged in performing their work tasks and are away from designated working areas.

Rest Room Visits

Workers generally do not have rights to privacy to stay in rest rooms for extended periods of time, particularly after being warned of such excessive respites and when the rest room visits are not medically related. However, if a medical condition justifies numerous trips to the bathroom (not for smoking or chatting), it may be wise for employers to avoid disciplining or terminating a worker without further investigation and careful planning in light of the increased protections and reasonable accommodation requirements afforded to covered employees under the ADA.

Corporate Owned Life Insurance Policies

It has recently been reported that large companies (especially in the banking industry) have profited from the deaths of its employees after taking out life insurance policies on them without their knowledge or consent. Also known as dead peasant policies, such corporate-owned life insurance policies (COLI) practices have been the subject of class action litigation throughout the United States. One Wal-Mart class action yielded a $10.3 million settlement in 2004 and a class action against Fina Oil reportedly settled for $4 million in 2005. The federal Pension Protection Act requires that employers get the written consent of rank-and-file employees insured under a COLI policy and notify them of the maximum amount of the policy. Get advice from a knowledgeable employment attorney if you believe your rights have been abused in this area.

Informants

Are company policies designed to encourage workers to inform on drug or alcohol abusers legal?

In one case, the NLRB ruled that the "informer" rule was valid. After noting that both management and the union agreed on the need to combat drug abuse, the referee decided that the basic premise of a drug-free atmosphere was vital and involved no violations of privacy.

STRATEGY: *Generally, an employee is under no ordinary obligation to divulge information on a coworker.*

Workplace Safety

Numerous changes benefiting workers have occurred in the area of health and safety. Federal and state laws give employees the right to refuse dangerous work and receive accurate reports concerning toxic substances in their working environment. Increased activity by representatives of the federal Occupational Safety and Health Administration (OSHA) has also played a large role in protecting employees from unsafe working conditions.

The 1970 Occupational Safety and Health Act requires employers to provide a safe and healthful workplace. This federal law applies to every private employer who is involved in interstate commerce, regardless of size. Additionally, some states have passed occupational safety and health plans approved by OSHA. Some of these laws are even stricter in their enforcement standards than the federal law.

The Occupational Safety and Health Administration (OSHA) is the federal agency created to enforce the law in this area. The law protects employees who band together to protest wages, hours, or working conditions. Under this law, workers are allowed to refuse to perform in a dangerous environment (e.g., in the presence of toxic substances, fumes, or radioactive materials) and to strike to protest unsafe conditions. Employees may also initiate an OSHA inspection of alleged dangerous working conditions by filing a safety complaint and cannot be retaliated against by taking such action when justified.

OSHA inspectors visit work sites to be sure that employers adhere to the rules. Penalties are sometimes imposed, including fines of up to $100,000 for each violation and/or imprisonment for up to three years for employers and key personnel who willfully or repeatedly violate OSHA laws or fail to correct hazards within fixed time limits.

The law includes an extremely broad general duty clause requiring all employers to furnish a workplace that is free from recognized hazards. This means that employers are required to comply with safety rules and are subject to inspections without notice (with an employee representative present) and that no employee who makes a complaint can be subject to retaliation, loss of work or benefits, or demotion.

Under this law, workers are allowed:

- To refuse to perform work in a dangerous environment (e.g., in the presence of toxic substances, fumes, or radioactive materials)

- To strike to protest unsafe conditions

- To initiate an OSHA inspection of dangerous working conditions by filing a safety complaint

- To participate in OSHA inspections, prehearing conferences, and review inspection hearings

- To assist the OSHA compliance officer in determining that violations have occurred

- To petition that employers provide adequate emergency exits, environmental control devices (e.g., ventilation, noise-elimination devices, radiation-detection tags, signs, and protective equipment), and the ready availability of medical personnel

- To request time off with pay to seek medical treatment during working hours

- To request eating facilities in areas that have not been exposed to toxic substances

- To request investigations when they are punished for asserting their rights

One of the most important aspects of the federal OSHA law is that it provides workers with protection against retaliation after asserting their rights. Employers cannot fire, demote, or transfer workers who assert their health and safety rights to any federal, state, or local agency empowered to investigate or regulate such conditions. Contact your union, regional office of the National Labor Relations Board, OSHA representative, lawyer, or state Department of Labor if you believe your rights have been violated.

STRATEGY: *It is not necessarily a good idea to suddenly walk off your job when you believe you are working in a dangerous or unhealthful environment unless it is likely that the work is placing* *you in imminent danger of serious injury. You should first attempt to discuss such conditions with your supervisor, union delegate, or OSHA representative. This will make your demands seem more reasonable and minimize potential conflict.*

However, if you feel you have been punished for complaining about your safety and health rights, speak with a representative of your nearest OSHA office immediately (i.e., within 30 days of the time you discover the retaliation). Request an attorney, OSHA, or union representative to file the complaint for you if you are too sick, since the complaint must be filed in a timely fashion to avoid dismissal under the statute of limitations.

Finally, be sure to fully discuss the facts with an OSHA representative before taking any action. After OSHA conducts the investigation, it may demand that your employer restore your job, earnings, benefits, and seniority if you have been illegally punished. OSHA is also empowered to institute a lawsuit in federal court to protect your rights, so be sure that you speak to a representative from your nearest OSHA office as soon as possible. You may also wish to retain an experienced employment attorney. All of these options should be taken immediately to protect your rights in this area.

Workers' Compensation Benefits

Each state has enacted its own particular laws with respect to workers' compensation benefits, which provide aid for employees who suffer job-related injuries and disease. Employers with more than several workers are obligated to maintain workers' compensation through an insurance carrier or be self-insured for the benefit of their employees (not independent contractors) out of which benefits are paid to injured employees. Workers' compensation reduces court battles because it shields employers from being sued for injuries sustained by workers during the course of employment, even when an accident is caused by an employer's negligence. Lawyers representing injured workers typically prefer that their clients not receive workers' compensation benefits because the monies paid are often inadequate and don't come close to the kinds of financial relief awarded by juries in personal injury lawsuits.

STRATEGY: *Since the outcome of each workers' compensation case varies depending on the particular facts and unique state law, always seek the advice of a lawyer specializing in workers' compensation law. Issues such as how long you may delay before filing a claim, whether coverage is available for stress-related injuries, and what kinds of injuries are covered, together with strategies to help maximize the benefits received, can become complicated and typically require a lawyer's assistance and advice.*

Benefits fall into three basic categories: cash to make up for lost salary, payment of medical bills, and the cost of rehabilitation. Each state has its own regulations regarding how much is paid for what kind of injury or illness. Workers usually receive a fixed weekly benefit based on a percentage of their regular salary, usually not exceeding 66 percent. You are eligible for a one-time payment to compensate for the decrease in earnings attributable to a permanent injury (e.g., $10,000 for the loss of a finger).

Always notify your employer when you are injured while working. This is your right and you cannot be retaliated against in any way for taking such action. Fill out all necessary forms. If no forms are available, contact your nearest workers' compensation office for details. Speak to a lawyer immediately if a claim is contested. Visit several doctors to obtain accurate evaluations of your condition. Be sure you understand your rights if you are a part-time worker or are injured during work-related travel.

Depending on state law, compensation may be available for the following kinds of injuries:

- Preexisting conditions that the workplace accelerates or aggravates, such as a bad back, even if pain from the injury is delayed until a later time

- Injuries caused during breaks, lunch hours, and work-sponsored recreational activities such as a company-paid New Year's Eve party, and on-the-job injuries caused by company facilities, such as a shower located on premises

- Diseases such as lung cancer, if contracted by asbestos or other carcinogenic exposure at work as a result of the usual conditions to which the worker was exposed by his/her employment

- Injuries resulting from mental and physical strain brought on by increased work duties or the stress caused by a requirement that the employee make decisions on other employee dismissals. In some states, this includes employees who develop a disabling mental condition because they cannot keep up with the demands of the job and a supervisor's constant harassment.

Not every on-the-job injury is covered under workers' compensation. State courts are divided on whether an employee can recover for an injury sustained during horseplay. Many states will not award benefits to a person who is injured while intoxicated or using drugs, who deliberately inflicts injury on himself, or who deliberately fails to use safety equipment. Furthermore, an employee who is injured while traveling to or from work is generally not entitled to benefits unless the employer has agreed to provide the worker with the means of transportation, pay the employee's cost of commuting, or if travel is required while performing his or her duties. For example, if the employee regularly dictates office memos into a dictating machine within a vehicle, the car may be deemed a part of the workplace.

If you leave the employer's premises to do a personal errand and are injured, no compensation may be due. However, if you are injured while returning from company-sponsored education classes, going to the restroom, visiting the cafeteria, having a coffee break, or stepping out of a nonsmoking office to smoke a cigarette and are injured, workers' comp boards and courts typically recognize that employees benefit from these "nonbusiness" employee conveniences and often award compensation.

An employer may not inquire whether you have ever filed for workers' compensation when you apply for a job. You also have the right to select your own physician for treatment, provided that physician is authorized by the state's workers' compensation board.

Immediately alert your employer if you are injured on-the-job. Under compensation laws in most states, each employer must promptly provide medical, surgical, optometric, or other treatment for injured employees as well as provide hospital care, crutches, eyeglasses, and other appliances necessary to repair, relieve, or support a part of the body. If your employer fails to give you a claim form to complete and submit along with related documents to the insurance carrier or to the workers' compensation agency in the state where you live, ask for it. Contact your state's workers' compensation agency if the employer doesn't have the claim forms.

Never be afraid to report an accident or file a claim. Employers are prohibited from firing, demoting, reassigning, or punishing an employee for filing or pursuing a valid workers' compensation claim. Speak to a lawyer immediately to protect your rights if you are harassed. File as quickly as possible so your case is not dismissed as being untimely. In some states, you only have a few days (or weeks) to notify your employer and report a workers' compensation injury. If you wait longer, you'll collect nothing.

Save all receipts for drug purchases, trips to the doctor (including tolls and cab fares), and all related purchases while you are receiving medical treatment. You may be entitled to full reimbursement for all direct out-of-pocket expenses, including payment for doctors, hospitals, rehabilitation and related therapy. The more documentation you provide, the more reimbursement you may receive.

Speak to a lawyer if the employer's medical team eliminates treatment. You may select your own physician for authorized treatment, provided that physician is approved by the state's workers' compensation board. Also, to review the medical care an injured worker is receiving, employers may engage the services of a competent physician, who may be able to determine, for example, whether less expensive home care is more appropriate than hospital care. A medical consultant can also evaluate claims from the employee's doctor to see if they are self-serving.

The type of disability you suffer (e.g., temporary, permanent, partial, and/or total disability) will determine the amount of money you receive each week and how long you will receive benefits. That is why you should consult a lawyer specializing in workers' compensation cases or a personal injury lawyer where applicable, particularly if your employer refuses benefits. The lawyer can protect your rights in many ways. For example, if anyone other than your employer or co-worker was even partly responsible for the accident, you may be free to file your own liability insurance claim against that person or business. If for any reason your accident is not covered by workers' compensation because you are an independent contractor or because the company has no coverage, you may be able to file a lawsuit against your employer in the same way that you can sue anyone who causes you personal injury. In such a case, additional damages, such as attorney fees, money for mental pain and suffering, loss of companionship to a spouse, and even punitive damages, may be awarded.

Under certain circumstances you may also be able to collect social security benefits, retirement benefits or unemployment compensation, and health insurance payments while you are receiving benefits. A lawyer who specializes in workers' compensation law can advise you. A lawyer's services may be required to argue your case at the hearing stage before an administrative law judge, especially when the issues are not clear-cut, such as when and where the accident occurred to determine initially if workers' compensation is applicable. The lawyer will assist you in preparing for the hearing and presenting witnesses, medical documentation, and other evidence and then at subsequent formal hearings if the matter is not settled. Lawyers handling workers' compensation matters are generally quite knowledgeable about medical conditions and dealing with doctors. Resolving the issue of whether an accident caused a partial or permanent disability can involve tens of thousands of dollars in future wages. (Note: Workers' compensation lawyers typically work on a contingency fee basis.) It may also be necessary to retain the services of a lawyer if you want to challenge an unsuccessful verdict at the appeals stage, if the employer contests a favorable decision on your behalf, or if you are awarded far less benefits than you deserve. Consult a specialist for advice and guidance where applicable.

After filing a claim, you will be notified by the employer's insurance carrier regarding the amount of compensation you will receive. Most jurisdictions permit the recovery of unlimited medical expenses so long as your condition necessitates continued treatment and care. Your employer may request you to be examined by a company doctor who may restrict the amount of care to be given, including physical therapy and vocational rehabilitation assistance. Should your claim for medical and related expenses and/or lost wages be partially or totally denied, you must initiate procedures for a hearing before a workers' compensation judge. Hearings also occur when employers disagree with the initial decision.

Your state workers' compensation board is an administrative agency empowered to supervise, administer, and adjudicate workers' compensation matters, subject to subsequent judicial appellate review. Procedures concerning hearings vary from state to state. Evidence relating to the extent and duration of your injuries, out-of-pocket losses, and diminished earning capacity will be presented at the hearing. Strict rules of evidence are not generally followed, although they can serve as a guide. If you are denied benefits at the formal hearing, you can appeal.

Once you begin receiving benefits, many states require you to update your condition periodically to ascertain your entitlement to continued eligibility. Subsequent hearings may be required to determine whether your benefits should stop or be reduced, especially if the employer believes you are capable of returning to work.

Visit your local workers' compensation agency to understand your rights and get all the facts if you don't receive such information.

Strategies to Win Workers' Compensation Cases

1. **THINK TWICE BEFORE FILING FOR WORKERS' COMPENSATION BENEFITS if it will result in the loss of more lucrative income.** For example, in order to receive workers' compensation benefits of $250 per week, you may have to forfeit $500 per week in short or long-term disability benefits. Depending on the facts, including the severity of your injuries, whether they are temporary or permanent, and how long you will stay out of work, it is important to consider your rights to unemployment insurance compensation, disability benefits, and damages under federal and state laws such as the ADA and the FMLA. There are legal consequences to seeking workers' compensation benefits which can exclude you from obtaining other benefits, so analyze your options carefully.

2. **SEND THE EMPLOYER A LETTER DOCUMENTING THE ACCIDENT and your injuries to prove the employer was timely notified.** Send the letter certified mail, return receipt requested, and save a copy for your records. An example of such a letter is found on page 170.

3. **KNOW THE LAW.** In order to obtain workers' compensation benefits, it is critical to prove that your injury arose out of and in the course of your employment. Once this is demonstrated and provided you gave timely notice of the accident to your employer, you must then prove medical expenses, lost wages, and other damages resulting from your work-related injury or illness. Most states forbid claimants from settling a claim for less than the statutory minimum.

4. **CALL YOUR STATE'S BOARD OF WORKERS' COMPENSATION OFFICE for advice, including how to properly complete all preprinted forms, and what lawyers representing claimants regularly appear before the Board at hearings.** For maximum success, hire a

specialist who knows all the judges at the Workers' Compensation Board.

5. DEMAND A HEARING IMMEDIATELY if the employer refuses to voluntarily pay medical expenses or lost wages. Most state laws require payment within a few weeks of the injury or illness. Additional statutory penalties may be awarded when you are not promptly paid or reimbursed for your expenses.

6. UNDERSTAND THE PROCEDURE FOR WORKERS' COMPENSATION HEARINGS. Inquire if reports from non-doctors, such as chiropractor and physical therapists, are acceptable and helpful to your case. If so, instruct your lawyer to use them where appropriate.

7. THOROUGHLY PREPARE FOR THE HEARING. Analyze all medical reports with your lawyer. Tell your lawyer about prior injuries. Ask your lawyer to review all the medical reports and surveillance information the employer has and plans to introduce. The employer may object to providing this information, but such evidence is discoverable. (Note: It is not uncommon for the employer or insurer to hire a private detective to engage in surveillance to determine if you are exaggerating your injuries. Don't be surprised if pictures or videos of you playing sports with your children or engaging in strenuous exercise is admitted at the hearing. Knowing what evidence the employer intends to submit at the hearing and reviewing all evidence ahead of time is crucial to winning a workers' compensations case.)

8. VISIT THE ACCIDENT SITE WITH YOUR LAWYER BEFORE THE HEARING. Take pictures where appropriate. Maps, diagrams, and pictures of the work site where the accident occurred can play a helpful role in convincing the hearing examiner the injury was work-related.

9. KNOW YOUR APPEAL RIGHTS. If you disagree with the initial determination and wish to appeal, be sure the appeal is filed in a timely manner acceptable to the Board.

10. UNDERSTAND YOUR RIGHTS TO REINSTATEMENT and the effect on workers' compensation benefits when you return to work. For example, suppose you hurt your back at work, undergo surgery and physical therapy, and return to work with a permanent restriction to avoid heavy lifting. Can you legally refuse a job that doesn't require heavy lifting without jeopardizing your workers' compensation benefits?

11. QUESTION AMBIGUOUS OR CONFUSING LANGUAGE IN THE SETTLEMENT AGREEMENT. Has your lawyer carefully prepared a settlement agreement which spells out your rights and benefits? Confirm that the Board approves the settlement. No attorney fees may be paid until this occurs.

12. AVOID WAIVING OTHER VALUABLE CLAIMS WHEN SETTLING A WORKERS' COMPENSATION CASE. In recent years, decisions by many state compensation boards and courts have greatly expanded the circumstances in which employees have been permitted to collect money for workplace related injuries, such as cardiovascular disease and cancer, injuries induced by workplace stress, and cumulative trauma and repetitive motion disorders. Some states have allowed employees to use the court system, rather than be bound by the exclusivity of a workers' compensation remedy, especially in cases of sexual harassment, wrongful discharge, and disability discrimination claims.

13. WHENEVER A SETTLEMENT IS REACHED IN A WORKERS' COMPENSATION CASE, and you are asked to sign a settlement agreement and release, be careful not to surrender other valuable potential claims, such as social security benefits. Get legal advice to protect your rights and discuss other potential legal causes of action you can assert in court before signing any settlement agreement. (Note: The failure to obtain available benefits or avoid needless liability can be grounds for malpractice against your lawyer.)

14. CONSIDER THE IMPACT A REFUSAL TO CONTINUE TO WORK OR ACCEPT A REASSIGNMENT WILL HAVE ON UNEMPLOYMENT COMPENSATION BENEFITS. Generally, one who leaves a job voluntarily without good cause is ineligible for benefits. More significant, however, is the fact that inconsistent statements uttered at unemployment hearings can be used against you at workers' compensation hearings. Since unemployment hearings usually come first, be sure your lawyer carefully reviews your testimony and prepares you for the tough questions you may face during cross examination to reduce the chances of making a statement that could doom a later workers' compensation claim.

15. UNDERSTAND HOW LEGAL FEES ARE PAID. Never volunteer to pay legal fees when you are not required to do so.

Sample Letter Detailing On-The-Job Injuries

Your Name
Address
Telephone Number
Date

Name of Officer
Title
Name of Employer
Address

Re: My Accident

Dear (Name of Officer)

Please be advised that on (date) at (time) I suffered the following on-the-job accident (specify). (State who you spoke to at the company, and what happened after the accident, and the assistance you received.) I am in the process of evaluating my injuries and it appears that (state the extent of your injuries and how long you will remain out of work, or the accommodations you require from the employer, such as reassignment to another job).

I will require (state the medical and physical therapy assistance you need). In that regard, it will be necessary for me to file a workers' compensation claim with your insurance carrier. Please advise how I should go about doing this and (state all other requests).

Thank you for your continued assistance and if you need further information or wish to speak to me, feel free to contact me at the above telephone number. As always, I appreciate your efforts on my behalf.

Very truly yours,
Your Name
Sent certified mail, return receipt requested

Sample Accident/Work Injury Report

(To Be Completed By Immediate Supervisor)
Date of this report:
Date of accident:
Name of employee:
Social security number:
Position:
Title:
Department:
Employment commencement date:
Number of months in this department or position:
Describe accident in detail (specify time, place, duties of employee, etc.):
Describe nature of injuries:
Names of witnesses (if any):
Have those witnesses been interviewed? If so, by whom?
Has a written statement of all witnesses been prepared?
If so, where is the report now and who has seen it? If not, by when?
Estimated medical consequence of accident/work injury to injured employee:
Estimated loss to Company from accident/work injury:

MANAGEMENT AUTHORIZATION

Name of Review:
Date:
Comments:
Action to be taken (specify, i.e., safety committee meeting, notify union or shop steward, replace position, etc.) and by when (specify date):

To minimize workplace accidents, it is a good idea for employers to implement the following :

1. Place OSHA workplace posters where all employees can easily see them.

2. Record all workplace fatalities, and report any serious accidents (e.g., accidents where five or more employees were injured seriously enough to be hospitalized) to a Federal or State OSHA Office within 48 hours of the fatality or serious accident.

3. Under OSHA, employers must maintain complete and accurate records concerning injuries and illnesses occurring on the job or as a result of conditions at the plant site.

4. Under OSHA, employers must consciously prepare and display an annual summary of workplace injuries and illnesses except if the company employs 10 or fewer employees, it may be exempt from OSHA record keeping requirements.

5. Notify employees of the procedures to follow in case of an emergency. This information should be contained in any employee manuals and company handbooks and all emergency phone numbers should be prominently listed.

6. Maintaining a safe workplace begins with the orientation of new workers. Set the stage from the beginning by letting the new employee know that safety is a very important focus at the workplace.

7. While job descriptions and work environment will determine what specific safety training must be given an employee, all new workers should receive an overall safety orientation.

8. Management's commitment to accident and injury prevention must always be conveyed.

9. Make clear that employee participation is needed to prevent accidents.

10. Request that workers notify management, without penalty, of any unsafe condition or potential hazard.

11. Constantly remind supervisors to maintain safe and productive work operations.

12. Advise workers not to undertake a task before learning the safe method of doing it and being authorized by a supervisor to proceed.

13. Remind new employees about hazard recognition and that any injury, even a slight one, must be reported and treated immediately.

14. Keep the workplace safe and train employees in safety on an ongoing basis.

15. Take a preventive approach to avoiding worker injuries and to insure a clean and healthful working environment.

16. Take steps to reduce worker stress, exposure to hazardous substances, vision impairment, repetitive motion injuries and exposure to computer terminal-caused injuries from video display terminals.

17. Work closely with employees and request regular employee suggestions to reduce potential safety violations.

18. Hire safety consultants to visit the work site and make suggestions. Many insurance companies provide this service at no cost.

19. Since safety training is mandated by federal regulation, regular training sessions for management and supervisors should be conducted to insure that employees know company policies and abide by the law.

20. Conduct follow-up field inspections to monitor compliance.

21. Publicize specific, strict rules regarding employee safety and related matters in company handbooks.

22. Statements on safety should include a list of prohibited forms of conduct and the consequences of committing such acts as well as a stated policy reminding workers how to report accidents, seek medical attention, and so forth.

Social Security Benefits

The federal Social Security Act guarantees benefits to people who qualify because of age, disability or hardship. Virtually all people who work, including employees, independent contractors, household workers, and federal, state and local government employees can participate, as well as people serving in the armed forces. It is a social insurance program funded through employee and employer payroll taxes. Being fully insured means that you can collect benefits when you reach retirement age or become disabled, and your dependents can also collect.

Benefits include social security retirement benefits and social security disability benefits. To be fully insured for retirement benefits, the Social Security Administration keeps track of the number of calendar quarters you worked (in which you earned more than $630) before reaching age 62, as well as the amount of social security contributions made by you or on your behalf by an employer. If you work more than 40 accumulated quarters of coverage in your working lifetime, you will become fully insured. Individual benefits are calculated by averaging the 35 years of your highest earnings through a formula that includes the period in which a worker contributed payments, the total amount you paid into the system, your age, and the type of benefits being applied for. Higher earnings result in higher benefits. Monthly old-age benefits commence at age 62 if you choose retirement from working. If you wait until 66 to begin collecting, the monthly retirement benefits are greater.

To confirm that you have received proper credit, you can apply for a statement of earnings every few years through a local office of the Social Security Administration. When seeking social security retirement benefits, apply for them a few months before eligibility, because there is a waiting period of several months before actual payments begin. There is no cap on lifetime benefits a person can receive from social security.

Since any missing years may reduce your benefit, it is important to save documents. If you can't find old returns or pay stubs, the government will still review your case based on secondary evidence, like a supervisor testifying to your salary. Call the Social Security Administration for information where applicable.

Aged, blind, or disabled workers and family members of deceased or disabled workers may be eligible to receive supplemental security income (SSI) and disability benefits. Unlike workers' compensation benefits, disability or death does not have to be job-related for you and your family to be entitled to Social Security benefits. Disability benefits begin for disabled workers at any age. Being disabled means you are incapable of engaging in any significant work activity and such disability has lasted or can be expected to last more than 12 months. To prove this, it is necessary to submit reports from doctors, hospitals, physical therapists, and other medical professionals.

Dependent benefits are available for spouses sixty-two and older, dependent unmarried children under eighteen (nineteen if full-time students), and disabled unmarried children eighteen and older if an adult wage earner becomes disabled. A wife can receive half of a husband's retirement benefits if she is still married to him when she reaches the age of sixty-six. A divorced wife is eligible for social security retirement and an ex-husband's disability benefits provided she was married to him for ten years or longer and is not currently married. If a female spouse worked, she can receive both her worker's retirement or disability benefit plus an amount by which her husband's benefit exceeds her benefit. A child under eighteen can receive approximately half of the monthly benefit a father or mother receives because of old age or disability.

Lump-sum death benefits are paid to the widow(er) of a deceased worker and dependent children, and the Social Security Administration provides dependents' benefits to all children who are dependents of a retired, disabled or deceased worker, including natural children, legally adopted children, stepchildren, and illegitimate children with inheritance rights.

When an issue arises concerning a dependent's (or any person's) eligibility for benefits and the amount of benefits to be paid, a multi-step process works this way:

INITIAL APPLICATION FOR BENEFITS. State disability determination services (DOSs) make most of the initial disability determinations for SSA and are subject to all of SSA's rules and regulations. The applicant for social security or SSI disability benefits files an application at the local social security office. A decision will be made whether you are eligible for benefits after an initial review. Generally, most applicants are denied Social Security benefits at the initial application level. After you file a claim for benefits, you should receive written notification informing you whether your claim has been approved or denied in 60 to 90 days. If accepted, the notice will explain what your benefits will be, and when the first check will be sent.

REQUEST FOR RECONSIDERATION. If your claim is denied, or if your benefits are reduced or terminated, a letter from the SSA will state the reasons. You can then request in writing that the initial adverse decision be reviewed by someone at SSA who was not involved in the decision. This must be done within 60 days after receiving a denial notice or notice of less benefits than you think you deserve. Contact a representative from your local Social Security office to learn what form to send, pertinent information to include, and to whom the form should be addressed. Submit detailed, additional evidence including letters from doctors stating why the initial decision was incorrect. Send the notice by certified mail, return receipt requested to prove the date your protest was sent. File a timely appeal in writing to preserve your rights. Since initial decisions are often reversed, you lose nothing by appealing the ruling.

At the reconsideration level, the DDS will conduct a paper review of the file. In most cases, the original decision will be upheld since a claimant's impairment is not severe enough to prevent him or her from working, or that your condition will improve within 12 months.

REQUEST FOR AN ADMINISTRATIVE HEARING. If, after several months, you receive an unfavorable decision after reconsideration, you have the right to appear before an administrative law judge (ALJ) at the Office of Hearings and Appeals of the Social Security Administration and present your case. This is a formal hearing where you will testify and submit evidence. Claimants often retain the services of an attorney to represent them at such hearings because a lawyer skilled in cross-examination of witnesses and knowledgeable as to social security laws and regulations can be useful.

Hearings usually occur a few months after a request. Use the time wisely. Schedule an appointment at a local SSA office to review your file to verify it contains all documents you submitted. If necessary, ask the judge to subpoena important witnesses who will not appear voluntarily on your behalf. For disability claims, develop a theme of the case with evidence and witnesses who can confirm your medical condition and why you cannot work. This includes letters from doctors, hospitals and clinics where you have been treated which discuss the medical condition that prevents you from doing any substantial gainful work (defined as any job that pays $500 per month or more). The letters should also state that your disability is expected to last for 12 months or is expected to result in death.

The hearing before the ALJ is the first level at which the decision-maker is to some degree independent. Often, the ALJ will look at all of the evidence fresh, and it is critical that the strongest factual and medical record possible be made at this step. You can represent yourself at this hearing or appoint someone else to represent you. Or, you can waive the hearing and have the case decided on the basis of written evidence submitted to the judge. The hearing is open to all interested parties and the ALJ is required to make a complete record of the proceeding.

The claimant has the burden of proving he cannot return to his past work. If the claimant can do this, the burden then shifts to the Social Security Administration to prove work exists in significant numbers in the national economy which the claimant can perform, taking into account his age, education, work experience, and residual functional capacity. In cases involving disability based on mental impairments, SSA evaluates the mental demands of past work and determines whether the claimant has the ability to meet these mental demands.

REVIEW BY APPEALS COUNCIL. The ALJ issues a written decision based on evidence included in the record and offered at the hearing. The decision gives findings of fact and reasons for the decision.

The ALJ decision is binding unless review by the Appeals Council is requested. If an unfavorable decision is rendered by an administrative law judge, you can request a final Appeals Council review by filing a notice, together with a legal memo supporting your position, in Washington, D.C. within 60 days of receiving written notification. The Appeals Council reviews all evidence in the ALJ hearing record and any additional evidence received. If the council agrees to review the case, it usually does not request another hearing because its job is to review the record of the earlier hearing to determine if the ALJ erred as a matter of law (but may do so if additional evidence is needed). The right to an Appeals Council review is not automatic and the council has the power to decide what cases it wants to review.

There are several reasons when the Appeals Council will review a case. These include (1) an abuse of discretion by the ALJ, (2) an error of law, (3) the action, findings, or conclusions of the ALJ are not supported by substantial evidence, or (4) a broad policy or procedural issue affecting the general public interest exists. Absent these factors the Appeals Council will deny the request for review.

FILING AN ACTION IN FEDERAL COURT. If the Appeals Council refuses to hear your case or hears your case but rules against you, you can then file suit in federal court. Generally, you have only 60 days to appeal each action to the next stage, and appeals to Social Security usually must be made on a special form available at your local Social Security office. Consider retaining the services of an experienced lawyer when appealing denials of a Social Security claim.

Understand how you will be charged for legal fees if you decide to file an action in a federal United States District Court. Unless you have deep pockets or the case involves a substantial amount of money and your chances of winning are good, do not hire a lawyer to provide litigation services on an hourly basis. Consider representation on a contingency basis to reduce your downside.

The appeals process pertaining to social security benefits and laws is extremely confusing and complicated. Always consult a knowledgeable lawyer to discuss your rights and options and possibly represent you. Although many claimants represent themselves, there are time limits for filing appeals and many people are unfamiliar on how to best represent themselves, especially at hearings. To determine if you qualify for benefits or have a matter that requires a specialist's services, speak to a representative at your local social security office for guidance.

Strategies to Receive Social Security Benefits

1. **MAINTAIN A RECORD.** Keep a full, organized account of your communications. When you file a claim, you are automatically assigned a SSA worker. Save this person's name and telephone number as well as copies of all forms or documents sent to the SSA.

2. **KEEP IN TOUCH WITH SSA TO AVOID INTERRUPTION OF BENEFITS.**

3. **BE THOROUGH.** When filing for disability benefits or contesting an initial adverse decision, submit a detailed list of the names, addresses and telephone numbers of doctors, hospitals, or institutions that have treated you for your disability, a summary of all the jobs you have held for the past 15 years, the type of work you performed, and claim numbers of any checks you receive for your disability. This is in addition to other documents, such as your birth certificate, copies of income tax returns and social security card.

4. **KNOW THE LAW.** Obtaining disability benefits often boils down to proving a legally recognized impairment. The Social Security Administration defines a disability as "the inability to engage in substantial gainful activity by reason of any medically determinable physical or mental impairment which can be expected to result in death or which has lasted or can be expected to last for a continuous period of not less than 12 months."

The disability must be medically certified. Some illnesses or handicaps are so serious that the SSA automatically treats them as disabilities, such as severe epilepsy or blindness; SSA has a list of such impairments. If you believe you are disabled, but your impairment is not on the list, you will have to prove that it is equally severe and disabling.

The SSA generally employs a five step evaluation procedure to determine if benefits should be granted. Failure to meet any of the following sequential tests often results in denial of benefits:

a. You must not be currently working and performing substantial gainful activity.

b. You must have a severe impairment or combination of impairments.

c. The impairment or combination of impairments must meet or equal one of the impairments in the Listing of Impairments.

d. Your impairment or combination of impairments must prevent you from doing work that you did in the past.

e. Considering your age, education, and work experience, there must be no other jobs you can perform, and no other jobs nationally that exist.

5. PREPARE FOR THE HEARING. Always review all medical evidence with your attorney before the ALJ hearing to be sure no existing records have been overlooked. The lawyer should write to all treating physicians as early as possible in the process to explain the importance of complete testing and to request the physician to schedule any additional testing at once so the results will be available when a final report is prepared.

Request a copy of the Exhibit file from the Office of Hearings and Appeals. The file contains all documents which have been filed by the claimant, as well as previous denials and medical records. Do this by letter and submit an Appointment of Representative form which has been executed by you and your lawyer if you have hired counsel to represent you.

Use medical advisors and vocational experts wherever practical and affordable. A competent medical expert will provide the ALJ with reliable testimony concerning your medical condition and jobs you can perform. Vocational experts testify as to your skills, the availability of significant jobs nationally you can perform, and other factors such as the transferability of your current skills to other work. Credible medical advisors and vocational experts can increase the chances of gaining disability benefits when used properly.

6. BE PREPARED TO TESTIFY. A successful case often hinges on the claimant's testimony. Your lawyer must fully understand your medical history and abilities and prepare you to properly answer a variety of questions at the hearing, including a description of:

- medical impairments
- history of your surgeries
- medications you take
- the pain you experience
- how often you leave home
- the doctors, hospitals, and physical therapists you have visited since the onset of your disability.

Providing compelling answers to these and other questions will give the judge a better understanding of your problems and hopefully persuade her to award disability benefits.

7. UNDERSTAND HEARING PROCEDURES. Hearings usually begin with an opportunity for your lawyer to make an opening statement. The ALJ will then swear in witnesses, enter the documents in the record, and begin the process of examining witnesses. Usually the claimant is questioned first by his or her lawyer. To ensure that the record is complete, the judge will inquire into all aspects of a claimant's condition and accept statements from social workers, friends, and co-workers regarding the limitations created by a person's impairments. Your lawyer will question you to develop a record. The ALJ will then ask questions, such as to describe an average day, beginning with what time you awake and whether you need assistance with dressing and grooming. Are you able to prepare meals, clean house or shop without assistance? Do you rely on others for transportation? What impairments affect your ability to stand, sit, walk, lift and carry?

After all the evidence and arguments are submitted and the testimony of the claimant, his or her witnesses (including medical advisors, vocational experts and others) are heard, the claimant and his counsel rest their case, leave the hearing, and wait for the written decision.

8. CONSIDER LEGAL REPRESENTATION AND UNDER-STAND HOW LEGAL FEES ARE COMPUTED. Before you have to pay anything, the person who represented you must file a petition with Social Security showing the fee requested, the nature and extent of the services performed, and the dates the services started and ended. Social Security usually decides the amount of the fee, but if you have to go to court, attorney's fees generally cannot exceed 25 percent of what you recover. If you disagree with the fee approved by Social Security, you can ask your local Social Security office to review it. You must make this request in writing within 30 days of the time you receive notice of the approved fee. Your representative, likewise, has a right to have the fee reviewed if he or she feels that it is too small.

If you are represented by an attorney, and your claim is successful, Social Security usually withholds 25 percent of your back payments for the attorney. If this is not enough to pay all of the attorney's fees as approved by Social Security, you may be liable to pay the difference.

9. BE CAREFUL WHAT YOU SAY AT OTHER HEARINGS. The purpose of unemployment insurance is to receive benefits while you are looking for work. You cannot receive such benefits and expect to receive social security disability benefits because these are paid to people who cannot work. As in workers' compensation claims, statements uttered at unemployment hearings can be used against you at social security benefits hearings. Accordingly, be sure your lawyer carefully reviews your testimony and prepares you for the tough questions you may face during cross examination.

STRATEGY: *The same is true for damages alleged in handicap discrimination lawsuits. In order to obtain disability benefits, claimants will often admit, under penalty of perjury, that they cannot perform any job with a current employer or within the economy. Their physicians will support benefits applications with acknowledgments that the individuals are incapable of performing any job duties, with or without accommodation, and that they are totally disabled. Such admissions and representations can defeat subsequent handicap discrimination claims.*

Thus, speak to a knowledgeable lawyer to analyze your competing legal claims so action taken in one area will not prejudice your rights to obtain greater benefits in another.

Right to Be Warned Before a Massive Layoff

Employees are entitled to be warned in advance of a large layoff or plant closing under the federal Worker Adjustment and Retraining Notification Act (WARN). The law applies to private companies, nonprofit employers and some quasi-public entities with at least 100 full-time employees. Employers with more than 100 workers are required to give employees and their communities at least 60 days' notice or comparable financial benefits (60 days' notice pay) of plant closings and large layoffs. A plant closing triggers the act if at least 50 workers lose their jobs. The law defines a plant closing as a permanent or temporary shutdown of a single site of employment or one or more facilities or operating units within a single site of employment. A personnel cutback qualifies as a mass layoff when during any 30 day period at least 500 employees at a company are laid off or 50 to 499 employees are laid off if they make up at least 33 percent of a workforce.

A WARN claim applies not only to union employees working at plants. It can be asserted when a private employer discharges large numbers of secretaries or dismantles an accounting, business, or financial department due to a reorganization. Speak to an experienced employment attorney or contact your nearest regional office of the U. S. Department of Labor for more information. Companies must be careful when contemplating a substantial reduction of their workforce, and a representative from the Department of Labor can advise you if your rights are being violated.

For example, a federal judge in New York found that a major law firm violated the federal plant closure law when the 125-partner firm failed to give its 250 former staff attorneys and clerical help the required 60 days' notice. To avoid damages, it was reported that the law firm offered former employees one week's salary in return for their promise to opt out of the case, and about 150 accepted the offer. The others remained in the case and will receive significantly more compensation: one day's back pay for each day of violation up to 60 days; the value of medical expenses and other benefits paid directly to the affected employee; and the value of actual payments made to third parties on behalf of the affected employee.

The following thumbnail sketch will highlight important aspects of the act; suggestions will then be offered on the law's possible effects on workers and employers throughout the United States.

The WARN Act prohibits employers from ordering a plant closing or mass layoff until 60 days after the employer has given written notice of this to:

1. Affected employees or their representatives;

2. The state dislocated-worker unit; and

3. The chief elected official of the unit of local government where the closing or layoff is to occur.

Employers are defined as business enterprises that employ more than 100 full-time workers (part-timers are characterized as those working fewer than 20 hours per week or less than six months in the preceding year) or who employ more than 100 employees who in the aggregate work at least four thousand hours per week excluding overtime.

Employment loss is defined under the law as "a termination other than for cause, voluntary departure or retirement, or a layoff for more than 6 months or a reduction in hours of work of more than 50 percent during each month of any 6 month period." A worker's last day is considered the date of his/her layoff and employees terminated after the first layoff must also receive 60 days notice.

The law does not affect governmental or nonprofit organizations, and many layoffs of small companies may not be affected by the act's requirements due to the number of persons affected. Additionally, if the plant closing or mass layoff was caused by a natural disaster (flood, earthquake, severe drought, etc.), or was due to the closing of a temporary facility or completion of a project whose employees were hired with the understanding that their work was of limited duration, the law will not adversely affect the employer. The same is true for problems caused by strikes, lockouts, or permanent replacement of strikers.

There are other exceptions as well. The 60-day rule does not have to be strictly followed if the employer, reasonably and in good faith, was forced to shut down the plant in a shorter time to obtain needed capital or business, or if the closing or mass layoff was caused by business circumstances not reasonably foreseeable at the time the required notice was to be given.

Finally, the law does not protect workers who lose their jobs less than 60 days after the effective date of a sale. This is because the act was intended to protect workers only from closings or layoffs prior to a sale. The law merely obligates the seller to give notice until the sale is completed; it is unclear to what extent, if any, the buyer would be liable thereafter.

Any employer who orders a plant closing or mass layoff without furnishing appropriate notice may be liable in a civil action to each affected employee for:

1. One day's back pay for each day of violation up to 60 days. This amount is calculated at the higher of the employee's average regular rate or final regular rate of pay less any wages paid during the layoff period and any voluntary or unconditional payments (e.g., severance) paid to the affected worker that were not legally required;

2. The value of medical expenses and other benefits paid directly to the affected employee; and

3. The value of actual payments made to third parties on behalf of the affected employee.

Employers are also subject to fines not to exceed $500 per day to the appropriate unit of local government where the closing or layoff occurs unless the employer continues to pay benefits to affected employees as described above within three weeks of the shutdown or layoff. However, this fine may be reduced by showing that a "complained of wrongful act or omission" was in good faith and that the employer had reasonable grounds for believing that the act or omission was not a violation of law.

Critics contend that the law is weak because federal courts do not have the authority to enjoin (force an employer to reopen or rehire) plant closings and layoffs. The act only awards the above-cited economic sanctions plus reasonable attorney fees and costs to the prevailing party. Some legislators interested in protecting the rights of employees are arguing that the act has no teeth and, at best, merely gives workers notice of the firing and possibly a small amount of severance pay if a job is eliminated prior to the 60-day notice period.

Some states, including New York and New Jersey, have recently enacted stronger laws to protect the rights of displaced workers with broader coverage and benefits than the federal WARN Act. For example, the New York law covers companies with at least 50 full-time employees, requires 90-day written advance notice for a mass layoff or plant closing, is triggered when at least 25 employees are laid off if they make up at least 33 percent of the workforce or when a company lays off at least 250 full-time employees, and empowers the state Labor Department to file lawsuits seeking penalties, back wages and benefits. The law is stronger because it protects more employees, is more easily triggered, requires more advance warning time before plant closings and mass layoffs, and empowers the state Labor Department to commence civil actions and recover attorneys' fees if successful. And the New Jersey law provides greater damages to a terminated worker. Instead of awarding pay and benefits for the notice period that should have been given, employees are entitled to receive severance pay equal to one week of pay for each full year the employee worked for the employer.

STRATEGY: *A recent study confirmed that the majority of WARN Act lawsuits filed nationwide were dismissed; in cases that were settled or decided in favor of the plaintiff, workers received a small fraction of what was due. Thus, do some research to determine if your state's law has more teeth and you qualify. Judges are required to enforce stricter state laws over the federal WARN Act for your benefit if one exists. Discuss this with co-workers, union officials and other pertinent individuals.*

There are many exceptions to the federal law that do not help you. For example, the layoffs of workers employed by the same company but located at different sites cannot be combined to meet the threshold minimum. However, you may be entitled to recover damages under the law if you are a traveling salesperson working for the company like others all over the country and the entire field sales staff is fired en masse. Also, companies that have filed for bankruptcy protection may not be subject to WARN Act requirements.

While employers must give as much notice as feasible, they are permitted to give less than 60 days notice if providing such notice would have precluded the faltering company from obtaining working capital to postpone a plant shutdown, or the employer experiences a sudden or unexpected termination of an important contract, a strike, government-ordered shutdown of a facility or a natural disaster.

The good news is that employment attorneys representing fired workers in class action lawsuits are suing equity holders and creditors of employers who fail to make WARN Act required payments with increasing regularity and success. For example, while shareholders in a company are ordinarily insulated from liability for the debts of the company, large holders of an employer's equity or debt can be potentially liable. Also, courts have adopted a five part test originally devised by the Department of Labor to calculate when a parent company may be responsible for WARN violations by its subsidiary or when a creditor company exercising control over the debtor company is subject to responsibility.

If you are affected by a closing or mass layoff, always:

1. Review the notice documents to determine if they comply with federal and/or state law.

2. Review the company's employee handbooks to insure the move complies with representations contained in such manuals.

3. Speak to co-workers to assess the validity of the move.

4. Prepare a list of questions to be answered by management and request a meeting with co-workers.

5. Determine whether the company will pay your earned sick leave, personal absences, bonuses, commissions, accrued expenses, and other payments. You may be entitled to receive such monies under federal and state laws. Question all attempts by the employer to deny paying you these monies. Speak to an employment attorney to discuss your rights and the steps to be taken to collect what you already earned or is due.

6. Confirm whether you have any bumping or seniority rights over other workers if you are a union member covered under a collective bargaining agreement. If you are a long-time union worker, you may learn that other workers must be eliminated before you and this can save your job. Also, do you have the right to re-apply for employment with the company any time after being displaced? Discuss these issues with your union delegate, attorney, HR director or management supervisor where applicable.

7. Discuss with management the possibility of being offered the opportunity to resign instead of being terminated in exchange for more severance, medical insurance, outplacement and other financial benefits. Recognize, however, that you may forfeit valuable unemployment insurance benefits by resigning.

8. Understand the effect of the plant closing or mass layoff on your entitlement to continued health benefits, pension and retirement plans, disability or medical leaves of absence, and workers' compensation claims. Experts suggest that employees on family or medical leave are sometimes forgotten when WARN Act notices are sent. If you are in this category and did not receive the required 60 days advance notice, speak to an employment attorney immediately to preserve and protect your rights. The lawyer can also explain how your long-term benefits will be paid, who is responsible for distributions, plus how to deal with the plan administrator after the formal mass layoff or plant closing occurs.

9. Check your state's law to determine that you qualify for unemployment insurance and continued health benefits. Fill out all forms requested by the employer, plan administrators, Department of Labor Unemployment

Insurance Division, and your state taxing authority where applicable to ensure medical, retirement plans, workers' compensation, disability, unemployment compensation, and other benefits.

10. Request a favorable letter of reference and outplacement benefits with management where applicable.

Employers covered by the law must carefully orchestrate all moves before closing marginally profitable plants. Obviously, affected workers and the community must be notified properly, and additional benefits will have to be given to comply with the act's provisions.

STRATEGY: *Now that you have a better understanding of the law, if you believe you are being victimized by a substantial reduction in force and the employer is not applying the law properly, speak to an experienced employment attorney immediately or contact your nearest regional office of the U.S. Department of Labor for more information. Companies must be careful when contemplating substantial reductions of their workforce, and a representative from the Department of Labor can hopefully advise you quickly if your rights are being violated.*

Employee Inventions and Suggestions

Workers frequently create valuable suggestions, comments, ideas, designs, manufacturing processes, and inventions. These suggestions often lead to money-saving and money-making devices. If the invention is created while on the job or is used by an employer, is the company obligated to pay the employee for the use of such an idea? Who owns the device or invention created?

This section will clarify ambiguous law and give you a better understanding of how to avoid problems and protect yourself in this area. To be able to implement many of the strategies contained herein, it is important to first understand the following basic concepts.

WORK FOR HIRE. A work for hire is defined as a work prepared by an employee within the scope of his or her employment or work specifically ordered or commissioned by the employer which the employee creates in reliance upon an express agreement. Thus, for example, when an employee is specifically engaged to do something (such as solve a problem, develop a new product, process, or machine), he or she is provided with the means and opportunity to resolve the problem or achieve the result and is paid for that work, then the employer is generally entitled to the fruits of the employee's labors. If a worker creates an invention while on the job, therefore, the invention may be owned by the employer under this legal principle.

THE SHOP RIGHT CONCEPT. If an employee is not hired to invent or solve a particular problem, does the employee have the right to claim any rights to his or her discoveries? Maybe, depending upon the particular facts involved.

For example, under the shop right concept, when an employee makes an invention or discovery that is outside the scope of his employment but utilizes the employer's resources (equipment, labor, materials, or facilities) in making the invention, that invention may be owned by the employee subject to a "shop right" on the part of the employer. This shop right in certain instances may give the employer a nonexclusive, irrevocable license to use the invention indefinitely, without having to pay a royalty.

VALUABLE IDEAS AS OPPOSED TO PATENTABLE INVENTIONS. Using a hypothetical case, Gwen develops a manufacturing process during nonworking hours which she thinks will save the company money. She tells her boss and the idea is incorporated into the company's production process. Gwen is not compensated for the idea. She resigns and sues to recover a percentage of the money saved by the idea's use.

Gwen's case is not as strong as it appears. The reason is that ideas, plans, methods, and procedures for business operations cannot normally be copyrighted. This is also true with respect to certain ideas as intellectual property. The law generally states that ideas belong to no one and are there for the taking.

Additionally, an idea is presumed to be a work made for hire and the property of the employer if an employee offers it voluntarily without contracting to receive additional compensation. Gwen would have a stronger case if she could prove that the idea was her own original, unique creation not requested or developed while working on company time or on the employer's premises, and that it was furnished because of a specific promise or understanding that she would be promoted or compensated once it was implemented by the employer.

Many workers are unknowingly exploited because they give away their ideas without understanding their rights. Review the following strategies if you wish to avoid being exploited in this area.

STRATEGY 1: *Articulate your idea, method, or process in writing. This is essential because it is difficult to prove you are the creator of a valuable idea unless it is set down on paper.*

STRATEGY 2: *Be sure the writing is detailed and specific. This can increase your chances of proving the idea is a protectable property interest. For example, if you write a proposal for a unique and original television show, be sure to fully describe the characters, budget, and script dialogue rather than briefly discussing the concept of the show.*

STRATEGY 3: *Avoid volunteering ideas. In one famous case a homemaker mailed an unsolicited cheesecake recipe to a baking company. The recipe was used and became a popular moneymaker. Although the woman sued the company for damages, she lost. The court ruled that no recovery was obtainable because the homemaker voluntarily gave her idea to the company.*

The lesson to be learned from this case is clear. Since employers generally have no obligation to compensate employees for ideas, inventions, or suggestions that are conveyed voluntarily, think twice before doing this, particularly if company policy states that there is no obligation to pay anything if the idea is used, or that any payments made will be purely discretionary (i.e., not linked to any predetermined formula such as a percentage of specific company savings, revenue, or profits generated from the idea).

STRATEGY 4: *Avoid signing any agreement or contract with work-for-hire provisions. Some companies request job applicants and employees to sign agreements stating that all inventions authored or conceived by the employee belong to the employer. Avoid this whenever possible.*

STRATEGY 5: *Negotiate a predetermined method of compensation and articulate your understanding in writing. For example, the agreement should mention the type of idea being conveyed and the manner of compensation for its use, and should stipulate that the employer will maintain the confidentiality of the idea and will not disclose, assign, or transfer the idea or its value to anyone else without your consent. The sample agreement below illustrates these points in greater detail. If compensation is difficult to ascertain at the time the acknowledgment is negotiated, the agreement can state that the employee will be compensated in a manner mutually agreed upon by the parties and that the idea will remain the property of the employee or individual until such formula is determined.*

Sample Acknowledgment of Receipt of Idea

Received on this day from (name of employee or individual) an idea concerning (specify) which was presented in the form of (specify) and which is hereby acknowledged.

The employer confirms that it has not used or implemented this idea in the past, that it is sufficiently original and has been conveyed with the expectation of receiving payment thereof, and, if used or implemented in any manner, shall cause (name of employee or individual) to be compensated according to the following: (specify).

The employer agrees to maintain the confidentiality of the material submitted herein by (name of employee or individual) and agrees not to disclose it, or the ideas upon which it is based, to any person, firm, or entity without (name of employee or individual)'s consent.

Accepted and consented to:
Name of Employer
By: Name of Officer and Title   Date:
By: Name of Employee or Individual   Date:

STRATEGY 6: *Get a receipt. If you are unable to receive a signed acknowledgment similar to the above, you must be able to prove delivery of a valuable idea to another in order to protect your rights. For example, it is often wise to send a certified letter indicating that your idea was submitted in confidence with the expectation of being paid for its use. The following letter illustrates this concept. Although such a letter cannot guarantee protection of your idea, it can increase the chances that you will not be exploited in this area. Try to send the materials by certified mail, return receipt requested, to prove delivery, and follow up the letter with a telephone call or another letter in the near future if you do not receive an immediate response. Finally, insist on having all materials returned, plus copies, if you receive an unfavorable reply; you don't want the materials floating around so other people can look at them and steal your idea.*

Sample Letter to Employer Concerning Your Idea

Your Name
Address
Telephone Number
Date

Name of Officer
Title
Name of Employer
Address

Re: The submission of my original idea regarding (specify) consisting of (specify)

Dear (Name of Officer),

Per our earlier telephone conversation on (date), I have enclosed, per your request, my original idea regarding (specify) consisting of (specify).

You indicated an interest in this concept and advised me that the materials would be reviewed in confidence with no disclosure to any other person, firm, or entity without my prior written consent.

Finally, it was agreed that these materials are submitted with the expectation of furnishing appropriate acknowledgment of my authorship and payment to me in the event they are used after my written consent has been given.

Thank you for your interest in the matter and I look forward to hearing from you after you have completed your review.

Very truly yours,
Your Name

Sent certified mail, return receipt requested.

STRATEGY 7: *Avoid signing releases. Many employers and individuals request that creators sign releases before they will agree to review their ideas. Such releases typically state that the individuals assume no liability regarding the receipt or use of such material. Avoid signing any such document because they defeat the purpose of the strategies discussed in this section.*

STRATEGY 8: *Keep copies of all materials and letters that you send to others. Some people mail an unopened copy of the package back to themselves for this purpose. In the event of a dispute, the postmark date on the front of the envelope may establish that you were the sender of the package.*

STRATEGY 9: *Consult a lawyer. If your idea is sufficiently unique or potentially valuable, you may wish to consult an experienced copyright or patent lawyer whom you can trust.*

5

All About Discrimination

Although employment discrimination is illegal, it is widely practiced throughout the United States. In fact, many hundreds of thousands of claims are filed each year with the various federal, state, and local agencies empowered to investigate, enforce, and protect the civil rights of workers.

Federal and state laws prohibit employers from discriminating against employees or potential employees on the basis of:

- Gender, marital status or pregnancy
- Age
- Race, color, creed or national origin
- Disability, physical or mental handicap
- Religion
- Retaliation

This applies throughout all stages of employment: recruiting, interviewing, and hiring; compensation, assignment, employee classification, demotions, transfers, promotions, wages, working conditions, testing, use of company facilities, training programs, fringe benefits, retirement plans, disability leave; and discipline, layoffs, and discharge procedures. An illegal act can be committed by any member of an employer's staff, from the president down to a supervisor or receptionist.

Retaliation and on-the-job harassment are also prohibited. This means that if you complain about discrimination to a supervisor or human resources officer (preferably in writing to prove the complaint), hire a lawyer to document your dissatisfaction, or file a charge of discrimination in good faith, you cannot be fired, demoted, or reassigned while the case is pending. Typical remedies for illegal conduct are significant monetary awards by judges, juries or arbitrators.

When a recently fired employee consults with me, one of the first points I consider is whether the individual has a valid claim of unfair termination based upon age, sex or race discrimination. For example, assuming equal work, did the company pay the same salary and benefits to women as to men? Was a black employee fired justifiably because of excessive absences and lateness? Was an elderly sales employee the first to be fired because of a slipping sales quota?

As you will learn in this chapter, recognizing and fighting back against job discrimination is not always easy. The subtleties of this become apparent with the examples used above. Suppose a company fired a 61 year old salesperson because he wasn't meeting quota. That sounds like a legitimate reason, right? Maybe, but what if the company's sales were down in many of its territories? Were younger salespeople fired as well, or were they merely given a warning and placed on probation?

Using the other examples, were white workers with the same record of absences and lateness merely warned and not fired? Was the female employee fired for complaining that she did not receive the same benefits as her male counterparts? If so, discrimination has occurred which must be redressed.

The information in this chapter will help you recognize when you have been victimized by discrimination. You will learn what practices are illegal and how to file a timely complaint, prove your charges, and collect damages for your claim. If you are being forced to work in a hostile and offensive environment and are the victim of sexual harassment, you will learn how to send letters to document the exploitation. Recent Supreme Court cases dealing with major discrimination subjects will also be analyzed to make this chapter as timely as possible.

Federal and State Discrimination Laws

The Civil Rights Act of 1991 implemented a series of sweeping changes in federal antidiscrimination laws. The legislation expanded procedural options and remedies available to workers and overruled a number of important U. S. Supreme Court decisions that limited employees' legal recourse. In doing so, Congress amended six different statutes that together prohibit discrimination based on age, race, color, religion, gender, national origin, and disability. Those statutes are Title VII of the Civil Rights Act of 1964, the Americans with Disabilities Act of 1990, the Vocational Rehabilitation Act of 1973, the Age Discrimination in Employment Act of 1967, The Civil Rights Act of 1866, and the Civil Rights Attorney's Fee Awards Act of 1976. Most employers are covered by these laws since they apply to companies employing 15 or more persons and affect private employers, employment agencies, and labor organizations.

Virtually all states and some major cities (such as San Francisco and New York) have enacted even stronger discrimination laws with greater coverage and penalties than federal law. These state statutes and the agencies that enforce them are highly significant. Although federal law does not recognize discrimination on the basis of a person's marital status or sexual preference, many state laws do. For example, New York recently added domestic violence victims as a protected class. This means that domestic violence victims are now protected under the state's human rights law from discriminatory employment practices in hiring, discharge, compensation and privileges of employment. Also, many small employers employing less than 15 persons not covered by Title VII fall within the jurisdiction of state law. Some local laws offer even greater protection; for example, age discrimination protection may apply to the young as well as those who are over 40, and white employees may sue for discrimination when blacks are perceived to receive better (unfair) treatment.

A question frequently asked is: Which law takes precedence? The answer is essentially the law that is the strictest and most inclusive. To ensure proper protection of your rights, try to be familiar with federal and state laws as well as those governing employment in your local business community or municipality. If there is a difference in coverage on the same subject, ask to enforce the law that is the most favorable to your situation. To learn whether you have greater protection and how it applies, contact an appropriate state or city agency and/or speak to a knowledgeable employment attorney for further details before taking action.

Prior to the Civil Rights Act of 1991, claimants could typically receive only their jobs back, together with retroactive job pay and restoration of seniority benefits. Now, in cases where intentional (i.e., willful) discrimination is proved, the act also authorizes jury trials, witness, and attorney fees to be paid to the individual harmed, punitive damages, compensatory damages up to $300,000 depending on the size of the employer, and additional penalties.

Compensatory damages are defined as money paid to compensate individuals for future pecuniary losses, emotional pain and suffering, inconvenience and mental anguish, loss of enjoyment and physical pain and suffering. Compensatory damages are typically available only for intentional discrimination and unlawful harassment, and do not apply where a job practice is not intended to be discriminatory but nonetheless has an unlawful impact on persons in a protected class, such as workers over forty.

In most sex, age and race disparate treatment discrimination cases, federal law requires judges and juries to review the facts and determine liability under a three-part burden-shifting test set forth in *McDonnell Douglass Corp. v. Green*. Initially, a claimant must make out a prima facie case of discrimination by using either direct, statistical, or circumstantial evidence proving: (1) membership in a protected class; (2) qualification for the employment position or benefit desired; (3) that the plaintiff suffered an adverse employment action; and (4) that the adverse employment action occurred under circumstances giving rise to an inference of discrimination.

Items one and two are generally easy to establish. Proving element three is more dicey. A plaintiff sustains an adverse employment action and thereby satisfies the third element of the prima facie case if he or she endures a materially adverse change in the terms and conditions of employment. Material adversity is more disruptive than a mere inconvenience or an alteration of job responsibilities. Whether a particular action is materially adverse depends on the circumstances of the case and is judged from the perspective of a reasonable person in the plaintiff's position, considering all the circumstances. Thus, if you are terminated or demoted by receiving less wages, salary or benefits, a less distinguished title, or significantly diminished important job responsibilities and can show such adverse action occurred under circumstances giving rise to an inference of discrimination, your case will be allowed to preliminarily go forward.

Once the plaintiff makes the de minimis showing, the burden of production shifts to the employer to provide a legitimate, nondiscriminatory reason supported by admissible evidence for its actions. If an employer articulates a nondiscriminatory justification for its conduct, the inference of discrimination raised by plaintiff's prima facie case disappears and the burden shifts back to the plaintiff to prove by competent evidence that the employer's nondiscriminatory explanation is pretextual.

To show that an employer's stated reason for firing or demoting you was pretextual, claimants are not required to show that the employer's stated reasons were false or played no role in the employment decision, but that they were not the only reasons, and that the prohibited factor was at least one of those motivating reasons. Your lawyer attempts to do this by demonstrating weaknesses, implausibilities, inconsistencies or contradictions in the employer's stated reasons so a judge will reasonably find such reasons to be unworthy of credence.

Proving discrimination can be difficult, especially when management-level employees have not made statements, remarks or threats; when there is no direct evidence; or when the claimant is unable to demonstrate statistical proof that the company had a practice of discrimination against workers in his/her protected class. This is why it is necessary in all discrimination cases to obtain the opinion of an experienced employment attorney before starting an action or proceeding with a trial.

STRATEGY: *If you are suing an employer under Title VII for discrimination based on sex, race, color, national origin or religion (but not age through an ADEA lawsuit), it may be easier for your lawyer to win the case by asserting the mixed-motive burden of proof standard. Unlike the McDonnell Douglas Corp. pretext theory which shifts the final burden of proof back to the employee, earning a mixed-motive jury instruction at trial is often better because a plaintiff is only required to show that race, color, sex, religion or national origin was a motivating factor for the employer's actions. Using this theory, especially in cases where there is only circumstantial evidence (i.e., no direct evidence), while a claimant may not completely disprove the employer's non-discriminatory reason, she can still win the case by persuading a jury that both legitimate and illegitimate reasons motivated the employment decision. Experts say whichever party doesn't have the burden of proof is more likely to win a discrimination lawsuit; using the mixed-motive theory to prove discrimination can be beneficial to the plaintiff's case. However, the law is unsettled and judges often do not allow plaintiff attorneys to utilize this burden of proof standard. Explore this option with your attorney whenever possible. Have your lawyer explain the kind of evidence that is required to request a mixed-motive instruction for the jury at trial.*

Strategies to help prove a case of discrimination are covered later in the chapter. We will now discuss the elements of sex, pregnancy, age, race, disability, religious and retaliation discrimination and related subjects in greater detail.

Sex Discrimination

Sex discrimination law encompasses many facets. The law mandates equal pay for equal work. It requires equal treatment, policies, standards, and practices for males and females in all phases of the employment relationship, including hiring, placement, job promotion, working conditions, wages and benefits, layoffs, and discharges. It is generally discriminatory in all states and under federal law to:

- Refuse to hire women with preschool-age children while hiring men with such children
- Require females to resign from jobs upon marriage when there is no similar requirement for males
- Include spouses of male employees in benefit plans while denying the same benefits to spouses of female employees
- Restrict certain jobs to men without offering women a reasonable opportunity to demonstrate their ability to perform the same job adequately
- Refuse to hire, train, assign, or promote pregnant or married women, or women of childbearing age on the basis of gender
- Transfer women to less-desirable positions with lesser benefits and opportunities or lowest paying/tip earning shifts than men
- Deny women overtime or the chance to attend career-enhancing seminars while offering these opportunities to men
- Deny unemployment or seniority benefits to pregnant women, or deny granting a leave of absence for pregnancy if similar leaves of absence are granted for illness
- Institute compulsory retirement plans with lower retirement ages for women than men
- Fire women because of their gender

Sex discrimination, also called gender discrimination, is legislated by Title VII of the Civil Rights Act of 1964 as well as the revised Civil Rights Act of 1991. Gender discrimination covers a variety of subjects and is protected by many laws, including the Equal Pay Act of 1963, which makes it illegal to discriminate against women concerning salary or wages, and the Pregnancy Discrimination Act of 1978, which prohibits discrimination on the basis of pregnancy, childbirth, and related medical conditions and health benefits. You may be the victim of sex discrimination when you are receiving disparate treatment (i.e., being treated differently from other employees), when you are denied employment opportunities primarily because you are a woman, or when the effect of a company policy or rule has a disproportionally negative effect on women in your company, causing an adverse impact. In certain cases illegal sex discrimination arises if you are a woman who is passed over for a promotion and eventually fired because of your gender, because you filed a charge of sexual harassment, or because you were pregnant (and not because of work performance).

In certain instances, it is also possible for you to be constructively discharged from a job even if you quit. Cases have been reported of women who were forced to resign from jobs out of fear they would have to keep working for a supervisor who sexually harassed them. If you are in such a situation and you resign, you may be able to argue successfully that you were a victim of wrongful discharge.

STRATEGY: *A charge of gender discrimination, constructive discharge, and retaliation can be made if you are excluded from meetings, observe that promotions and senior management positions are given to less qualified men, and are fired or resign after complaining about such alleged illegal treatment. Being purposely excluded from new opportunities may constitute workplace bias and gender discrimination if you are fired from a job because of an alleged corporate restructuring or downsizing, are not rehired several months later following the termination and learn that a less qualified male was offered your position. Consult an experienced employment attorney for advice where warranted.*

It is also illegal for companies to use advertising that denies women a chance to apply for a job or screening procedures that eliminate female applicants because the requirements are too demanding (e.g., requiring a college degree for secretarial work). No longer can women not be considered for physical jobs, nor is it lawful for employers to refuse jobs to women because they think that their turnover rate is higher, they take more sick leave, or they may become pregnant. As mentioned in Chapter 1, any questions to women regarding their families or childbearing plans are illegal. In certain cases the law is also making it easier for women to claim that the reason they were passed over for a promotion, such as not being made a partner in an accounting firm, was their gender and not their work performance (which is sometimes offered by employers as a pretext). Speak to a lawyer for more details.

Be aware that numerous cases of women winning large verdicts for sex discrimination have been reported. For example, a major oil company reportedly agreed to pay more than $8 million to settle a class action filed by 777 female employees who claimed they were discriminated against in terms of pay, promotions, and assignments. In another case, a judge upheld a $7.1 million sex discrimination jury verdict against a company after the plaintiff successfully alleged that senior managers removed her accounts she had helped build and gave them to male brokers. After 12 years with the company, the woman was accused of poor productivity and fired. The verdict included a $5 million punitive damages award.

A large grocery retailer reportedly agreed to pay $81.5 million to settle a class-action lawsuit by 150,000 women who accused the big grocery chain of relegating them to dead-end, low-paying jobs. The settlement applied to all women who worked at any of its stores in Florida, Georgia, South Carolina, and Alabama since 1981. The suit was brought in 1995 by eight women who accused the employer of passing them over for raises and repeatedly denying them management jobs. They and four others who quickly joined the case said they watched as men with less experience and less seniority got promotions.

Some said their requests were met with unwanted sexual advances from managers. The EEOC later joined the suit, and it was expanded to a class action covering past and current employees.

Although the settlement is the largest involving supermarket chains, another company reportedly paid $107 million to 14,000 women to settle similar allegations, and a different employer reportedly settled for $7.5 million in a sex discrimination suit covering 20,000 employees in California.

In a suit against a well-known insurance company, $250 million was reportedly paid to women who said they were denied or deterred from positions as insurance agents. And a well-known retailer faces a similar challenge from more than 20,000 current and former female employees who filed a class-action lawsuit claiming the company's personnel structure is set up to limit their access to sales jobs and supervisor and manager positions. The lawsuit claims women are placed in positions with fewer opportunities, while men are given jobs with greater advancement potential. The suit also alleges a pattern of sexual harassment and unequal pay. And recently a major university agreed to salary hikes and payments totaling more than $300,000 to several female professors who were illegally paid less than male professors of the same rank.

When a recently fired female employee consults with me, one of the first things I consider is whether she was fired because of gender. For example, I initially ask if the company has a history of laying off predominately more senior female executives than male executives.

Suppose a company fired a sixty-year-old salesperson because she wasn't meeting quota. Although that sounds like a legitimate reason, the employer may be committing sex discrimination if its sales were down in many of its territories and younger, male salespeople were not fired but merely given a warning or placed on probation.

Suppose a female worker was fired for lateness. In such a case, careful investigation might reveal that male workers with the same records of absences and lateness were merely warned but not fired. What if a female employee was fired in retaliation for complaining that she did not receive the same benefits as her male counterparts? If this is proved, illegal discrimination may have occurred.

Although this section stresses gender-based discrimination problems, other forms of discrimination, including age, race, national origin, disability, and religious discrimination may also be involved, because women who assert sex discrimination claims after a firing are often victimized due to other personal characteristics.

Equal Pay

The federal EPA prohibits covered employers with two or more employees from paying unequal wages to male and female employees who perform substantially the same jobs. For example, a major university was ordered to pay 117 women an award of $1.3 million after a federal court judge ruled that the university paid less money to women on the faculty than to men in comparable posts.

While the EPA and the Civil Rights Act of 1964 both prohibit sex discrimination in the workplace, the EPA applies only to wage inequities between the genders. Under the Equal Pay Act, employers are barred from paying women less than men if they are working on jobs that require equal skill, effort, and responsibility and if those jobs are performed under similar working conditions. This includes everyone from hourly workers to salaried employees engaged in executive, administrative, and professional functions, such as teachers. The courts have held that the jobs need not be identical, only "substantially equal." Further, an employer may not retaliate against a female worker, such as by firing her, because an EPA charge was initiated.

Fringe benefits are included in the definition of wages under the law. Thus, employers may not differentiate with items such as bonuses, expense accounts, profit-sharing plans, or leave benefits. Under EPA, it is not a defense to a charge of illegality that the costs of such benefits are greater with respect to women than to men, since the law is designed to ensure that women do not receive lower salaries and benefits than their male counterparts.

There are loopholes in the law, however. Employers may pay different wages if there is a bona fide preestablished seniority system, a merit system, or a system that measures earnings by quantity or quality of production. Differential pay is also permitted when the jobs are different or are based on a legitimate factor other than gender.

For example, a company began operations in 1995. Initially, 11 production assistants were hired, all male. Many of them are still employed by the company. In 2012 the company expanded and hired ten more production assistants, six of whom were women. Although all production assistants perform the same job, many of the older male workers receive greater hourly pay rates because of their seniority and number of years with the company. This is legal.

Determining if a job is different is not always clear-cut. A major problem arises when two jobs are similar but one includes extra duties. Although it is legal to give higher pay for the job with more responsibilities, a judge will scrutinize if the greater-paying jobs are given only to males at a particular company. This is often the case and may be illegal depending on the facts.

A female worker may seek damages in federal or state court or through the EEOC and may obtain a trial by jury when asserting an EPA violation. Successful litigants are entitled to recover retroactive back pay, liquidated damages, reasonable attorney fees, and costs. If willful violations (defined as reckless disregard for the law) are found, double back pay may be awarded. Employers are obligated to maintain and save records documenting wages and benefits paid to all employees. Once a complainant shows that she is working in the same place, is doing equal work under similar working conditions, and is paid less than employees of the opposite sex, the burden shifts to the employer to show an affirmative defense that any wage differential is justified by a permitted exception. Practices that perpetrate past sex discrimination are not accepted as valid affirmative defenses.

If a violation is present, you can sue the employer privately instead of filing a charge of sex discrimination, such as failing to promote you or firing you. Any other form of sex discrimination must be filed under Title VII or various state discrimination laws. The advantage of utilizing the EEOC is that the agency may include a charge of sex discrimination if the employer failed to promote you or fire you.

To avoid charges of EPA violations, employers are instructed to prepare precise job descriptions that demonstrate different duties and job responsibilities for different pay. When offering jobs with different salaries and benefits, companies are instructed to assign those higher-paying jobs on the basis of such factors as technical skills, additional education, work experience, and knowledge required, rather than gender.

STRATEGY: *If you believe that your company is exceeding predetermined salary ranges by offering higher salaries to males who are performing essentially the same job, speak to an employment attorney. This is a violation of EPA even if the reason is to attract minority applicants. And being denied equal pay because you are married, have children, or are a victim of gender-based stereotypes violates the law.*

Congress enacted the Lilly Ledbetter Fair Pay Act in January of 2009. Experts suggest the law has far-reaching implications for victims of unequal pay as well as disabled and elderly Title VII compensation discrimination claimants under the ADA and ADEA. The new law extends the time within which an employee can assert a charge of pay discrimination from 180 days of the making or adoption of a company's discriminatory rule to 180 days of the receipt of any wages, benefits or compensation affected by the decision. Thus, the time to file a charge of illegal treatment has been extended until 180 days from the receipt of the last paycheck based on an allegedly discriminatory pay act.

Since the law defines an unlawful discriminatory practice occurring when "a person" is affected, such broad language may also allow pay discrimination lawsuits to be filed by non-employees, such as the spouses of deceased workers, if such individuals were damaged by the employer's discriminatory acts.

New revisions in the law make it more difficult for employers to defend against wage disparity claims because objective performance-based specifics with supporting documentation must now be offered to support compensation decisions. All compensation decisions must be consistently and uniformly applied to all classes of workers without regard to gender, race or ethnicity.

The law states that an unlawful employment practice occurs with respect to disparate pay when a discriminatory compensation decision or other practice is adopted, affecting an individual to a discriminatory compensation practice each time wages, benefits or other compensation is paid.

No employee's pay may be reduced when enforcing the law. Rather, the pay of the lower paid worker must be increased. Also, the EPA applies only to employees, not job applicants.

Thousands of wage bias lawsuits are filed each year with the EEOC. Experts suggest passage of the Lilly Ledbetter Fair Pay Act will dramatically increase the number of lawsuits annually commenced against employers.

The following suggestions may be helpful in determining if you are a victim in this area:

1. Question all non-objective pay decisions which unfairly affect you, especially decisions implemented by an immediate supervisor without knowledge, input, or approval from the company's compensation committee, upper management, or human resources department.

2. Since all compensation decisions must be uniformly and consistently applied, speak to co-workers to determine what people at your salary grade are making. When in doubt, request information from management about your pay relative to co-workers and the criterion used in making salary, bonus, benefits, and compensation decisions.

3. Schedule a meeting with a human resources officer or management supervisor if you are underpaid or subject to unfair pay differentials because of a transfer, promotion or demotion (especially if you believe a factor was your gender, race or ethnicity). Prepare a written memo which clarifies the issues. Present the document at the meeting. Don't be afraid to voice your complaints because federal and many state laws prohibit employers from not allowing employees to discuss wages and/or retaliating against those who speak up.

4. Question all unfair or biased pay decisions given by managers during a pay review. Write a rebuttal immediately if you receive an evaluation which is factually incorrect or subjectively unfair. Present it to a higher ranking officer, manager or human resources officer. Schedule a meeting with such individual(s) to discuss the evaluation.

5. Speak to a lawyer immediately to discuss the correct course of action to take and protect your rights if you are the victim of unequal pay caused by your gender, ethnicity or race, or are retaliated against by protesting such illegal treatment.

Sexual Harassment

Another prohibited form of sex discrimination is sexual harassment. In 1986 the Supreme Court ruled that sexual harassment was actionable under Title VII of the Civil Rights Act of 1964. Many thousands of cases are filed yearly with the EEOC and state agencies. In fact, studies indicate that the vast majority of working women (more than 85 percent) believe they have been sexually harassed on the job at one time or another.

The newspapers are full of large verdicts that women are receiving in this area. In one case a former airline employee was awarded $7.1

million in punitive and compensatory damages for a sex-discrimination-harassment charge. In another case the EEOC obtained a $1.85 million settlement in a sexual harassment case on behalf of a group of ten women who had worked for a company as secretaries or executive assistants. The women complained that the company's chairman sought sexual favors in exchange for job benefits and had engaged in a pattern and practice of harassment against them by forcing them to discuss sex acts, touching them in their private parts, and other harmful acts. The money is to be divided among the women based primarily on their seniority. Additionally, as part of the settlement, the employer must provide individualized counseling and training for all its employees nationwide, hire an outside consultant and several new employees to respond to sexual harassment complaints, and institute a toll-free number for reporting sexual harassment.

Sexual harassment cases are on the rise in a variety of nontraditional areas. For example, sexual harassment was found in one case when female employees were required to wear revealing uniforms and suffer derogatory comments from passersby. In another case a jury awarded $196,500 in damages to a man who claimed his supervisor demoted him because he refused her sexual advances. According to court testimony, the employee and his supervisor met one night in a hotel room, but the man refused to continue the relationship. The man proved he was demoted and passed over for a promotion as a result. In another case the termination of a male employee for rejecting the advances of his homosexual male supervisor proved costly to a company.

The Supreme Court has also ruled that same-sex sexual harassment is actionable. This means that anyone who is sexually harassed by supervisors or employees of the same sex may proceed with sexual harassment cases in federal and state courts.

Imaginative lawyers representing claimants in sexual harassment suits are also asserting other nontraditional causes of action in federal and state courts. These include wrongful discharge, fraud, intentional infliction of emotional distress for outrageous conduct, invasion of privacy, and assault and civil battery. Additionally, the Supreme Court in *Harris v. Forklift Systems, Inc.,* in 1993 made it easier for plaintiffs asserting such actions by ruling that they were not required to prove that any abusive conduct actually caused an injury or affected the person's psychological well-being. Lawyers representing claimants now only have to show that a "reasonable person" would have found the conduct to be offensive.

Unwelcome sexual advances, requests for sexual favors, and verbal or physical conduct of a sexual nature all constitute sexual harassment when:

- The person must submit to such activity in order to be hired;

- The person's consent or refusal is used in making an employment decision (e.g., to offer a raise or promotion); or

- Such conduct unreasonably interferes with the person's work performance or creates an intimidating, hostile, or offensive working environment (e.g., humiliating comments are repeatedly addressed to the complainant).

Defining what constitutes sexual harassment depends on the facts of each particular case. In quid pro quo cases (instances when employees of either gender are propositioned for sexual favors in order to receive a job, raise, or promotion), the issue may be clear-cut. If a person is passed over for a promotion or denied benefits in favor of an individual who submitted to sexual advances, the passed-over person is considered to be a victim of sexual harassment under federal and state guidelines.

Additionally, if a worker initially participates in social or sexual contact, but then rejects continued advances, that constitutes sexual harassment in most instances. The fact that the person does not regularly communicate her negative reaction may not exculpate the company from liability.

In hostile, intimidating, and unprofessional work environment cases, the issues are not always clear-cut. Typically, to establish a prima facie case, the employee must prove that:

1. The employer subjected the employee to unwelcome sexual conduct;

2. The unwelcome sexual conduct was based on the employee's gender;

3. The unwelcome sexual conduct was sufficiently pervasive or severe to alter the terms and conditions of the employee's employment and create an abusive or hostile working environment; and

4. The employer knew or should have known of the harassment and failed to take prompt and reasonable remedial action

Courts have ruled the following to constitute sexual harassment with respect to hostile, intimidating work environment cases:

- Extremely vulgar and sexually related epithets, jokes, or crusty language, provided the language is not isolated and is continuously stated to the complainant

- Sexually suggestive comments about an employee's attire or body

- Sexually degrading words describing an employee

- Repeated touching of the employee's body, provided the touching is unsolicited and unwelcome

- Showing lewd photographs or objects of a sexual nature to employees at the workplace

- Offensive or repeated requests for dates, even if the calls are made to the complainant after work

- Continued advances of a sexual nature that the employee rejects, even after the parties break off a consensual sexual relationship

- Requiring females to wear revealing uniforms and suffer derogatory comments from nonemployees

How the company investigates and acts on complaints may be a major factor in determining whether it will end up in court and incur substantial damages. In 1998 the Supreme Court clarified the law on sexual harassment in the workplace, making some lawsuits against employers easier to win while also possibly limiting the legal exposure of companies that have effective anti-harassment policies in place (provided the effect of any harassment was not recognizable or severe). In a series of cases decided together, the Court first ruled that employers are strictly liable for the acts of their supervisors and managers when the harassment results in tangible harmful action, such as discharge, demotion, transfer, or other retaliation of the complainant. This is so regardless of whether the employer knew or should have known that harassment was taking place. Thus, when you can prove that serious harassment from a supervisor took place and resulted in damages (such as a lost job opportunity), the employer will probably lose the case.

However, when there has been no detrimental action taken (for example, an employee, although propositioned repeatedly by a supervisor, refuses his advances and gets promoted anyway), an employee is allowed to proceed with a lawsuit and recover modest damages, but the employer may defend itself by proving it has taken reasonable care to prevent and promptly correct any sexually harassing behavior (such as by adopting an effective policy with a complaint procedure) and proving that the employee failed to unreasonably take advantage of such corrective mechanisms by remaining silent instead of coming forward to complain.

As a result of these cases, courts will now carefully look to see if a comprehensive policy against sexual harassment was in place at the time the incidents occurred and whether the employer acted properly and promptly when notified of the complaint. When policies are vague or the complaint is not immediately and adequately investigated, or if the complainant is punished in any way for coming forward, the company may be found liable if the facts are true. For example, in one case, after a company investigated a sexual harassment charge and found that it had merit, the employer did nothing further but warn the supervisor only once. When the supervisor continued his unlawful conduct (by showing lewd pictures to the complainant), the female worker quit her job and filed a complaint with the EEOC. She was awarded $48,000 when the court ruled that the company had failed to act on its investigation.

Current law on sexual harassment in the workplace makes some lawsuits against employers easier to win while also possibly limiting the legal exposure of companies that have effective anti-harassment policies in place (provided the effect of any harassment was not recognizable or severe). Experts suggest that the practical effect of these rulings will be for employers to take a more active role in eliminating workplace harassment, such as by training workers in identifying and preventing lewd behavior.

Many employers have begun disseminating periodic reminders in policy manuals, journals, and letters distributed to employees that the company does not tolerate sexual harassment of any kind on the job, that anyone who experiences or observes such treatment should report this to management or their immediate supervisor (but not to the one doing the harassing) immediately, and that all communications will be held in strict confidence with no direct or indirect reprisals to the informant or complainant. In addition, companies are taking steps to instruct supervisors about sexual harassment and other forms of discrimination, what the adverse effects on the company could be, and ways to handle problems if they arise.

Courts consider the nature and frequency of the acts, the conditions under which the conduct occurred, whether the company was promptly notified by the complainant, and what steps, if any, the company took after being notified. To prove a case of sex harassment, it is crucial to take prompt steps to document your claim. For example, if you are being teased on the job, it is wise to complain to a supervisor or manager in writing immediately after the incident occurred. Judges, arbitrators, and EEOC hearing officers are more willing to award damages for sex harassment when a formal complaint was made requesting that the offensive conduct stop and the request was ignored.

In one case, a woman was the only female traffic controller stationed at an air traffic center. While working there she was subjected to substantial sexual slurs, insults, and innuendo by other employees, including supervisory personnel. When the woman alerted her supervisors of this in a letter, several suggested that her problem might be solved if she "submitted to one of the controllers."

The court held that the woman proved that sexually harassing actions took place, that such acts were offensive and severe, and that the employer did little to stop them after receiving a warning through her letter. She was awarded substantial damages as a result. Thus, by sending a letter similar to the one on page 218, you may be able to prove a repetitive pattern of conduct and demonstrate that the offensive acts were not condoned.

STRATEGY: *By sending a letter you notify the company of the allegations. When an employer does not properly investigate a claim, it can further compound the problem and be legally exposed. Most important, you have proof that a formal complaint was made. If the company then takes any negative action against you in retaliation, you may be able to prove the retaliation occurred after and because the letter was sent.*

Send a copy of this letter to the president or other high officer of the company. Always keep a copy for your files. Save the receipt to prove delivery. If you feel you are the victim of harassment, discuss the incident with the other employees you trust to discover if they have suffered similar abuse. By doing so, you may strengthen a claim and be less at risk for making a complaint, since there is always safety in numbers. For example, it was recently reported that a sexual harassment and discrimination lawsuit against a well-known investment firm was amended to include 20 more women in a total of 11 states. The newest plaintiffs joined the action (which was started by one woman only) and alleged being subjected to lewd language, unwelcome touching, and being denied opportunities and privileges afforded men. The suit seeks class-action status on behalf of all women employed by the firm, in part for the company's alleged explicit descriptions and sexual talk in the basement of one of its offices.

If possible, collect and save evidence (e.g., the pornographic pictures shown to you). Maintain a diary of all incidents of harassment recalling the location, events, time, persons involved, and name of any witnesses who may have observed the illegal conduct. Recall whether supervisors participated in creating or tolerating a sexually poisoned atmosphere.

Speak to an experienced employment attorney immediately if:

- The matter is not resolved satisfactorily

- You are retaliated against for making a complaint, such as being demoted, reassigned, denied benefits or a promotion, receive an unfavorable job evaluation, or are fired

- You feel uncomfortable while being questioned about the events (i.e., the company is not conducting a fair and unbiased investigation and is accusing you of contributing to or causing the harassment by your dress, behavior, or language)

- The employer fails to take speedy action to investigate your complaints

- You wish to pursue money damages for stress, mental suffering, and physical injuries caused or induced by the harassment

- The company mistakenly determines that no harassment occurred, that the acts do not constitute harassment, that it had no knowledge of the incident and thus is not responsible, or fails to make a decision in an objective manner

- The employer disparages your character, job performance, or family life

- The employer refuses to allow you to grieve the incident through its complaint procedures

An experienced employment attorney can tell you whether it makes sense to confront the harasser, use a company complaint procedure, immediately file a claim in court or with an appropriate federal agency (such as the EEOC) or a state agency, or, if more desirable and/or advantageous, to contact the employer and try to settle the matter out of court in negotiations.

Sample Letter Protesting Sexual Harassment

Your Name
Address
Telephone Number
Date

Name of Supervisor or Officer
Title
Name of Employer
Address

Dear (Name)

While working for the company, I have been the victim of a series of offensive acts that I believe constitute sexual harassment.

On (date), I (describe what occurred and with whom). I immediately (describe your reaction) and ordered that such conduct stop. However, on (date), another incident occurred when (describe what occurred and with whom).

I find such behavior intimidating and repugnant. In fact, (describe the physical and emotional impact on you), causing me to be less efficient on the job. Please treat this letter as a formal protest of such conduct. Unless such conduct ceases immediately, or in the event the company illegally retaliates against me for writing this letter, I will contact the Equal Employment Opportunity Commission to enforce my rights.

I do not wish to take such a drastic measure. All I want to do is perform my job in a professional environment.

Thank you for your cooperation in this matter.

Very truly yours,
Your Name

Confidential

Sent certified mail, return receipt requested.

Most states have laws that expressly prohibit sexual harassment; there are occasions when it may be advantageous to apply state law and file charges with a state agency instead of the EEOC. Talk to your lawyer about this. Consider filing a private tort lawsuit for assault, battery, or infliction of emotional distress if you are touched, kissed, or rubbed without your consent. The advantage of being able to file a lawsuit is that you may receive greater damages for your injuries and may be able to file a charge more than 300 days after the acts occurred. Claimants who are not able to file a discrimination charge because the statute of limitations has expired may still be able to commence a private lawsuit in some cases under state or local anti-discrimination laws or codes. (However, a discrimination claim under Title VII cannot be maintained unless you filed a charge of discrimination with the EEOC within 180 days of the incident and the EEOC has issued you a "right to sue" letter.)

In any event, do not be afraid to assert your rights when subjected to conduct you find uncomfortable. Implement some course of strategy immediately so that you don't suffer more abuse and to protect your rights in this area. Consider filing a police action if the touching was severe. If you delay contacting an appropriate agency or a lawyer, your inactivity may be viewed as a waiver of your rights or an acceptance of such illegal acts, which can jeopardize a claim.

Discrimination Against Gays and Lesbians

Some states and municipalities have passed laws that forbid employers from discriminating on the basis of an individual's sexual preference, although such discrimination is not prohibited by federal law. A gay or lesbian faced with hostile conduct, denied employment opportunities, or fired primarily because of sexual orientation should seek legal advice about relevant state and local ordinances and rulings. Lawyers representing gays and lesbians who practice in states where such discrimination is prohibited are suing employers and supervisors for invasion of privacy and other causes of action.

Work-Related Stress

Even when harassment is not sexual in nature, it can give rise to a valid legal claim when it results in documented physical and mental injuries, especially when you are forced to resign. Some female claimants have also successfully asserted that such conduct is a form of sex discrimination when the acts complained of were directed to them because of their gender.

It is often easier to win sex-related harassment cases because the law specifically authorizes claimants to collect damages for illegal acts and proof of physical or mental injuries is not necessary. For nonsexual harassing acts, you must prove the acts were so severe that they caused you harm (e.g., forced you to quit). This is often difficult to do. The author has been consulted by female clients who request legal assistance as a result of nonsexual harassment (such as verbal abuse from a supervisor). Most of the time the author declines representation because the law does not ordinarily provide protection. In most situations, perhaps the best strategy is to discuss the problem with someone from personnel and request that the harassment stop. Most supervisors are cognizant of the potential causes of action arising from physical and mental distress claims and are instructed to avoid contributing to these problems where possible. You can also write the company a letter protesting such activity. If you do, however, you may be fired for making a complaint and the law may not protect you in this area.

Confer with a lawyer to explore your options if you are the victim of extensive nonsexual harassment. The lawyer may advise you to consult a physician, take prescribed medication, or institute other steps without delay to prove the extent of your injuries and enforce a claim. For example, a workers' compensation claim was awarded to a female employee whose mental troubles arose because she was repeatedly singled out for public criticism and who proved that coworkers were not subjected to this treatment. The employee eventually developed a fear of going to work, which led to a disabling "panic disorder."

Hazardous Jobs

The Supreme Court has ruled that employers cannot ban women from certain hazardous jobs, even if the motive is preventing birth defects in fetuses those female workers may be carrying. In an important ruling, the Supreme Court decided that a manufacturer acted illegally by prohibiting women capable of bearing children from holding jobs involving exposure to lead during the manufacture of batteries. The Court determined that such a policy forces some women to choose between having a child and keeping a job, and this violated federal laws against sex discrimination. And sex discrimination against working mothers is prohibited by Title VII even if the employer does not discriminate against women with children.

The same holds true for employers who don't allow a mother or pregnant worker to accept a new position due to a concern that the reassignment will be too stressful or exhausting. Enforcement Guidelines promulgated by the EEOC forbid employers from making assumptions about the ability or commitment of women or pregnant workers to perform certain tasks. Thus, it is illegal to place a pregnant worker on an unpaid leave of absence status due to a belief the worker would be unable to fulfill the requirements of the job or be continuously absent due to physical sickness or emotional stress.

Discrimination in Benefits

Sex discrimination laws also apply to benefits. Retirement, pension plans, and fringe benefits must be equally applied, since any program that favors one sex over another violates federal and state discrimination laws. Be aware that the following practices have been declared illegal in the application of fringe benefits pertaining to vacation, insurance coverage, pensions, profit-sharing plans, bonuses, holidays, and disability leaves:

■ Limiting the benefits available to employees and their spouses and families to those employees who have a particular status in the family (e.g., "head of household" or "principal wage earner")

■ Making certain benefits available to wives of male employees but denying them to husbands of female employees

■ Basing provisions of a pension plan on norms applied differently according to gender

■ Denying a job or benefit to pregnant employees or applicants

These are just some of the ways employers commit violations relating to benefits. If you have doubts about any current practices, seek competent legal advice.

Hiring Interviews

Many employers ask illegal questions of females at job interviews, particularly with respect to their marital status. EEOC guidelines and most state regulations declare that the only lawful question that may be asked of a female applicant at an interview or on a job application form is "What is your marital status?" It is a good idea to familiarize yourself with the kinds of questions that are illegal at job interviews. If you refuse to answer such questions and are denied a job, you may want to consider filing charges with the EEOC or an appropriate state human rights organization or agency alleging sex discrimination on the basis of such illegal inquiries.

Finally, recognize that female independent contractors (such as insurance agents) cannot sue for sex discrimination under the laws of many states. This means that if you were fired because of your sex but were an independent contractor, you may not prevail regardless of the facts of your case.

Pregnancy Discrimination

In 1978, Congress enacted the Pregnancy Discrimination Act (PDA) as an amendment to Title VII. Specifically, the PDA provides that pregnancy-based discrimination falls within the confines of Title VII's prohibition of gender-based discrimination. The PDA prohibits discrimination by employers based on pregnancy, childbirth, or related medical conditions.

Thousands of pregnancy-related discrimination lawsuits are filed each year; the kind of mistreatment varies. Experts suggest that staff cuts and management overhauls have given companies opportunities to save money by unloading workers whose personal circumstances, they think, may require special attention. Some pregnant workers who return to work do not suffer outright terminations, but come back to positions with fewer responsibilities and get pushed off the fast track.

In one case, a female lawyer sued her former employer. She claimed that the law firm refused to give her work after she returned from maternity leave. Shortly after her return to work, she was told that she was required to leave the Tokyo office where she was stationed. She refused and was eventually fired.

Her employer argued that the decision was purely one of economics, since it could not afford to keep the Tokyo office open. Jury members, however, appeared skeptical of that line of defense and seemed incensed by the law firm's lack of effort in finding another office to which she could transfer. The jury also heard testimony from fellow employees who overheard a managing partner say that women who have children do not return to work with the same commitment to their jobs. The case was settled out of court just before the jury gave its verdict.

Childbirth leave and pregnancy-related disability are protected by numerous federal and state laws. Employers cannot treat pregnancy-related disability or maternity leave differently from the way they treat other forms of disability or leaves of absence. The law requires employers to review their health, disability, insurance, sick leave, benefit, job reinstatement, and seniority policies to ensure that they treat pregnancy-related disability and maternity leaves of absence the same as other temporary absences for physical disabilities.

The following general rules illustrate what employers may and may not do in this area:

- Employees who are on maternity leave (defined as the childcare period commencing after disability from the pregnancy and birth has ended) are entitled to accrue seniority, automatic pay increases, and vacation time on the same basis as other employees on medical leave.

- Employers may not require pregnant workers to exhaust vacation benefits unless all temporarily disabled workers are required to do the same.

- Employers may require a physical examination and doctor's certification of ability to return to work only if such is required of all temporarily disabled workers.

- Although employers may require workers to give notice of a pregnancy, such requirement must serve a legitimate business purpose and must not be used to restrict the employee's job opportunities.

- Employers are prohibited from discriminating in hiring, promotion, and firing decisions on the basis of pregnancy or because of an abortion.

- After a birth, an employer cannot prohibit a woman from returning to work sooner than company policy dictates.

- Employers are barred from forcing pregnant workers to take mandatory maternity leaves (i.e., forcing a woman to leave work against her wishes in anticipation of giving birth) as long as the employee is able to do her job.

- The decision as to whether payment for pregnancy disability leave will be given must be in accord with policies governing other forms of disability leave; if paid leave is provided for workers with other disabilities, the employer must provide pregnant workers with paid leave for their actual disability due to pregnancy and related childbirth.

■ Time restrictions based on pregnancy-related leaves (e.g., that pregnancy leaves not exceed four months) must be reasonable and job-related; if not, they may be illegal. In addition, employers are generally required to provide disability benefits for as long as a pregnant woman is unable to work for medical reasons.

■ It is illegal to place pregnant workers on involuntary sick leave if the company has no policy of placing workers with other forms of disabilities on involuntary leave; if a worker is physically able to work, the company cannot force her to leave merely because she is pregnant.

■ An employer cannot refuse to hire a pregnant worker because it does not want to find a replacement when the employee takes a leave to give birth if her skills and qualifications meet or exceed those of other applicants.

■ Women who take maternity leave must be reinstated under the same conditions as employees who return from leaves for other disabilities. For example, if an employer reinstates a worker who was absent from work due to a case of chronic bronchitis, the employer must reinstate a worker after childbirth to avoid violating Title VII.

■ If an employer accommodates partially disabled workers who cannot perform certain job assignments (such as lifting heavy objects because of a strained back), the employer is obligated to make similar arrangements for a pregnant worker.

■ Employers cannot limit pregnancy disability benefits to married employees. Federal law states it is illegal to fire female workers who get married if the employer does not fire male workers who get married. Many state laws have gone even further to protect women; statutes have been enacted that prohibit employers from making any adverse decisions on the basis of a person's marital status even if the employer applies its policies equally to males and females.

- At the hiring interview, you cannot be asked questions about childbearing plans or pregnancy.
- Employers are not allowed to ask a pregnant employee to choose between a lower-level job and resignation.

The above rules may or may not apply, depending on the law and the particular facts and circumstances of your case. Know your rights regarding pregnancy and when you want to return to work after giving birth. Time and time again, women are fired after returning from maternity leave. Typically, firms will cite a poor attitude, tough economic times, or declining work quality to support their decision. You should point to excellent work reviews and argue that the employer has invented or magnified the criticisms (and possibly prepared phony documentation for your personnel file) from the moment you announced your pregnancy. Always consult an experienced employment attorney for advice and guidance.

Speak to a competent lawyer if you feel you have been discriminated against on the basis of pregnancy. Women who are fired while pregnant should naturally suspect that pregnancy was the reason for the discharge. Consider filing a claim alleging pregnancy discrimination with the EEOC or appropriate antidiscrimination agency. The filing is free, and you do not need a lawyer to assist you in the process. Information on how to file a discrimination charge is given later in this chapter.

Employers are often advised that even when a decision to fire has nothing to do with a woman's pregnancy, it may be wise to continue her employment until she voluntarily leaves to give birth, rather than fire her several months before the birth, to avoid the added costs and burdens of contesting a charge of pregnancy discrimination. Employers are also advised by their attorneys that if they must fire a pregnant worker, they should be sure that her file supports the decision (i.e., that unfavorable job performance appraisals and repeated written warnings are present in the file and the worker was repeatedly warned about her performance before the company was notified of her pregnancy).

In one reported case, six workers who said they were laid off after asking for lighter duties because of pregnancy sued their employer in federal district court. One of the plaintiffs, a train operator, asked for light-duty assignment when she announced her pregnancy. According to the court papers, she was then placed on involuntary unpaid leave despite the fact that she was ready, willing, and able to continue working and that appropriate work was available. The suit also charged that the women who were laid off were unable to collect unemployment insurance because the employer advised the unemployment insurance department that they had gone on voluntary leaves. The employer argued that no employee is allowed to remain on light duty longer than 14 days, whether pregnant or disabled by any other condition.

Although pregnant workers have been subject to poor treatment from employers in the past, the laws are now attempting to put pregnant women on equal footing with other employees. While it is estimated that approximately 84 percent of women expecting children work into the final month of pregnancy and that approximately one-third return to work within eight weeks and half return within three months after giving birth, millions of women have lost their jobs after giving birth. Fortunately, as a result of the passage of the FMLA, pregnant women who work for employers with more than 50 full-time employees are guaranteed equivalent jobs when they return.

Winning a pregnancy discrimination case after a firing is often difficult, and women lose their claims because they fail to prove their case or fail to ask for accommodations beyond the minimum provided by law. During an economic downturn, employers often attempt to mask pregnancy discrimination as layoffs and downsizing, which often makes it harder to prove the underlying discriminatory motive.

The following two cases illustrate the problems often associated with winning pregnancy discrimination lawsuits.

A woman 19 weeks pregnant asked for reassignment to a job that did not require heavy lifting. She was given a job at the service desk, which required evening and weekend work. She was unable to work those hours because of family conflicts and declined the assignment.

The company fired her and she sued for pregnancy discrimination. She lost her case because she failed to prove a disparate impact (i.e., that other employees who were reassigned for medical reasons and objected were not terminated). The judge commented that the law does not guarantee that pregnant workers not suffer any adverse employment decisions. He wrote that "the law protects against decisions which, for discriminatory reasons, are different from decisions relating to persons who are not pregnant."

In another case, a female salesperson suffered severe morning sickness during her first trimester and was often late in reporting to work. The woman was placed on part-time status but continued to report to work late. After several warnings and being placed on probation, the company fired her. Although she was fired one day before taking maternity leave, the court ruled that the fact did not warrant a finding of liability because the company was free to fire anyone who could not work due to a medical condition, whether pregnant or otherwise.

STRATEGY: *The salesperson's case might have been strengthened if she had found other nonpregnant workers who had not been fired due to excessive absences or right before taking a leave of absence. And although the company was guilty of poor timing, the woman failed to introduce significant evidence at trial, including damaging statements made to her indicating that the reason given for the firing (i.e., excessive lateness) was really pretextual (i.e., unfounded) and offered just as an excuse to terminate because she was pregnant. Given the absence of important comparisons and other evidence, she lost her case. This is the kind of evidence you may be required to prove with your lawyer for success in any pregnancy discrimination case.*

It is strongly recommended that you tell your supervisor and other bosses immediately after you learn you are pregnant. Some litigants lose their cases because they cannot prove that the company knew they were pregnant before taking adverse action. Once you become pregnant you enter a protected class under the law, and the company may have to reevaluate any decision to fire you if that was being considered before the news. Thus, recognize that in marginal performance cases, becoming pregnant could give a woman added job security. Do not be afraid to tell key people at the job site that you are pregnant because this may work to your legal benefit and strengthen a claim.

Additional Strategies to Strengthen a Claim

1. Understand your options to take paid short-term and long-term disability leaves and unpaid leaves.

2. Be aware of how the company treated pregnant workers in the past for comparison purposes.

3. Remember that the payment of costs for pregnancy-related conditions may be limited to a specific dollar amount stipulated in an insurance policy, collective bargaining agreement, or other statement of employee benefits, provided limits are imposed for other health conditions.

4. Always read and understand your employer's health insurance policies and coverage before incurring medical treatment.

5. If you are offered a choice between enrolling in one of two health insurance plans, be sure to choose the one that covers pregnancy-related conditions so that you will be reimbursed on the same basis as for other medical conditions.

6. Employers are not generally responsible for providing health insurance covering abortions. However, they are required to offer sick leave and other fringe benefits as a result of abortion. Additionally, while some health plans do not pay for abortions, they do cover complications resulting from the procedure, such as treatment due to excessive bleeding. Always read the fine print of your policy to determine your options.

Pregnancy as a Disability

The ability of pregnant workers to succeed in demanding special accommodations has been strengthened by the passage of state and local laws. Although the ADA does not consider pregnancy a covered disability (since it is classified as a temporary non-chronic impairment with no long-term impact), some state laws have ruled it is a per se disability requiring a company to make reasonable accommodation when requested by an employee. Under these state laws, the physical demands of pregnancy may require companies to allow pregnant workers to work at home or rearrange their work schedules. When a woman seeks reasonable accommodation during pregnancy, an employer should be responsive to the particular physical limitations that the employee brings forward on a case-by-case basis. Employers unwilling to comply with such a request are required to justify their decisions by demonstrating that compliance would create an undue hardship.

STRATEGY: *Check your state's law on this issue to understand the extent of protection available to you. If you find the law is favorable, consider requesting reasonable accommodation (such as reporting to work an hour later each day or being allowed to work from bed if you risk losing your baby without extensive bed rest). Speak to a lawyer for more details.*

Breastfeeding

A number of states have laws allowing workers to breastfeed and/or express breast milk while on-the-job. This is an important development since most employers frown on the practice and there is no federal legislation to protect the rights of women in this area. Employees who claim breastfeeding discrimination by their employers have been unsuccessful under existing federal law, such as Title VII and the Pregnancy Discrimination Act (PDA). Research the law in your state to determine if you are substantially protected or consult an experienced employment attorney to determine your rights where applicable.

Pregnancy Leave, Other Unpaid Leave and Reemployment

Passage of the FMLA guarantees that pregnant workers who work for companies with 50 or more employees will get their jobs back after birth. The act affects private and nonprofit employers as well as federal, state and local government employers. It applies to companies that employed 50 or more employees within a 75 mile radius for each working day for each of 20 or more calendar workweeks in the current or preceding calendar year. This is about half the nation's workforce. Part-time employees and employees on leaves of absence are counted in this calculation provided they are on the employer's payroll for each day of the workweek. Employees who began employment after the beginning of a workweek, were terminated prior to the end of a workweek, or who worked part-time on weekends are not included in the equation.

Since companies with fewer than 50 employees are exempt, analyzing the number of employees who must be counted becomes an important consideration for organizations close to the "magic" 50 number. If a company hires temporary contract employees or part-time workers who work 25 or fewer hours a week to get under the number, they will not be subject to the law's provisions. However, be sure to research for the existence of comparable state and local laws, which may apply to companies with fewer than fifty employees.

Speak to a knowledgeable lawyer if you return from pregnancy leave or unpaid child care leave to a different position. This is advised because receiving a job of equal pay and grade may still violate the law if it is a different job. The following hypothetical scenario may be instructive in this area:

> Joan works for a large company as a supervisor. She takes unpaid leave to care for her sick husband. When she returns ten weeks later, she is given a new job at the same rate of pay. But the new job has fewer duties (she supervises only two people instead of five), and she is required to perform

clerical functions not present in her prior position. Joan advises management that she is dissatisfied with her new position and that the company has violated the FMLA by not giving her old job or an equivalent one back. The company states that it reorganized her department while she was on leave.

Joan consults a lawyer for advice. Rather than sue her employer, she is told to first try to negotiate better benefits. Joan listens to the lawyer. She receives another week of paid vacation, an office with a window, a prime parking spot, and her employer's promise not to terminate her for at least two years. She is also promised her old job back if it becomes available. Joan is pleased with the negotiation efforts.

Speak to a lawyer immediately or contact your nearest Equal Employment Opportunity Commission district office or state commission on human rights office if you believe you were fired, demoted, or denied benefits on the basis of pregnancy. An experienced employment attorney or agency representative can help you weigh your options to achieve the quickest and most satisfactory results.

Do not be pressured or intimidated into accepting a decision that appears to be unfair. To avoid misunderstandings, request a full explanation of your benefits and options with a duly authorized representative of the company. Go in with a ballpark proposal and be prepared to negotiate certain benefits, because many items are negotiable (no matter what you are told). Then if you are unsatisfied, weigh all your options carefully and be apprised of the law in this area to protect your rights. Remember, all actions taken by the employer must be justified under the law. The burden of proving that decisions are appropriate and necessary falls on the employer, since any practice that excludes employment or denies benefits on the basis of pregnancy is closely scrutinized. In addition, if there is an investigation into such charges, a company faces the risk of having the Equal Employment Opportunity Commission and other agency investigators evaluate treatment accorded other employees returning after non-maternity leaves of absence.

Thus, never be afraid to assert your rights. You may discover that the employer will have no choice but to respond favorably to your demands to avoid potential problems and investigations.

Age Discrimination

Federal and state discrimination laws are designed to promote employment of older persons based on their abilities, irrespective of age. The most important federal law, the Age Discrimination in Employment Act (ADEA), protects workers between the ages of 40 and 70 from being arbitrarily fired, refused a job, forced to retire, or treated unfairly with respect to pay, promotions, benefits, health care coverage, retirement plans, and other employment opportunities because of age.

The ADEA governs all private employers with 15 or more workers. It also protects employees of labor organizations, unions, and local, state, and federal government. Many states have enacted even tougher laws protecting workers by reducing the number of employees an employer must have to be subject to the law or reducing the cut-off age for inclusion into a protected class (i.e., age 30 in a few states).

The following thumbnail sketch outlines what employers can generally do under the ADEA and state discrimination laws pertaining to age:

- Fire older workers for documented, inadequate job performance or good cause (e.g., excessive tardiness or absences)

- Entice older workers into early retirement by offering additional benefits, such as bigger pensions, extended health insurance, or substantial severance packages that are voluntarily accepted

- Force employees to retire if the worker is 65 or older, has worked as an executive for the past two years, and is entitled to a pension exceeding $44,000, or if the job calls for physical fitness (e.g., airline pilots or police officers) and age is recognized as a bona fide occupational qualification (BFOQ) factor in fitness and job performance. (An employer that sets age limits on a particular job must be able to prove the limit is necessary because a worker's ability to adequately perform that job substantially diminishes after the age limit is reached)

- Lay off older workers when younger employees are similarly treated
- Make adverse decisions provided the acts are taken as a result of a demonstrated good-faith business decision that does not have a discriminatory impact on all older workers at the company

Some employers may legally discriminate against older workers when they hire independent contractors (which the law doesn't generally protect) or employ fewer than 15 workers and there is no state antidiscrimination law to protect the rights of older workers. However, a number of cases decided throughout the United States suggest that a company may be held liable for discrimination by third parties, including independent contractors, authorized by the employer to make decisions on its behalf. In one case, a pro se litigant filed a lawsuit after he was told by an agent hired by the employer he was "too old" for the job. The court ruled that ADEA prohibits employers and intermediaries from hiring any individual on the basis of age, allowing the case to proceed to trial.

Always check the law of your state to see what protection is available if you work for a small employer or are an independent contractor. Additionally, since some state agencies process discrimination cases more quickly than the EEOC and provide greater damages and remedies under applicable state law, consider pursuing your rights with a state agency or in state court (instead of the overburdened federal EEOC) after discussing your options with an employment attorney.

The following actions are generally prohibited by federal and state law:

- Denying an older applicant a job on the basis of age
- Imposing compulsory retirement before age 70
- Forcing older employees into retirement by threatening them with termination or loss of benefits, unless the company has instituted a valid seniority system or retirement plan
- Firing older workers because of age
- Denying promotions, transfers, or assignments because of age
- Penalizing older employees with reduced privileges, employment opportunities, or compensation because of age

You may recover significant damages if you receive unfair treatment because of age. These may include job reinstatement in the event of a firing, wage adjustments, back pay and double back pay, future pay, promotions, recovery of legal fees, witness fees, and filing costs, compensatory damages up to $300,000 depending on the size of the employer, and punitive damages. Recourse can also include the institution of an affirmative action program on behalf of fellow employees, counseling, and enhanced outplacement assistance.

The U.S. Supreme Court made it a little easier for older workers by ruling that when a fired over-40 employee files an age discrimination suit, courts cannot insist that his or her replacement must be under 40 to be actionable. The Supreme Court stated that the fact that the replacement is "substantially younger" is a far more reliable indicator of age discrimination than whether the replacement is older or younger than forty. Thus, for example, an age-discrimination case will be allowed to proceed if a 58-year-old employee's job is replaced by someone 42 years of age.

STRATEGY: *Whenever an older employee (over 40) is fired and consults me, the basic issue I must decide is whether the company's decision was made because of age or was the result of a reasonable nondiscriminatory business decision.*

Because direct evidence is often difficult to obtain, the client must typically use circumstantial evidence to prove that an employer's motive was improper. This is sometimes done by demonstrating that the client was between 40 and 70 years of age, was doing satisfactory work, was fired, and the position was then filled by a substantially younger employee. In the case of a female employee, if a younger male employee replaces her, she may also have a claim for sex discrimination. However, when employers support firing decisions with documentation of poor work performance or other factors, an older worker's chances of proving age discrimination diminish.

It is easier to prove age discrimination when age-related statements are made to or about the claimant ("You are too old and set in your ways", "Why don't you retire?") or by using statistics (e.g., that the company fired ten older workers in the past six months and replaced them all with substantially younger employees). This is because courts have been known to uphold age bias suits brought by senior employees because they were subjected to demeaning jokes and adverse remarks about their age before being fired. In fact, many companies try to head off such suits by issuing instructions to indoctrinate employees against discriminatory chatter.

But sometimes a valid case can exist when there is no documentation supporting the employer's reason for discharging the older worker. A sudden drop in performance rating may be viewed with suspicion by juries, particularly when a supervisor failed to give any notice to the employee of the apparent dissatisfaction with the employee's performance. In cases where the worker recently received a raise or bonus for good work and had not been warned, reprimanded, or criticized about his or her performance before being fired, the employer's reason may be a pretext for age discrimination.

As with other forms of discrimination, to establish a prima facie case of age discrimination, a plaintiff must show that (1) he belonged to a protected class (e.g., was over 40), (2) was qualified for the position he held or sought, and (3) suffered an adverse employment action (4) under circumstances giving rise to an inference of discriminatory intent.

Thus, if you are over 40 and are replaced in a job by someone who is 29 you may satisfy the fourth prong of proving a case. Examples of materially adverse changes include termination of employment, a demotion evidenced by a decrease in wages or salary, a less distinguished title, a material loss of benefits, or significantly diminished important job responsibilities.

Once a plaintiff establishes a prima facie case in indirect or circumstantial evidence cases, there is a presumption of unlawful discrimination. The burden then shifts to the employer to offer a legitimate, nondiscriminatory rationale for its actions. If the employer is able to demonstrate such a rationale, for example through a series of negative performance reviews regularly given to the plaintiff, the presumption of discrimination drops out and the plaintiff must prove the legitimate reasons offered by the defendant were not its true reasons, but were a pretext for discrimination.

Showing that an employer treated older workers differently than younger ones is a common and often effective method of establishing a prima facie case of age discrimination. A plaintiff's burden is often not overwhelming. A plaintiff's initial burden is to show that he or she was between 40 and 70 and suffered an adverse employment action (e.g., firing or demotion) by the employer. If the plaintiff meets this initial burden, it is the employer's burden to articulate a legitimate non-discriminatory reason for its actions. Like the plaintiff's initial burden, this is generally not a difficult burden to meet. This is because it is not a court's role to second-guess an employer's personnel decisions, even if foolish, so long as they are non-discriminatory. If the employer meets its burden of articulating a legitimate, non-discriminatory reason for its actions (and employers generally have little trouble doing so), then the plaintiff must prove that the employer's stated non-discriminatory reasons are pretextual.

To show that an employer's stated reason for firing or demoting you was pretextual, you are not required to show that the employer's reasons were false or played no role in the employment decision, but that they were not the only reasons and that the prohibited factor was at least one of the motivating reasons. Your lawyer attempts to do this by demonstrating weaknesses, implausibilities, inconsistencies, or contradictions in the employer's stated reasons so a judge or jury will reasonably find such reasons to be unworthy of credence.

Proving age discrimination can be difficult, especially when management-level employees have not made age-related statements, remarks, or threats; the employee is unable to demonstrate statistical proof that the company had a practice of firing older workers and replacing them with younger ones; or there is no direct evidence.

In addition, the Supreme Court has ruled that an employer's decision to lay off mostly older workers close to receiving vested retirement benefits did not, in and of itself, constitute age discrimination. In that case, the Court found that since the employer proffered a rational business justification for firing a large number of older workers (i.e., to save the company money, since older workers with the most seniority had the highest salaries), no illegality occurred even though the older workers were more severely affected by the discharge! (The Supreme Court did say the individuals might consider filing ERISA claims to protect forfeited retirement and severance benefits as a result of the company's actions.)

PRE-EMPLOYMENT SCREENING. Employers sometimes set requirements that are too high or commit violations through illegal ads. Many make statements or ask questions during the hiring interview that are illegal. For example, discrimination against older applicants occurs when they are told by an interviewer that:

- They are "overqualified"
- They lack formal education credits even though they are highly qualified by previous work experience and a college degree is not necessary for successful job performance

- They must take a pre-employment physical that is unnecessary, not job-related, or not requested of all other applicants
- They are required to answer questions such as "How old are you?", "What is the date of your birth?", or "Why did you decide to seek employment at your age?"

With respect to pre-employment questions concerning age, be aware that under federal and state guidelines, employers can only ask the applicant if he or she is between 18 and 65, and if not, to state his or her age. Any other type of question concerning age is illegal. If you refuse to answer such a question and believe you were denied a job as a result, consider contacting the EEOC, a local human rights commission office, or your state attorney general's office to pursue your rights.

PHYSICALS. Companies sometimes require potential employees to take pre-employment physicals. This is not legal as a result of the passage of the Americans with Disabilities Act. Physicals can be given only if they are directly related to successful job performance (e.g., a firefighter's job) and are required by all employees after a job has been offered, not before. Thus, employers are allowed to offer a job that is conditioned on passing a physical exam.

ADVERTISING. Pay special attention to language in advertisements used to attract job candidates. As stated in Chapter 1, the ADEA prohibits companies from publishing advertisements indicating any preference, limitation, specification, or discrimination based on age. Thus, targeted advertisements containing language such as "Industrial management trainee, recent college degree," "Sales trainee, any recent degree," "Prefer recent college grad," or "Corporate attorney, two-to-four years out of law school" are illegal. However, help-wanted notices or advertisements that include a term or phrase such as "college graduate" or other education criterion, or specify a minimum age less than 40, such as "not under 21" are not prohibited by federal statute.

JOB REQUIREMENTS. When preparing criteria for a particular job, companies sometimes set a higher requirement than is necessary to attract higher-caliber applicants. This may discriminate between classes of applicants. If you are an older applicant and believe a potential employer has established unwarranted requirements (such as a college degree) that are not job-related, be aware that you may have a valid case of age discrimination.

Simply showing that a younger individual was hired over a qualified older applicant does not prove age discrimination if the employer can show its decision was based on an honest evaluation of the candidate's qualifications (e.g., the rejected applicant would be bored or likely to leave upon finding a better job, or both). Furthermore, an employer is under no obligation to provide a laid-off employee with a job for which that person is overqualified. And when eliminating a position, an employer does not assume an obligation to retain or create a position for the displaced employee simply because the employee is within a protected class, such as being a female or over forty.

PROGRESSIVE DISCIPLINE AND WARNINGS. The practice of progressive discipline, in which notice is given to the employee of alleged work performance dissatisfaction, is frequently used by employers to reduce the risk of discrimination and wrongful termination lawsuits. By documenting the incidence of employee disciplinary measures through precise records of conferences, warnings, probationary notices, remedial efforts, and other steps, employers sometimes demonstrate that an eventual termination was not due to a discriminatory motive but stemmed from a good-faith business decision.

Many companies, however, apply their system of discipline and warnings in a haphazard fashion and fail to use the same punishment for similar infractions. This may invite a discrimination lawsuit if there are several employees with a chronic problem (e.g., absenteeism) and the older worker is the first to be fired for that reason, while substantially younger workers or those under 40 are only given a warning.

If you are an older worker who believes that an employer is treating you more harshly than younger workers for identical infractions, or you are receiving dissimilar, unfair on-the-job treatment with respect to benefits, promotions, or other matters, speak to an employment attorney for advice.

STRATEGY: *When you receive a performance review that is unfair, incorrect, or subjective, write a rebuttal and give it to the supervisor or manager who wrote the review. Send a copy to your company's human resources officer. Keep a copy for your records and store it in a safe place. A rebuttal memo can demonstrate that you did not agree with the review and can come in handy later in the event you sue the company for age discrimination after a firing.*

FAILURE TO PROMOTE. Another form of discrimination that is regularly practiced by employers against older workers, minorities, and females is the failure to promote a person and give plum jobs and job assignments to workers in a protected class. Unfortunately, employers often use subjective criteria in their decision-making process rather than consider the employee's actual skills, past performance, achievements, or other objective criteria. However, in the absence of direct evidence (e.g., actual discriminatory statements made by a supervisor or co-worker), it is difficult to prevail in a discriminatory failure to promote case. The reason is that federal and state courts require a plaintiff to demonstrate he was vastly superior and qualified for the job such that no reasonable person could have chosen the candidate selected over you.

To survive a motion for summary judgment and not have the case dismissed, it is not enough to merely prove you should have been promoted for the position because you were over forty and better qualified than the individual chosen. Cases reveal that the disparity in qualifications has to be so apparent as to "virtually jump off the page and slap you in the face." Always be aware of this stringent legal standard when considering filing an action to protest perceived illegal action and understand that recent Supreme Court rulings pertaining to the burden of proof in age discrimination cases is generally becoming harder to establish. In certain situations it may be necessary to prove that age was the key factor in an employment decision, even though there is some evidence that age played a role. Being able to prove age was the "but-for" cause of the challenged adverse employment action as opposed to proving the lesser standard that age was a motivating or substantial role (e.g., not the only or principal reason for the complained-of employment action) is difficult. That is why experienced employment attorneys often try to utilize more liberal state law where applicable. Always discuss the applicable burden of proof standard required to win an age discrimination case under federal, state and local law with your lawyer to gain more insight in this area.

Seniority Rights and Vacation Time

Nothing in the federal laws barring age discrimination prohibits employers from altering the terms of a benefit seniority system provided the new system is not a subterfuge for engaging in arbitrary age discrimination. For example, when companies change vacation pay policies by putting a cap on the amount of annual paid vacation a person can take (this penalizes older workers when all employees regardless of seniority must take the same number of days off) or reduce medical insurance and retiree benefit plans, such acts are legal when justified by significant cost considerations. However, the burden falls on the employer to prove that its actions are lawful.

Retirement Plans and Forced Retirement

This is an area where older executives are sometimes exploited. Most pension or retirement plans require employees to be a certain age or to have worked a minimum number of years before they can begin drawing the maximum pension payment per month. Some plans permit employees to draw monthly pension payments before reaching the age specified in the plan for eligibility of full benefits. When an employee takes "early retirement," he or she generally receives less in monthly benefits. The advantage of taking early retirement is that while monthly payments are less, they are often paid sooner.

A "forced" retirement occurs when companies illegally exert pressure on older employees to opt for early retirement or face firing, demotion, a cut in pay, or poor recommendations. The law requires that employers contemplating a large layoff or seeking to reduce payroll through early retirement incentives must do so carefully to avoid charges of age discrimination.

Under the ADEA and in most states, it is illegal to impose compulsory retirement before age 70 unless the employee is a "bona fide executive" receiving an annual company-paid retirement benefit of at least $44,000 per year after reaching 65 or is in a "high policy-making position" during a two-year period prior to reaching age 65. (What constitutes an executive or high policy-making position depends on the unique facts of each case. Thus speak to an employment attorney for more details).

Many states have passed similar laws to protect older employees from being victimized by forced retirement and mandatory retirement plans. For example, New York has a law that prohibits most public employees from being forced to retire, no matter how old they get. Private sector employees (with limited exceptions for some executives and tenured college faculty members) are also protected.

It is also illegal to deny early retirement incentives to employees based on their age. For example, an early retirement program limited to workers between the ages of 57 and 62 penalizes employees older than 62. Furthermore, eligibility to receive Social Security benefits cannot be used as a factor in deciding which employees will be laid off.

If the employer can show that a retirement plan is "bona fide" (e.g., plan benefits are based on an employee's length of service), that the employee's decision to accept early retirement is voluntary, and that the reasons for the plan are nondiscriminatory (i.e., not based on age), a plan may not violate the ADEA. If an employee can no longer perform her job duties, the employer may be allowed to discharge her or, alternatively, force her to retire (depending on the circumstances).

The ADEA explicitly requires equal treatment in pension plans regardless of age. Employers may, however, set a limit on the maximum number of years of service they will credit to employees. It is also legal for employers who offer retiree health benefits to offset the value of these benefits against an employee's entitlement to severance benefits as a result of a reduction in force, a layoff, or a plant closing. Employers may also reduce life insurance benefits for older workers to keep premium costs equal.

Many executives are willing to retire by the age of 65 provided there is sufficient financial incentive. Be sure you understand how much in additional benefits you will be receiving. Speak to your accountant, lawyer, or other professional adviser and do the arithmetic before accepting any early retirement package.

Any retirement incentive program that forces older employees to leave is unlawful. The key question is whether the employee voluntarily accepted the incentive. Implied or direct threats that you will be fired or demoted after not taking the benefit can make the offer unlawful. Speak to an employment attorney immediately if you feel such pressure.

Just because you are encouraged to take a severance package does not mean your company has violated the ADEA. Employers have no reason to shy away from discussing severance options with eligible older employees. As long as the severance package is not specifically based on age (e.g., $x for people 55 to 60, $Y for people over 60), it is probably legal.

STRATEGY: *If you are fired and the company's pension or retirement plan permits early retirement, investigate whether you qualify and whether the termination can be treated instead as a voluntary early retirement. This is an important consideration to be asserted through negotiation. If you are fired several months before*

*qualifying for early benefits, try to get the company to agree to place
you on "unpaid leave status" for the remaining period of time so you
can bridge the gap and qualify.*

You may be able to achieve this benefit if you are fired just before
the vesting of a pension. If this happens to you, always argue that the
timing of the firing is suspect and that public policy requires the
employer to grant your pension. If the employer refuses, consult an
experienced employment attorney immediately.

Another important yet frequently overlooked consideration in
deciding whether to accept an early retirement package is whether the
employer will honor its promises in subsequent years and be around to
pay the benefits. Whatever decision a company makes about retirement
benefits, its plan must have the likelihood of standing up in court.

For example, 50,000 early retirees who took packages between
1974 and 1988 sued General Motors after the company amended their
lifetime health benefits plan. The claimants argued that the automaker
was required to provide free health care benefits to retirees instead of
altering the package a few years later and billing them for co-payments.

The company argued that when it made the offer of free health
benefits for life, it reserved the right to "amend, modify, suspend and
terminate" such benefits. The retirees claimed that the offer of free
lifetime medical benefits with no co-payment was a compelling factor
in why they agreed to retire prematurely in the first place. The court
agreed with the workers and ruled that a promise is a promise.

But the opposite result occurred in another important case. As far
back as 1946 a company unilaterally provided group life and health
insurance for its salaried, nonunion employees. The company's benefit
literature stated that the company would provide group insurance for
all retirees and their dependents. However, the company specifically
reserved the right to terminate the insurance "should business
conditions warrant it."

Thirty-six years later, retirees were shocked to receive a notice that all retiree health and life insurance benefits would be terminated. The president told them the company could no longer afford the coverage.

The U.S. Court of Appeals ruled that since the company at all times had clearly reserved the right to amend or kill the insurance program and that since no written promise of lifetime welfare benefits was made, the company had not breached any legal obligation to provide continuing benefits.

STRATEGY: *The consequence of this case is clear: never assume that retiree benefits you are to receive will continue undisturbed. Many times an offer to pay retiree benefits is merely a gratuitous offer that a company can legally modify or revoke. It is rare that such benefits are guaranteed (e.g., in certain ironclad union contracts). Remember this and confer with legal counsel for more advice.*

Case decisions in this area have become difficult to predict. More companies are attempting to reduce or eliminate retiree health benefits as the cost of medical prescriptions has skyrocketed. The success of a case often depends on where the lawsuit is brought as well as its facts. While the 6th Circuit Court of Appeals is more likely to rule in favor of retirees, the reverse is so in the 3rd, 4th, and 7th Circuits. Each of the federal circuit courts imposes a different standard on employers and retirees to prove a claim or interpret the contractual rights of the parties under ERISA and the Labor Management Relations Act (LMRA). Most courts state that employers with contracts that reserve the right to cut or eliminate benefits later have the legal right to do so. Until the Supreme Court finally rules on the question, there is the distinct possibility an ex-employer will successfully reduce or terminate your retiree health coverage benefits. Thus, never assume such benefits are sacred and will continue in the future undisturbed.

Finally, if you sign a release or waiver after voluntarily accepting an early retirement offer, you may have a difficult time repudiating the agreement if you later change your mind. In one case, for example, a company offered all salespeople over 55 an early retirement option that included a year's severance pay, medical benefits for life, supplemental life insurance, and retirement benefits computed as if the workers had reached 65. Although the employees accepted the package, they later charged that the plan violated the ADEA.

Despite the fact that the salespeople claimed that a supervisor threatened them to take the offer or else their jobs might be eliminated, the court ruled that "vague impressions" or threats in the absence of objective factors indicating age discrimination are insufficient to support a constructive discharge claim. The court also noted that the salespeople had signed an acknowledgment stating that the decision to accept early retirement benefits was made freely with no coercion, that they could have changed their minds shortly after signing the waiver (i.e., within seven days) but didn't, and that the benefits received as consideration for accepting the package were considerable.

Ask yourself the following questions if you believe you were fired because of age:

- Did you request a transfer to another position before you were fired? Was it refused? If so, were similar requests granted to younger workers?

- How were you terminated? Were you given false reasons for the termination? Did you consent to the action or did you protest (such as by sending a certified letter to the company refuting the discharge)?

- Were you replaced by a younger worker under 40 (or between 40 and 50 if you are between 60 and 65)? Were younger workers merely laid off and not fired (i.e., rehired several months later)?

Positive answers to these questions may prove you were fired as a result of age discrimination. Your case will be strengthened when fellow employees are also victimized. In one case, for example, 143 persons were forced to retire prematurely from an insurance company at the age of 62. The large number of older employees all the same age made it difficult for the company to claim it was a valid reduction in force (called a RIF), and the workers collectively received more than $6 million in back wages.

Before implementing a RIF, companies must take steps to ensure they have acted properly. For example, if they have a practice of permitting bumping or transfers before a discharge, not extending such opportunities to older workers during a RIF may give rise to a claim of disparate treatment. Moreover, selection of individuals for layoff based on their current cost of retention may also be unlawful where wage and benefit rates are found to be a function of length of service and, as such, an arguable product of age.

In one case, a federal court jury found a large bank guilty of age discrimination in dismissing five customer service representatives. The employer was ordered to pay more than $700,000 to the plaintiffs who were allegedly dismissed as a result of corporate restructuring. Their ages and seniorities were:

Plaintiff 1: age 45, 18 years of service
Plaintiff 2: age 43, 25 years of service
Plaintiff 3: age 59, 19 years of service
Plaintiff 4: age 62, 14 years of service
Plaintiff 5: age 42, 12 years of service

The lawyer representing the five customer service representatives said there were other positions they could have been offered (but weren't) and that shortly after the dismissals the bank advertised for replacements. Each of the five was awarded $141,000 for back pay (doubled as a result of the jury's finding of wrongful discrimination), $408,750 for lost future wages and benefits, and $25,000 for emotional distress.

The case is instructive in several respects. It demonstrates that you don't have to be in your late sixties to win an age claim when you are fired. Furthermore, a case may be strengthened when, despite having greater seniority, you and other senior workers are terminated (instead of junior employees) in an alleged downsizing, but your jobs are filled by new, inexperienced workers soon thereafter.

STRATEGY: *A reduction in workforce due to legitimate economic conditions (demonstrated by a fiscal crisis, cost cutting measures or a hiring freeze) does not generally constitute a discriminatory act. Cronyism, preferential treatment and favoritism, while unjust and unfair, are not unlawful forms of discrimination and a supervisor's decision on who to select for a RIF may go undisturbed. But a violation of ADEA may be found when age is a motivating factor in the selection of an employee targeted for layoff during the course of a RIF and the claimant proves the decision was partly based on an intentionally false internal appraisal of the complainant's work. Thus, while an employer may reduce its workforce in order to effectuate cost savings and other legitimate business considerations, such a reduction does not insulate it from claims of intentional discrimination under the ADEA and the employer bears the burden of explaining whether there was a reasonable explanation other than age for acts disproportionately affecting older workers. Smart employers terminate people from all ages when instituting a RIF to avoid claims of illegal treatment. Get advice from an experienced employment attorney when substantially all of the employees terminated at your company due to a RIF are over 40.*

STRATEGY: *It is always helpful to gather all available information to support your case. Plan ahead if you think you may be fired because of your age. This includes checking your files for documents that show you have been productive and a high performer. Such documents include positive letters of reference from customers and/or supervisors, excellent employee evaluations, and a history of salary raises, job enhancements and other cash incentives.*

Always document comments made to you, such as offhand remarks that reveal a desire to hire younger employees. For example, if you're told, "You're slowing down," write who said this to you, the date, time and location and whether or not it was stated in the presence of a witness. Gathering information showing the company unfairly favored a less qualified, younger worker will help your case.

After you have collected this information, it is a good idea to consult an experienced employment attorney who has handled many age discrimination cases and obtain an opinion as to whether your case has merit and how to proceed. The lawyer may recommend that you contact the ex-employer on your own to settle the matter or retain her to send an initial demand letter to the employer in an attempt to obtain an out-of-court settlement. The following letter illustrates the kind of letter your lawyer may preliminarily send.

The tone, language, and substance of an initial demand letter will vary depending on your lawyer's style, preference and the facts. The purpose is to get the company's attention so that the lawyer will receive a favorable response. Hopefully, a dialogue and an appropriate settlement will ensue prior to the institution of further legal proceedings.

Sample Attorney Letter on Behalf of Terminated Employee

Law Offices of Steven Mitchell Sack
110 East 59th Street, 19th Floor
New York, NY 10022
Telephone (917) 371-8000 or (212) 702-8843
Fax (516) 623-9115
E-Mail Address: stevensackatty@hotmail.com

Date

Name of Company Officer
Title
Company Address

Re: Termination of (Name of Client, "Wilma Jones")

Dear (Name):

This office has been retained by Wilma Jones concerning her dismissal from employment with your company. On (specify date), Ms. Jones, who is 63 years of age, was dismissed from employment after 12 years of exemplary service in the highly competitive and sophisticated field of publishing. She was replaced by an inexperienced, unqualified, younger woman (specify name).

No articulable reason was provided to Ms. Jones at the time of her discharge other than that the company was downsizing. (Name of supervisor) told my client she was to be terminated, and Ms. Jones was given only one hour to clean out her desk and vacate the premises. Upon further inquiry Ms. Jones learned that your company has not engaged in downsizing as stated.

My client demonstrated a wide variety of valuable skills in her work. She was never criticized or warned that her job was in jeopardy. The woman who replaced her is much younger (under forty), is not technically skilled in her field, and is inexperienced. Ms. Jones always received favorable performance evaluations during her tenure.

The manner of my client's discharge was both humiliating and distressful. Ms. Jones is confused, deeply pained, and upset at what prompted her dismissal without explanation or notice. Your offer to pay only four weeks' severance is inadequate in light of my client's long-term contributions and achievements. Furthermore, I have been advised that other executives with similar long-term service have received substantially greater severance packages.

My client's replacement by a much younger, less competent woman causes me to conclude that your company terminated Ms. Jones because of her age. Under this state's laws and federal laws, the circumstances surrounding her discharge and replacement reflect a strong indication of age discrimination. As such, I have advised my client she is entitled to be compensated for the arbitrary manner in which she was treated. As a result of the termination, Ms. Jones also suffered the loss of the medical, dental, and profit-sharing benefits she was receiving while employed and which she relied on for her future welfare. At her age it is doubtful she will obtain gainful employment soon, and she was counting on working several more years before her retirement. The discharge is even more damaging in view of the fact that Ms. Jones is a widow with little means of support.

Finally, the manner in which she was terminated caused her additional harm and distress in that she was not notified of her continuation of medical benefits under federal COBRA law.

In light of the foregoing, I request that either you or your representative contact this office immediately in an attempt to resolve these and other issues in an amicable fashion to avoid expensive and protracted litigation.

Hopefully this can be avoided, and I thank you for your immediate attention and cooperation in this matter.

Very truly yours,
Steven M. Sack

Sent Via Messenger

If you don't take prompt action, your rights may be extinguished. If the initial attempts to obtain voluntary redress from the employer fail, you should consider filing a formal charge of age discrimination. No matter what course of action you consider, do not delay unnecessarily. You must normally file a formal administrative complaint within 180 days of the time the alleged act(s) occurred to avoid the expiration of the statute of limitations. Some complainants take their time and unfortunately discover their cases are dismissed because they waited too long to file.

This is typically done at a local EEOC office and/or state antidiscrimination agency. To avoid having your case dismissed and losing your right to later sue for age discrimination under the ADEA you must file a claim with the EEOC and/or comparable state administrative agency within 180 days of a firing or notification that you were being fired. In some states, you are permitted to file an action within 300 days of the harmful act(s), so check your state's law.

If an EEOC claim is dismissed for not being timely filed, you will have lost your right to sue for age discrimination under the ADEA. Before throwing in the towel, a discrimination victim in such circumstances should check state and local laws to see if there are any state or local code provisions under which a lawsuit can be maintained in state court. Many states have filing deadlines which are just as strict as the EEOC filing deadlines. Others are not so strict. In addition, some localities (and large cities in particular) have code provisions that allow a discrimination victim to file a discrimination suit in state court without first pursuing remedies before the EEOC or comparable state administrative agencies. It is therefore critical that you know your options for pursuing redress under state and local law as well as federal law.

Information on how to present your case properly to the EEOC, what to do once you obtain a finding of probable or no probable cause at the initial administrative level, and how to proceed with a lawsuit in federal or state court are explained in greater detail at the end of this chapter and Chapter 9.

Releases and Waivers

To avoid charges that an employee was not given sufficient time to reflect and weigh the options of an early retirement offer and thus was constructively discharged, employers are now required to prepare written releases that give retirees and older workers time to consider the offer, seek advice from a lawyer, and even repudiate the decision within seven days of signing the document. Historically, Congress did not recognize the ability of employers to enforce a waiver of age discrimination claims. As a result, some lucky workers who signed releases prior to 1990 were able to cash their settlement checks and still sue an employer thereafter.

Enactment of the federal Older Workers Benefit Protection Act (OWBPA) in 1991 eliminated confusion provided its provisions are properly followed. The act makes clear that in relation to the firing or resignation of a worker over forty, a company can protect itself from potential violations of ADEA claims by utilizing waivers, provided:

1. The waiver is part of an agreement that specifically states the worker is waiving his or her ADEA right and is not merely a general release;

2. The agreement containing the waiver does not disclaim any rights or claims arising after the date of its execution;

3. The worker receives value (e.g., an extra month of severance pay) in exchange for signing the agreement;

4. The worker is advised in writing of his or her right to consult a lawyer of his or her choosing before signing the agreement;

5. The worker is advised in writing of his or her right to consider the agreement for a period of 21 days before it is effective; and

6. The worker is given at least seven days following the execution of the agreement to revoke it.

When employers request the signing of releases or waivers in connection with mass termination programs and large-scale voluntary retirement programs, the act is even stricter. All individuals in the program must be given at least 45 days to consider the agreement, and each employee must also be provided with numerous facts such as the class, unit, or group of individuals covered by the program, any eligibility factors for the program, time limits applicable to the program, the job titles and ages of all individuals selected for the program, and the ages of all individuals not eligible for the program. The cover letter and release beginning on page 255 illustrates the kind of document that is often prepared by employers to comply with the OWBPA.

A benefit of the OWBPA is that all voluntary early retirement programs are now scrutinized closely to determine that no threat, intimidation, or coercion is directed to the worker to whom the benefit is offered. Older employees must now be given sufficient time to consider the offer and receive accurate and complete information regarding benefits.

STRATEGY: *If you are an older worker being terminated after working years for an employer, always try to negotiate a better severance package. Information on how to do this successfully is included in Chapter 7. When companies agree to pay more money in severance and/or benefits, they typically prepare releases for individuals to sign. Carefully review any such document. Question all ambiguous or confusing language. Consult an experienced employment attorney for advice and guidance where necessary. Do not be afraid to do this, since the release, to be valid, must specifically allow the right to consult a lawyer of your choosing. Take advantage of this provision. The lawyer you consult may advise that the company has violated the ADEA and you are entitled to a greater settlement before signing away your rights.*

Sample Cover Letter and Release
(Specifically Waiving an Age Discrimination Claim)

To: Severed Employee
From: The Company
Re: Older Workers Benefit Protection Act

This communication apprises you of your rights under the Older Workers Benefit Protection Act (OWBPA), which amends the Age Discrimination in Employment Act (ADEA) that Congress passed. The OWBPA establishes certain standards as regards waivers that the Employer obtains from its Employees.

The OWBPA amends the ADEA by adding a new section which establishes standards for a "knowing and voluntary" waiver:

1.   The waiver has to be part of an agreement between the employee and the employer and it has to be written in understandable English;

2.   The waiver must refer specifically to rights or claims arising under the ADEA;

3.   The waiver cannot cover rights or claims that may arise after the date on which it is signed;

4.   The waiver must be exchanged for consideration, and the consideration must be in addition to anything of value to which the employee is already entitled;

5.   The employee must be advised in writing to consult with an attorney before signing the agreement;

6.   The employee has to be given a period of at least 21 days to decide whether to sign the waiver; and

7.   The employee is entitled to revoke the waiver within seven days after signing it, and the waiver does not become effective or enforceable until the revocation period has expired.

Sample General Release

FOR GOOD AND VALUABLE CONSIDERATION, the adequacy of which is hereby acknowledged, in the form of payment to Employee of a severance benefit in the amount of ($XX) _____ salary less withholding for federal and state taxes, FICA, and any other amounts required to be withheld, Employee agrees that he/she, or any person acting by, through, or under Employee, RELEASE AND FOREVER DISCHARGES (Name of Employer), and its parent company and subsidiaries, affiliates, successors, and assigns, as well as the officers, employees, representatives, agents and fiduciaries, de facto or de jure (hereinafter collectively referred to as "Released Parties"), and covenants and agrees not to institute any action or actions, causes or causes of action (in law unknown) in state or federal court, based upon or arising by reason of any damage, loss, or in any way related to Employee's employment with any of the Released Parties or the termination of said employment. The foregoing includes, but not by way of limitation, all claims which could have been raised under common law, including retaliatory discharge and breach of contract, or statute, including, without limitation, the Age Discrimination in Employment Act of 1967, 42 U.S.C. Sections 621-634, as amended by the Older Workers Benefit Protection Act of 1990, Title VII of the Civil Rights Act of 1964, 42 U.S.C. Sections 2000e et seq. and the Employee Retirement Income Security Act of 1974, 29 U.S.C. Sections 1001 et seq. or any other Federal or State Law; except that this General Release is not intended to cover any claim arising from computational or clerical errors in the calculation of the severance benefit provided to Employee, or retirement benefit to which Employee may be entitled from any plan or other benefits to which Employee may be entitled under any plan maintained by any of the Released Parties.

Employee covenants and agrees to forever refrain from instituting, pursuing, or in any way whatsoever aiding any claim, demand, action, or cause of action or other matter released and discharged herein by Employee arising out of or in any way related to Employee's employment with any of the Released Parties and the rights to recovery for any damages or compensation awarded as a result of a lawsuit brought by any third party or governmental agency on Employee's behalf.

Employee further agrees to indemnify all Released Parties from any and all loss, liability, damages, claims, suits, judgments, attorney's fees and other costs and expenses of whatsoever kind or individually Employee may sustain or incur as a result of or in connection with matters hereinabove released and discharged by Employee. Employee warrants that he/she has not filed any lawsuits, charges, complaints, petitions, or accusatory pleadings against any of the Released Parties with any governmental agency or in any court, based upon, arising out of, or related in any way to any event or events occurring prior to the signing of this General Release, including, without limitation, his/her employment with any of the Released Parties or the termination thereof.

Employee acknowledges, understands and affirms that: (a) this General Release is a binding legal document; (b) (I) Released Parties advised him/her to consult with an attorney before signing this General Release, (ii) he/she had the right to consult with an attorney about and before signing this General Release, (iii) he/she was given a period of at least 21 calendar days in which to consider this General Release prior to signing, and (iv) he/she voluntarily signs and enters into this General Release without reservation after having given the matter full and careful consideration; and (c)(I) Employee has a period of seven days after signing this General Release in which he/she may revoke this General Release, (ii) this General Release does not become effective or enforceable and no payment shall be made hereunder until this seven-day-revocation period has elapsed, and (iii) any revocation must be in writing by Employee and delivered to (specify), Human Resources, within the seven-day-revocation period.

IN WITNESS WHEREOF, the Employee signs this General Release this ___ day of ____ (year)

_____

Employee's Name (please print)

WITNESS:

_____

Signature   Date

ACKNOWLEDGMENT

I HEREBY ACKNOWLEDGE that (Name of Employer) in accordance with the Age Discrimination in Employment Act, as amended by the Older

Workers Benefit Protection Act, informed me in writing: (1) to consult with an attorney before signing this General Release; (2) to review this General Release for a period of 21 days prior to signing; (3) that for a period of seven days following the signing of this General Release, I may revoke this General Release, and this General Release will not become effective or enforceable until the seven-day-revocation period has elapsed; and (4) that no payment shall be made until the seven-day-revocation period has elapsed.

    I HEREBY FURTHER ACKNOWLEDGE receipt of this General Release for my review on the _____ day of _____. (year)

Employee: _____
                 (Print or Type Name)

_____
              Signature of Employee

Witness:_____

STRATEGY: *If you have signed an employment contract containing an arbitration clause, a claim you make as a fired employee under the ADEA may fall within the scope of the clause and you may be forced to litigate an age discrimination dispute in arbitration rather than in a court before a jury. This can work to your disadvantage because in most instances arbitrators are not empowered to award punitive damages, injunctions to stop further harassment, or legal fees. Furthermore, arbitrators are usually lawyers and their philosophical orientation is often not as closely aligned to an individual's rights as a jury. Arbitration awards tend to be smaller than jury awards for discriminatory harms committed. It is important to understand the ramifications of any arbitration clause in an employment agreement before you sign it. Seek legal advice when presented with a comprehensive employment contract for an important job.*

    Recognize that waivers signed by a departing worker may not protect the employer if the worker later applies for a job. One 55-year-old executive was dismissed in a downsizing move. He accepted an enhanced severance package (twice the usual severance) and signed a waiver relinquishing his right to sue the company. A year later, still unemployed, he saw his old job advertised in the newspaper. With the encouragement of a former superior, he applied for the position. He lost out to a much younger worker under 40 with little experience.

The man sued, claiming that he was a victim of age discrimination. The trial court dismissed the case as a result of the waiver he had signed. But the appeals court noted that the ADEA disapproves people waiving age discrimination claims. It ruled that although the waiver would normally preclude the worker from suing the company, it did not cover discriminatory events that occurred after the waiver was signed and that illegal treatment had occurred.

STRATEGY: *The OWBPA provides possible legal protection if your employer offers you the opportunity to participate in a staff reduction program. I frequently represent groups of employees who are told they will be fired as part of a downsizing or reorganization. When you and other departing employees make a counteroffer (e.g., you request that the severance package currently on the table be tripled), your employer may be inclined to settle (e.g., at double the present offer) just to get rid of you and others and avoid a potential age discrimination lawsuit. Thus, if at all possible, try to negotiate the terms of your departure either separately or collectively with coworkers after receiving notification of a staff reduction.*

Tax Treatment

Damages received for personal physical injury or sickness (e.g., a bleeding ulcer caused by workplace stress) pursuant to an award or out-of-court settlement of an age discrimination claim may be excludable from gross income and therefore not taxable. However, damages for back pay, liquidated damages, and damages for nonphysical personal injuries from emotional pain, sickness, or distress pursuant to the ADEA are taxable. Money received as punitive damages is also taxable. Consult a knowledgeable lawyer for more advice on this subject where applicable.

Since most ADEA awards are not tax-free, they are treated as wages subject to FICA, FUTA, and income tax withholding. Employers who are liable for such awards may also be liable for tax penalties for failing to collect withholding on these awards and failing to pay the employer portion of FICA.

Race Discrimination

Title VII of the Civil Rights Act and various other federal and state laws prohibit intentional discrimination based on ancestry or ethnicity. Some employers discriminate by paying lower salaries and other compensation to blacks and Hispanics. Others deny promotions and jobs to individuals on the basis of race or color. Federal laws prohibit employers of 15 or more employees from discriminating on the basis of race or color. Virtually all states have even stronger antidiscrimination laws directed to fighting job-related race and minority discrimination. In some states, companies with fewer than eight employees can be found guilty of discrimination.

Both federal and state laws generally forbid employers from:

- Denying an applicant a job on the basis of race or color
- Denying promotions, transfers, or assignments on the basis of race or color
- Penalizing workers with reduced privileges, reduced employment opportunities, and reduced compensation on the basis of race or color
- Firing a worker on the basis of race or color

For example, in one recent case 3,500 black and Hispanic employees of a city's Parks Department and their lawyers received $21 million in settlement of an eight-year-old lawsuit claiming discrimination in promotions and compensation as well as an allegation that minority employees who complained about unfair treatment suffered retaliation.

COMMON AREAS OF EXPLOITATION. Although it is legal for employers to pose questions at the hiring interview that test your motivation, maturity, willingness to accept instruction, interest in the job, and ability to communicate, inquiries made to further discriminatory practices are illegal. Common areas of exploitation encompass questions pertaining to color, national origin, citizenship, language, and relatives. For example, it is illegal to ask the following questions under federal Equal Employment Opportunity Commission guidelines and state regulations:

Color: What is your skin color?

National origin: What is your ancestry? What is your mother's native language? What is your spouse's nationality? What is your maiden name?

Citizenship: Of what country are you a citizen? Are your parents or spouse naturalized or native-born citizens? When did they acquire citizenship? Are you a native-born citizen?

Language: What is your native tongue? How did you acquire the ability to read, write, and speak a foreign language?

Relatives: Names, addresses, ages, and other pertinent information concerning your spouse, children, or relatives not employed by the company. What type of work does your mother or father do?

STRATEGY: *You have the right to refuse to answer any of the above questions at the hiring interview. If you choose not to answer them, you can politely inform the interviewer that you believe the questions are illegal and refuse to answer them on that basis. If you are then denied the job, you may have a strong case for damages after speaking with a representative from the EEOC, your state's human rights commission, or a knowledgeable lawyer provided you can prove the denial stemmed from a refusal to answer such questions.*

Another common area of race discrimination occurs when companies deliberately impose higher hiring standards than necessary, which tends to exclude minorities. All employment requirements must be directly related to the job; minorities cannot be excluded unnecessarily.

Typically, the EEOC or related state agency will investigate charges of race discrimination or race-related retaliation. The EEOC has broad power to secure information and company records via subpoena, field investigations, audits, and interviewing witnesses, both employees and outsiders. Statistical data may be presented to demonstrate a pattern or practice of discriminatory conduct. As in other forms of discrimination, the contents of an individual's personnel file and the files of others in similar situations are often examined. Data on workplace composition may reveal a pattern or practice of exclusion. Regional or national data may shed light on whether a decision locally made was, in fact, racially discriminatory.

In cases where circumstantial evidence is presented to prove race discrimination, the burden is on the plaintiff to raise an inference of discrimination. This is often done through the use of statistics and payroll records.

Proving you were individually excluded from a job based on your race or color may be difficult. It is often helpful to obtain statistical data to show that the employer's practices are illegal. For example, if ten positions for an engineering job were filled and none of the jobs was offered to a minority (or a woman), that may be sufficient to infer that the company violated the law. You would need assistance from a competent lawyer or discrimination specialist to prove this because the rules necessary to prove statistical disparities are complex.

You may have an easier time of demonstrating race discrimination when you are directly treated unfairly on the job. For example, if you are repeatedly harassed and called names on the job, or are treated differently from non-minorities (e.g., you are absent several days from work and are suspended or placed on formal probation, while white workers with the same or a greater number of absences are only given an informal warning), it is best to gather this factual information for discussion with an executive or officer in your company's personnel department.

The job of a plaintiff's employment attorney in a race discrimination case is to submit evidence convincing a reasonable fact-finder
that the alleged misconduct was motivated by racial animus. This is
often done by demonstrating the work environment was pervasively
hostile and abusive and that the illegal acts were not isolated but
occurred on a regular basis over several years. Cases are strengthened by
the presence of blatant racial stereotypes (e.g., pictures and newspaper
clippings attached to the employer's walls) and/or evidence of reported
threats, insults and ridicule regularly directed at the complainant and
other minority workers.

In one case a judge allowed a race discrimination case to proceed
when a Puerto Rican plaintiff applied for a position as a waitress and
wasn't hired after being told "You have a Latino accent," "You don't
speak white," and "You are Ghetto." The plaintiff adequately plead
race discrimination after the defendant didn't prove the woman could
not adequately perform the duties of the job. Interestingly, the court
stated that an adverse employment decision may be predicated upon an
employee's accent, but only when it interferes materially with job
performance.

In another case, a federal appeals court reinstated a white city
worker's lawsuit which claimed he was denied a promotion because of
his race. The claimant proved his supervisors, both black, made several
racist remarks, including "white people are lazy," and they were "out to
get him" and "make his life miserable." From such statements the
judge ruled that a reasonable jury could find that the denial of the
promotion was race-based due to the supervisor's hostility. (Note: The
case is also instructive due to the fact that white workers may also sue
for race discrimination.)

You may have an easier time proving race discrimination on an
individual basis as opposed to relying on statistical disparities. This is
because in certain cases employers now have to offer only a business
justification for actions that are shown by statistics to have an unfair
impact on minorities. The burden then shifts to the complainant to
demonstrate that the alleged business justification is not legitimate.

STRATEGY: *Employers often defend themselves in race discrimination lawsuits by alleging that any racial comments made were isolated and discrete, and that the complainant was unable to absorb the new tasks a job required, refused to follow reasonable instructions, had an attitude problem, or was guilty of misconduct.*

A plaintiff may meet the burden of establishing an inference of discriminatory intent through a number of ways, such as the incorrect criticism of the workers' performance in ethnically degrading terms, invidious comments about others in the employee's protected group, or the more favorable treatment of employees not in the protected group. But if you are fired for documented and proven poor work performance or similar issues, the odds increase dramatically you will lose the case.

The use of federal affirmative action programs that award benefits on the basis of race has diminished due to a number of Supreme Court rulings. While the Office of Federal Contract Compliance Programs (OFCCP) charged with overseeing and administering the largest affirmative action program in the United States (more than ninety thousand companies have contracts with the federal government valued at $50,000 or more) still administers such programs, the OFCCP desires that its affirmative action program be different from preferences or set-asides and does not amount to reverse discrimination.

While many employers desire to implement employment practices aimed at increasing their racial and ethnic diversity, a 2009 Supreme Court ruling may put a damper on such plans. In *Ricci v. DeStefano*, a 5-4 majority of the Supreme Court held that the City of New Haven, Connecticut unlawfully discriminated on the basis of race when it refused to certify results of promotional exams in which white firefighters outperformed minority co-workers. The court rejected the city's argument that it disregarded the test results to avoid violating Title VII's disparate impact provisions. Companies wishing to promote diversity in the workplace by correcting for disparate-impact discrimination based on race or ethnicity are now subject to lawsuits by nonminority employees alleging disparate treatment discrimination.

The ruling also jeopardizes diversity considerations in termination RIF decisions.

While the ruling restricts (but does not eliminate) a company's ability to take diversity into account in employment decisions, any employer who hires or promotes employees based on an exam will be required to hire based on the exam's results and not diversity. Going forward, experts predict it will be harder for employers to have minority hiring programs and for minorities to force employers to address complaints about a potentially biased test.

Employers who adopt an employment practice to promote or maintain a diverse workforce must now be careful of the risks involved. As a result, many employers are now abandoning or eliminating any race or gender based preferences in their hiring policies and modifying or deleting stated goals in company handbooks and employee manuals. An employment program with numbers, goals, or timetables that can even remotely lead to quota preferences may be illegal. Speak to an employment attorney to determine your rights and options where applicable.

Religious Discrimination

Title VII of the Civil Rights Act of 1964 prohibits religious discrimination and requires employers to reasonably accommodate the religious practices of employees and prospective employees. Various state laws also prohibit discrimination because of a person's observance of the Sabbath or other holy day. In many states employers may not require attendance at work on such a day except in emergencies or situations in which the employee's presence is indispensable. Absences for these observances must be made up at some mutually agreeable time or can be charged against accumulated leave time.

One terminated worker sued after she was fired for refusing to work overtime on Saturdays due to her religious beliefs. In this particular case, an auto manufacturer hired the woman to work on an assembly line. The job did not initially conflict with her religious beliefs (which required that she not work from sunset Friday to sunset Saturday) because the assembly line operated only from Monday through Friday. However, when the company began requiring mandatory overtime on Saturdays, the worker refused on religious grounds, and she was fired after missing a series of Saturday work shifts.

The woman brought suit in federal court, alleging that the company violated Title VII of the Civil Rights Act, which makes it unlawful to fire or discriminate against an employee on the basis of race, color, religion, gender, or national origin, and that a 1972 amendment to the law requires employers to prove they are unable to accommodate an employee's religious practice without "undue hardship."

The primary issue before the trial court was whether the company had made a bona fide attempt to meet the needs of the employee. The court ruled that the woman's absence did not injure the company and that her request was not unreasonable. She was awarded $73,911 in back pay and benefits, despite the employer's argument that the proper running of the business would be affected by high absenteeism rates on Saturday, complaints from coworkers that she not receive special privileges (i.e., it was unfair to require them to work on Saturday while allowing the woman to take time off), and waiting lists of more senior employees requesting transfers to departments with no Saturday work.

The Supreme Court let the lower ruling stand, commenting that the company could have acted on the employee's request without undue hardship through the use of people employed specifically for absentee relief.

The following points summarize what companies are obligated to do to avoid lawsuits:

1. Employers have an obligation to make reasonable accommodations to the religious needs of employees.

2. Employers must give time off for the Sabbath or holy days except in an emergency.

3. If employees don't come to work, employers may give them leave without pay, may require equivalent time to be made up, or may allow employees to charge the time against any other leave with pay, except sick pay.

4. Employers may not discriminatorily apply personal appearance rules to religious observers.

5. Employers may not fire workers as a result of their religious beliefs.

Employers may not be required to give time off to employees who work in key health and safety occupations or to those whose presence is critical to the company on any given day. Employers are not required to take steps inconsistent with a valid seniority system to accommodate an employee's religious practices. They are not required to incur overtime costs to replace an employee who will not work on Saturday. Employers have no responsibility to appease fellow employees who complain they are suffering undue hardship when a coworker is allowed not to work on a Saturday or Sabbath due to a religious belief while they are required to do so. Finally, employers are generally not required to choose the option the employee prefers as long as the accommodation offered is reasonable. However, penalizing an employee for refusing to work on Christmas or Good Friday most likely constitutes religious discrimination, depending on the facts.

The definition for a "religious belief" is quite liberal under the law. If your belief is demonstrably sincere, the belief can be considered religious even though it is not an essential tenet of the religion of which you are a member. The applicant's or employer's knowledge that a position will involve a conflict does not relieve the employer of its duty to reasonably accommodate, absent undue hardship.

In most cases, the court weighs the facts to determine whether the employer offered a reasonable accommodation or that undue hardship existed; the plaintiff will attempt to show that the hardship was not severe or that the accommodation offered was not reasonable. What constitutes undue hardship varies on a case-by-case basis. Generally, undue hardship results when more than a de minimis cost (i.e., overtime premium pay) is imposed on the employer.

For example, four uniformed public-safety officers wearing dreadlocks in adherence with their Rastafari beliefs settled an EEOC complaint against an employer for $40,000 in emotional damages. The employer's policy required workers to maintain a neat appearance and trimmed hair, and the employees were verbally reprimanded for failing to fully tuck their locks into their uniform hats. The officers offered to tie their hair in neat ponytails but this was rejected. They also stated a company demand to trim their beards was wrong because it violated Rastafari custom. The EEOC's attorney successfully argued that their sincere religious practices necessitated accommodation which did not create an undue hardship for the employer.

Also, a Muslim Wall Street analyst who claimed he was wrongfully fired because of his religion and national origin recently received a $1.55 million settlement. The employee alleged that inappropriate discriminatory comments were made to him in the workplace, including that he was not allowed on the trading floor because "you are from a country which has a high risk factor and a threat" and, "Quants were like Israelis, and traders were like Palestinians." The employer alleged he was fired due to a department elimination but the evidence revealed all other workers were reassigned within the company, one employee was promoted, and he was the only one fired.

The lawsuit requested damages for loss of back pay and future benefits, pain and suffering, attorney fees and costs of the suit, punitive damages, an injunction preventing the company from discriminating against employees in the future, and an order requiring the employer to institute policies providing equal employment opportunities for all employees.

STRATEGY: *Like other forms of discrimination discussed in previous sections of the chapter, proving that insensitive remarks were made strengthened the case and helped prove a discriminatory bias toward the complainant. The case is also instructive because*

sometimes finding liability for claims of a litigant's religious beliefs
and national origin are hard to separate.

The "undue hardship" defense is an exception that companies try to assert to successfully circumvent current law in this area. When you request time off for religious practices, document the date and nature of the request and the reasons given by the employer (or the alternatives it considers) in meeting or denying that request. Speak to counsel to fully explore your options, such as filing a charge of religious discrimination with the EEOC or a state agency or suing the employer in either state or federal court, whichever is applicable. You have certain rights if you are a true religious observer whose beliefs conflict with your work schedule and you are fired as a result.

One worker claimed he was fired merely because he kept a Bible in his drawer, displayed religious plaques in his office, and had his secretary type his Bible study notes after hours. The employer argued he was fired for poor performance, but an Iowa jury awarded him $325,540 for back pay, front pay, and consequential damages for his emotional pain and suffering.

Experts suggest that religious harassment cases are on the rise, and the number of religious discrimination cases filed annually with the EEOC has gone up dramatically. Another related key issue that is often involved concerns freedom of expression in the workplace. For example, can employers bar employees from wearing any sort of religious symbols or garb at work or from discussing religion at work? Lawyers representing employees who are fired from their jobs as a result claim that people are free to discuss their religious beliefs while working. However, reported case decisions generally indicate that you cannot do so if it intrudes on another person's ability to work or you are asked to stop but persist.

Handicap Discrimination

The federal Americans with Disabilities Act (ADA) was enacted in 1990 to widen the scope of protection available to disabled workers. Employers with 15 or more workers must avoid disability discrimination in all phases of the job. In many states, people who work in small firms (i.e., those having five or more employees) are also protected against disability discrimination under more stringent state laws, so it is important to be familiar with your state's law as well.

Employers are required to eliminate any inquiries on medical examinations and forms designed to identify an applicant's disabilities. Employers cannot deny employment opportunities to an employee because of the need to make reasonable accommodation for a disability, and persons with disabilities cannot be fired because of the inability to perform nonessential or marginal functions of the job.

The main object of the ADA is to protect any person with a physical or mental impairment that substantially limits one or more life activities. This covers a broad range of disabilities, including deafness, AIDS, cancer, and learning disabilities. It does not include compulsive gambling or pregnancy. (State law may be more inclusive as to what constitutes a covered disability so speak to a lawyer for more details.)

Every aspect of the employment relationship is protected, from employee compensation, terms, and privileges to job classifications, fringe benefits, promotions, training opportunities, and discharge. Although the ADA does not require an employer to give preferential consideration to persons with disabilities, such persons cannot be excluded for consideration for a raise, promotion, or an on-the-job opportunity because of an inability to perform a marginal function. The law also states that persons associated with those who have a disability, such as an individual who does volunteer work with AIDS patients, cannot be fired because of that relationship or association.

Persons with disabilities cannot be disqualified from applying for a job because of the inability to perform nonessential or marginal functions of the job. Employers must scrutinize all job requirements so they do not inadvertently screen out qualified disabled applicants. Under the ADA, it is unlawful to refuse to hire people with disabilities who have equal skills after the employer provides reasonable accommodation, such as purchasing a telephone headset for a person with a hearing impairment.

The following list will familiarize you with typical obligations employers must generally follow during the hiring process:

- Employers cannot ask disability-related questions in interviews (such as "Do you presently have a disability?" or "Do you have any impairments that prevent you from performing the job you've applied for?")

- Employers cannot inquire about the kind of accommodation a person needs in order to perform the job properly if hired

- A medical exam can be requested only after hiring, provided it is an essential condition for employment for all entering employees in that position

- All contracts with employment agencies, unions, and insurance plans cannot be discriminatory

- Employers cannot deny employment opportunities to an applicant or employee because of the need to make reasonable accommodation for a disability

- Employers must avoid employment tests or selection criteria that have a disparate impact on individuals with disabilities unless the tests or criteria are shown to be job-related and supported by business necessity

- Employers may deny jobs to handicapped workers if they can demonstrate the position poses a danger to the individual's health and welfare or that hiring would significantly interfere with productivity or create dangers to others

To establish a prima facie case of disability discrimination, you must show (1) that the employer is subject to the ADA, (2) you are disabled within the meaning of the ADA or perceived to be so by the employer, (3) that you were otherwise qualified to perform the essential functions of the job with or without reasonable accommodation; and (4) suffered an adverse employment action because of the disability.

In the first category, you will be considered disabled if you (1) suffer from a physical or mental impairment that (2) affects a major life activity, and (3) the effect is substantial.

With regard to the second element, to prove a disability under the ADA, you must show (1) a physical or mental impairment which substantially limits one or more major life activities, (2) a record of having such an impairment, or (3) being regarded as having such an impairment.

Alcoholism and drug addiction are impairments under the ADA. However, the mere status as an alcoholic or substance abuser does not necessarily imply a limitation under the second part of that definition (i.e., that it affects a major life activity). To prevail, you must show not only that you were actually addicted to alcohol or drugs in the past, but also that the addiction substantially limits one or more of your life activities. Some courts now hold that alcoholism and drug addiction do not constitute disabilities under the ADA because they are not permanently disabling.

To be substantially limited you must have an impairment that prevents or severely restricts you from doing activities that are of central importance to most people's daily lives (e.g., caring for oneself, performing manual tasks, walking, seeing, hearing, speaking, breathing, learning) and the impairment's impact must also be permanent or long-term.

However, the impairment must not be so disabling that you are not able to perform the functions of the job. If it is, then your case will be dismissed.

Finally, plaintiffs who allege violations under the ADA may proceed under any or all of these theories: disparate treatment, disparate impact, and failure to make reasonable accommodation (discussed below).

Congress expanded coverage of the ADA in 2009 with the ADA Amendments Act (ADAAA). The law now requires courts to more broadly include people with disabilities from discriminatory acts by employers. People with disabilities now include persons with conditions that flare up only occasionally or conditions in remission (provided the impairment substantially limits a major life activity). The definition of a major life activity has been expanded to include hearing, breathing, reading, learning, caring for oneself, performing manual tasks, thinking, concentrating, communicating and working. Even if such conditions can be mitigated by using medication or prosthetics, the only exclusion now recognized by the ADAAA will be for ordinary eyeglasses and contact lenses. Experts predict these changes will make it easier to sue employers on the basis of disability discrimination and more claimants will be included. Speak to an experienced employment attorney for advice and guidance where applicable.

THE EMPLOYER'S OBLIGATION TO MAKE REASONABLE ACCOMMODATION. The law does not cover workers who cannot work because of a total disability; the law protects only workers with disabilities who are capable of continuing working if the employer provides reasonable accommodation. On-the-job accommodations that must be provided to handicapped employees include:

- Restructuring or modifying work schedules
- Offering part-time work
- Permitting the employee to work at home
- Reassigning an individual to a vacant position
- Providing readers or interpreters for blind or deaf persons
- Acquiring or altering equipment or devices
- Making existing facilities readily accessible to the disabled
- Adjusting marginal job requirements

■ Allowing flexibility in arrival and departure times for people who require special vehicles for transportation or who are confined to wheelchairs

Employers are required to make such accommodations only if the disability is known, if the accommodation requested is reasonable, and if the employee is truly partially disabled. An employer is relieved of responsibility to accommodate a disabled employee when to do so would impose an undue hardship. Factors considered in determining whether undue hardship exists are the nature and the costs of the accommodation to the employer, the overall financial resources of the employer (i.e., number of employees, overall size of the business, etc.), and other related factors. Courts will look at the type of the operation, overall size, budget, profitability of the employer, and the financial impact of the suggested accommodation in determining whether undue hardship exists. The facts concerning what constitutes undue hardship vary from case to case; however, if the employer can afford to accommodate, it must generally do so.

Is an obligation of accommodation owed to an employee who does not request specific accommodation? Generally, the ADA contemplates that employers must engage in an interactive process with their employees and work together to assess whether an employee's disability can be reasonably accommodated. Thus, ignorance is not an excuse if a jury finds it was reasonable for an employer to conclude that an employee was disabled yet failed to engage in an interactive process and didn't offer reasonable accommodation.

As a result of the ADA and various state laws, employers now have enhanced obligations to current employees who develop disabilities while working. In particular, wrongful discharge of workers who contract the AIDS virus, develop alcohol problems affecting their attendance or performance, or even become "morbidly obese" can result in severe penalties.

Interestingly, rulings around the United States suggest employers may have a legal duty to pay for expensive weight-loss surgery after an employee is injured on-the-job and becomes disabled. In one case a worker developed arthritis in a knee he injured on-the-job. The court stated the employer was required to pay for gastric bypass surgery to ensure the effectiveness of knee replacement surgery. Another case with the same result was also decided for a 340 pound employee requiring back surgery for a work-related back injury.

Under the ADA, while you cannot be refused a job or be fired because of past drug addiction, there is no protection for current drug use. You can be legally terminated for using drugs on the job or working in an impaired state because of current drug use. Also, you can be legally terminated for taking an excessive amount of time off due to illness.

Although employers are generally permitted to terminate workers who become completely disabled, they must give handicapped workers the opportunity to work at less demanding jobs or offer other accommodations. Employers must also provide such workers with existing short or long-term disability benefits and other medical coverage (as well as an enhanced severance package if the worker can negotiate it) before they leave. Thus, always try to obtain the best post-termination benefits if you are fired and possess a disability.

STRATEGY: *Employers sometimes innocently make statements useful to proving a discriminatory motive. Pay special attention to comments made by supervisors, officers, and other personnel such as "We need someone at the top of their game," "We need someone who can handle the pressure," or "What's the matter with you, why aren't you your old self?" Proof of such statements dramatically improves a claimant's chances of success in disability and other discrimination lawsuits brought under federal, state, and local laws. It is essential to recollect and record all harmful statements as soon as possible after they are made so you won't forget them. Maintain a diary and record the date, time and place the words were spoken, what was stated, and whether any witnesses overheard the comments. If so, record their names as well. Remind your lawyer to consider using this evidence as proof of discriminatory intent for maximum benefit.*

The author has represented clients who were considered an important asset of the firm until they announced a disabling medical condition, such as skin cancer. Employers then often began treating such individuals differently — for example, not inviting them to frequent lunches, not giving them periodic raises, or leaving them out of the loop. This kind of unfair treatment is subtle, but its victims are probably not imagining it. If you feel you were treated differently or were fired after becoming disabled, contact an employment attorney immediately to discuss your rights and options.

As an example, in a boost to the rights of cancer patients undergoing chemotherapy, the New York State Division of Human Rights represented a legal secretary who was fired after her treatment of breast cancer began. The woman missed three days of work following a mastectomy. After three days of halftime work, she resumed working full days. A few weeks later, she took one day off because she felt weak from chemotherapy. She returned and worked full-time the rest of the week but was fired a week later. She sued her former law firm employer in state court because the five-attorney firm was too small to be covered under the federal ADA. She was awarded $20,000 in lost pay for the year following her dismissal and $50,000 for mental anguish. The state human rights agency noted that she lost her job even though she had enough sick days to cover the time projected to be lost due to ongoing treatments. The agency also noted that while someone suffering from an illness must still be able to perform his or her job in a reasonable manner (which is not defined as flawlessly or with perfect attendance), employers have an affirmative duty to reasonably accommodate a disabled employee.

Although it is permissible to fire workers who use illegal drugs, alcoholism is considered a protected disability. Generally, workers cannot be fired for drinking excessively off-premises if they are participating in an alcohol rehabilitation program. However, an employer may prohibit the use of illegal drugs and alcohol at the workplace and require that employees not be under the influence of alcohol while at work (since they may be considered a direct threat to the health or safety of other workers or customers).

You can still be fired (for gross misconduct, for example) even if your mental disability was the cause of the act (e.g., stealing). But some experts suggest that these guidelines will unfairly help a person who doesn't get along with coworkers to hire a doctor to say that he or she has a mental disability, thus making it much more difficult legally to be fired. The benefit to employees is that EEOC regulations now significantly expand protections for mental disabilities as the following case demonstrates.

In that case, after one employee started receiving medical treatments for manic-depression, he asked his employer of 14 years to adjust his work schedule to the day shift only, rather than nights and sometimes days. This was based on a doctor's advice that he needed a regular sleeping pattern. Shortly after making the request, he was fired. He sued the company under the ADA and obtained a six-figure settlement.

STRATEGY: *Always seek the advice of a knowledgeable employment attorney if you believe you were fired or treated unfairly because of a bona fide physical or mental disability.*

Retaliation Discrimination

Perhaps the most common form of illegal treatment that employees suffer is retaliation discrimination. Employees who legitimately assert discrimination rights by filing charges in federal or state court, with the EEOC, or through state agencies, complain to the employer before taking action, testify on behalf of another party, assist another party in administrative or judicial proceedings, or advise fellow employees of their rights under the discrimination laws are protected from adverse retaliation by an employer. If you reasonably believe that a Title VII violation was committed, an employer cannot take any action adverse to such rights, such as failing to promote, discharging, or unduly criticizing you as a direct result of that action.

Acts taken by an employer as a direct result of your filing charges or threatening to go to the EEOC or commence a lawsuit are viewed by the courts as retaliatory. Many employers who are accused of discrimination have valid defenses and can overcome such charges. However, they foolishly take steps deemed to be in retaliation against an individual's freedom to pursue such claims and eventually suffer damages resulting from the retaliatory actions, not the alleged discrimination.

The following list identifies common areas where retaliation occurs:

- Transfer or reassignment that is undesired (even with no loss in pay or benefits)
- A transfer out of the country
- Threats, when repeatedly made and when disruptive to your job performance
- Harassment on the job
- Giving unfavorable references to a prospective employer, or otherwise interfering with your efforts to obtain a new job, or wrongfully refusing to write a recommendation on your behalf
- Firing you or forcing retirement by eliminating the position and offering only lesser alternative positions
- Denying or suspending severance payments
- Retroactively downgrading your performance appraisals and placing derogatory memos in your personnel file
- Refusing to promote or reassign you or adding preconditions for a requested reassignment
- Transferring you to a job with fewer amenities, such as no office, phone or business cards

- Increasing your workload without good reason
- Adversely changing or decreasing your wages, vacation time, or benefits
- Delaying the distribution of tax and Social Security forms
- Interfering with an employment contract

The burden of proof necessary to prevail in a retaliation lawsuit is similar to other kinds of discrimination actions and utilizes a burden shifting framework. Thus, a plaintiff bears the initial burden of establishing a prima facie case of retaliation by showing (1) he exercised rights protected under Title VII, FMLA or other protected federal, state or local law, (2) he was qualified for his position, (3) he suffered an adverse employment action, and (4) the adverse employment action occurred in circumstances giving rise to an inference of retaliatory intent.

If this burden is met, a presumption of retaliation is created and the burden of production shifts to the defendant to articulate a legitimate, non-discriminatory reason for the alleged wrongful act. If the employer does so, the presumption of discrimination is rebutted and the burden shifts back to the plaintiff to show, without the benefit of any presumptions, that more likely than not the employer's decision was motivated, at least in part, by a discriminatory reason.

Proving discriminatory intent is often made by direct statements to the complainant such as "you are a pain in the ass," or "I'm tired of your complaints." It also helps if the adverse act (e.g., a firing) takes place within a short period of time after the complaint is made. In one case for example, a teacher had received excellent evaluations, letters of praise, and commendations from colleagues from the previous administration. But after engaging in activities as a member of the local teachers' union, she received unsatisfactory performance evaluations, was cited for alleged incidents of professional misconduct, and was denied tenure. The court ruled that since all of this occurred after she was elected as the union's co-chapter leader, it was likely that illegal retaliatory conduct had occurred.

A plaintiff need only establish general corporate knowledge rather than proving that the ultimate decision-maker was aware of a complaint. Generally, as long as you complain (preferably in writing) to someone whose job is to investigate and resolve such complaints and suffer an adverse action, a retaliation lawsuit will be allowed to proceed to trial. The following hypothetical illustrates this:

> *Alexa has been sexually harassed on the job. Before being harassed, she was given a poor work evaluation and was told she was being placed on probation. Although she disagreed with the company's position, she is trying her best to demonstrate satisfactory work to remove herself from probation status.*
>
> *Alexa is concerned that if she complains to management about the sexual harassment, she will be fired. She consults an employment attorney. Alexa learns that by sending a letter to her company documenting and complaining about the illegal incidents, she may be protecting her job, because if she is then accused of poor work performance and fired, she can assert that the employer's adverse action was in retaliation for her filing a valid discrimination charge.*

Recognizing what constitutes retaliation is not always clear. In one case, for example, a New York court ruled that the loss of an office and phone previously provided to an employee who was informed of a termination decision and was waiting out his numbered days on the payroll searching for a new job does not, in and of itself, amount to adverse employment action. Nor does preparing a poor performance review in the absence of evidence that the employer gave the negative evaluation in bad faith. Thus, you may not be able to sue over every action that causes you dismay. The acts must be serious and provable — that is, there must be a causal connection between the protected activity and the adverse employment action.

Never falsely accuse an employer of a wrongful act in the attempt to obtain leverage, because you may not be legally protected if you then suffer harmful retaliation. However, you are protected against retaliation in a variety of nondiscriminatory areas such as complaining about overtime policies, safety (OSHA) violations, and filing a workers' compensation claim. Most federal laws, such as the Civil Rights Act of 1964, the Family and Medical Leave Act, and the Americans with Disabilities Act prohibit retaliation against anyone filing a charge. So do many federal and state whistleblower statutes.

STRATEGY: *Do not stand idly by when an employer fires or demotes you, gives you an unfair or harsh evaluation, or singles you out in a negative way. This also includes giving a bad reference after you leave.*

Constructive discharge, defined as conduct forcing you to resign, is an indirect violation of the same laws, and the employer cannot mistreat you to the extent that you suffer intolerable working conditions and are forced to resign. If you prevail in such a case, damages you may receive include reinstatement, back pay, attorney fees, punitive damages, and front pay with interest.

Often a supervisor will say to a worker, "If you don't like it, quit." Reconstruct such statements (e.g., note the time and place it was said and who overheard the remarks). Speak to those witnesses and prepare a diary to document what was said. If you state in court that you quit because this is what your supervisor told you to do, your case can be strengthened, depending on the facts.

Always view suspiciously an employer's actions if you are transferred or demoted after complaining about alleged discrimination. Demand specific factual reasons for any company action if this occurs. If you believe the reasons are false, or you were treated unfairly as a result of complaining about an employer's illegal acts, speak to an employment attorney immediately for advice and guidance.

Strategies to Enforce Your Rights

Recognizing discrimination is only part of the battle; you must take the proper steps to enforce your rights. The law entitles victims of discrimination to recover a variety of damages. These may include reinstatement or job hiring; receiving wage adjustments, back pay, and double back pay; receiving promotions and future pay; recovering legal fees, filing costs, and fees paid for expert witnesses; receiving punitive damages and compensatory damages up to $300,000 depending on the size of the employer; and other damages depending on the facts of your case. Even if you work in a right-to-work state and can be fired easily, it is illegal to be fired because you belong to a protected class, such as being a woman, over forty, a minority, handicapped, or a religious believer.

In seeking to enforce your rights, you will not be alone. More than 100,000 formal complaints are filed each year with the EEOC, and thousands of private discrimination lawsuits are tried in court annually. This does not include the many hundreds of thousands of complaints brought to state and local agencies and other institutions.

If you believe you have been victimized by employment discrimination, consider filing a charge with the Equal Employment Opportunity Commission and/or your state agency. The EEOC is a federal agency responsible for investigating claims of discrimination under various federal laws, including the Americans with Disabilities Act, Title VII of the Civil Rights Act, and the Age Discrimination in Employment Act. The headquarters of the EEOC are in Washington, D.C., and there are numerous regional and local offices throughout the United States.

In some states, filing a charge with either the EEOC or a state agency will be treated as a filing with both. Although some state agencies permit a longer period (e.g., up to 300 days depending on state law), to be timely you must file a charge with the EEOC within 180 days of the date the last incident occurred. You should also know that the EEOC is authorized to contract with state agencies to handle some of its cases, so it is possible your case will automatically be turned over to a state agency.

STRATEGY: *Before deciding whether to file with the EEOC or a state agency, speak to an employment attorney for advice, because some state discrimination statutes provide greater protection and some state agencies have more powers than the EEOC. For example, although the EEOC cannot investigate charges of discrimination with companies that have fewer than 15 full-time employees, most state agencies can.*

You must also first decide whether to commence a private discrimination lawsuit in state court or file a charge with the EEOC or a state agency. The advantage of commencing a private lawsuit may be the more liberal statute of limitations if you are concerned that the time to file may soon expire. It is also possible to recover more damages under some state laws. You may also be able to receive a judgment quicker, since the EEOC is understaffed. Cases often take years to be decided, and obtaining a favorable decision (i.e., a letter stating your case has probable cause) does not automatically mean you will receive an award of any size, much less that you will receive big bucks. The employer may appeal an EEOC or state agency decision and force you to sue it in federal court or have the case remanded to a state administrative hearing. This could effectively stall any financial recovery for many more years. If you decide to file a private lawsuit, however, you will probably need to hire a lawyer to represent you in court, and this can be expensive.

The advantage of initially commencing a claim through the EEOC or a state agency is that it costs you nothing. Once a claim is accepted by the EEOC or state agency, an investigator in charge of your case will attempt to resolve the complaint through investigation and conciliation. The agency may render a nonbinding decision only when an informal settlement cannot be reached.

The EEOC performs the following general functions in any discrimination charge for free:

1. It will conduct interviews with you to obtain as much information as possible about the alleged discrimination and to explain the investigative procedure.

2. It will notify the employer about the charge that has been filed.

3. It will investigate the charge. This includes interviewing witnesses and reviewing all pertinent records, documentation, and other written materials.

4. It will attempt to resolve the matter amicably between the parties.

5. It will drop your case if it determines that it does not have merit.

6. It may conduct a fact-finding conference with all parties present in one room.

7. It will decide whether discrimination took place (i.e., issue a formal decision of probable or no probable cause.)

Once you file a charge with the EEOC, you cannot litigate the matter privately until the EEOC dismisses your case (finds no probable cause), rules in your favor, or permits you to do so (i.e., issues a "right to sue letter"). In these situations, you will have 90 days to file a private lawsuit to be timely after receiving a final disposition notice right-to-sue letter from the EEOC.

To start the ball rolling, it is necessary to file a formal charge. No one can stop you from filing a complaint; the law forbids employers from threatening reprisals or retaliation (such as loss of a promotion) when action is taken. The following must be included in the complaint:

1. Your name

2. The names, business addresses, and business telephone numbers of all persons who committed and/or participated in the discriminatory act(s)

3. Specific events, dates, and facts to support why the act(s) was discriminatory (e.g., statistics, whether other employees or individuals were discriminated against, and if so, the person(s) victimized, and by whom)

The complaint must be signed and sworn to by the complainant. However, it is not necessary for the complaint to be lengthy or elaborate. The main purpose is to make sufficient allegations to trigger an investigation. That is the advantage of filing charges with an appropriate agency; charges of discrimination are initiated and investigated at no cost to you. An investigator from the EEOC or state agency prepares and types the complaint. If your claim seems plausible, the EEOC or other agency will develop the claim on your behalf. A copy of the complaint, together with a request for a written response, is then sent to the employer. The employer must respond to the charges within several weeks. This is done either by a general denial of the claim or by the filing of specific facts and reasons to support the employer's position.

The following text illustrates the brevity of a valid complaint:

> *I am a female. On (date) I was notified by my supervisor (name) at (name of employer) that I was fired. I asked (name) to tell me why I was fired; he said it was because I called in sick six times in the past year. I know of several male employees who called in sick more than six times and who were not fired.*
>
> *Based on these facts I believe I have been discriminated against on the basis of my gender.*

After charges and countercharges have been examined by an investigator, the employer and the complainant may eventually be invited to attend a conference if the investigator believes the complainant's charges possibly have merit. Cases that are deemed to be too far-fetched or insufficient on their face are dismissed before the no-fault conference. If you receive a notice from the EEOC that your case has been dismissed (sometimes referred to as lacking probable cause), it must advise you of your rights. The letter will state that if you wish to proceed with your case, you must file a formal lawsuit in federal court within 90 days or forfeit your claim. This is called a right-to-sue letter.

The purpose of a no-fault conference is to discuss your case. At that time the investigator may make arrangements to visit the employer's premises, examine documents and other pertinent records, and interview key employees and witnesses. Because an employer may have an incentive to dispose of the matter early on to save excessive legal fees, lost manpower time, and potential damages, approximately 40 percent of all complaints are disposed at the settlement conference.

STRATEGY: *Although it is not necessary to retain a lawyer to represent you at or before the no-fault conference, the chances of settling your case are much higher with a lawyer present. An employer will bring its counsel and you may be intimidated. Additionally, an experienced lawyer can evaluate your claim and advise how much it is realistically worth. Since many EEOC claims take years to be heard, a lawyer will advise you whether a settlement offer is valid and should be accepted, particularly after considering the lengthy delays that are frequently involved. The conference is conducted by an investigator. Pressure may be placed on the employer to offer a monetary settlement or some other form of restitution (such as a promotion) to avoid the large legal expenses that would be incurred in the course of an ongoing investigation and eventual hearing. And some employers may be fearful that the investigator will examine its business records, including employment applications, interoffice memos, and pay records if a settlement is not reached.*

If your case cannot be settled at the conference, many options are available, including:

- ▪ Hiring a lawyer privately and suing the employer in a civil lawsuit, typically in federal court
- ▪ Representing yourself pro se (without a lawyer) and suing the employer in federal or state court

■ Having the agency act on your behalf to protect your rights and proceeding to a fact-finding hearing and determination

■ Having the EEOC or Department of Justice commence a lawsuit for you and/or others similarly situated in a class-action lawsuit

■ Hiring a lawyer and commencing a private lawsuit in state court and, if applicable, alleging other causes of action as well as violations of discrimination laws

The advantage of suing an employer privately is that you may receive a quicker settlement. The EEOC and other agencies have many thousands of claims to process and follow; your case could take years before it is acted upon. Even if you receive a favorable decision (referred to as a finding of probable cause), the employer can appeal the agency's decision, adding years to the delay before an administrative trial is commenced. A lawyer working for you may be able to move the matter along more quickly. However, private lawsuits can be very expensive. That is why it is best to initially contact the nearest district office of the EEOC or state agency and speak with an intake person or investigator, or contact an employment attorney and discuss your options before taking action.

State and local laws are often more favorable than federal law in terms of the standards of proof required, the amount of damages awarded, and other factors. It may be advantageous to file charges with these agencies instead, so do not automatically assume your case must be filed with the EEOC. Talk to an employment attorney to discuss your options and maximize a claim.

When you retain a lawyer, he or she may first contact the employer by letter. The letter may specify the potential charges and invite the employer to discuss settlement before the matter proceeds to the next step. Cases are often settled this way before a formal discrimination charge is filed.

No matter what course of action is considered, do not delay unnecessarily. In many situations you must file a formal complaint within 180 days of the time the alleged act(s) occurred to avoid the expiration of the statute of limitations. Some complainants take their time and unfortunately discover their cases are dismissed because they waited too long to file.

Summary of Steps to Maximize a Discrimination Claim

1. If you believe you have been victimized by employment discrimination, consider filing a discrimination charge with the EEOC and/or your state agency. In some states, filing a charge with either the EEOC or state agency will be treated as filing with both. Speak to an employment attorney for advice, because some state statutes provide greater protection and some state agencies have more powers than the EEOC.

2. EEOC offices are listed in the telephone directory under United States Government or on the Internet. State agencies can be located by calling your state's Department of Labor or an EEOC office in your area.

3. Typically, you must give your name if you want an investigation to proceed, but you cannot be retaliated against for filing a charge.

4. Although some state agencies permit a longer period (e.g., up to 300 days depending on state law), to be timely, you must file a charge with the EEOC within 180 days of the date the last incident occurred.

5. Although you may file a private lawsuit in federal court, once you file a charge with the EEOC you cannot litigate the matter privately until the EEOC dismisses your case (finds no probable cause), rules in your favor, or allows you to opt out. In either situation you then have 90 days to file a private lawsuit after receiving a final disposition notice (a right-to-sue letter) from the EEOC to be timely.

6. Obtaining a favorable decision does not automatically mean that you will receive big bucks. The employer may appeal a state agency or EEOC decision and force you to sue it in federal court.

7. Call the EEOC officer assigned to your case regularly to determine the status of the investigation and action taken in your case. Be assertive and follow the progress of your case. Whenever you receive a request for information, provide this immediately to the investigator.

8. If you are unhappy with the progress of the investigation or how the case is being handled, consult an employment attorney for guidance and advice. Consider joining a class-action lawsuit if one already exists against your employer or ex-employer. By doing so, however, you may have to withdraw from your own action.

9. Be patient. The EEOC often takes years to render its decision and the employer may delay the final outcome years more by refusing to settle and appealing the case further. Some investigators leave the agency while working on a case and a new investigator has to be assigned, causing further delay. Thus, recognize that in most situations, even with a good case, you may not receive justice for many years.

PART III
■　■　■　■　■　■　■　■　■
How to Avoid Being Fired Unfairly and What to Do if You Are

Until recently, employees had few options when they received a "pink slip." This was because of a legal principle called the employment-at-will doctrine, which was generally applied throughout the United States. Under this rule of law, employers hired workers "at will" and were free to fire them at any time with or without cause and with or without notice. From the nineteenth to the mid-twentieth century, employers could discharge individuals with impunity for a good reason, a bad reason, or no reason at all with little fear of legal reprisal.

Some state legislatures began scrutinizing the fairness of this doctrine beginning in the 1960s. Courts began handing down rulings to safeguard the rights of nonunionized employees. Congress passed specific laws pertaining to occupational health and safety, civil rights, and freedom to complain about unsafe working conditions.

Now there has been a gradual erosion of the employment-at-will doctrine in many areas. Some states have enacted public policy exceptions that make it illegal to fire workers who take time off for jury duty or military service. Some courts have ruled that statements in company manuals, handbooks, and employment applications constitute implied contracts which employers are bound to follow. Other states now recognize the obligation of companies to deal in fairness and good faith with longtime workers. This means, for example, that they are prohibited from terminating workers in retaliation when they tattle on abuses of authority (i.e., whistle-blowing), or denying individuals an economic benefit (a pension that is vested or about to vest, commission, bonus, etc.) that has been earned or is about to become due.

Given the changed legal climate, it is understandable that more people are seeking information about their rights and are fighting back after being fired. For example, they are requesting and receiving benefits that include severance pay greater than the company's last offer, accrued bonuses, continued medical, dental, and life insurance coverage, office space, telephones, secretarial help, resume preparation, and outplacement guidance while looking for a new job.

This section of the book deals with important considerations to remember and follow when you are fired.

In Chapter 6 you will learn how to recognize when you are fired illegally. This is the first step in understanding when you have been exploited and collecting what you are due. Among other subjects, the chapter covers statutory restrictions to firings, public policy exceptions, being fired for serving in the military, and breach of contract actions after being discharged contrary to oral representations or written promises in contracts. You will learn how to gather information from personnel records and discreetly collect evidence to strengthen a claim. Strategies are included to help you recognize the warning signs of an impending firing so you will be in a better position to prepare for the inevitable and maximize a legal case if necessary.

Information in Chapter 7 will help you take charge and employ effective negotiating strategies to maximize severance and termination benefits. The chapter breaks down all the components of a potential package with numerous fall back tips. You will learn the correct way to act, the right questions to ask, and all of the points to clarify at the termination session to increase what can be obtained. Additionally, you will discover what to look out for when requested to sign a release or settlement agreement prepared by your employer.

Chapter 8 covers a number of important post-termination issues affecting all terminated workers. This includes how to win benefits at unemployment hearings, how to resign properly without losing valuable benefits, plus how to avoid being sued for violating restrictive covenants, gag orders in written contracts, or misusing trade secrets and confidential information. Also included are important strategies telling you the steps to take when an ex-employer harms your chances of future employment by defaming you or failing to give a positive reference to a prospective employer.

6

Recognizing When You Have Been Fired Illegally

Not every firing is illegal. If you are fired in a state that still recognizes the employment-at-will doctrine, you may have little bargaining power in getting your job back. However, you are still entitled to monies earned and due before the firing, such as commissions, profit sharing, and perhaps bonuses, even in states that follow this doctrine.

And notwithstanding this law, you may still have a statutory right to fight the discharge. This is because all states have laws protecting workers who are fired due to discrimination, whistle-blowing, and other acts; these laws operate independently of the employment-at-will principle.

The first step in determining when action should be taken is to know the particular laws in your state. This can be done by consulting an experienced employment attorney or investigating the law yourself in order to determine whether you have been fired illegally.

Statutory Restrictions

A variety of federal and state statutes restrict an employer's freedom to discharge employees. These form the legal basis for many challenges to firings. The most comprehensive and significant federal legislation is Title VII of the Civil Rights Act of 1964, as amended by the Equal Employment Opportunity Act of 1972. Under this law, employers cannot fire workers based upon personal characteristics of gender, age, race, color, religion, national origin, and non-disqualifying physical handicaps or mental impairments unrelated to job qualifications. If you believe that your termination from a job was due to discrimination, see Chapter 5 for information on discrimination and the law. The law also protects workers who exercise their First Amendment and other rights from reprisals. If you have lost your job because you spoke up about health and safety conditions, or because you refused to take a lie-detector test, see relevant portions of Chapter 4. Other factors may enter into the legality of a firing, and a discussion of these follows.

Credit Problems

The Consumer Credit Protection Act of 1973 forbids employers from firing workers whose earnings have been subjected to a wage garnishment arising from a single debt. However, employees may presumably be fired after other garnishments. Some states have enacted laws that give workers additional protection; check the applicable law in your state.

Severance and Retirement Benefits

The Employee Retirement Income Security Act of 1974 (ERISA) prohibits the discharge of any employee who is prevented thereby from attaining immediate vested pension rights or who was exercising rights under ERISA and was fired as a result.

You are also entitled to certain rights as a participant in an employer's pension and/or profit-sharing plans. ERISA provides that plan participants are entitled to examine without charge all plan documents, including insurance contracts, annual reports, plan descriptions, and copies of documents filed by the plan with the U.S. Department of Labor. If you request materials from a plan (including summaries of each plan's annual financial report) and do not receive them within 30 days, you may file a suit in federal court. In such a case the court may require the plan administrator to provide the materials and pay you up to $100 a day until you receive them (unless the materials were not sent for reasons beyond the control of the administrator). Consult Chapter 7 for more about your rights under ERISA.

Asserting a Sexual Harassment Claim or Charge of Retaliation

Federal law prohibits employers from retaliation after an employee complains about sexual harassment, files formal charges with the EEOC or a state agency, or commences a lawsuit in court. Consult Chapter 5 for more information about this subject.

Fired as Part of a Large Layoff

If you are part of a massive layoff and not given at least 60 days' notice or 60 days' severance pay, this is a violation under the federal Worker Adjustment and Retraining Notification Act (WARN). This law prohibits employers from ordering a plant closing or massive layoffs until 60 days after the employer has given written notice of this to affected employees or their representatives, the state dislocated-worker unit, and the chief elected official of the unit of local government where the closing or layoff is to occur. If you are fired suddenly and are part of a massive layoff, consult a lawyer immediately to discuss your rights and options under WARN. Information about WARN is contained in Chapter 4.

> **STRATEGY:** *This claim does not only apply to union employees working at plants. As noted earlier, it can be asserted when a private employer lays off hundreds of executives at one time or when a company discharges large numbers of secretaries or dismantles an accounting, business, or financial department due to a reorganization.*

Asserting Union Rights

The National Labor Relations Act prohibits the firing of any employee because of his or her involvement in union activity, because of filing charges, or because of testifying pursuant to the act. Contact the closest regional office of the National Labor Relations Board if you believe you have been fired for one of those reasons.

The law also protects employees who band together to protest about wages, hours, or other working conditions. For example, if a group of nonunion employees complains about contaminated drinking water or about failure to receive minimum wages or overtime pay, their employer could be prohibited from firing them if their charges are proved.

Fired for Serving in the Military

Congress passed the Uniformed Services Employment and Re-employment Rights Act (USERRA) in 1994 to protect the rights of veterans and military personnel. The law, together with revisions in 1996 and 1998 and the Veterans Benefits Improvement Act of 2004, expanded protections previously offered by the Veteran's Re-employment Rights Act and the Military Selective Service Act. The USERRA provides reemployment protection against job denials or demotions for returning and/or injured soldiers, prohibits on-the-job discrimination and retaliation against any employee or applicant because of the individual's past, present, or future application for uniformed services or performance of such service, and provides health insurance protection for service members and their families.

The Civil Rights Division of the U.S. Department of Justice is the agency responsible for enforcing the law and suing employers who fail to promptly reemploy returning service men and women. Complaints alleging violations of the USERRA can be filed with the Veterans-Employment Service of the United States Department of Labor. Veterans have different methods of enforcing USERRA rights depending on whether the employer is a federal agency, state agency, or a private company.

The law covers all people who perform service on a voluntary or involuntary basis. This includes people serving in the Armed Services (including the Coast Guard), the National Guard (both active and inactive-duty training), commissioned corps of the Public Health Service, and the reserve components of each of these services.

The USERRA applies virtually to all U.S. employers regardless of size and covers all jobs. The only civilian jobs not protected are seasonal or temporary jobs with no reasonable expectation that employment would continue. To be covered, you must hold a civilian job; give reasonable notice (preferably by certified mail or in person to prove delivery) of leaving the job for participation in the uniformed services; leave the employer for no more than five years; obtain an honorable discharge (as opposed to a dishonorable or bad conduct discharge); and report back to the civilian job or submitted an application for reemployment in a timely manner.

The law requires immediate reinstatement if you were gone 30 days or less and within a few days if you were away more than 30 days unless business circumstances have changed so much that it is an impossible or unreasonable burden on the employer. You must be offered a job with the same pay, rank, and seniority upon your return. The employer is prohibited from forcing you to use vacation time for military training. Employers are obligated to assist employees who return from military service and cannot deny promotions, seniority, or other benefits because of military obligations. For example, if you were promoted or promised a raise right before a call-up, you must receive a job in line with the promised promotion and raise upon return, together with reinstatement of all benefits and those benefits (e.g., additional pay) that would have been earned if you continued to work.

If requested, health insurance and continuation coverage for a period up to 24 months must be offered to employees on military leave and their families at a cost of no more than 102% of the full premium under the plan. Veterans and their families may choose to go back on the company health plan immediately when they are re-hired with no waiting period and no exclusion for pre-existing conditions.

The law guarantees all defined benefit or defined contribution pension plan benefits that accrued during military service. Employers must prove reasonable accommodation for any disabilities incurred in military service unless the employer can demonstrate undue hardship. Most importantly, the law guarantees job security of at least one year if you worked at the company more than 180 days before taking military service or six months if you worked at the company between 31 and 180 days before serving in the military. This means you cannot be fired for any reason other than misconduct or cause in retaliation for seeking re-employment.

STRATEGY: *The thrust of the USERRA is to prohibit employment discrimination due to past, present or future military membership in all aspects of employment including hiring, retention, promotion, reemployment, discharge and benefits. If you are forced to wait a long period of time (e.g., nine months) before getting your old job back, are fired shortly after returning to work through no fault of your own, are not allowed to use any previously accrued paid vacation or annual leave, are offered an alternative position with substantially less pay or a longer commute, or are denied a promised promotion, contact an official or attorney at the U.S. Department of Labor or private lawyer to enforce your rights. Recoverable damages include getting the job back and receiving lost back pay and benefits such as pension adjustments, vacation pay, forfeited promotional opportunities and a corrected personnel file, plus attorneys' fees, liquidated damages and the costs of the lawsuit, including reasonable expert witness fees. In one recent case for example, an employer reportedly settled a case with an Army National Guard member who was denied a promotion upon returning for $20,000. Thus, get advice where applicable.*

Attending Jury Duty

The Jury System Improvements Act of 1978 forbids employers from firing employees who are impaneled to serve on federal grand juries or petit juries. Most states have enacted similar laws.

Reporting Railroad Accidents

Two federal laws govern here. The Federal Railroad Safety Act prohibits companies from firing workers who file complaints or testify about railroad accidents; the Federal Employer's Liability Act makes it a crime to fire an employee who furnishes facts regarding a railroad accident.

Public Policy Exceptions

Many courts and state legislatures have carved out other exceptions to the employment-at-will doctrine based on public policy considerations. For example, workers are protected from discharge who refuse to violate criminal laws by committing perjury on the employer's behalf, participating in illegal schemes (e.g., price-fixing and other antitrust violations), mislabeling packaged goods, giving false testimony before a legislative committee, altering pollution control reports, or engaging in practices abroad that violate foreign, federal, and state laws. Also protected are workers who perform a public obligation, exercise a public duty (e.g., attend jury duty, vote, supply information to the police about a fellow employee, file workers' compensation claims) or observe the general public policy of the state (e.g., refuse to perform unethical research).

Whistleblowing

Tattling on abuses of authority, or whistleblowing, is now protected conduct under federal and state law. The Sarbanes-Oxley Act (SOX) prohibits publicly traded companies from discharging, demoting, suspending, threatening, harassing, retaliating against, or in any other manner discriminating against their employees in the terms and conditions of employment for providing information or otherwise assisting in the investigation of conduct that they reasonably believe constitutes wire fraud, bank fraud, securities fraud, or violation of any rule or regulation of the Securities and Exchange Commission (SEC).

SOX grants employees a civil cause of action for alleged violations. Cases interpreting the law suggest that an employee's report, complaint, or communication may be covered and the worker protected against retaliation when it describes fraudulent activity against the shareholders that had occurred or was being attempted even though such remarks don't formally or specifically accuse the employer of acting fraudulently.

SOX protection does not apply if you work for a small private employer. Coverage becomes unsure if you work for a nonpublic subsidiary of a public company, but probably doesn't exist when there is no evidence that the parent company is not intimately involved in the subsidiary's employment practices.

An employee alleging retaliation for engaging in protected whistle-blowing activity must file a complaint with the Occupational Safety and Health Administration within 90 days after the alleged violation occurred. This can be done in person, or by mail, fax, or e-mail.

STRATEGY: *File a claim with OSHA immediately if you believe you were victimized by asserting your whistleblower rights. Seek competent legal advice before engaging in whistleblowing activity since the law is often unclear and each case is decided upon its own merits. An employment attorney can help you draft a letter or e-mail for you to send to prove you made a concrete, verifiable complaint that will hold up in court.*

Your credibility in a SOX whistleblower case alleging unnecessary spending, waste, or other inappropriate financial practices will be enhanced if you have access to or copies of financial records or work in the controller's office. Whether you are allowed to retain private company records to prove a claim is not always clear-cut. You must also be able to demonstrate a complaint was made for the right reasons and not because you decided to protect your job after being warned of a possible discharge due to poor performance. That is why it is necessary to consult an experienced employment attorney to discuss your rights, options and strategies.

An advantage of SOX is that the Department of Labor can order the employer to immediately reinstate you (if you were previously fired) for reporting fraud if an investigator determines "probable cause" in your favor. You also have the right to commence a private action in federal district court if the Department of Labor has not issued a final order within 180 days of the filing of the complaint with OSHA. Commentators state this is an extraordinary remedy since the employer may be required to take such action after a probable cause finding even though no formal evidentiary hearing was held allowing the company to dispute the whistleblower's allegations.

The American Recovery and Reinvestment Act of 2009 prohibits employers, including contractors, subcontractors and others conducting business with the government or receiving stimulus funds, from retaliating against an employee who discloses information that he or she reasonably believes evidences gross mismanagement of an agency contract or grant relating to stimulus funds, a substantial and specific danger to public health related to the use of stimulus funds, or a violation of law, rule or regulation related to an agency contract, grant or award related to stimulus funds. Unlike the anti-retaliation provisions found in SOX (which protect only the reporting of fraud or violation of U.S. Securities and Exchange Commission regulations) the act applies to complaints of gross mismanagement, gross waste, or an abuse of authority. Employees who believe they have been subjected to a prohibited reprisal must submit a complaint to the appropriate inspector general of a federal agency under their domain, such as the departments of Agriculture, Commerce, Defense, Education, etc. Seek legal advice from a knowledgeable employment attorney about the unique aspects and features of this law where warranted.

Most states also recognize whistleblowing by statute. These laws typically protect employees from retaliation after they report suspected violations of laws or regulations, and provide specific remedies including reinstatement with back pay, restoration of seniority and lost fringe benefits, litigation costs, attorney fees and fines. Be aware however that not all conduct is protected. New York, for example, only protects plaintiffs who prove they were discharged in retaliation for disclosing a policy of a former employer that constituted an actual violation of the law and created a substantial and specific danger to the public health, such as the improper quality of patient care at a hospital. Thus, the New York law is designed to essentially support the rights of only health care and nursing home employees. Since the law is not broadly applied in New York, many companies have fired workers with impunity who questioned internal management systems, "blew the whistle" without properly investigating the facts, bypassed management, or tattled in bad faith. That is why it is critical to research the unique law in your state and confer with counsel before proceeding in this area.

People who work for federal agencies are also protected from being fired for whistleblowing. In one case a nurse was dismissed after reporting abuses of patients at a Veterans' Administration medical center. She sought reinstatement and damages before a federal review panel. The panel ordered that she be reinstated and awarded her $7,500 in back pay.

The following true cases illustrate examples of firings that were found to be illegal in this area as a public policy exception to the general longstanding employment-at-will rule:

- A quality control director was fired for his efforts to correct false and misleading food labeling by his employer.
- A bank discharged a consumer credit manager who notified his supervisors that the employer's loan practices violated state law.

■ A financial vice-president was fired after reporting to the company's president his suspicions regarding the embezzlement of corporate funds.

Implied Contract Exceptions

In addition to federal and state statutory restrictions on an employer's freedom to discharge employees and the public policy exceptions outlined above, there are newer protections that may restrict the at-will authority of employers to terminate employment without having to state a reason for the termination. This protection is in the form of "implied contract" terms created by representations and promises published by employers in their employee handbooks.

During the first half of the twentieth century, a number of state courts ruled that company retirement, sick leave, and fringe benefit plans described in their employee manuals were enforceable promises of compensation. Today, rights to your employer's retirement and benefit plans are protected by federal law under ERISA (Employee Retirement Income Security Act).

But ERISA did not affect the right of an employer to terminate your job "at will" without having to give the reason for firing you. Employers then began to use their employee handbooks to dress up their images as good places to work by promising job termination only for "good cause" or under specified procedures. A number of state courts began to view these promises as enforceable "implied contracts," even though they may not have been read by the employee until after accepting employment and they were not signed by either party, as is customarily required to enhance contract enforceability.

Many state courts have ruled that the promises in employee handbooks may be legally enforceable as implied contracts. In spite of this progress, many questions still exist. What if the employer promises, then makes a disclaimer, equivalent to taking back the promise? What if after you are hired your employer changes the employee handbook, taking back some of the promises contained in the version in effect when you were hired and upon which you relied? For how long are the promises effective? And there are more questions.

Basically, the first step to protecting your rights in this area is to investigate whether the company has enunciated its firing policies in writing. If such statements exist in work rules, policy manuals, periodic memos, or handbooks, these must be analyzed to determine if the words are sufficiently definite to constitute promises you can rely upon. Courts are sometimes ruling that statements in employee handbooks are not legal promises but merely sales puffery aimed at enhancing morale. And the existence of disclaimers may be legally sufficient to void the enforceability of such promises. So, too, may the same result occur if the company reserves the right to print revisions to the manual after you are working, revisions that eliminate promises contained in earlier editions of the manual you were given, and relied upon, when being hired.

Since each case must be analyzed on its particular facts, if you believe that you are being deprived of your rights as stated in your employer's employee manual, see an attorney experienced in employment rights. The lawyer may find that an implied contract exists.

The implied contract exception to the employment-at-will doctrine may extend to oral promises made at the hiring interview. For example, if you are told by the company president at the hiring interview, "Don't worry, we never fire anyone around here except for a good reason," a legitimate case might be made to fight the firing provided you could prove that the words were spoken and that it was reasonable to rely on them (i.e., that they were spoken seriously and not in jest).

However, be aware that not all oral promises are enforceable against an employer, particularly when you are promised "a job for life." Promises of lifetime employment are rarely upheld due to a legal principle referred to as the statute of frauds. Under this law, all contracts with a job length exceeding one year must be in writing to be enforceable. As a result, courts are generally reluctant to view oral contracts as creating permanent or lifetime employment. Usually, such contracts are viewed as being terminable at will by either party. Thus, a "lifetime contract" may theoretically be terminated after one day!

Some states have laws that limit the duration of an employment contract to a specified number of years (e.g., seven). Thus, if you currently have a contract that you believe is for lifetime employment, it may not be enforceable. Consult an experienced employment attorney if you hope to obtain such a contract in the future.

STRATEGY: *To successfully assert this claim, it is essential to have previously received a copy of the company's manual and read it carefully. If you can prove that promises are clearly contained in a manual, and you relied on them to your detriment, you may be able to assert a valid lawsuit under the laws of some states. Remember, if a company fails to act in accord with published work rules or handbooks, it may be construed as violating an important contract obligation in certain situations.*

Types of promises to look for (which may give you additional rights during and after a firing) include:

- Allowing you to appeal or mediate the decision through an internal nonbinding grievance procedure
- Requiring the employer to give reasonable notice before any firing
- Stating you can be fired for cause only after internal steps toward rehabilitation have been taken and have failed
- Guaranteeing the right to be presented with specific, factual reasons for the discharge before the firing can be effective

Fired in Breach of Contract Rights

If you are fired in a manner inconsistent with or different from rights in a written contract or collective bargaining agreement (if you belong to a union), you may be entitled to damages. If a contract exists, examine it upon termination. The failure to give timely notice as required by a contract, or failure to follow the requirements set forth in a contract, may expose a company to a breach of contract claim. In some instances, it can even cause the agreement to be extended for an additional period.

Implied Covenants of Good Faith and Fair Dealing

Courts in some states have further eroded the at-will doctrine by imposing a duty of good faith and fair dealing on long-term employment relationships. Typically, the duty of employers to act in good faith and fair dealing only applies to cases where an employee has been working for the company for many years or where a person is fired just before he or she is supposed to receive anticipated financial benefits (commissions, bonuses, accrued pension, profit sharing, etc.).

But not all longtime workers are entitled to such protection. Remember that if an employer fires you for a lawful reason (i.e., for cause), the fact that you have been with the company for a substantial time or are eligible for a substantial benefit may not make the firing illegal under a covenant of good faith and fair dealing theory.

STRATEGY: *If you are fired at the end of the year and are denied a year-end bonus or other benefits about to vest in the following year, consult a lawyer immediately to enforce your rights. Pension or stock option benefits about to vest within six months to a year of a firing can often be obtained via negotiations. For a bonus, a stronger claim can be made if you are fired within three months of the expected payment date. Sometimes a company will agree to keep you on unpaid leave status during the appropriate period as a way of qualifying. Speak to your lawyer about this negotiating strategy for more details.*

If you cannot get your job back using a violation of good faith and fair dealing argument, you or a lawyer may be able to negotiate for you to obtain benefits you were expecting and would have received but for the firing. You should also consider asserting a claim for benefits based on ERISA rights. However, if an employer fires you for a lawful reason—that is, for cause—the fact that you are about to become eligible for a substantial benefit may not make the firing illegal.

Firing Due to a Legitimate Illness or Absence

You cannot be fired if you were injured on the job and file a workers' compensation claim, or are absent for a medical reason relating to pregnancy or for taking maternity leave of less than 12 weeks in any given one-year period (in violation of the federal FMLA if you work for an employer with more than 50 full-time employees). However, an employer may have the right to fire a worker who is excessively absent due to illness. In that case a viable option might be for you to file for and collect benefits under the company's short or long-term disability plan.

The above legal theories are exceptions to the traditional employment-at-will rule and may be useful in recovering greater benefits or damages when you are fired. The law varies greatly from state to state, and each case warrants attention based upon its particular facts and circumstances. However, this information should help you determine if you have been fired illegally or unfairly. For example, you should now understand many of the instances when firings become suspect. These include:

- When you are about to receive a large commission or vested stock option rights
- If the company fails to act in a manner specified in its employment applications, promotional literature, policy statements, "welcome aboard" letters, handbooks, manuals, written contracts, correspondence or memos, benefit statements, or disciplinary rules
- If you are fired right after returning from an illness, pregnancy, or jury duty
- If you are fired after complaining about a safety violation or other wrongdoing
- If you are over 40, belong to a minority, are partially disabled, or are a female and believe you were fired primarily because of such personal characteristics

- If you are a longtime worker and believe the firing was unjustified
- If you received a verbal promise of job security or other rights that the company failed to fulfill

In many situations the company may still have a right to fire based on the traditional employment-at-will rule. But even in those states that adhere to the rule, you can obtain additional benefits by demonstrating your knowledge of the above exceptions and appealing to the company's sense of decency and fair play.

Since laws change rapidly, consult with an experienced employment attorney or research current case decisions and statutory developments in your state to be sure you know your rights in this area whenever you are fired or treated unfairly.

Many employers fire workers without warning—for obvious reasons. By firing workers suddenly, employers believe they will keep workers off balance, without sufficient time to anticipate the discharge and plan ahead.

No matter how you learn the news, it is important to remain calm so you can carefully consider your options. The fact that you are fired suddenly (as opposed to being given a warning) does not mean you should accept fewer benefits than you deserve.

The first question to ask yourself when you are fired is whether the employer had a valid legal basis for doing so. The preceding material mentioned various instances where employers are prohibited from discharging workers, even those employed at will. However, these are not the only prohibited kinds of actions. For example, do you have a written contract? If so, what does it say? Employers cannot fire you in a manner inconsistent with the terms of the written contract. Thus, if you are hired for a definite term (for example, one year), you cannot be fired prior to the expiration of the contract term except for cause.

Written Promises of Job Security in Contracts

Review what your contract says about termination. For example, many companies have written contracts with their executives. Some of these agreements run for a period of one year and state that if timely notice of termination is not given at least 30 days prior to the expiration of the one-year term, the contract will automatically be extended and renewed under the same terms and conditions for an additional year. If the company fires the executive two weeks before the end of the year, or forgets to send timely notice, the employee could have a legal basis to insist on working for an additional year. He or she would then have a strong claim to negotiate for additional compensation rather than filing a lawsuit.

This is illustrated by the following example: "This agreement is effective for a period of one year commencing on February 1, 2011, and terminating on January 31, 2012." If so, the employer can only terminate you prior to the effective termination date—January 31, 2012—for cause.

The following are examples of cause that justify contract terminations:

- Theft or dishonesty
- Falsifying records or information
- Punching another employee's time card
- Leaving the job or company premises without prior approval from a supervisor
- Insubordination or disrespect of company work rules and policies
- Willful refusal to follow the directions of a supervisor (unless doing so would endanger health or safety)
- Assault, unprovoked attack, or threats of bodily harm against others

- Use of drugs or possession of alcoholic beverages on company premises or during company-paid time while away from the premises

- Reporting to work under the influence of drugs or alcohol

- Disclosing confidential and proprietary information to unauthorized third parties

- Unauthorized possession of weapons and firearms on company property

- Intentionally making errors in work, negligently performing duties, or willfully hindering or limiting production

- Sleeping on the job

- Excessive lateness or irregular attendance at work

- Failing to report absences

- Sexually harassing or abusing others

- Making secret profits

- Misusing trade secrets, customer lists, and other confidential information

Does the contract restrict you from working for a competitor or establishing a competing business after termination? This is referred to as a restrictive covenant or covenant not to compete, which may or may not be enforceable depending on the particular facts and circumstances. (Restrictive covenants are discussed in detail in Chapter 8.)

Thus, remember that your rights may be enhanced or diminished depending upon the type of contract in existence.

Oral Promises of Job Security

Courts in some states are ruling that employees have the right to rely on oral representations made before hiring or during the working relationship. Interviewers, recruiters, and other intake personnel are often careless and make statements that can be construed as promises of job security. They sometimes use words such as "permanent employment," "job for life," or "just cause termination" and make broad statements concerning job longevity and assurances of continued employment (such as "Don't worry—no one around here ever gets fired except for a good reason.") or specific promises regarding career opportunities.

When such statements are sufficient to be characterized as promises of job security, when you can prove the actual words were spoken, and when you can demonstrate that you relied on such statements to your detriment, you may be able to contest the firing if you work in a state that recognizes this exception to the employment-at-will doctrine. The following actual case is a good illustration.

An executive worked for a company for 32 years without a written contract. The man was suddenly fired. He sued his company and argued that he had done nothing wrong to justify the firing. At the trial the executive proved that:

- The company's president told him several times that he would continue to be employed if he did a good job
- The company had a policy of not firing executives except for cause
- The man was never criticized or warned that his job was in jeopardy
- He had a commendable track record, his employment history was excellent, and he had received periodic merit bonuses, raises, and promotions

The executive won the case because the facts created an implied promise that the company could not arbitrarily terminate him.

STRATEGY: *Try to remember and document what was said, when, where, who said it, and the names of any witness(es) who were present whenever such promises were made. This may help your case at a later date if you are fired in a manner inconsistent with such promises.*

A word of caution: Some employers design employment applications or contracts that specify that employment is at will, that no one has made additional promises regarding job security, and that you acknowledge not receiving such promises. You may have a difficult job arguing this point (regardless of verbal promises) when you sign such a document.

Written Promises of Job Security in Company Manuals

If company manuals promise job security, has the employer followed stated policy? It is important to review all manuals, handbooks, memos, correspondence, benefit statements, "welcome aboard" letters, employment applications, policy statements, and disciplinary rules. Know what they say regarding firings. For example:

- Can you appeal the decision?
- Must the employer give you a warning before firing?
- Are there specific rules regarding severance?
- Can you be fired at will or only for cause?
- Is there a system of progressive discipline, or can you be fired immediately without notice?
- Are there internal grievance policies?
- Can you arbitrate the dispute rather than litigate?
- Do you have the right to receive a written reason for the firing?
- Do you have the right to review your personnel file after the firing?

You may be able to contest the firing and sue for damages if the employer has favorable policies in writing that aren't followed. Thus, review all company policies as soon as possible to determine if promises have been broken.

STRATEGY: *Sometimes it is difficult to review these materials after a discharge. You may not be on the premises and may be unable to obtain such documents because many employers insist that* *ex-employees return all company property upon being fired. If this is the case, ask friendly coworkers to lend you their materials for review. Photocopy relevant text as soon as possible. Better still, if you have suspicions you may be fired, plan ahead by gathering copies of these materials before you are asked to leave. Bring this information to your lawyer at the initial consultation. This will enable him or her to give you a more accurate opinion as to whether the employer has violated an implied contract term. For example, if the employer has a written policy allowing terminated employees to appeal the firing to a grievance committee, you may wish to do so. If the employer refuses to allow you to file such an appeal despite its stated policy, you might be able to contest the firing as a result.*

Whenever an individual is fired, the author seeks an advantage for a client by scrutinizing all company policies regarding firings to see if they were followed. If not, this is used as leverage in negotiating for additional severance and other benefits.

Personnel Records

Some states permit workers to review and copy the contents of their personnel files. In such states an employee is to be given access to personnel files used to determine his or her qualifications, promotions, pay raises, discipline, and discharge. Other states allow both employees and terminated employees to inspect personnel files maintained by employers. Some states also permit inspection by a representative designated by the employee.

Additionally, most states give employees the right to review information supplied to the employer by a credit reporting agency under the Fair Credit Reporting Act of 1971, as well as to review all medical and insurance information in the file. However, confidential items such as letters of reference, records of internal investigations regarding theft, misconduct, or crimes not pertaining to the employee, and confidential information about other employees are generally prohibited from being viewed.

Sometimes these files do not support firing decisions because they contain favorable performance appraisals, recommendations, and memos. If you can only be fired for cause and the employer gives you specific reasons why you were fired, your file may demonstrate that such reasons are factually incorrect and/or legally insufficient. If this occurs, you may have a strong case against the employer for breach of contract.

STRATEGY: *Try to make copies of all pertinent documents in your file while working for the employer (particularly favorable records). If you have received excellent performance reviews and appraisals and the file indicates you received large merit salary increases and other benefits, you may be able to contest the firing and be rehired. Or you may use this information to successfully negotiate more severance than the company is offering.*

In some states you can bring legal proceedings to expunge false information that is contained in your file and is known by the employer to be false. These states even allow you to collect attorney fees, fines, court costs, and damages in the event you discover false information or records of off-premises activities (political, associational, etc.) that do not interfere with your work duties.

Refusals to Pay Expected Financial Benefits

Many companies fire workers to deprive them of the fruits of their labors. This includes a year-end bonus, commissions, wages, accrued vacation, or pension benefits that are about to vest. In some states, if an employer fires someone just before he or she is supposed to receive anticipated benefits, the firing may be illegal.

Even if the firing is legal, you may be entitled to collect this money in negotiations or during a lawsuit. For example, the Department of Labor in most states requires employers to pay accrued vacation and earned wages to terminated workers. Additionally, you may be able to receive a pension if you are about to qualify for a vested pension but are fired. This is because employers are forbidden in most states and under the federal Employment Retirement Income Security Act from firing longtime workers who are close to receiving such benefits. Consult an experienced employment attorney immediately if you believe you have been victimized in this area.

Salespeople who earn commissions are now receiving additional statutory protections in this area. Many states now require that companies promptly pay commissions to their independent sales representatives (or agents) who are fired. When prompt payment is not made, companies may be liable for penalties up to three times the commission amount plus reasonable attorney fees and court costs if the case is eventually litigated.

Additionally, you may have a valid claim if you are fired right before the payment of a year-end bonus. Some employers require workers to be employed on the day bonus checks are issued as a condition of payment. However, workers are sometimes fired unfairly and are denied bonuses that have been earned. The author represented a man who had worked a full year and was expecting a bonus of $22,500 to be paid on February 15 of the following year. The company's policy required workers to be employed on the date of payment in order to receive the bonus. The client was fired on February 10 for alleged misconduct due to an unauthorized absence taken the day before. The employer refused to pay severance or the bonus.

I proved that the client had a justifiable excuse for missing work on the day in question and argued that the employer's policy of paying earned bonuses only if the worker was still employed the following year was unfair. Although I was unable to obtain his reemployment, the client obtained severance pay equivalent to two weeks for every year of employment, as well as the expected bonus.

STRATEGY: *Always request a bonus if you are fired close to the end of the year and are entitled to a bonus by contract or job history (i.e., you consistently received bonuses in prior years). If the employer tells you that bonuses are only paid if you are still working on the day the check is issued and that you were fired before then, argue that you would have received the bonus but for the firing. And argue that you are entitled to a pro rata share of the bonus if you are fired close to but before the end of the year. For example, if you are fired on December*

1, negotiate to receive eleven-twelfths of the bonus you were expecting.

Offers of Severance Pay

Although there is generally no legal obligation to pay severance monies, most employers in the United States do offer such payments when a firing is due to a group layoff, business conditions outside the employee's control (such as reorganization), or reasons other than employee misconduct. However, there may be a legal obligation to pay severance when:

- You have a written contract stating that severance will be paid
- Oral promises are given regarding severance pay
- The employer voluntarily promises to pay severance
- The employer has a policy of paying severance and this is documented in a company manual or employee handbook
- The employer has paid severance to other employees in similar firings and thereby has created a precedent

If you are fired and are not offered severance, it is advisable to request a meeting with a qualified representative of the employer to discuss clarification regarding severance and available wage equivalents.

Many employers are fearful of the increasing amount of employee-related litigation and are flexible in easing the departure of terminated individuals. Thus, you should begin the discussion by appealing to corporate decency and fair play. For example, it might be stated that severance pay is needed because you anticipate it will take longer to find a suitable job than the amount of severance currently offered. Always be polite and act professionally; being vindictive or making threats won't solve anything.

Most employers have different policies regarding severance depending on the industry and company. However, it is recommended that you attempt to receive one month of severance for every year worked as a starting point. If this can be achieved, you can leave the company knowing that you have received a fair severance offer.

Although severance pay is a common problem for individual employees whose employment has been terminated, the extensive merger and acquisition activity in recent years has caused the issue of severance pay to become one of large-scale financial and legal significance. If your company is sold and you continue to work for the new employer, you may be able to assert rights under ERISA and welfare benefit plans in the event the new employer denies severance to a group of workers at a later date.

Additionally, you may have grounds for a valid lawsuit in the event you have a vested pension but are fired just weeks short of becoming entitled to greater severance, larger monthly pension payments, and improved medical and insurance benefits.

Cases demonstrate the responsibility of employers to comply with all pension laws and ERISA regarding severance when a business is sold or when company policy has created an expectation that the purchasing company will continue an established severance policy crediting employees with prior years of service from the selling company.

If you begin working for a new employer who ceases business operations (i.e., declares bankruptcy) within a relatively short period of time after the hiring, you may have a valid claim of severance from the selling company under certain conditions.

Courts are beginning to recognize the rights of employees to severance in many situations, particularly when there is a massive layoff or group sale of assets due to a merger or acquisition.

STRATEGY: *You should not automatically acquiesce to a denial of benefits if you are fired and not offered severance, whatever your particular situation. Most workers are now receiving severance when they are fired; others are negotiating and receiving greater severance than the company's first offer. Statistics from the author's law practice support this.*

Reliance on Hiring Promises

What if you resign a current job because you are offered a position with a new employer, but the job offer is then withdrawn? What happens if you are fired immediately after starting the new job? Unfortunately, this happens to thousands of workers each year in the United States.

Fortunately, you may be protected by a legal principle called promissory estoppel. In one case, for example, the court rejected the company's argument that employers should be permitted to change their minds regarding job offers when they hire at will.

The author represented a man who flew to Texas and was offered a prestigious sales position. He resigned from a lucrative job to begin working for the new employer. Two weeks later he was fired when the company stated he "didn't fit in." The man attempted to get his old job back but was unsuccessful. The author was hired to collect damages resulting from this unfair treatment. The case was settled satisfactorily out of court after a lawsuit was commenced on his behalf.

STRATEGY: *Always obtain a written contract with a new employer before you resign from a current employer. The contract should guarantee employment for a minimum period of time (such as three months) to avoid exploitation.*

Recognize that you may have rights if you are offered a job and rely on this promise of employment to your detriment. Consult an experienced employment attorney immediately if this happens to you.

Issues for Older Workers

The Age Discrimination in Employment Act (ADEA) prohibits employers from firing workers between the ages of 40 and 70 because of their age. Similar discrimination laws have also been enacted in most states.

If you are an older worker and are being pressured to retire voluntarily by accepting an early retirement option or face the risk of being fired, demoted, or given a cut in pay, you may have grounds for an age discrimination complaint with the Equal Employment Opportunity Commission (EEOC) or a state agency such as the division of human rights. See Chapter 5 for information on age discrimination and the law.

Early retirement programs in and of themselves are legal and do not violate federal age discrimination laws so long as participation is voluntary. However, if you are offered a financial package containing early retirement inducements, be sure that it really contains worthwhile incentives such as additional pension benefits (i.e., extra years of age and service for pension calculations), lump sum severance payments (e.g., an extra year's pay), cash inducements, and retirement health programs.

Avoid accepting early retirement packages that penalize you if you return to the workplace with a new job. Some companies permanently discontinue health coverage when the employee takes another job where coverage is provided. The problem here is that you could wind up working for the new employer for a short period of time (say, six months) and find yourself out of a job. Accepting this condition would cause you to forfeit valuable health benefits that are essential during your older years.

Be aware that if you are offered lifetime retiree benefits, the company may seek to cut or eliminate such benefits in the future, especially when it reserves the right to do so by contract. Many employers are successfully circumventing their obligations in this area. Never assume such benefits are sacred and will continue in the future undisturbed. Get legal advice if the offer of lifetime benefits is an important consideration in your decision to accept an early retirement package.

If the employer offers decreasing benefits with increasing age, this may penalize you unfairly. Before accepting an early retirement package, understand that you may have a difficult time finding a new job or starting your own business because of your age. You should also recognize that inflation may eat away at your pension if you don't have a secure financial nest egg. Finally, if you are an older worker being asked to sign a waiver or release in exchange for more severance or early retirement inducements, be aware that the federal Older Workers Benefit Protection Act may give you added protection and should be reviewed with your employment attorney.

Massive Layoffs and Plant Closings

You may be entitled to receive WARN benefits including salary and/or severance for an additional period up to 60 days if you weren't given ample notice before losing your job. The application of the Worker Adjustment and Retraining Notification Act is detailed in Chapter 4.

Speak to an experienced employment attorney immediately if you believe that the law is not being properly followed in your case. Additionally, you may be entitled to receive free training in your local community where the plant closing or discharge en masse occurs. Contact the nearest U.S. Department of Labor office for further details if you are victimized in this area.

Recognize the Warning Signs

Experts suggest that it takes roughly one month for every $10,000 of salary to find a comparable job after a termination. Thus, for example, if you make $50,000 a year, chances are you may not be reemployed within five months after being fired. While unemployment benefits will provide you with several hundred dollars of weekly income up to a maximum of 99 weeks in most states, anticipate that you may have problems paying a mortgage or rent and other regular expenses if you do not have substantial savings

That is why it is essential to heed the warning signs as soon as possible. The time to make the right moves, such as trying to establish a line of credit (which is always easier to get while you are employed) or selling a large house to avoid a potentially devastating cash drain (which takes at least several months after the decision to sell is made), is before a firing whenever possible. It is also easier to get copies of important information and documentation from your files while you are still on the payroll.

Being aware can help you detect early signs of an impending discharge. If you are left out of important meetings, hear whispers when you walk down the hall, your boss doesn't look you squarely in the eye anymore, you are not promoted, do not receive an expected raise or promotion, are given unfavorable performance reviews or final warnings, or aren't paid an expected year-end bonus, the employer may be telling you that you are headed for the door. If your senses tell you something negative is going on, it is time to swing into action.

Even if your concerns are unfounded, the following strategies will not harm you in any way but may help prioritize your efforts to protect the current job or enable you to look more effectively for a new one.

1. REVIEW YOUR CONTRACT. As previously mentioned, if you signed a written contract, reread it. Review what it says about termination. For example, can you be fired at any time without cause, or must the employer send you written notice before the effective termination date? Many independent sales agents, brokers, and reps receive written contracts from their principals requiring either party to give 30 to 60 days' notice before the contract can be effectively terminated. Remember that the failure to give you timely notice, or any notice at all, may place the company in breach of contract if notification is required. To map out an effective action plan, be sure you know exactly what the contract says.

You are increasing your chances of recovering damages in a lawsuit when you are hired for a fixed term of employment. This is because the burden of proof falls on the employer to demonstrate the specific actions constituting a legitimate reason to fire before the expiration of the fixed term. Often it is difficult to do this. Thus, where possible, always try to negotiate for a fixed term of employment before being hired.

Review if the contract prohibits additional benefits on termination. Some agreements specify that employees have no additional claims for damages after discharge. Others place a limit on benefits (e.g., "Upon termination for any reason, the employee will be limited to receiving severance equivalent to two weeks' pay for each full year of service"). By signing a written contract containing such a clause, you may be minimizing your post-termination negotiating power.

Does the contract restrict you from working for a competitor or establishing a competing business after termination? This is referred to as a restrictive covenant or covenant not to compete, which may or may not be enforceable depending on the particular facts and circumstances.

Remember that your rights may be enhanced or diminished depending on the type of contract in existence. That is why it is important always to negotiate a fair agreement before accepting a job.

STRATEGY: *If you remember signing a formal employment contract but do not have a copy, discreetly ask the human resources department to make you a copy of the original. If you are asked why, just say that you misplaced or accidentally destroyed your copy recently and need it for your records.*

2. ACCUMULATE AND SAVE COPIES OF ALL PERTINENT DOCUMENTS AND RECORDS.

Now is the time to collect all correspondence, records, and documents that may confirm your deals, the company's actions or promises (e.g., you have been told, "You are doing a great job here, so we would never fire you without adequate notice except for cause"), or show that you are doing a great job (e.g., a recent letter from the company president thanking you for a job well done or recommending you for a raise or promotion). Accumulating such evidence can help your case immeasurably in the event you are fired unfairly and decide to take legal action down the road.

Hopefully, you have taken steps right along to indicate your dissatisfaction with unfair company actions so that a court will not conclude that you accepted such actions by your conduct. As an example, many employees refuse to sign unfair and subjective employee evaluations. This is not recommended. Rather, it is better to sign the review with a notation that you are attaching a rebuttal as part of the evaluation. This is the way to properly document your dissatisfaction, and the rebuttal can protect you against subsequent illegal action by the company.

Firing and/or disciplining workers is not as simple as it used to be. Because many terminated individuals are now consulting lawyers, companies are being instructed to "set you up" (i.e., document problems in your personnel file). The reason is that when employers have failed to note performance problems on appraisals and lack sufficient documentation to prove inadequate job performance, they may not have a legal basis for firing an employee (since a poor performance excuse may then be viewed as a pretext) and may be leaving the company open to a ready-made claim of gender, race, or age discrimination if the employee fits into one of these protected categories. Thus, it is a good idea to protest (always in writing preferably) company actions you do not agree with.

If you believe that a future lawsuit with your employer is inevitable, get the edge by planning ahead. It is easier to obtain pertinent documents, including a copy of your employment contract, employee handbook, performance reviews, and favorable recommendations contained in your file from coworkers and management while you are still working at the company.

The author represented a man who worked for a prestigious financial institution. He was part of a four-member team responsible for devising and selling tax shelters on behalf of the employer. The man had worked about nine and a half years for the company and was earning an annual base salary of $125,000. Each year he had consistently received large year-end bonuses (the previous year's bonus had been $50,000).

The man was suddenly fired in late November. The company claimed that his work performance was not satisfactory and that he did "not fit the image of an investment banker." The client hired me because he believed his job performance was excellent. He also felt cheated because the company offered no severance benefits, would not allow him to receive a pension that was due to vest within six months, and refused to pay him a bonus for the substantial portion of the current year he had worked.

After thoroughly investigating the matter, I inquired if the client had collected copies of pertinent information from his personnel file. Fortunately, he produced a number of excellent performance reviews. In addition, he was able to locate a memo that had been circulated throughout the company and delivered to the company's president. The memo congratulated each member of his group by name for placing a large tax shelter that year, and each member (including my client) was cited for outstanding work.

During negotiations, management was informed of the existence of this memo. I argued that in view of the client's history of receiving large raises and year-end bonuses, excellent performance evaluations, and the favorable memo, his firing was unjustified and was probably done to save the company a large sum of money. The company was advised that a jury would probably take a dim view of what had transpired.

After several meetings with management and opposing counsel, an out-of-court settlement was obtained that included a year-end bonus, severance pay representing one month's salary for every year of employment, the company's agreement to qualify my client for a substantial pension, continuation of employer-paid medical insurance for six months, substantial payment for an outplacement employment search (up to $7,500) by a reputable firm, and a favorable recommendation in writing.

It is highly doubtful I would have been able to negotiate such a favorable settlement without a copy of the "kudo" memo collected by the client. Thus, never underestimate the importance of collecting all favorable documents while working for a company.

Even if you did not keep copies of such material, don't despair entirely. Employees may have access to their personnel files as part of the discovery process during a lawsuit even in those states that do not ordinarily allow access.

Some states have passed laws allowing employees access to their personnel records. If your state permits this, it is a good idea to view information in your file and correct incomplete or inaccurate information before you are terminated. In some of these states, you may not be allowed to copy any of the documents in the file except those you previously signed (e.g., an employment application or a performance review), but you are allowed to make notes. And in other states, you may not even have the right to review your records, so check the law in your state. (The Federal Privacy Act, which deals mainly with access to employee records, forbids federal government employers from disclosing any information contained in employee files without the written consent of the employee in question. Discuss the ramifications of this federal law with your employment attorney.)

Even in states where access to records is not permitted, employers are generally prohibited from distributing confidential information, such as medical records, to nonessential third parties and prospective employers, and you are generally permitted to inspect all your files containing confidential medical and credit information. Some union employees covered under collective bargaining agreements have the right to examine their own records and to be informed of what information is used in making decisions relevant to their employment.

Since it is often difficult to review the contents of your personnel file, make and save copies of all documents the minute you receive them so you don't have to retrieve them later. In most arbitrations and lawsuits, employers are prohibited from introducing "memos in the file" that were never read or signed by you. This means that the company cannot attempt to prove an issue at a trial, such as your alleged misconduct, by submitting to a judge or jury a warning memo that was never given to you or that you never saw. During litigation, a few employers advise supervisors to prepare harmful documents after the fact, so be aware and advise your lawyer about this.

Some states permit workers to place a rebuttal statement in their personnel file if incorrect information is discovered. Other states allow employees to do this when the employer will not delete such comments. A few states have laws that require employers to send copies of rebuttal statements to prospective employers or other parties when information pertaining to workers or their employment history is conveyed. Since each state treats the subject differently, review your state's law.

Some states require employers to seek workers' approval before employee records can be collected, distributed, or destroyed, and it may be illegal to distribute personal information without your consent. With respect to medical records and investigations, the law generally recognizes that a duty of confidentiality can arise to protect this information and avoid dissemination to nonessential third parties. Under emerging state laws and case decisions, employers who request medical information may be liable for the tort of intrusion and for the tort of public disclosure of private data. Several states have recognized a claim for negligent maintenance of personnel files when files containing inaccurate medical information are made available to third parties. For example, Connecticut has enacted a statute requiring employers to maintain medical records separately from personnel files and permitting employees to review all medical and insurance information in their individual files. Thus, know your rights and review your state's law.

3. MAINTAIN A DIARY. It is easier to remember important incidents while they are happening instead of trying to remember and writing them down later. Your main focus in any diary is to reconstruct harmful events, workplace discrimination, oral promises of job security, or statements to show you are being treated unfairly by a supervisor or manager. Keeping a regular record of promises made and not kept concerning your job can assist you if you decide later to pursue legal action. A diary will also help construct a time frame and chronology of important events and ensure that your memories are accurate. Thus, wherever possible, if you sense your job is in jeopardy, start making daily entries such as the date, time, place, and comments you heard, noting exactly what was said and the names of witnesses who overheard the statements.

Interviewers, recruiters, and officers make oral statements that can be construed as promises of job security. They sometimes use words like "permanent employment" or "job for life," make broad statements concerning job longevity, and give assurances of continued employment or specific promises about career opportunities. When such statements are sufficient to be characterized as promises of job security, when you can prove the actual words were spoken, and when you can demonstrate that you relied on such statements to your detriment, you may be able to contest a firing. The following true case illustrates this.

An executive who worked for a company for 32 years without a written contract was suddenly fired. The man sued the company and argued that he had done nothing wrong to justify the firing. At the trial, he proved that the company's president told him several times that he would continue to be employed if he did a good job. He also proved that the company had a policy of not firing executives except for cause and that he was never criticized or warned that his job was in jeopardy. He also proved that he had a commendable track record, his employment history was excellent, and he had received periodic merit bonuses, raises, and promotions. He won the case because the facts created an implied promise that the company could not arbitrarily terminate him.

Try to document what was said, when, where, who said it, and the names of witnesses who were present whenever promises were made. This may help your case at a later date if you are fired in a manner inconsistent with such promises and your state recognizes this exception to the employment at-will rule. Maintaining a contemporaneous diary will help you prove that such statements were actually made because you will be able to remember them in court and your recollection may be viewed as being more reliable because you could refer to a diary.

4. CONSIDER MEETING WITH A LAWYER BEFORE YOU RESIGN OR ARE FIRED. Show the lawyer the documentation you have accumulated. If you perceive problems that are valid, your lawyer may be able to recommend additional strategies, such as sending a final letter of protest or requesting a meeting to discuss and attempt to resolve the difficulties. These options may not be available after your firing and can enhance your case if litigation proves necessary

The lawyer can give you a better evaluation of the possibility of success with your case when he or she has viewed all pertinent records and documents. That is why it is important to collect key evidence for presentation to your lawyer before a case is litigated. Be aware of this and act accordingly.

5. START LOOKING FOR NEW EMPLOYMENT. The best time to seek reemployment is while you are still working. There is less pressure to find a replacement job when a steady paycheck is still coming in. You also have the luxury of not appearing as hungry, since the prospective employer knows you are currently employed. This means you may have more clout and be able to command a higher salary or more benefits during negotiations.

People often ask if it is legal to look for a job while they are still employed. The answer is yes, provided you do so discreetly and not on company time. Thus, schedule your telephone calls and interviews during lunch hours or after work. If you have to prepare for and attend an important interview, take a vacation day.

If you are employed full-time but also work for a competitor or hold another job, that is probably illegal without your employer's knowledge and consent. For instance, one salesperson was accused of violating his duty of loyalty by distributing a competitor's catalog to his customers while still working for his company.

In preparation for quitting a job, you are generally allowed to look for another job without advising your employer. You can quietly advise customers and friends of your intention to leave and even take minor steps to compete and organize a new company while still working (e.g., prepare stationary and business cards or arrange for a new telephone number if you are going into business for yourself).

What you cannot do is take active steps, such as solicit business for the new entity, while on your present employer's payroll, hurt its reputation by talking poorly about your employer, or lie down on the job by not taking orders or working as diligently as before.

Start calling business contacts for leads. Prepare long and short lists of all the people you would call if you did lose a job and start calling them regularly. It is essential to maintain an active network of business associates, and now is the time to start. You may want to make a personal copy of your Rolodex™ for this purpose.

Update your résumé. Schedule an appointment with a career counselor or an employment agency for advice and guidance.

In addition, some employees believe that if they are fired illegally, they can delay going back to work because their former employer will have to pay them damages. This approach is wrong for two reasons. First, a person should never assume that his or her lawsuit will succeed. Second, even if you sue your former employer and win, your damages will be cut back severely if you fail to mitigate your damages — i.e., you fail to take active steps to find comparable employment.

What is comparable employment? The answer may be somewhat subjective, but, for example, a terminated physician cannot be required to accept employment as a gardener to mitigate her damages.

By the same token, a security guard at an office complex would probably not be justified in failing to pursue or accept employment as a security guard at a residential complex. The result here would be different if the security guard position at the residential complex required an additional 15-20 hours per week of work. The bottom line is that the new position should be similar to the former position, but it need not be identical. Therefore, do not pass up a job that is similar to the one from which you were terminated.

Finally, if you think you were fired in violation of your rights, either contractual or statutory, it is essential that you maintain a post-termination diary documenting all of your efforts to find suitable alternative employment. Every letter, phone call, newspaper clipping, review of websites, etc. should be documented. The more detail the better. If you file a lawsuit and have not thoroughly documented your efforts to find suitable alternative employment, the judge or jury will likely conclude that you failed to mitigate your damages, and any award that you might have otherwise received may be substantially reduced as a result. Don't make this mistake.

6.   REMOVE PERSONAL DOCUMENTS FROM YOUR OFFICE.
After being fired, you may have difficulty removing personal effects and business materials from your office. In fact, many employers, after suddenly notifying you that you are fired, will escort you back to your office and stay there to approve the materials you want to pack up and take home. Plan ahead to avoid this potential problem.

The author represented a female employee who resigned from a job. She returned the next morning to retrieve the personal contents from her office. However, many of these items were not given to her. The company claimed that boxes of expensive items (including textbooks, course materials, and technical manuals) were purchased with company funds and remained the property of the company. The woman hired the author to retrieve these valuable materials.

You can avoid this kind of aggravation by being discreet and removing valuable items now. But be sure not to take company property to avoid being accused of theft or conversion.

7.   MAKE SURE THAT YOU ARE NOT IN POSSESSION OF ANY CONFIDENTIAL INFORMATION OR TRADE SECRETS.
The computerization of the workplace has caused some subtle but very important changes in the employee-employer relationship. Unlike the workers of yesteryear, most of today's workers conduct at least some amount of business from cell phones and home computers, blurring the physical boundaries of the employment relationship. This blurring of the boundaries means that the separation process is often more complicated than it used to be.

Hoping to dissuade former employees from suing, many employers go on the offensive when accused of violating the law. It is therefore crucial that employees act calmly and appropriately when fired, even if the firing is unlawful and unfair. After being fired, employees who have signed agreements restricting their post-employment access to confidential information should therefore promptly and calmly offer to return any confidential computer files or other company documents that they possess, and request a written confirmation that such information was in fact returned. Remember, information does not have to rise to the level of a trade secret to be confidential. You may need the assistance of a lawyer to determine what is and what is not confidential.

If the employee has a claim that is at least partially evidenced by documents in his possession, then the employee would be arguably justified in not destroying or deleting copies of all confidential information returned to the employer. For example, if the employee has e-mails to and from the client which corroborate his claim that he facilitated the sale and therefore deserves the commission, he will understandably be reluctant to part with such information for fear that the former employer would destroy such evidence. Likewise, an hourly employee may have e-mails or computer files which contain data showing when it was created or modified, and which can therefore be used as evidence to help corroborate that he worked the hours that he said he did. Or perhaps the employee has e-mails evidencing unlawful discrimination. Moreover, the employee may be legitimately concerned about defending himself in the event the employer files a lawsuit claiming that the employee never had any right to be in possession of materials he returned to the employer immediately after his termination; if the employee destroys every copy of the computer files and e-mails transmitted to the employer after his termination, how will he have any proof as to what was and was not returned?

If any of these circumstances is present, the employee should (1) immediately return copies of all of the computer files and e-mails in question, and (2) offer to return or destroy his own copies of such information provided that the employer can think of some way in which the employee can be truly assured that such evidence will be available later on for the employee to prosecute his claims or defend against the employer's claims. If the employee is represented by counsel, he may wish to ask his attorney to draft a stipulation stating that only his counsel will have access to the files and will only discuss them with his client to the extent that it is necessary for counsel to understand the parties' claims and defenses. If the employer does not agree to such a stipulation, at least there will be a record of the employee having made a good faith effort. And while there is no guarantee that a court would overlook the employee's failure to immediately destroy all copies of his own copies of the e-mails and computer files, the odds of being punished for preserving data needed to prosecute a claim or defend against a claim is greatly reduced, especially if the good faith steps outlined above are followed.

A former employee has no right to acquire documents or information directly from his former employer unless such information is distributed freely by the former employer. Nor is a current employee free to go digging into his employer's confidential files to collect information before an impending termination. If the confidential information in question was not in the employee's possession in the course of performing his job duties, but rather as a result of surreptitiously rifling through the employer's files, then the employee's claim may end up being dismissed, and the employee may be held liable for theft.

In addition, if you receive any company related phone calls on your personal cell phone or e-mails on your personal computer, be sure to promptly forward them to the company, and maintain a record of your having done so. If a company client asks you what happened, simply state that you are no longer with the company, and do not say or do anything to denigrate the ex-employer. If a company client asks you to do work for them, you may be prohibited from doing so if you are bound by a restrictive covenant. Further, regardless of whether there is a restrictive covenant, you can be held liable if you persuade a company client to break its contract with the company and hire you instead. (And if the client breaks a contract with the employer and hires you instead, the company may accuse you of having caused the contract to be breached.) Remember, civility can be disarming, even to an employer that has mistreated you. By contrast, needless rancor can cause an employer to dig in its heels and commit vast resources to defeating you in court.

8.   TALK TO FELLOW EMPLOYEES. It is easier to learn about a company's termination and severance policies while you are still on the premises. Find out all you can about what was paid to other employees when they were fired. This information can be quite useful to your lawyer during severance negotiations. For example, if you belong to a protected class (e.g., are a woman, over 40, a minority, or handi-capped), your lawyer can argue that the company violated its policy or engaged in discrimination by not paying you the same rate of severance as other non protected employees.

9.   ANALYZE YOUR FINANCIAL SITUATION. How much cash do you currently have on hand to pay your bills? If you do not have at least a six-month cushion, you should consider planning for the termination by reducing your overhead, bills, and lifestyle. Of course you will be reluctant to do this, but it makes sense to consider an austerity budget before the ax falls.

Speak to your accountant or financial planner for guidance. Experts suggest it is a good idea to pay off large credit card bills with high interest rates while you are still receiving a regular paycheck. Look into refinancing your mortgage and consolidating all your debts for this purpose. Worse, if you live above your means and the chances of being reemployed at your current level of salary may not materialize for many months, you may be forced to sell your house to lower your debt. But selling can take many months, so plan ahead if this is a viable option.

10. FIND SOURCES OF CASH. Think about trying to obtain a cash infusion until you find a new job. One way to do this is to establish a line of credit or taking out a home equity loan. Do this before being laid off, because banks generally don't lend to the unemployed.

Liquidate long-term accounts like CDs and place ample funds into checking accounts so that you can use the money immediately without paying a penalty. Although you may get less interest, availability should be your concern and you don't want the money tied up.

Consider borrowing from your company's 401 (k) plan or IRA's if applicable. If you are in the process of buying a home, you may want to postpone the decision if you can get out of the transaction.

If all else fails and you have no other possible sources of funds, speak to family members or friends about short-term loans. Consult your accountant to get advice about whether the interest payments on such loans are tax-deductible and how to structure them in your best interest. If you can take out a personal loan from a bank so much the better.

11. SUSPEND PAYMENTS ON LOANS IF POSSIBLE. Some lending institutions will let you suspend payments on school loans and other loans without penalty when you are unemployed. Inquire if this is feasible and whether your future credit will be impaired.

12. START A PART-TIME BUSINESS OR FREELANCE JOB NOW. Such a business has the potential of keeping you going after you are laid off and may even expand into your next career.

13. REVIEW YOUR PENSION PLANS AND RULES. Confirm that the amounts you will receive on termination are accurate. By asking for a current statement, you can ascertain that your years of service are properly credited and that your income is properly reported in the final computation. Now is the time to check for mistakes so you can receive the money immediately after a termination if you need it. Check to see that there is no break in service or that the benefits have not been reduced for technical reasons (e.g., because the company you work for was acquired by another). Ask for copies of pertinent company plans and review what they say. If someone asks why you want this, just say "because I have the right to this information by law." Write a letter to the plan administrator if you cannot obtain a copy or do not agree with the numbers.

After reviewing and approving the amount, you can compute what your monthly income will be after counting expected pension or profit-sharing monies plus unemployment payments for the first 26 wecks after you are unemployed (and possibly for another 73 weeks depending on your state or federal law at the time you receive such benefits).

14. CONSIDER YOUR ELIGIBILITY FOR BONUSES, STOCK OPTIONS, PROFIT-SHARING MONIES, OR COMMISSIONS ABOUT TO BECOME DUE. Be aware of the date when the money will be vested or when it is supposed to be paid. Do not allow the company to fire you to deprive you of these expected benefits.

15. REVIEW YOUR HEALTH BENEFITS TO BE SURE YOU ARE PROPERLY COVERED. Your entitlement to continued health and medical benefits under federal COBRA law is discussed in Chapters 3 and 7. But if you anticipate special needs for yourself and your family, or are worried that company supplied benefits may be too costly, it may be wise to shop around for a more attractive policy before you are laid off.

16. CONSIDER SENDING DEMAND LETTERS. Sending demand letters to confirm all actions or complain about illegal treatment may strengthen a legal claim. The time to demonstrate your non-acceptance of a company's act is before you are fired, not after. Complaining in writing after a firing may not mean as much and be viewed merely as sour grapes. Examples of sample letters are included in Chapter 9.

If you complain about illegal treatment before a firing, your employer may be advised by its legal counsel not to fire you (since the action may be viewed as illegal retaliation). In some cases, you can save your job or forestall the firing by complaining in writing. This action may also enable you to recover additional damages if you are fired. However, it is best to do this only after speaking with an employment attorney.

17. AVOID RESIGNING. Never resign from a job just because you suspect you are about to be fired. By resigning you may forfeit valuable benefits. I repeat: Do not resign for this and many other reasons (to be discussed in Chapter 8). Seek legal guidance to avoid acting incorrectly or irrationally.

Take It in Stride

Being out of work is not the end of the world. Many clients receiving a severance package with income for a lengthy period and unemployment compensation benefits take precious time off to travel, get in shape, pursue a hobby, go back to school, re-establish personal relationships with family members and friends, re-evaluate their careers, work part-time as a consultant, pursue a job in another field, or start their own businesses (without a boss). Looking for employment is stressful but it can also be an opportunity to pursue your dreams, especially if you can afford not to jump at the first unattractive offer that comes along.

Experts say it's important not to become discouraged or depressed when looking for a job. Visit a career or outplacement center and speak to a counselor for advice. Join a support group so you don't isolate yourself. Learn about changes in the job market and how to make yourself a better candidate. Live within your means. Look for bargains and cut back where you can. Network. Assess your situation objectively. Register with a temp agency to ensure a steady source of pay. Release feelings of anger and resentment. Recognize that no job lasts forever. Focus on the future and not the past. Update your résumé. Practice and hone effective interviewing techniques. Visit employment agencies in person or via the Internet. Map out a game plan and stick to it. Go to your local library and read books and articles on successful career planning and transitioning. Keep your spirits up. Maintain a good positive outlook. Avoid taking your frustrations, fears and insecurities out on loved ones. Take one day at a time. Trying your best is all you can do.

7

Facing the Music and Taking Charge

Being notified that you are fired can come as a shock even when you are prepared for it. Most people experience strong feelings of panic because they suddenly have no control of how they will maintain their present lifestyle, pay debts, become reemployed, and tell their friends and loved ones. Some become physically sick. Others feel deeply embarrassed. Many feel used and resent the years of loyal and dedicated service they gave without being more fully appreciated. A few clients say that being fired is a relief.

Terminated workers basically share one common denominator: they all feel cheated and want to even the score.

Whether you are fired for a valid reason (such as for poor performance, misconduct, dishonesty, or being accused of sexual harassment) or due to a downsizing or reorganization, you expect that your employer will treat you with respect and dignity. This means, for example, that you will not suddenly be fired before a vacation, during an office Christmas party, or in the presence of a large group of your colleagues. The firing should be discreet and professional. All precautions should be taken to avoid embarrassing you in front of coworkers. No information about the dismissal should be revealed to nonessential third parties.

Marshall Loeb tells people to remember these three rules for negotiating your exit: "(1) Never quit; make the company fire you; (2)

He who acts first, loses; and (3) Your pride is the company's best weapon. Don't get proud, get even."

This chapter will answer many questions you'll have if you are fired. Helpful strategies will enable you to begin the process of getting the most out of your separation package with or without a lawyer, protect and enhance your reputation, and help you feel you did everything possible to rectify a situation that may have been caused through no fault of your own. More important than trying to get your job back or discovering the true reasons for your discharge is getting the most money possible in your situation.

Learning Why You Were Fired

An initial inquiry should be to ascertain whether the employer had a valid reason to fire you. This is important because it can impact your severance package and whether you are entitled to receive severance and other benefits in the first place. Many employers will not offer you post-termination benefits if you are fired for misconduct (i.e., cause) unless you are an important officer or executive.

There is a manual that arbitrators use to assist them in rendering employment decisions. The manual lists standards for "just cause" firings, which are given here in modified form for their importance and instruction.

Every company official entrusted with hiring and firing employees should be familiar with the following guidelines:

1. Did the company have a clear rule against the kind of employee behavior for which discipline was administered?

2. Is the rule reasonably related to the orderly, efficient, and safe operation of the company's business?

3. Has the company provided employees reasonable opportunity to learn the company's rules?

4. Has the company provided employees reasonable opportunity to learn the possible consequences of disregarding the rules?

5. Has the company administered and enforced the rules evenhandedly and without discrimination among the employees?

6. Did the company investigate fairly the circumstances involved in an alleged offense?

7. Did the company, through its investigation, obtain substantial evidence of guilt?

8. Was the degree of penalty imposed for a fairly investigated, fact-supported offense reasonably related to (a) the seriousness of the proven offense and/or (b) the nature of the guilty employee's past record?

The burden of proving these points rests with the company.

If you are fired for cause, you may not be able to collect unemployment insurance and your COBRA health benefits may be impaired. The employer may also decide to give you a poor reference. Thus, consult an employment attorney if you are terminated for cause, because the lawyer may be able to help you regain benefits.

A young man faced many obstacles due to an innocent lapse of judgment. The 29-year-old client managed a Broadway theater and was doing a terrific job. He worked 80-hour weeks, had received a raise, and was in line for a Christmas bonus.

Someone who worked for the company staging the current production at the theater told the client she was leaving to get married and asked if he could give her a T-shirt souvenir. These souvenirs were handed out regularly to customers attending the show as a free Christmas promotion gift.

The client went upstairs to the main star's dressing room and removed a T-shirt from his locked cabinet. He was spotted by an assistant, who alerted management. The client was suddenly fired for stealing. Devastated, the man came to the author for help. He related how he had keys to every office, door, and locked closet in the theater and didn't feel he was required to ask anyone's permission just to remove a T-shirt. Besides, he said, the company gave away thousands of garments that week after every performance.

I conveyed this to management and pleaded that the client's firing was unjustified due to his record of loyalty and hard work. I argued that he was being used as a scapegoat. There was no malicious motivation behind the act because he was taking the item for a friend, not himself (this was confirmed in a letter which the woman signed to support the client's story), and it was not taken for resale. As a last resort an offer was made that he be briefly suspended without pay for his actions.

Although the ex-employer refused to give him back his job or pay him severance, I did manage to recover a small year-end bonus. The company agreed it would not contest his application for unemployment insurance and he was allowed to collect benefits. I also received a letter confirming that no record of the true reason for the discharge would be revealed to third parties in the future. Hopefully, the client is managing another theater these days, which was his passion.

To learn if the employer's reason for firing you was valid, you must first discover the reason. If you are terminated illegally, there are usually several causes of action that can be asserted in court before a jury.

The best way to discover the reason for your discharge is to ask. Inquire why you are being let go. If the employer refuses to answer, an effective method of getting the employer to talk is to state that you need to know what happened so you don't act the same way in your next job. Although the law in most states does not obligate employers to spill the beans, a jury may well believe that decency and compassion require, at a minimum, that the employer provide you with an honest explanation.

Although you may not be able to get your job back, a lawyer may be able to use the following reasons as leverage in the attempt to get you more severance and other benefits. When a terminated worker consults with me regarding his or her discharge, I consider the following factors to determine whether the firing was justified and/or legal:

- Are there mitigating factors that excuse or explain the employee's poor performance or misconduct?

- Was the employee victimized by a supervisor's bias or subjective evaluations rather than objective criteria?

- How long has the employee worked for the company? What kind of overall record does the employee have?

- Is termination appropriate under all the circumstances? Does the punishment fit the crime?

- Has the employer followed a consistent policy of terminating workers with similar infractions?

- Is the employer retaliating against the employee because of a refusal to commit illegal or unethical acts (such as falsifying records), for obeying a subpoena (in a legal case involving the employer), or for serving on extended jury duty or in the military rather than due to a bona fide business reason, disciplinary problem, or poor performance?

- Has the employee been fired because she filed a sexual harassment complaint, is pregnant, or refused to submit to demands for sexual favors?

- Is the fired employee being deprived of severance or other financial benefits that are due? Is this contrary to the employee's contract, letter agreement, company handbook, or employee manual? Is the firing contrary to a written contract?

If any of the above considerations apply to you, consult an employment attorney immediately.

How to Properly Handle the News

Typically, you will be called into a supervisor's, manager's, or executive's office when being informed of the firing. Decisions such as who should tell you, where, and when have already been made. The employer should decide these matters with an eye to minimizing your discomfort and embarrassment, and increasing the chances you will have an opportunity to regain your composure and begin taking steps to find employment elsewhere. People who quickly find satisfactory replacement jobs are less likely to sue ex-employers. Smart employers know this and should be willing to do everything possible to help you in this pursuit.

Some companies will fire you at the end of the week (so they don't have to pay you for any remaining days that week) and order you to leave the premises immediately. Other companies often escort fired employees out of the building, sometimes shipping their belongings to their homes.

If you are requested to leave the premises, do so quietly. The decision to fire you has already been made. Typically, it is final and not appealable in most cases. However difficult it may be, the trick is to stay calm when you are told the news. Raising your voice and arguing will get you nowhere and burn bridges.

Asking the person to reconsider is generally a waste of time unless he or she is a trusted friend and your request has a good chance of paying off or the employer has a stated policy of allowing workers to grieve and/or appeal a termination decision. If you are aware of such a policy, consider taking appropriate steps immediately, since you have nothing to lose. Thus, if the policy requires you to appeal the decision in writing no more than X (e.g., three) days after being fired, do so to avoid a claim that your appeal was not filed timely or properly. Just don't get your hopes up, because requests for reconsideration rarely work.

Although the author disagrees, some experts advise against asking the employer to reconsider under any circumstances. This minority view is that your acquiescence may be viewed positively (as a relief) and the company may reward you for "not rocking the boat" by giving you a generous severance package. Since each situation depends on the unique facts and personalities of the players involved, it is always recommended you seek the advice of an experienced employment attorney before embarking on a particular course of action.

There are situations, however, where the employer may have a confirmed progressive discipline system in place. To combat the trend toward awarding fired workers large verdicts in discrimination and breach of contract cases and to avoid looking foolish or biased to a jury, most employers are being advised by their lawyers to enact a progressive discipline system before firing workers (especially those over forty, women, or minorities). They are advised to structure the discipline so that it appears rational and proportional. This includes first giving employees notice that their performance is unsatisfactory and extending an opportunity to improve. If they do not meet expectations, workers then receive a written warning that sets deadlines for improvement. When there is no improvement after a final warning, termination follows, with the decision to terminate being reviewed and independently approved by several people (such as a supervisor, the president, and an executive from the human resources department) before it occurs.

If you believe the company has a policy of giving written warnings before a firing but you were not given the same opportunity to improve as other coworkers, ask the employer to reconsider, or consult a lawyer for advice. Many employers violate the law when they fail to apply a system of progressive discipline consistently, properly, or fairly.

When companies decide to terminate workers in a large layoff or restructuring, the same executives typically review the ages and personal characteristics of all those chosen to be fired to be sure the layoffs are not skewed and predominantly affect one protected class of workers (such as older workers). Again, if you are part of a protected class and believe that a predominant number of women, older workers, or minority workers were fired en masse along with you, speak to an employment attorney for guidance.

A request to reconsider, however, if presented in a calm and professional manner, may cause the owner or president to gain sympathy for your predicament. This can translate into more severance and post-termination benefits if you play your cards right.

There may also be occasions when it is wise to request that the decision be postponed. These include if you are close to earning a vested pension or profit-sharing benefit, commission, bonus, or stock option grant and need the additional time to "bridge the gap." Request this when applicable, because you have nothing to lose. If you feel the decision was financially driven and you need to stall the effective termination date, consider telling the employer you might take a cut in pay in return for a higher bonus or commission. If you are told you were fired for poor performance, ask to be placed on final warning or probation and given one last chance. And if you must stay on the payroll a little longer because you desperately need the money that a regular paycheck will bring (e.g., to pay for your child's large tuition bill that is due in a few weeks), tell the employer you are willing to work different or part-time hours, or will accept a transfer or even a temporary demotion if this is applicable.

This is a very important concept to think about and act on. Too often, employees accept a firing very close to the vesting of a significant financial benefit without a fight.

You may also have grounds for a valid lawsuit in the event you have a vested pension but are fired just weeks short of becoming entitled to greater severance, larger monthly pension payments, and improved medical and insurance benefits.

Cases demonstrate the responsibility of employers to comply with all pension laws and ERISA provisions regarding severance when a business is sold or when company policy has created an expectation that the purchasing company will continue an established severance policy crediting employees with prior years of service from the selling company.

Stay Calm

Your goal when being informed of the termination decision is to increase the chances of getting more severance and other post-termination benefits. Don't panic, lose your temper, or passively accept the package offered. Yelling will not help your cause. I frequently advise my clients to act composed, surprised, and hurt, even if this is out of character. You want the employer to feel sorry for you. Representing thousands of terminated workers from all walks of life and job levels has taught me that sympathetic employers are more amenable to offering a generous severance package than irritated or angry ones. Sending obnoxious letters, screaming, fighting, making threats, or otherwise acting improperly will only reaffirm the employer's decision to fire you and may cause the employer to refuse to negotiate a severance package with you or your lawyer in the future.

Stay calm and collected, even if it kills you, since you don't want to be labeled a troublemaker due to an angry outburst. Employers are quite familiar these days with stories of angry ex-employees who resort to violence to even the score. Never even remotely create the impression that this is possible.

Do not let the employer know what you are thinking when you initially hear the news. Be reserved. Listen to what the employer says (especially what the initial severance package comprises). When presented with an initial package, act noncommittal. Marshall Loeb states that the best way of getting even is to keep your cool during that most stressful moment when the boss calls you in and wields his terrible swift sword. He recommends that you should say almost nothing; you don't want to start negotiating now. Instead, carefully write down what your boss is saying. This may make him or her be more conciliatory. It also sends a signal that you're not about to surrender, and so the company had better prepare to deal with you.

STRATEGY: *Taking notes during the meeting conveys the message that you're compiling information that someone else, like a lawyer, will review. It also signals that you may be documenting the substance of the conversation for possible use in a future lawsuit. Write down everything you hear. If the supervisor asks why you are taking notes, state, "It's very important for me to understand everything you're saying." Take notes even if you are told that a formal severance package in writing will be coming shortly. Try not to act positive or negative once you hear the company's initial offer.*

Simply repeat the terms as you've written them down, saying, "I just want to make sure I have this right."

Stall for Time

Try to stall for time when you are fired. Stalling for time can help you learn more important facts. This includes many of the points previously discussed (e.g., requesting to see your personnel file to review and collect favorable documents; learning who made the decision to fire you to see if there is a possibility of appealing that decision or whether that person had proper authority to terminate you; reconstructing promises of security that were made; reviewing employment manuals). This information can help you in negotiations for additional severance and other benefits.

Get the Best Package

After you have been fired and decide not to accept the company's initial offer, it is critical to prepare a proper battle plan to maximize your severance package. Understand what you want to ask for, whom you will talk to, and what you want to achieve before you attend the negotiation session. Prioritize the critical elements of the package and try to obtain them in order of importance.

Always Ask for More

Do not accept the company's first offer of severance if possible. Always request a negotiating session to obtain more benefits. If you're pressed to accept the package offered or to sign any type of form, refuse. Tell the employer that you need time to consider without specifying whom you'll be discussing it with. Make an appointment for another meeting several days later. This will give you time to speak to your lawyer or advisor and formulate a response to the initial severance offer.

After contacting employers to negotiate more generous severance packages on behalf of fired workers, not once has an employer revoked the initial offer made to a client. In a minority of instances, they will say, "Mr. Sack, it's the best we can do, take it or leave it (by X date)." But employers or their counsel have never revoked the offer in spite because they were contacted. This is probably due to the fact that since there is generally no legal obligation to offer severance, the fact that an offer was made can be viewed as an employer's attempt to buy peace and avoid litigation.

Although there is generally no legal obligation to pay severance monies, employers in the United States do offer such payments when a firing is due to a group layoff, business conditions outside the employee's control (such as a reorganization, downsizing, job elimination, or other "neutral" factors), or for reasons other than employee misconduct. However, there may be a legal obligation to pay severance when:

■ You have a written contract stating that severance will be paid

■ Oral promises are given regarding severance pay

■ The employer voluntarily promises to pay severance

■ The employer has a policy of paying severance, and this is documented in a company manual or employee handbook

■ The employer has paid severance to other employees in similar firings and has thereby created a precedent

If you are fired and are not offered severance, it is advisable to request a meeting with a qualified representative of the employer to discuss clarification regarding severance and available wage equivalents. As you will learn, there is generally nothing to lose and plenty to gain.

The amount of severance pay offered is typically derived from a formula based on a person's length of service (e.g., two weeks for every year of work), but each company and industry is different. People who work in publicity-conscious industries, such as advertising, often receive greater severance packages than those working for heavy-manufacturing concerns, especially when they worked many years or made significant achievements or revenue for the company.

The ability to request a better severance package is greatest when you alone have been singled out for firing. When a job elimination affects a large group of workers, each will have a tougher time getting a better package. In such a case, a company's standard response is often: "We would like to offer you more, but then we have to offer the same benefits to everyone fired in your department to be fair and consistent, and we can't afford it."

Even if you are fired as part of a group, you should still request an appointment to ask for a better package. Go for it, since you have nothing to lose. The goal is to try to demonstrate that you are different from the pack, that your special achievements warrant a better package, or that your personal situation (e.g., caring for an infirm parent) requires that you be treated differently. Your efforts can work if the company believes giving you more is fair or decent and you will keep your mouth shut and not reveal the more favorable terms to others. If applicable, tell the company that you will sign a gag order clause in a separation agreement, with hefty penalties if you ever reveal the terms of the settlement to anyone other than your lawyers, accountant, or spouse. The company may be willing to accommodate you provided you sign a release, especially if you are over forty, a female, a minority, or in a protected class. It may view giving you additional benefits worth it when you sign a release agreeing not to sue and agreeing to keep quiet.

STRATEGY: *Ask for more severance and other perks when you are fired, regardless of the circumstances. This is so even when you are told the company never deviates from its established policy. Bosses who do the actual firing are not typically the ones who negotiate the package. This is done by someone from human resources or a company lawyer. If your proposal is presented early and professionally, it may be viewed as an honest attempt to reach an agreement, regardless of how much more you're asking for and even if you were fired along with others in your department. You've already been terminated: what more harm can an employer do to you?*

Stay On at a Lower Pay and Grade

There is, of course, another negotiating strategy to consider taking, especially when you simply can't afford a layoff, must continue working to receive important medical coverage for a sick spouse, or are a few months shy of a vested retirement benefit and need the extra time to "bridge the gap." Consider asking for and accepting a job at the company with a lower title and salary grade if necessary. Offering to work reduced hours with no overtime, agreeing to accept less benefits, or accepting a temporary furlough might be sufficient incentive for the employer to reverse its decision and keep you employed, especially when you are well-liked by your boss, there is an opening for another position, you are able to swallow your pride, and the company promises to reinstate you to the former position in better economic times. However, your company may be prohibited from doing this pursuant to an existing collective bargaining agreement or the National Labor Relations Act if you are a union employee. Also, granting your request but denying it to a minority worker might lead to a discrimination lawsuit and be an important reason why your request is denied.

Consider asking for project work as an independent contractor outside of the office if you receive a negative response to the above request but are leaving on good terms and your skills are highly regarded. This happened to a client who worked many years as the editor of a well-known magazine. She inquired if the company needed her services on special projects after she was fired for budgetary reasons. The company accepted her request and benefitted from her expertise while paying her a lower contract rate per magazine issue with no benefits.

STRATEGY: *If such an arrangement is offered, be sure it does not impact any severance or post-termination benefits you may be receiving. Don't ask for projects if you need valuable time to look for permanent employment elsewhere. Negotiate a fair daily rate for your efforts. Always discuss important aspects of the arrangement,* *such as deadlines, reimbursement of expenses, use and return of company property, when your fees will be paid, and other details to avoid misunderstandings. Ask for a written e-mail memo or letter which includes all the points that were agreed upon. For maximum protection, send a letter to the company yourself or hire an employment attorney to assist you if you don't receive one.*

Appeal to Decency and Fair Play

This is the most effective way of getting a better package. Most employers are fearful of the increasing amount of employee-related litigation and are flexible in easing the departure of terminated individuals, especially those who can sue for discrimination (i.e., people over forty, women, minorities, and others in a protected class). After you are granted an appointment, you should begin the negotiating session by appealing to corporate decency and fair play. For example, you may state that severance pay is needed to carry you over while you look for a new job or that more severance is needed because you anticipate it will take longer to find a suitable job than the amount of severance currently offered will cover. Tell the employer that experts state it takes an average of one month for each $10,000 of salary to find a replacement job.

Rather than state, "If you don't give me more money, I'll sue," it is more effective to say, "I have two children in college, an expensive home with a hefty mortgage that I can barely afford, and I recently lost a parent (or spouse) (or have just gone through a nasty divorce). If I don't receive more severance pay, I may have to foreclose my home, file for bankruptcy, and tell my kids they'll have to drop out of school. By not offering more money, I'm afraid you're putting me on the road to financial ruin."

Employers are often sympathetic to this approach. Be polite; being vindictive or making threats won't solve anything. But acting in a polite way doesn't mean that you can't be demanding and forceful during the presentation. Recognize that most companies want you to feel you've "won" something from them So they may be inclined to offer you at least some of the extras they have quietly granted to others in your situation. That way, you'll be less likely to bad-mouth your ex-employer to customers or the press, hire a lawyer (which companies want to avoid whenever possible), or file a lawsuit, which can cost the company valuable time and expense even if it wins. This is why you should not believe a company's claim that it cannot afford to pay you more because word may get out to others and create a precedent.

If your efforts are unsuccessful with the HR person or bureaucrat, go back to your boss and explain that you are being treated unfairly. By then guilt may have sunk in and the ex-boss could want to get it over with, and that's when exceptions are made.

Most important, you must know what you want out of the negotiations before you begin. The following material explains in detail each of the major elements you should be discussing and fallback strategies to employ if you don't initially get what you want. This is the same information I give to my clients to help them obtain a better severance package. Recognize that this information can help you obtain more money and benefits, whatever your situation.

Negotiating Strategies to Achieve Maximum Compensation

If possible, do not accept the employer's first offer regarding severance. Always request a negotiating session to obtain more benefits. Prioritize the critical elements of the package and try to obtain them in order of importance similar to the guidelines on the following pages.

Wages

The longer you've worked at a company and the better your job reviews have been, the more leverage you may have. Most employers have different policies regarding severance wages depending on the industry, company, and your title, job status, and achievements. Although you may initially be offered between one and two weeks of pay for each year worked, ask for more. Avoid accepting the employer's first offer; negotiate, negotiate, negotiate. I recommend that you attempt to receive one month of severance for each year worked as a starting point. Ask for an additional month of pay for every dependent you claim on your tax return. If this can be achieved, you can leave the company knowing that you have received a fair severance offer.

Stall for time while you are negotiating the package. Delaying the start date before the package kicks in means that you will receive more money in the aggregate. You are in good shape while your regular salary and benefits continue, since you are still being paid. Most terminated employees forget to negotiate this simple point.

Avoid arrangements where you are offered severance for a specified period (e.g., six months) that automatically ceases when you obtain a new job. Rather, make the offer non-contingent on new employment, or arrange that differential severance will be paid in a lump sum when you obtain a new job prior to the expiration of the severance period. For example, arrange that three months' worth of severance will be paid in a lump sum if a new job is obtained three months before the six months of salary continuation expires.

STRATEGY: *If the company offers you three months' severance, for example, and you want more, tell the company you will accept this provided you receive an additional month of severance (up to three months) for every month you continue to remain unemployed after the initial three-month period from the date of your discharge. Many employers will agree to this because they believe the goal of severance is to help you survive while you are out of work.*

If severance pay is to be paid in a lump sum, ask for it immediately, not in installments over time (e.g., 20 percent now and 20 percent every month for the next four months). Some employers insist on structuring severance this way as a guarantee that you will not violate the terms of a restrictive covenant or reveal the terms of the settlement to others, knowing that if you do, all payments will stop. Avoid this arrangement whenever possible.

Since severance pay is taxable, it may be advantageous to defer a portion of the income into the next tax year, when you may pay less in taxes. Speak to your accountant or financial adviser for more details.

If you are being paid severance regularly over time, negotiate for the employer to continue to provide paid medical, dental, and hospitalization coverage for you and your family while you are receiving severance wages. Some of my clients also successfully negotiate to receive regular 401 (k), pension, and profit-sharing contributions from the employer during the severance continuation period. This can add up to plenty of extra compensation.

In some states, if you receive salary continuation with benefits, you may be ineligible for unemployment compensation, But if you receive salary without benefits or are paid in a lump sum, you may be able to file for and receive unemployment benefits immediately, The rules are often tricky, and it is important to understand your state's regulations before you begin severance negotiations.

If you are offered a choice between a lump sum and salary continuation, discuss the advantages and disadvantages of each arrangement with your lawyer, accountant, or financial adviser. Call your local unemployment insurance department for details. Find out under what conditions you qualify. If you learn you may not qualify, weigh if it is advantageous to receive benefits instead of unemployment compensation before making your decision. Compute the economic effect of receiving paid medical and pension contributions and whether this outweighs the maximum $400+ per week of taxable money you will receive from unemployment compensation. If you elect to defer unemployment benefits or do not presently qualify, you are still entitled to receive unemployment benefits if you are out of work when your salary continuation expires.

In addition to receiving immediate unemployment benefits, there are other advantages to being paid severance in a lump sum. One benefit is that all contact with the former employer ceases. You don't have to worry that you were overpaid or that periodic payments may stop. Getting a lump sum also gives you the ability to invest the funds immediately or pay bills. But once you accept a lump sum package, your fringe benefits (if any) will stop and you will not receive any more assistance from your ex-employer.

The key advantage of being paid salary continuation is that valuable fringe benefits may continue.

If money is your main concern, there are strategies to receive more cash in lieu of benefits. If the company offers to provide you with paid outplacement assistance, job-hunting, or relocation expenses, negotiate to trade off these benefits for cash if you don't need them. For example, many of my clients receive outplacement assistance that may cost a former employer up to $10,000. You may be able to substantially increase a severance package by accepting a lesser amount (say $3,500) in lieu of this benefit. This is a good idea if you know you will find another job quickly and don't need outplacement assistance.

The same is true with respect to medical benefits. If your spouse works and you can be covered under the spouse's plan at no additional or nominal cost, why not thank the company for its offer of paying continued premiums for your medical coverage and receive, say, 50 percent of that cost in cash?

Other Compensation

If you have relocated recently at the request of the employer, try to obtain additional relocation allowances. This can amount to a large sum if you recently sold your house at a loss in order to move per the ex-employer's demands, or must return to a distant state to be with your family and look for work there. Additional expenses to ask for where applicable include expenses incurred to transport your personal possessions back to another state or travel and lodging expenses incurred to find a replacement job in a distant locale.

Discuss accrued salary, vacation pay, overtime, and unused sick pay. Be sure you are paid for these items. In most states, there is no legal obligation for a company to pay you unused vacation or sick time. Check your company handbook to determine what rules, if any, apply.

Hopefully, there was no company policy stating that vacation or sick days are forfeited if they are not used in a given year.

If you worked for a sufficient time (e.g., more than six months) during the year, you may have accrued vacation time. It is illegal in most states for employers to withhold accrued vacation money even if you are fired for cause. Although each company is free to implement its own rules governing vacation pay, employers must apply such policies consistently to avoid charges of discrimination and breach of contract.

Inquire and demand to be paid for all earned, accrued vacation, sick leave, and overtime pay at the final negotiating interview. Chapter 9 contains various letters that you can send to enforce your rights if the company refuses to pay you accrued benefits.

Some employers are not inclined to pay more (or any) money unless you sign a release. But it is generally illegal for the company to refuse to pay your salary, wages, overtime and accrued vacation pay earned through the termination date at the time of discharge. There can be no strings attached; you are entitled to receive the money immediately regardless of whether you decide to sign a release or not. If you do not receive such monies immediately after a firing, contact a lawyer or your nearest Department of Labor office for advice.

Overtime is not generally available for salaried workers who work in executive, administrative, or professional jobs (called exempt employees). But if you are a salaried worker, your company is not generally allowed to deduct a few hours off your weekly paycheck for time off for any reason, including personal time. If it does, you may be determined to be an hourly worker, capable of receiving overtime for up to three years.

If you are an hourly worker and worked overtime, discuss the amount of money due you (at time-and-a-half rates) with your company. Tell the ex-employer you may contact a representative at your state's Department of Labor or the Wage and Hour Division of the U.S. Department of Labor for help if the ex-employer fails to respond to your request.

If you were fired without notice, ask for two additional weeks of salary in lieu of the employer's lack of notice. This is an effective strategy to help get more severance. Even if the employer is not willing to pay you more severance, this is the one area where your request has a good chance of being accepted.

If commissions are due or are about to become due, insist that you be paid immediately; do not waive these expected benefits. Salespeople who earn commissions are now receiving additional statutory protections in this area. Many states now require that companies promptly pay commissions to their independent sales representatives (or agents) who are fired. When prompt payment is not made, companies may be liable for penalties up to three times the commission amount plus reasonable attorney fees and court costs if the case is eventually litigated. Check your state's sales rep law or speak to a knowledgeable employment attorney for more details.

Bonus

Understand how your bonus is computed. If you were entitled to receive a bonus at the end of the year, ask for it now. If you were fired close to the end of the year, and the company says it has no legal obligation to pay you a bonus because you didn't work the full year or are not on the payroll the day the bonus is paid per company policy, argue that the firing deprived you of the right to receive the bonus, especially if you were terminated through no fault of your own (not for cause). If this request is rejected, insist that your bonus be prorated according to the amount of time you worked during the year. If this request is denied, ask for your full bonus but settle for less (e.g., half). Speak to a lawyer to analyze and enforce your rights in this area where applicable.

Retirement and Savings Plans

Understand if you are a participant in any retirement or savings plan and be aware of all plans, funds, and programs that may have been established on your behalf. You are not legally entitled to define benefit plan monies until you become vested. Once vested, your money becomes non-forfeitable. Each pension plan has rules to determine when vesting occurs. If you are fired just before the vesting of a pension (e.g., one month before your fifty-fifth birthday or the vesting date), argue that the timing of the firing is suspect and that public policy requires the employer to grant you your pension.

Although federal law states that employers generally do not have to change their pension rules to accommodate individual cases, the author has represented many employees who were terminated close to a vesting date and has negotiated for the employee to be placed on unpaid leave status or to receive a small monthly check for several months and stay on the payroll as a way of qualifying for the pension. This is called pension bridging and can be done in special circumstances.

If you are fired just before qualifying for a long-awaited pension and the employer refuses this request, consult an experienced employment attorney immediately. ERISA prohibits employers from terminating employees to avoid paying some or all pension benefits due the employee or that will become due the employee when he retires.

The fact that you are fired before receiving full pension benefits (because you did not reach the age of 65, work 20 or more years, or some other requirement) may not preclude you from receiving a monthly pension, albeit a smaller one. Where applicable, evaluate whether it pays for you not to start receiving your pension immediately after a termination, especially if the few additional years of postponement will mean more hefty vested monthly benefits later. Speak to your accountant or financial adviser for more details, and ask the employer if you can agree to defer your benefits for more money later.

In some states, if you begin receiving pension benefits, the amount of unemployment compensation you will receive weekly will be reduced accordingly. Always take this into account.

Some plans permit early retirement with a smaller monthly pension. If you are terminated, you may, depending on your age and length of service, still be eligible to receive reduced benefits. Be sure you understand your rights with respect to smaller vested benefits.

Negotiate to receive full enhanced pension benefits as consideration for accepting early retirement. If this cannot be done, think twice before accepting early retirement. Investigate the amount of pension reduction or penalty for early withdrawal. Inquire if the employer will augment additional employment served so you may qualify for an early pension.

Although your pension and other contributions from the employer may stop on termination, ask the employer to continue to contribute these benefits while you are receiving salary continuation. Getting the employer to agree to this can mean thousands of additional dollars to you.

Ask for a copy of pertinent plan summaries and statements of benefits when you learn of your firing. Carefully review these and other documents. Talk to a benefits officer or someone in the personnel department if you do not understand something. Do not rely on oral promises; ask for all explanations in writing. If there is any doubt concerning your rights, write to the plan administrator for a written explanation.

Demand in writing that the employer and/or plan administrator provide you with a copy of the employer's pension and/or profit-sharing plans from the plan administrator if the employer refuses to furnish you with accurate details. A sample demand letter is contained following this paragraph. (You may have to pay for the cost of photocopying said plans when requesting them.) ERISA provides that plan participants are entitled to examine without charge all plan documents filed with the U.S. Department of Labor, including detailed annual reports and plan descriptions. If you request materials and do not receive them within 30 days, you may file suit in federal court. In such a case, the court may require the plan administrator to provide the materials and pay up to $100 a day until you receive the materials, unless the materials are not sent for reasons beyond the control of the administrator.

Sample Letter Requesting ERISA Plan Documents from the Department of Labor

Your Name
Address
Telephone Number
Date

[Name and Address of Plan Administrator]

Re: Request for Plan Documents

Dear Sir or Madam:

As an employee of [name of company] whose employment terminated earlier this year, I am writing to request that you send me copies of the following documents relating to the company's profit sharing/401 (k) Plan:

(1) The SPD
(2) Any documents which modified the SPD, including, without limitation, any SMM or Summary of Material Modifications
(3) The last two Summary Annual Reports issued
(4) An Individual Benefit Statement

In addition, please let me know whether the Annual Report (Form 5500 Series) and the Documents under which the plan is established and operated are available in PDF form or in paper form free of charge. If they are available in paper form free of charge, please mail them to me. If you cannot mail them to me in paper form free of charge, then please e-mail them to me in PDF form at the following e-mail address: [insert your e-mail address here] If they are not available in paper form free of charge, and do not exist in PDF form, please advise me in writing as to the applicable copy charges. Thank you.

Sincerely,
Your name

Sent certified mail, return receipt requested.

If you are satisfied that all monies due you have been accounted for, you will have to decide whether to keep the funds in their present accounts, withdraw the funds for your personal needs, or transfer the funds into other investments. The questions of where to put the money and whether you will suffer harmful tax consequences should be answered by a competent accountant and/or financial adviser. Some company plans allow participants to roll benefits over so you do not get hit with hefty early withdrawal penalties. I strongly recommend that my clients seek professional tax and financial advice when retirement and savings plan monies are involved at the time of a termination. It is also a good idea to speak with the person in charge of the company's benefits or investments before making an informed decision in this area.

Stock Options

Your right to continued stock options will either vanish or be substantially impaired once you are fired. This is especially true if the employer claims you were fired for misconduct. But if you were fired through no fault of your own (e.g., due to a downsizing or job elimination), try to negotiate an arrangement that accelerates the vesting of stock options. If you cannot obtain this, discuss taking less severance pay if the company will vest your options now or stretch out the deadline for exercising them. Tell the company this is a win-win for both parties because it will cost the employer less money in the short term and you can get more money in the future if the value of the company stock appreciates. Review these strategies with your employment attorney.

Medical, Dental, and Hospitalization Benefits

Have your benefits explained to you at the negotiation session so you'll understand them. For example, does coverage stop the day you are fired or is there a grace period? Ask for a copy of all applicable policies and review them carefully. Negotiate to extend coverage beyond the grace period, especially if you are responsible for maintaining your family's health coverage and do not expect to find a replacement job in the near future.

Ask the employer to continue paying your medical and health premiums for another six months (or a year) while you are receiving salary continuation. Many employers will grant this request if you ask for it. The advantage of this arrangement is that in addition to receiving free medical coverage for several months, you may have the right to receive COBRA health benefits at your expense up to 18 months after the employer-paid-for benefits during the salary continuation period stop.

Some employers will concede this request in order to make a departing worker feel that he or she was treated fairly during negotiations. It is one of the most important benefits you can ask for and is often granted by an employer. Always ask for this during negotiations where appropriate.

Although most plans terminate automatically at the date of your discharge, inquire if you can assume the policy at your personal cost and find out the required time frame to implement coverage. This is referred to as a conversion policy. Such policies may also apply to long- and short-term disability insurance and life insurance plans in existence at the time of your firing.

If you are married and your spouse is working, you may be covered under your spouse's policies. If so, you may not want to continue paying for your own policies.

Be sure the employer has notified you regarding your COBRA rights. This must be done in writing within 30 days after you are fired and you then have several weeks to advise the company in writing if you will continue your health benefits. If you desire to continue coverage, you should promptly remit the first month's premium.

Under federal law, private employers who employ more than 15 workers on a typical business day must continue to make group health insurance available to workers who are discharged from employment. If you work for a smaller company, you may still be protected under state law. Check your local Department of Labor or department of insurance for details.

Most people benefit from COBRA, since the cost of maintaining insurance is reasonable; rather than the cost of an individual policy, you pay for coverage at the employer's group rate plus a 2 percent administrative fee.

If you don't receive the initial COBRA notification letter from the ex-employer immediately after a firing, call the company and speak with the person in charge of benefits or personnel. Demand to receive a formal notice. This is your right. To ensure that your coverage will not lapse, send payments directly to the ex-employer (not the insurance carrier unless you are instructed otherwise in writing) regularly and timely.

Never ignore the notice once it is received. Send your initial check back immediately with a letter by certified mail, return receipt requested, to prove delivery. Make a copy of your check and letter and keep the canceled check as proof that payment was made and received. Contact the insurance company separately to verify that the carrier was notified that your payment was received. You can't do enough to ensure that your coverage exists and is being maintained.

Under the law, all employees who are discharged as a result of a voluntary or involuntary termination (with the exception of those who are fired for gross misconduct) may elect to continue plan benefits currently in effect at their own cost provided the employee or beneficiary makes an initial payment within 30 days of notification and is not covered under Medicare or any other group health plan. The law also applies to qualified beneficiaries who were covered by the employer's group health plan the day before the discharge. Thus, for example, if the employee chooses not to continue such coverage, his or her spouse and dependent children may elect continued coverage at their own expense.

In the event the employer fails to offer such coverage, the employer may be required to pay the employee a penalty equal to $110 per day for each day the employee is not covered.

Due to burdensome record-keeping requirements, it isn't surprising that many companies run afoul of the law and fail to follow properly rules regarding notification requirements, conversion privileges, excluded individuals, and time restrictions, because the law does not provide much guidance or instruction. In fact, good-faith compliance may not be sufficient to protect the employer, as a California ruling demonstrates. The employer, a mental health residential treatment facility, offered its two health care plan options to a laid-off employee. When the plan chosen by the ex-employee went bankrupt, only the second plan (an HMO) remained. All current employees of the company were in the plan's geographic area and they signed up with the HMO. Since the ex-employee lived outside the area, she was left without any health continuation coverage. She sued her former employer for the health care coverage that was her right under COBRA and prevailed. Although IRS regulations require only that COBRA coverage be the same as insurance offered "similarly situated beneficiaries" as the employer argued the US. District Court ruled that the employer had not satisfied its obligations.

The law is now being interpreted very broadly, and the courts are ruling regularly that COBRA coverage be provided. Because the cases typically pit a former employee or an employee's dependent with substantial medical expenses against the employer or an insurance company, many courts are willing to interpret and apply COBRA with a view toward extending coverage wherever possible.

In one case, an employee incapacitated by a series of strokes was maintained on her employer's group health insurance policy. After about a year, the employee was taken off the company rolls. At that time, she was in a coma and the COBRA continuation notice was sent to her husband. Misunderstanding the intent of the offer, and thinking his wife was still covered under the employer's group plan without premium payments, he waived his wife's insurance continuation rights. Later, as legal guardian, the ex-employee's husband tried to regain the option of COBRA coverage, but the insurance company refused. The husband sued and won; the court ruled that the employer should have included the summary plan description with the COBRA notice sent to the husband and that without the summary he was unable to make an informed decision.

Be sure you know your rights under COBRA in the event you are fired. This is especially true if you or a spouse or dependent is sick and needs the insurance benefits to pay necessary medical bills. You are entitled to such protection even if you have worked for the employer for only a short period of time. In fact, under the law as it presently exists, most short-term employees can generally enjoy COBRA protection for periods exceeding the length of their employment. The only requirement is that you must have been included in the employer's group plan at the time of the firing.

Remember, however, that you may not be able to obtain benefits if you are fired for gross misconduct. This term is relatively ambiguous; the burden of proof is on the employer to prove that the discharge was for a compelling reason (fighting on the job, stealing, working while intoxicated, etc). Also be aware that some employers reduce a person's working hours to a point that makes them ineligible for group health coverage.

If an employer refuses to negotiate continued health benefits as part of a severance package or fails to notify you of the existence of such benefits, contact the human resources office immediately to protect your rights. If the employer refuses to offer continued COBRA benefits after a discharge for any reason, consult an employment attorney immediately.

Life Insurance Benefits

Inquire if you can convert any life insurance policies at your own cost. There may also be equity in a life insurance plan that may accrue to you upon termination. Ask about this and also obtain a copy of all policies presently in effect.

Outplacement Assistance

Many employers offer paid outplacement assistance as part of a severance package. What terminated workers do not realize is that it is usually short (e.g., no more than six months) and may consist only of simple resume preparation, modest typing, a short seminar on proper interviewing skills, and irregular assistance. Your goal is to negotiate the best assistance possible. This should include unlimited use of a private office or cubicle space, your own personal telephone line and answering service, a secretary, and mail facilities to assist you in your job search. These services should be offered for as long as you are unemployed (or at least for a year if necessary). Many different kinds of plans are typically offered by outplacement assistance firms to employers at various costs. Since not all services are the same, try to get the company to pay for the best plan available.

Do your homework and interview various firms. If you are impressed with a particular one, ask the company to pay for the firm of your choosing. Look for a firm that designates a personal counselor to meet with you weekly. Select a firm that goes the extra mile, such as one that screens topical newspaper ads or transmits your resume to headhunters and important employment agencies in your region.

Extra Benefits

Depending on your particular situation, there is no limit to the kinds of benefits you can request. Skilled lawyers often throw ten darts at a wall during negotiations in the hope that several will stick. That is an effective way you, too, can try to obtain extra benefits.

Ask the employer to provide the same benefits you would ordinarily expect from an outplacement firm. This includes continued use of an empty office, computer or laptop, pager, secretary, mail facilities, and telephone reception to assist you while your job search continues. Ask the company to keep your voice-mail service active until you find a new job. That way, you can hunt from home, without prospective employers knowing you are out of a job. Tell the company why you still need these items. Convince the company to allow you to use such property (as a courtesy) especially if it is inexpensive to the employer.

Request the continued use of your company car if you have one. Ask to buy the car or take over the lease at a reduced rate if appropriate. On numerous occasions, I have obtained favorable auto deals for my clients at substantially lower-than-market rates simply by asking for this concession. Perhaps the employer will allow you to keep the personal computer it purchased several years ago if you request it.

If appropriate, request a loan to tide you over while looking for a new job. Or, if the parting is amicable, perhaps you can convince the employer to continue paying for the degree program you have started, especially if you were fired at the beginning of a semester and you only have one more semester of courses to take. Some companies may provide tuition assistance or a pay-for-retraining stipend to help you switch careers (e.g., take courses in computer training) or enhance your skills.

Ask the employer to reimburse you for job-hunting expenses. Specify the kinds of expenses you should be reimbursed for. This may include travel to and from interviews, typing, résumé preparation and printing, postage and book purchase costs. If the employer refuses, explain why this is necessary. As a last resort, tell the employer that you will accept a modest amount with a cap.

You have nothing to lose and everything to gain by asking for these benefits. Be imaginative. Marshall Loeb reports there are executives who have successfully requested reimbursement for country club dues (or yacht slips) as an inexpensive way for the company to preserve goodwill.

The more things you ask for, the more concessions you will probably get. Even if the company refuses to provide you with many of these extra perks, you may still receive an enhanced severance package as a compromise. Prepare a detailed list of proposed benefits. Discuss these intelligently with the employer. If you're leaving on good terms, you should even consider requesting the employer to hire you as a freelancer.

Golden Parachutes

Determine if you are entitled to receive additional benefits under a severance contract or golden parachute. Generally, golden parachutes are arrangements between an executive and a corporation that are contingent on a change in control of a corporation. Typically, additional cash and other economic benefits are paid to a terminated individual following the discharge (provided the employee is not fired for cause). Although most companies cover only a limited group of key employees with golden parachutes, some companies have determined that it is appropriate to cover a much larger group.

Speak to an employment attorney immediately to protect your rights if the employer refuses to provide all the benefits specified in your contract.

Maximum Tax Advantage

During the process of negotiating a severance package or settlement, be mindful of the after-tax consequences. Try to get the employer to agree on a package that saves the company real dollars while creating greater after-tax benefits for you. For example, when settling a sex discrimination case, instead of getting $50,000 in back pay (which is completely taxable), have your lawyer or yourself try to structure the settlement in terms of money for attorney fees, interest, physical pain and suffering, and back pay. By structuring the arrangement in this fashion, you would not necessarily be required to pay tax on the money paid directly to your lawyer for legal fees, for interest, and for physical pain and suffering, and the company would avoid paying Social Security, Medicare and FUTA taxes on these amounts.

Most payments made to you after a firing are taxable. Severance pay and money paid to compensate you for an earned bonus, overtime, vacation pay, or commissions are taxable. So, too, are damages paid to settle an age, gender, race, handicap, retaliation, or other discrimination claim. Damages for back pay and emotional distress pursuant to discrimination, defamation, or breach of contract charges are now taxable.

However, damages received for personal physical injury or sickness (e.g., a bleeding ulcer caused by workplace stress) pursuant to an award or settlement of a discrimination claim is excludable from gross income and is not taxable.

Get professional advice when negotiating tax-free benefits with your employer. Consider innovative ways to reduce taxes, such as for interest-free loans or the sale of company property (e.g., computers and company cars) to you.

Since money received by a judgment or settlement in a lump sum or as periodic payments as damages for personal physical injuries or sickness is not taxable, it pays to understand basic IRS rules after speaking with your accountant, financial advisor, or lawyer. The tax consequences of employee-related severance negotiations and settlements present opportunities for both parties to save money.

The trick is to be as specific as possible when drafting or reviewing the settlement document. Be sure its language complies with the IRS code.

Once a tax-wise settlement based on economic realities is made, it should be adhered to by both parties. An IRS audit can be triggered when a particular allocation is agreed on but you claim a different amount on your tax return. If this happens, both you and the company could be liable for hefty penalties and interest.

Cover Story and Job References

Clarify how the news of your departure will be announced. Discuss and agree with management on the story to be told to outsiders. Consider whether you want it to be known that you resigned for personal reasons or that you were terminated due to a "business reorganization." These are neutral explanations that are preferable to firings caused by misconduct or poor performance.

If the company agrees to release a positive announcement, ask to review the final draft before it goes out. Ask that the memo list your major accomplishments and state a neutral reason for your departure, such as that you are leaving to "pursue new career opportunities."

The Resignation Dilemma

Recognize that if you resign you may be forfeiting unemployment benefits. My advice is to avoid resigning wherever possible. Although you may prefer that outsiders be told you resigned for personal reasons, confirm with the employer that you will be able to apply for unemployment benefits. That way your local Department of Labor will be advised that there was a termination (as opposed to a resignation, since that is what really happened) and you can still tell outsiders that you resigned.

Recommendation

Request that a copy of a favorable letter of recommendation be given to you before you leave the company. The letter should state the dates of your employment, the positions held, and that you performed all your job duties in a diligent and satisfactory fashion. If possible, the letter should be signed by a qualified officer or supervisor who worked with you and knows you well. Do not rely on promises that the employer will furnish prospective employers with a favorable recommendation, since many fail to do this after employees leave the company. Thus, always attempt to have such a letter in hand before you leave. The letter below is an example of the kind of recommendation you may find acceptable.

It is best not to include the specific reason for the parting in such a letter. This will enable you to offer whatever reasons you feel are appropriate under various circumstances.

Sample Letter of Recommendation

Date

To whom it may concern:

I am pleased to submit this letter of recommendation on behalf of (name of employee).

(Name of employee) worked for the company from (date) through (date). During this period (name of employee) was promoted from (specify title) to (specify title).

During the past (specify) years, I have had the opportunity to work closely with (name of employee). At all times I found him/her to be diligent and dependable and (name of employee) rendered competent and satisfactory services on the company's behalf.

I heartily recommend (name of employee) as a candidate for employment of his/her choosing.

Very truly yours,

Name of Officer
Title

Notification of Departure

Request that key members of the company be notified of your departure in writing. If possible, approve the contents of such a memo before distribution. Written memos can dispel false rumors about your termination. A positive memo may assist you in obtaining a new job. Remember, news of a firing usually spreads rapidly; you don't want to be the subject of false rumors or innuendo.

Protecting the Severance Arrangement

After you have negotiated your severance package and are satisfied that you have adequately covered all of your options and benefits, you must decide whether to accept the company's final offer or retain a lawyer in the attempt to obtain additional compensation.

Before retaining a lawyer, be sure that you feel comfortable with him or her and that the lawyer will be able to render competent services on your behalf. This can be accomplished by following many of the strategies contained in Chapter 10.

STRATEGY: *When you are owed wages, accrued overtime pay, vacation pay, an earned bonus, commissions, stock options, or other compensation, or believe the employer violated the law, a lawyer may first advise you to send letters of protest on your own in the attempt to obtain an amicable settlement. The letters serve several functions: in addition to helping you settle the matter privately (and saving money allocated for legal fees), they can help your lawyer if the company refuses to respond or responds inaccurately or negatively. A letter can help you document your claim and often places the employer or its actions in a poor light.*

When you hire a lawyer, it is important that the lawyer get started on your matter immediately. Time is crucial in all termination cases; action must be taken immediately to demonstrate the seriousness of your resolve. In fact, the longer a lawyer waits before contacting the employer, the weaker a case can become. That is why the author prefers to contact the employer within a week or two after the individual has been fired.

When the author is retained to represent a terminated individual, a letter is sent to the employer by fax and mail, usually the day I am hired. This ensures that the employer is notified quickly that I have been hired to discuss and negotiate the circumstances surrounding the person's termination, the inadequacy of the severance offer, the amount of money in commissions or other benefits still due, and other considerations. The initial demand letter is kept brief because I do not want to "tip my hand" and state my case to someone I have never spoken with. Of course, it is always desired that the employer contact me as soon as possible. This helps my negotiating position.

A variety of techniques are used during negotiations; the author typically stresses that the employer should offer more to settle the matter amicably and avoid time-consuming and expensive legal action.

An officer of the employer or a company attorney usually contacts me after receiving such a letter. Negotiations then ensue to determine if the matter can be settled out of court. Usually it is due to several factors. First, most employers want to avoid the poor publicity that can arise from a protracted court battle. Second, when companies are contacted by attorneys representing terminated employees, they must weigh whether it is wise to offer additional compensation to settle out of court versus spending thousands of dollars in legal expenses and lost work hours resulting from defending the charges in formal litigation. Finally, if the firing is illegal, company exposure can amount to hundreds of thousands of dollars in actual damages (which doesn't include interest, attorney fees, and costs that are sometimes awarded).

A pragmatic approach is often taken and most matters are settled. The employee receives additional severance and other benefits and the employer avoids a lawsuit. Remember that the mark of a good settlement is that no side is truly happy with the result. The employer believes too much money was paid to settle; conversely, the employee sometimes feels that he or she received too little. However, given the confines of the legal system (the long delays before the case is actually tried, the tremendous expenses involved, etc.), many terminated employees often achieve a fair out-of-court settlement for their troubles.

If you decide that contacting a lawyer is not necessary when you obtained a fair and equitable settlement on your own, request that the employer confirm the deal in writing. Such a letter will clarify the points agreed upon and document the severance arrangement that has been made. If the employer fails to abide by an important term (such as a promise of salary continuation for six months), the letter can increase your chances of success if you decide to sue for breach of contract.

The following letter was given to a client who negotiated to receive an additional one year's severance arrangement and other benefits with my assistance. Note the protections insisted on by the employer in the latter part of the agreement.

Sample Employer Confirmation of Severance Agreement

Date

Name of Employee
Address

Dear (Name of Employee),

This will confirm our agreement regarding your employment status with (name of employer).

We agreed as follows:

1. Your services as Vice President of (specify division) will terminate by mutual agreement effective (date).

2. Although your services as Vice President will not be required beyond (specify date), you agree to be available to (name of employer) through (specify termination date) to render advice, answer any questions, and provide information regarding company business.

3. Through (specify termination date) except as provided in paragraph 4 below, you will continue to receive your regular biweekly salary of (specify) and you may continue to participate in those company benefit plans in which you are currently enrolled. In addition to your final paycheck, you will receive from the company on or about (specify termination date) or given as provided for in paragraph 4 hereunder, the sum of (specify) less applicable deductions for local, state, and federal taxes, as a bonus for the present year.

4. If you obtain other regular, full-time employment prior to (specify termination date), then, upon commencement of such employment (date of new employment), your regular biweekly salary payments and your participation in company benefit plans, as described in paragraph 3 above, shall cease; however, medical and dental coverage previously provided you shall be continued for an additional period of three months at a cost to be borne by (name of employer). In such event, you will receive in a lump sum, less applicable deductions for taxes, the remaining amount you would have received on a biweekly basis from the date of new employment through (specify termination date) plus the (specify sum) bonus, less taxes, payment referred to in paragraph 3 within two weeks of your date of new employment. You agree to notify

the company immediately of the date on which such regular full-time employment will commence.

5.   You acknowledge that the sums referred to in paragraphs 3 and 4 above include any and all monies due you from the company, contractual or otherwise, to which you may be entitled, except for any vested benefit you may have in the (name of employer) Savings and Investment Plan and the Pension Plan.

6.   (Name of employer) will provide you with available office space, telephone service, and clerical help on an as-needed basis at (address) until you obtain other regular full-time employment or (date), whichever occurs first.

7.   You agree to cooperate fully with (name of employer) in their defense or other participation in any administrative, judicial, or collective bargaining proceeding arising from any charge, complaint, grievance, or action which has been or may be filed.

8.   You, on behalf of yourself and your heirs, representatives, and assigns, hereby release (name of employer), its parents, their subsidiaries and divisions, and all of their respective current and former directors, officers, shareholders, successors, agents, representatives, and employees from any and all claims you ever had, now have, or may in the future assert regarding any matter that predates this agreement, including, without limitation, all claims regarding your employment at or termination of employment from (name of employer), any contract, express or implied, any tort, or any breach of a fair employment practice law, including Title VII, the Age Discrimination in Employment Act, and any other local, state, or federal equal opportunity law.

9.   You acknowledge that you have had the opportunity to review this agreement with counsel of your own choosing, that you are fully aware of the agreement's contents and of its legal effects, and that you are voluntarily entering into this agreement.

10. You agree that any confidential information you acquired while an employee of the company shall not be disclosed to any other person or used in a manner detrimental to the company's interests.

11. Neither you nor anyone acting on your behalf shall publicize, disseminate, or otherwise make known the terms of this agreement to any other person, except to those rendering financial or legal advice, or unless required to do so by court order or-other compulsory process of law.

12.   The provisions of this agreement are severable and if any provision is held to be invalid or unenforceable it shall not affect the validity or enforceability of any other provision.

13.   This agreement sets forth the entire agreement between you and the company and supersedes any and all prior oral or written agreements or understandings between you and the company concerning this subject matter. This agreement may not be altered, amended, or modified except by a further writing signed by you and (name of employer).

14.   In the event (name of employer) becomes insolvent, bankrupt, is sold, or is unable in any way to pay the amounts due you under the terms of this agreement, then such obligations shall be undertaken and assumed by (specify parent company) and all such sums shall be guaranteed by (name of parent company).

15.   In the event that any monies due under this agreement are not paid for any reason, then the release referred to in paragraph 8 shall be null and void and of no effect.

If the foregoing correctly and fully recites the substance of our agreement, please so signify by signing in the space below.

Dated:

Very truly yours,
Name of Employer
By: Name of Officer, Title

Accepted and agreed:
Name of Employee

In the event the employer refuses to provide such a letter, it is advisable to send a letter to the company by certified mail, return receipt requested, confirming the arrangement that has been made. The letter should state that if any terms are ambiguous or incorrect, a written reply will be sent to you immediately. If no response is received, you will be able to rely on the terms of the letter in most situations. The following is a good example.

Sample Employee Confirmation of Severance Agreement

Your Name
Address
Telephone Number
Date

Name of Corporate Officer
Title
Name of Employer
Address

Re: Our severance agreement

Dear (Name of Corporate Officer),

This will confirm our discussion and agreement regarding my termination:

1.   I will be kept on the payroll through (specify date) and will receive (specify) weeks' vacation pay, which shall be included with my last check on that date.

2.   (Name of company) shall pay me a bonus of (specify) within (specify) days from the date of this letter.

3.   (Name of company) will purchase both my non-vested and vested company stock, totaling (specify) shares at the buy-in price of (specify) per share, or at the market rate if it is higher at the time of repurchase, on or before (specify date).

4.   (Name of company) will continue to maintain in effect all medical, dental, hospitalization, and life insurance policies presently in effect through (specify date). After that date, I have been advised that I may convert said policies at my sole cost and expense and that coverage for these policies will not lapse.

5.   I will be permitted to use the company's premises at (specify location) from the hours of 9:00 A.M. until 5:00 PM. This shall include the use of a secretary, telephone, stationery, and other amenities at the company's sole cost and expense to assist me in obtaining another position.

6.   I will be permitted to continue using the automobile previously supplied to me through (specify date) under the same terms and conditions presently in effect. On that date, I will return all sets of keys in my possession together with all other papers and documents belonging to the company.

7.   (Name of company) will reimburse me for all reasonable and necessary expenses related to the completion of company business after I submit appropriate vouchers and records within (specify) days of presentment thereto.

8.   (Name of company) agrees to provide me with a favorable letter of recommendation and reference(s), and will announce to the trade that I am resigning for "personal reasons." I am enclosing a letter for that purpose which will be reviewed and signed by (specify person) and returned to me immediately.

9.   Although unanticipated, (name of company) will not contest my filing for unemployment insurance benefits after (specify date), and will assist me in promptly executing all documents necessary for that purpose.

10.   If a position is procured by me prior to (specify date), a lump sum payment for my remaining severance will be paid within (specify) days after my notification of same. Additionally, the stock referred to in paragraph 3 above will be purchased as of the date of my employment with another company if prior to (specify date) and will be paid to me within (specify) days of my notification.

If any of the terms of this letter are ambiguous or incorrect, please advise me immediately in writing specifying the items that are incorrect. Otherwise, this letter shall set forth our entire understanding in this matter, which cannot be changed orally.

(Name of corporate officer), I want to personally thank you for your assistance and cooperation in this matter and wish you all the best in the future.

Very truly yours,
Your Name
Sent certified mail, return receipt requested.

Be sure to draft the agreement accurately, since all ambiguities are usually construed against the person who writes such a letter. In addition, be prepared to send follow-up letters. Using the preceding case as an example, it would be wise to notify the company in writing if you obtained another job prior to the severance cutoff date. This is confirmed as shown in the following sample.

Sample Letter Requesting Unpaid Severance

Your Name
Address
Telephone Number
Date

Name of Corporate Officer
Title
Name of Company
Address

Re: Subsequent development to our agreement dated (specify)

Dear (Name of Corporate Officer),

I hope all is well with you and yours.

As a follow-up to our letter of agreement dated (specify), I am informing you that I have accepted employment with another company effective (specify date).

Therefore, I expect to receive a lump sum payment representing all unpaid severance through (specify date) plus (specify) weeks of vacation pay on or before (specify date).

Furthermore, I believe I am entitled to compensation for my stock totaling (specify amount) within (specify number of days).

As of this date, I am returning all keys to the office by messenger together with keys to the company car. I have also included the last voucher for company-related expenses.

Thank you for your prompt cooperation in these matters.

Very truly yours,
Your Name

Enc.

Releases

Always be cautious if the employer asks you to sign a release. Generally, releases extinguish potential claims. Employees sometimes voluntarily sign such documents when they are fired, without fully understanding the ramifications of such an act. Later they regret taking such action after consulting a lawyer and learning they forfeited valuable rights without receiving much in return.

Since you may be out of luck if you sign such a document, consider the following strategies whenever you are asked to sign a release:

1. NEVER SIGN A RELEASE UNLESS YOU ARE SATISFIED WITH THE COMPANY'S OFFER. This is reasonable because you should never relinquish a potentially valuable right without obtaining something of value in return.

2. READ THE RELEASE CAREFULLY BEFORE SIGNING IT. Most releases are complicated documents. Many have settlement agreements, releases, waivers, and nondisclosure provisions all rolled into one document.

For example, what exactly does the release say? Are you prohibited from telling others about the terms of your settlement? This is referred to as a "gag order" provision. Many employers insert gag order clauses into releases that require all settlement monies to be forfeited and returned in the event you reveal the terms of the settlement to others. Obviously, you should question this provision and avoid signing it if possible.

Does the release prohibit you from working for a competitor or starting a competing business? Without such a clause you are free to work for the employer of your choosing. This is a valuable right that should never be given up easily.

3. NEGOTIATE ADDITIONAL CLAUSES FOR YOUR PROTECTION. First, make sure the release will be null and void if any monies due under the agreement are not paid. Second, include a guarantee that obligates the parent company to pay all remaining sums due under the agreement in the event a subsidiary corporation becomes bankrupt, insolvent, or fails for any reason to pay the amount due. These are examples of the kinds of points to consider and implement in your agreement.

4. OBTAIN MUTUAL RELEASES WHERE APPROPRIATE. Try to get the employer to give you a release whenever you are giving one to the employer. This is because you want to be sure that the employer can never sue you at a later time for something you did.

5. SPEAK TO A LAWYER IMMEDIATELY WHENEVER THE EMPLOYER REQUESTS THAT YOU SIGN A RELEASE. Not understanding the consequences of their actions, people often waive important rights by signing such agreements. For example, you may be waiving valuable claims based on discrimination, breach of contract, unfair discharge, or additional commissions or other monies owed. Never sign such a release until you are knowledgeable about all potential rights that you are giving up.

The cover letter and releases beginning on page 255 illustrate the kinds of documents you may be requested to sign depending on your particular circumstances.

A competent lawyer can also take other practical steps for your protection. For example, he or she can insist that the release be held in escrow until all sums due under the agreement have been paid. This means that the employer could not rely on the signed release until it had fully performed all of the obligations required by the release. This is important and should never be overlooked.

STRATEGY: *If you believe that you signed a release under conditions of fraud, duress, or mistake, it can be rescinded in special cases if you act promptly. Although it is generally difficult to overturn a release, always consult a lawyer immediately if you believe you were tricked into signing one.*

One client, an African-American woman over 40, once found herself in such a situation. She thought that she was fired illegally because of her race and age. She was told to sign a release in order to receive severance. But the release she signed was quite short (just a few sentences) and was not artfully drafted. For example, the release did not say that she had 21 days to review it, that she could revoke it up to seven days after signing, or that she had the right to consult a lawyer.

When she met with me, I told her that she had received very little in return for signing the document. I also advised her that she had a decent chance of fighting the release on legal technical terms because it was drafted so poorly.

The woman hired me to contact the company and negotiate a better package. Through my efforts, I was able to disallow the release and get her another $8,000 in severance. In hindsight, the company probably thought that $8,000 wasn't worth a lawsuit and the poor publicity and wasted manpower that go along with it.

Finally, recognize your rights with respect to releases under the federal Older Workers Benefit Protection Act (OWBPA). The act makes it clear that, in relation to a firing or a resignation of a worker over 40, a company can protect itself from potential violations of ADEA claims by utilizing waivers, provided:

1. The waiver is part of an agreement that specifically states the worker is waiving ADEA rights and is not merely a general release;

2. The agreement containing the waiver does not disclaim any rights or claims arising after the date of its execution;

3. The worker receives value (such as an extra month of severance) in exchange for signing the agreement;

4. The worker is advised in writing of the right to consult an attorney of his or her choosing before signing the agreement;

5. The worker is advised in writing of his or her right to consider the agreement for a period of 21 days before it is effective; and

6. The worker is given at least seven days following the execution of the agreement to revoke it.

When employers request the signing of releases or waivers in connection with mass termination programs and large-scale voluntary retirement programs, the act is even more strict. All individuals in the program must be given at least 45 days to consider the agreement, and each employee must also be provided with numerous facts, such as the class, unit, or group of individuals covered by the program, any eligibility factors for the program, time limits applicable to the program, the job titles and ages of all individuals selected for the program, and the ages of all individuals not eligible for the program.

A benefit of the OWBPA is that all voluntary early retirement programs are now scrutinized closely to determine that there is no chance of threat, intimidation, or coercion to the worker to whom the benefit is offered. Older employees must now be given sufficient time to consider the offer and receive accurate and complete information regarding benefits.

Ask a lawyer to advise you of your rights if you are asked to sign a complicated waiver that you believe does not comply with the requirements of this law.

Finally, as previously stated, the federal Older Workers Benefit Protection Act codifies existing law by providing that an older worker may not waive rights or claims of discrimination under the Age Discrimination in Employment Act unless the waiver is clear, voluntarily signed, part of an agreement where additional severance pay, early retirement benefits, or other monies are given, and the individual is given at least 21 days to consider the agreement containing such a waiver and seven days to change his or her mind after he or she signs it. Speak to a lawyer to advise you of your rights if you are asked to sign a complicated waiver that you believe does not comply with the requirements of this law.

Summary of Things to Know if Your Job is in Jeopardy

1. It may be illegal for a company to fire you to deprive you of large commissions, vested pension rights, a year-end bonus, or other expected financial benefits.

2. It may be illegal for a company to fire you after returning from an illness, pregnancy, or jury duty.

3. It may be illegal to fire you for complaining about a safety violation or other wrongdoing.

4. It may be illegal to fire you in a manner inconsistent with company handbooks, manuals, written contracts, and disciplinary rules.

5. It may be illegal to fire you if the decision to fire you is motivated, in whole or in part, by your age (if you are between 40 and 70), your race or ethnicity, or your gender.

6. It may be illegal to fire a large number of workers and/or close a plant without giving at least 60 days' notice or 60 days' severance pay.

7. It may be illegal to fire you if you received a verbal promise of job security or other rights that the company failed to fulfill.

8. It may be illegal to fire a long-term worker when the "punishment does not fit the crime" and other workers were not similarly treated, particularly if you are over 40, belong to a protected minority group, or are a female.

9. If you signed a written contract, reread it. Review what it says about termination, because if the company fails to act according to the contract, your rights may be violated.

10. Try to make copies of all pertinent documents in your personnel file while working. If you have received excellent performance reviews and appraisals and the file indicates you received merit salary increases, you may be able to use this information to successfully negotiate more severance than the company is offering.

11. Refuse the company's offer to resign whenever possible. This is because if you resign you may be waiving your claim to unemployment and other severance benefits.

12. Avoid accepting the company's first offer of severance. Stall for time and follow the negotiating strategies given in Chapters 6 and 7. By doing so, you can increase the chances of obtaining more severance pay and other post-termination financial benefits than the company initially offered.

Finally, as with the other recommendations in this book, the above 12 strategies are merely suggestions and are not intended to be legal advice per se. Therefore, always seek competent legal advice where warranted.

Summary of Negotiating Strategies to Maximize Severance Pay and Retirement Benefits

1. Generally, there is no legal obligation for a company to pay severance unless you have a written contract stating that severance will be paid, oral promises are given regarding severance pay, there is a documented policy of paying severance in a company manual or handbook, the employer voluntarily offers to pay severance, or other employees in similar positions have received severance pay in the past.

2. If you are fired, request an additional negotiating session to discuss your severance package.

3. Stall for time and try not to accept the company's first offer.

4. Appeal to corporate decency and fair play at the initial meeting. For example, it is better to say, "I am 58 years old and have to pay for two children in college right now, and your offer of just four weeks' severance will probably put me on the road to financial ruin, since it is unlikely that I

can find another comparable job in four weeks," rather than, "If you don't pay me more money, I will sue."

5. Follow the negotiating strategies given in Chapters 6 and 7 to maximize your chances of obtaining additional financial and other post-termination benefits. Recognize that by asking for many (e.g., 15) items, you may be able to get the company to settle for some (e.g., five).

6. Confirm all arrangements in writing to document the final deal of severance and post-termination benefits; do not accept the company's promise that "everything will work out."

7. Insist on receiving more money and other benefits before signing any release or waiver of age discrimination claims.

8. Do not rely on promises from the company that you will receive a favorable job reference. Rather, draft your own favorable letter of reference and get an officer or your supervisor to sign the letter of reference before you depart.

9. Do not be intimidated or forced into early retirement. Recognize that you may have rights, particularly if your early retirement causes you to lose large, expected financial benefits.

10. Be cautious when the employer asks you to sign a release, because you may be waiving valuable rights and benefits in the process.

11. Never resign from a job unless absolutely necessary. If you are given the choice between resigning or being fired, get fired.

12. Select the most favorable or sympathetic person at the company to initially negotiate the deal with.

13. Go above him or her if you don't achieve what you're seeking.

14. Never be pressured by the employer into signing a release or making a fast decision.

15. Be persistent; don't become demoralized.

16. Know your rights, ask questions, and demand answers.

17. Have a game plan in place to help you get what you want.

18. Rehearse what you will say and why it is fair for you to get a better package.

19. Consider early retirement options or other ways to keep you on the payroll such as working freelance or as a consultant where appropriate.

20. Analyze the tax aspects of any settlement.

21. Negotiate for nontaxable benefits or convert unneeded benefits (such as outplacement assistance) into more severance pay when practicable.

Finally, since the above 21 strategies are merely suggestions and are not intended to be legal advice per se, always seek competent legal advice where warranted.

Summary of Negotiating Tips
Wages (Also Referred To As Salary Continuation)

1. Try to stay on the payroll as long as possible.

2. Negotiate for the employer to continue to provide medical, dental, and hospitalization coverage (paid for by the employer) while you are receiving severance wages.

3. Avoid arrangements where you are offered severance for a specified period (e.g., six months) that automatically ceases when you obtain a new job. Rather, make the offer non-contingent on new employment or arrange that differential severance will be paid in a lump sum if you obtain a new job prior to the expiration of the severance period. (For example, arrange that three months' worth of

severance will be paid in a lump sum if a new job is obtained three months before the six months of salary continuation expires.)

4. If severance pay is to be paid in a lump sum, consider asking for it immediately, not in installments over time.

5. Recognize that if you receive salary continuation rather than a lump sum payment, you may be ineligible in some states for unemployment benefits until the salary continuation payments cease; thus, consider the benefits of a lump sum payment rather than extended salary continuation where warranted.

6. Avoid accepting the employer's first offer: negotiate, negotiate, negotiate.

7. Attempt to receive at least four weeks' severance for every year of employment.

Other Compensation

1. If you have relocated recently at the request of the employer, try to obtain additional relocation allowances.

2. Discuss accrued vacation pay, overtime, and unused sick pay. Be sure you are paid for these items.

3. If you were fired without notice, ask for two additional weeks of salary in lieu of the employer's lack of notice.

4. If commissions are due or about to become due, insist that you be paid immediately; do not waive these expected benefits.

Bonus

1. Understand how your bonus is computed.

2. If you were entitled to receive a bonus at the end of the year, ask for it now.

3. Argue that the firing deprived you of the right to receive the bonus if the employer refuses to pay; or,

4. Insist that your bonus be prorated according to the amount of time you worked during the year if this argument is rejected.

Pension And Profit-Sharing Benefits

1. Ask for details regarding the nature of your benefits. Under federal law, you are entitled to an accurate, written description of all benefits.

2. Be aware of all plans, funds, and programs that may have been established on your behalf.

3. If you are fired just before the vesting of a pension (e.g., two months before the vesting date), argue that the timing of the firing is suspect and that public policy requires the employer to grant your pension. If the employer refuses, consult an experienced lawyer immediately.

4. Demand a copy of the employer's pension and/or profit-sharing plans from the plan administrator if the employer refuses to furnish you with accurate details. (You may have to pay for the cost of photocopying.)

5. Contact the plan administrator immediately to protect your rights if your claim is denied or if you have not received a proper accounting or payment of your retirement benefits from your employer.

Other Benefits

1. Request continued use of an office, secretary, telephone, or mail facilities to assist you in your job search, if appropriate.

2. Consider requesting a loan to tide you over while looking for a new job, if appropriate.

3. Consider requesting continued use of your company car or ask to buy the car or take over the lease at a reduced rate, if appropriate.

4. Request that the employer pay for outplacement guidance, career counseling, and resume preparation services including typing and incidental expenses, if appropriate.

Medical, Dental, And Hospitalization Coverage

1. Does coverage stop the day you are fired, or is there a grace period? Ask for a copy of the applicable policy.

2. Can you extend coverage beyond the grace period?

3. Be sure to have your benefits explained to you if you do not understand them.

4. Can you assume the policy at a reduced personal cost? This is sometimes referred to as a conversion policy.

5. If you are married and your spouse is working, you may be covered under your spouse's policy. If so, do you want to continue paying for your own policy?

6. Be sure the employer has notified you regarding your rights under COBRA.

Life Insurance

1. Can you convert the policy to your benefit at your own cost? Don't forget to inquire about this.

2. Is there any equity in the employer's life insurance plan that accrues to you upon termination? Inquire about this and ask for a copy of all policies presently in effect.

Your Cover Story

1. Clarify how the news of your departure will be announced. Discuss and agree with management on the story to be told to outsiders.

2. Consider whether you want it to be known that you resigned for personal reasons or that you were terminated due to a "business reorganization." These are neutral explanations that are preferable to firings for misconduct or poor performance.

3. Recognize that if you resign, you may be forfeiting unemployment benefits. Thus, avoid resigning wherever possible. Although you may prefer that outsiders be told you resigned for personal reasons, confirm with the employer that you will be able to apply for unemployment benefits. That way your local Department of Labor will be advised that there was a termination (as opposed to a resignation, since this is what really happened) and you can still tell outsiders you resigned.

4. Request that a copy of a favorable letter of recommendation be given to you before you leave the company. The letter should state the dates of your employment, the positions held, and that you performed all of your job duties in a diligent and satisfactory fashion. If possible, the letter should be signed by a qualified officer or supervisor who worked with you and knows you well. Do not rely on promises that the employer will furnish prospective employers with a favorable recommendation, since many fail to do this after employees leave the company. Thus, always attempt to have such a letter in hand before you leave.

5. Request that key members of the company be notified of your departure in writing. If possible, approve the contents of such a memo before distribution. Written memos can dispel false rumors about your termination. A positive memo may assist you in obtaining a new job. Remember, news of a firing usually spreads rapidly; you don't want to be the subject of false rumors or innuendo.

Golden Parachutes

1. Determine if you are entitled to receive additional benefits under a severance contract or golden parachute.

2. Speak to an experienced employment attorney immediately to protect your rights if the employer refuses to provide all the benefits specified in your contract.

8

■ ■ ■ ■ ■ ■ ■ ■ ■

Post-Termination Issues

Unemployment Hearings

Many people who are fired forfeit valuable unemployment insurance benefits. This is because they do not know how to act or represent themselves properly at unemployment hearings. Many are told by unemployment personnel that a lawyer or other representative is not required and that preparation for the hearing is unnecessary. They then attend the hearing and are surprised to learn that the employer is represented by experienced counsel who has brought witnesses to testify against their version of the facts. Additionally, some are unprepared for the grueling, humiliating cross-examination lasting several hours that they may be subjected to. Other people lose at the hearing because they do not know the purpose of their testimony or what they must prove to receive benefits.

This section will offer strategies to increase your chances of obtaining benefits at unemployment hearings when your case is contested by a former employer.

1. **KNOW THE LAW.** Each state imposes different requirements for collecting unemployment benefits, such as the maximum amount of money that may be collected weekly, the normal waiting period required before payments begin, the length of such benefits, and the maximum period you can wait before filing and collecting. States also differ on standards of proof required to receive such benefits. You must

know such essential details before filing. This can be done by contacting your nearest unemployment office.

The following questions are some of the points to consider asking:

- How quickly can I file?

- When will I begin receiving payments?

- How long will the payments last?

- What must I do (i.e., must I actively look for employment in order to qualify and continue receiving benefits)?

- How long did I have to work for my former employer in order to qualify?

- What must I prove in order to collect if my ex-employer contests my claim?

- When will the hearing be held?

- Will I have an opportunity to review the employer's defense and other documentation submitted in opposition before the hearing?

- How can I learn whether witnesses will appear on the company's behalf to testify against me?

- How can I obtain competent legal counsel to represent me?

- How much will this cost?

- Is a record made of the hearing? If so, in what form?

- Is the hearing examiner's decision final and binding, or can the decision be appealed?

- Can I recover benefits if I was forced to resign?

- Is the burden on the employer to demonstrate that I was fired for a good reason (such as misconduct), or is the burden on me to prove that I did not act improperly?

- Can I subpoena witnesses if they refuse to appear voluntarily on my behalf? Will the hearing examiner assist me in this regard?

- Are formal rules of evidence followed at the hearing?

As you can see, collecting benefits may not be a simple matter, especially if your claim is contested by an ex-employer.

When a terminated worker comes into my office, one of the first points I consider is whether the employee was discharged for a valid reason. In most states you can collect unemployment benefits if you were fired due to a business reorganization, massive layoff, job elimination, or other reasons that were not your fault. In many situations you can even collect if you were fired for being unsuited or unskilled for the job or for overall poor work performance. However, you generally cannot collect if you resign voluntarily (unless you were forced to resign for a good reason) or if you were fired for misconduct.

The following are common examples of acts that often justify the denial of unemployment benefits based on misconduct:

- Insubordination or fighting on the job
- Habitual lateness or excessive absence
- Intoxication or drug abuse on the job
- Disobedience of company work rules or policies
- Gross negligence or neglect of duty
- Dishonesty or unfaithfulness

Although these examples appear to be relatively straightforward, employers often have difficulty proving that such acts reached the level of misconduct. This is because hearing examiners typically seek to determine whether a legitimate company rule was violated and whether or not that rule was justified.

Hearing examiners, judges, and arbitrators use guidelines in making decisions at unemployment hearings and arbitrations. Many of these guidelines are relevant to successfully asserting one's claim for unemployment benefits and are repeated here for your benefit.

- Did the employer have a clear rule against the kind of behavior that resulted in the firing?

■ Is the rule reasonably related to the orderly, efficient, and safe operation of the employer's business?

■ Did the employer provide all employees with a reasonable opportunity to learn the company's rules?

■ Did the employer provide all employees with reasonable notice regarding the consequences of violating such rules?

■ Has the employer administered and enforced the rules consistently and without discrimination among all employees?

■ Did the employer take steps to fairly investigate the circumstances involved in the alleged offense?

■ Did the employer obtain substantial evidence of the alleged act through this investigation?

■ Did such acts meet the standard of law required to prove misconduct?

■ Are there mitigating factors that reasonably explain the employee's conduct?

■ Was the firing fair under all of the circumstances?

■ Were the employer's witnesses credible in proving the action taken?

These considerations demonstrate the degree of sophistication that is often required to prevail at unemployment hearings. That is why you should carefully consider whether you require representation by experienced counsel at the hearing. If you are anticipating receiving the maximum benefits allowed (in some states this may exceed $425 per week) and expect to be unable to find gainful employment for a long period of time (e.g., six months), it may be advantageous to hire counsel.

2.   **PREPARE FOR THE HEARING.** Once you file for unemployment insurance and learn that the employer is contesting your claim, it is your responsibility to follow the progress of the case carefully. Plan on attending the hearing on the date in question. If you cannot be present, speak to a clerk responsible for scheduling, explain your reasons, and

ask for another convenient date. This should preferably be done in person. Indicate future dates when you know you can appear. Call that individual the day before the old hearing date to confirm that your request has been granted.

An unemployment hearing is not different from a trial. Witnesses must testify under oath. Documents, including personnel information, warnings, performance appraisals, and so on, are submitted as exhibits. The atmosphere is rarely friendly. Thus, you must prepare in advance what you will say, how you will handle tough questions from the employer, and what you will try to prove to win the case.

When preparing for the hearing, be certain that all your friendly witnesses (if any) will attend and testify on your behalf. If necessary, ask a representative from the unemployment office to issue a subpoena compelling the attendance of key disinterested witnesses (such as coworkers) who refuse to voluntarily attend and testify. Unfortunately, people who tell you they will appear do not always do so, and it may be necessary to subpoena them. If the unemployment representative has no authority to do this, wait until the first day of the hearing. Explain to the judge or hearing examiner the necessity of compelling the appearance and testimony of key witnesses. The judge may grant your request depending on the relevance and reasonableness of it.

Organize your case before the day of the hearing to maximize your chances of success. Collect all evidence so it can be produced easily at the hearing. Practice what you will say at the hearing. This will relax you and help you to organize the important facts. You can even prepare an outline of key points to be discussed and questions to ask each witness and employee of the ex-employer.

3.   ATTEND THE HEARING. Arrive early on the hearing day and advise a scheduling clerk of your appearance. Bring your evidence and come properly attired (preferably in business clothes).

STRATEGY: *In some states you can review the entire contents of your unemployment file before the hearing; don't forget to show up early and ask for this if appropriate.*

When your case is called, all relevant witnesses will be sworn in. Stay calm. The judge or hearing examiner will conduct the hearing and ask you questions. Speak directly and with authority. Show the judge your evidence. Talk directly to the judge and respond to his or her questions. Show respect. Always refer to him or her as "Your Honor" or "Judge" and never argue with the judge. If you are asked a question while speaking, stop immediately and answer it. Make your answer direct and to the point.

Avoid being emotional. Avoid arguing with your opponent at the hearing and avoid interrupting his or her presentation.

After your opponent finishes testifying, you will have the opportunity to cross-examine such testimony and refute what was said. In addition, do not be afraid if the employer is represented by an attorney. If you feel intimidated, tell the judge that you are not represented by counsel and are not familiar with unemployment hearing procedures. Ask the judge to intercede on your behalf when you feel your opponent's attorney is treating you unfairly. Most judges are sympathetic since unemployment hearings are specifically designed for you to present your case without an attorney.

4. OBTAIN A DECISION. Decisions are not usually obtained immediately after the hearing. You will probably be notified by mail (sometimes one to four weeks later). Be sure to continue filing for benefits while waiting for the decision. Many people forget to do this and lose valuable benefits in the process.

You should begin collecting weekly or biweekly benefits immediately after receiving a favorable decision. Additionally, you should receive a lump sum check representing benefits previously due.

5. DECIDE IF YOU SHOULD APPEAL. If you are notified that you lost the decision, read the notice carefully. Most judges and hearing examiners give specific, lengthy reasons for their rulings. If you feel that the ruling was incorrect or you disagree with the judge's opinion, you may wish to file an appeal and have the case reheard. However, it is best to speak with an experienced attorney to get his or her opinion before doing so. You may discover that your chances of success with the appeal are not as good as you think. Appeals are not granted automatically as a matter of right in many states. If the judges on the appeals board believe that the hearing judge's decision was correct factually or as a matter of law, the decision will go undisturbed.

Recognize that the odds of winning the appeal are not in your favor. Often, the amount of time needed to review the transcript or tape of the proceeding(s), prepare an appeal brief, and reargue the case makes it too expensive and time-consuming. Thus, depending on the particular facts of your case, appealing the hearing may not be worth it. However, if new material facts come to light or relevant witnesses are willing to come forward and testify at the appeal hearing, this could make the difference. That is why you should always consult with an experienced employment attorney before making such a decision.

Resigning Properly

Most people do not know how to resign properly. The slightest mistake can expose you to a lawsuit or cause the forfeiture of valuable benefits. Some people resign without receiving a firm job offer from a new employer. Later, after learning the new job did not materialize, they are unable to be rehired by their former employer and spend months out of work unnecessarily.

It doesn't have to happen this way. Problems such as these can be avoided by thinking ahead. A proper resignation occurs when you are able to step into a new job with increased benefits without missing a day's pay, have no legal exposure, and collect what you are owed from the former employer. Take the following hypothetical for example:

Bari is called into her boss's office and told that she is being summarily discharged. However, the company states that she can resign by signing a letter of resignation, which it has prepared and presents to her.

Bari thinks it is better to resign than to be fired, so she signs the letter of resignation and leaves the premises. When she files for unemployment benefits, she learns she is not entitled to benefits unless she can prove that she was forced to resign. The company introduces the letter of resignation as evidence that no pressure or undue influence was forced on Bari and it was her voluntary decision; she is denied unemployment insurance benefits.

Bari consults an employment lawyer. She learns that had she not resigned she would have received severance. She also learns that she could have made a deal with her employer (and confirmed it in writing) that although the company would agree to inform prospective employers that she resigned for personal reasons, it would not contest her unemployment benefits or deny paying her other benefits she would have received had she allowed the company to fire her. The lawyer also explained that if she was close to earning a vested pension, profit-sharing benefits, or year-end bonus, her resignation would seriously undermine a claim for those expected benefits.

The golden rule is never to quit a job if you can help it. Refuse an employer's offer to resign whenever possible. This is because if you resign you may be waiving a claim to unemployment and other severance benefits, including earned commissions. This is a trap many employees fall into.

However, there are occasions when you may receive a better job offer and decide to resign from your current position. Information in this section will tell you how to do so properly to increase the chances that the job at your new employer will not be short-lived.

For maximum protection, review and implement the following strategies where possible.

1.   SIGN A WRITTEN CONTRACT WITH A NEW EMPLOYER BEFORE RESIGNING. A written contract with a definite term of employment (for example, six months or one year) can protect you from situations where the new employer changes its mind and decides not to hire you, or fires you after a short period of time. This often happens with devastating consequences but can be avoided by insisting on a valid agreement with job security before starting work. If the new employer does not agree to this, think twice before jumping ship.

Many clients wish to learn what rights they have after resigning from a job and accepting a position with a new employer. Generally, they forget (or are afraid) to get a firm commitment of job security from a new employer before they resign from a good job. On some occasions, unfortunate workers sell their homes and relocate their family to a distant locale, only to discover they aren't happy or that the employer is not satisfied with the arrangement shortly after the move is made. They ask if they can sue the new employer for promissory estoppel, misrepresentation, and other related legal causes of action as a result of the new job going sour.

While it is possible to recover money as a result of the new employer's broken promises, this could have been avoided had they insisted on receiving an employment agreement that contained a definite promise of job security.

Remember, a job is like a romance. Companies woo applicants with promises of fulfillment and riches. Then, when the honeymoon is over, even highly qualified people find themselves being treated unfairly. This is the nature of the working world. Remember this for your own good. Never leave a good job voluntarily without a strong employment agreement from your new employer if you can help it.

2. REVIEW YOUR CURRENT CONTRACT OR LETTER OF AGREEMENT. If notice is required to be given, do this so you will not violate the contract's obligations.

This is an important concern. For example, if your contract requires you to give 30 days' notice before leaving, you must do so to avoid the company claiming you are in breach of contract. If you do not resign properly, you may be sued for damages. Damages in such cases are typically calculated at the employer's cost of training a replacement. However, if you resign prematurely at an important time (e.g., during market week if you are a salesperson, or right before a customer is consummating an important deal in which your services are required, but the deal is blown because you leave), the damages could be significant.

There are occasions where an employer will release you from your obligations immediately after you give proper notice. This is because the employer may not want you around for, say, 30 days after it knows you will be leaving. If your contract requires notice, offer it but anticipate, discuss, or seize the opportunity that you may leave suddenly at the employer's request. If the employer agrees, ask to receive the wages you would have earned during the notice period as part of a severance package. Some employers may be amenable to this.

Finally, since the employer may tell you to get out immediately after you give notice, anticipate this may occur and plan accordingly. Consider removing valuable contents from your office before giving notice, because the employer may tell you to vacate the premises and you won't have this opportunity later. Get your affairs in order. Select the best time to resign to suit your needs knowing this may occur.

3. GET LEGAL ADVICE IF YOU BELIEVE YOUR CURRENT EMPLOYER WILL REJECT (OR REJECTS) AN OFFER TO RESIGN. On rare occasions, an employer may be inclined to do this, especially if you have an important job and your presence is essential to completing a major task or project. This could happen when you have a written employment contract with a definite term (say for a year) and you wish to resign six months into the contract period.

If you choose to leave anyway, you may be subjecting yourself to a breach of contract lawsuit. An employment attorney may advise that the most obvious damages you would suffer might be the employer's costs to train a suitable replacement. If the company was forced to hire a replacement at a higher salary or with greater benefits, the difference in pay might also be cause for damages.

Fortunately, in many cases, the damages typically asserted by an employer against someone breaking a contract and leaving a job prematurely are speculative and hard to prove. I have observed that the vast majority of employers are inclined to set you free because keeping you around is dangerous (you could be sharing information with a competitor) and bad for morale (since you will probably not be giving your best when forced to remain).

All of these factors should be considered before you decide to break a contract. As consideration, a lawyer may recommend that you continue to work for the company as a consultant with less compensation in return for getting the employer to "let you out" of the contract. To minimize the risks of a lawsuit, these and other ideas should sometimes be explored before the decision to leave is made.

4. GIVE NOTICE ONLY WHERE NECESSARY. In many jobs, giving notice is not required or necessary (contrary to the public's misconception) especially if you are hired at will. However, the employer will usually benefit when you offer notice because it may then have time to seek and train a replacement. It may also give you the opportunity to bargain for additional financial benefits before walking out the door.

Two weeks' notice is probably more than adequate; avoid giving more notice than necessary. Do not offer notice if you must start a new job immediately and believe this will jeopardize your new position. However, if you are entitled to a large bonus or commission in the near future, postpone resigning until you have received such a benefit.

Many employers often summarily reject an employee's notice and ask you to leave the minute they are notified of your intentions. The reason is that some employers believe you will copy pertinent documents or cause trouble. Don't be surprised if this occurs. Anticipate it and plan ahead.

5. SHOULD YOU RESIGN BY LETTER? Only when it is used to clarify resignation benefits, request prompt payment of monies previously due, confirm unfair or illegal treatment, or put you on record that the resignation will not be effective until some later date. If these reasons are important, always resign by letter. When you do, keep the letter brief and avoid giving reasons for the resignation without having a lawyer review the letter first. The reason is that the letter may be used as evidence at a later trial or proceeding and can preclude you from offering other reasons for the resignation or tipping your hand in the event of a lawsuit.

The example on page 407 is the kind of resignation letter you may wish to draft. You should deliver it by hand or send it by certified mail, return receipt requested, in order to prove delivery.

6.   NEVER RESIGN IF GIVEN THE CHOICE. Many employers have written policies that state that no severance or other post-termination benefits will be paid to workers who resign. Additionally, in many states, you are not entitled to unemployment insurance benefits after voluntarily resigning from a job. If you are a commission salesperson, it is often more difficult to argue that you are entitled to commissions due on orders shipped after a resignation (as opposed to after a firing).

STRATEGY: *Think twice if the employer gives you the option of resignation or discharge. Talk to a lawyer for advice. It is generally preferable that clients be fired rather than resign, since potential damage claims and severance benefits may remain intact. If you are worried what others may think, you can always negotiate that the employer will tell outsiders that you "resigned for personal reasons" (even if you were fired).*

---

7.   KEEP QUIET. Tell friends and business associates of your decision to resign after telling your current employer, not before.

8.   AVOID BAD-MOUTHING. It is not a good idea to tell others about the circumstances surrounding a resignation, particularly if you are leaving on less-than-pleasant terms. Many employers have sued former employees for defamation, product disparagement, and unfair competition on discovering that harmful oral or written comments were made. Additionally, when the statement disparages the quality of a company's product and at the same time implies that an officer or principal of the employer is dishonest, fraudulent, or incompetent (thus affecting the individual's personal reputation), a private lawsuit for personal defamation may be brought. Some companies withhold severance pay and other voluntary benefits as a way of getting even. Thus, avoid discussing your employer in a negative way with anyone.

9. RETURN COMPANY PROPERTY. Disputes sometimes occur when property belonging to the employer is not returned. You probably must return such property (automobile keys, confidential customer lists, samples, etc) immediately on resignation to avoid claims of conversion, fraud, and breach of contract.

If you return items by mail, get a receipt to prove delivery. A few states permit you to retain company property as a lien in the event you are owed money that the employer refuses to pay. However, since many states do not recognize this, speak to an employment attorney before taking such action.

Sample Letter of Resignation

Your Name
Your Address
Telephone Number
Date

Name of Officer
Title
Name of Employer
Address

Re: My Resignation

Dear (Name of Officer):

Please be advised that I am resigning from my job as (title) effective (date).

As of this date, I believe that (describe what salary, commissions, other benefits) are due and I look forward to discussing my termination benefits with you.

I shall be returning all property belonging to the company (specify) by (date) and will be available to assist you in a smooth transition if requested.

Thank you for your attention to these matters.

Very truly yours,

Your Name

Sent certified mail, return receipt requested

Restrictive Covenants, Trade Secrets, and Gag Orders

Employees often resign from a job or are lured away to a rival company to compete directly against their former employers. Sometimes they take valuable customer lists, trade secrets, and confidential information (such as prices and requirements of key customers) with them. When the former company discovers this, a lawsuit may be filed to stop the employee from using such information. In other instances, a former employer may attempt to stop the individual from using information that was learned and acquired while working. Can this be done? This section discusses lawsuits often commenced by employers to restrict a workers' ability to work or discuss important information after quitting or being fired. The following information can decrease the chances that such problems will occur and give you a better understanding of the legalities in this area.

RESTRICTIVE COVENANTS. Restrictive covenants, also referred to as covenants not to compete, are clauses in written employment contracts, confidentiality agreements, or termination agreements that are used for many purposes. Depending on the facts, when properly drafted and when state law allows, such clauses may:

- Restrict an employee from working for a competitor of the former employer

- Restrict an employee from starting a business or forming a venture with others that directly competes against the former employer

■ Restrict an employee from contacting or soliciting former or current customers or employees of the employer

■ Restrict an employee from using confidential knowledge, trade secrets, customer lists, and other privileged information learned while working for the former employee

■ Restrict an employee from any of the above in geographic or time limitations

The above points are illustrated by the following actual clauses often used in agreements:

"For a period of one (1) year following the termination of your employment for any reason, it is agreed that you will not contact, solicit, or be employed by any person, firm, association, or corporation to which you sold products of the Employer during the year preceding the termination of your employment."

"During the period of this Agreement and for a period of one (1) year thereafter, the Employee agrees that he or any company he is affiliated with, either directly or indirectly, shall not induce, hire, solicit, or otherwise utilize the services of any employee or sales rep currently employed by the Company."

Without a written contract containing a restrictive covenant, employees generally cannot be stopped from working for a competitor or starting a competing business after they resign or are fired from a job. This is especially true if you resigned for a good reason (e.g., were not being paid in a timely fashion) and have not stolen trade secrets or confidential information. In situations where employees signed an agreement with a covenant-not-to-compete clause either before or after commencing work, the general trend is that such restrictions may not be enforceable because they unfairly inhibit a person's ability to earn a living at his or her chosen profession.

The enforcement of any written covenant varies on a state-by-state basis and usually depends on a number of factors unique to each particular case. Many states, such as New York, have left the issue to the courts to decide. Other states, including Oregon, Louisiana, and Texas, have responded legislatively by enacting statutes regulating the

410 The Employee Rights Handbook

enforceability of such clauses. In those states where restrictive covenants are not automatically illegal (as they are generally when they restrict independent contractors, sales reps and agents, brokers, and professional such as doctors), the primary focus of a judge is usually the reasonableness of the covenant in terms of geographic scope, time restraints, and purpose.

An employer may increase the chances of having such a clause enforced when the covenant is short in terms of geographic location (i.e., the ex-employee is prohibited from calling on only a few large customers located within the county where the ex-employer's main office is located, instead of the entire United States); when such customers were procured by the employer's efforts and not the employee's; and when the prohibition does not exceed six months to a year.

Thus a restrictive covenant prohibiting a lighting-services employee from competing in the lighting retrofitting business within a hundred-mile radius of his former employer for five years after termination was found to be unreasonable and unenforceable by the Nevada Supreme Court.

STRATEGY: *A non-solicitation provision may bar you from calling on specific customers but does not generally prohibit you from taking orders if customers independently call you. Remember this and act accordingly.*

Courts sometimes respond more favorably to situations where companies have paid the employee extra consideration, such as $2,500 or an extra week's vacation before signing a contract containing such a provision, or negotiating a greater severance package in consideration for signing a contract with such a clause. And in some states, if the agreement provides that the ex-employee will receive his or her regular salary while the covenant is being enforced so that no loss of salary takes place during the restricted period, some judges may enforce the clause depending on other factors.

These factors often include an examination into whether the ex-employee's services are special, unique, or extraordinary; whether the restriction is necessary for the company to protect its business; and whether the person is in possession of trade secrets and other confidential information that, if disclosed or used in competition, would severely damage the company. When the employer prepares a restrictive covenant that is signed by the employee and is found to be enforceable, the restrictions may also apply to competing businesses conducted by the employee's family members with background help from the employee even though they did not sign any agreements.

In order to establish that an employee is "unique," the employee must generally show more than that the employee excels at his work or that his performance is of great value. The employer generally has the difficult burden of proving that the employee's services are of such character as to make his replacement impossible or that the loss of such services would cause the employer irreparable injury. This is often difficult to prove.

In some states, if you are required to sign an agreement containing a restrictive covenant after you begin working, the court may find such an agreement to be unenforceable because no additional consideration was conveyed. In such states, a judge will not enforce it unless the company gives a corresponding benefit (e.g., an increase in salary, a bona fide promotion, or a beneficial change in job status). Other states may rule in the company's favor on this point, however, finding that the additional consideration was the ability to keep the job (which would be lost if someone refused to sign the document). Since state laws vary substantially as to what constitutes sufficient consideration to enforce covenants in these cases, speak with a knowledgeable employment attorney to explore your options.

Be aware that some kinds of noncompete pacts stand a better chance of being upheld than others. These include a situation where a business is sold and the seller (who was an employee) agrees not to compete with the buyer for a specified period of time after the sale.

The following strategies may be helpful for protection in this area.

1. AVOID SIGNING ANY AGREEMENT CONTAINING A RESTRICTIVE COVENANT. Even if you work and/or live in a state that does not recognize such clauses, it is still not a good idea to sign any agreement containing such a clause. The reason is that a restrictive covenant provision may have a chilling effect and impair your ability to get to keep another job.

Restrictive covenants carry the implied threat that the company may institute legal action after your resignation or termination. This may effectively discourage you from contacting prospective employers or customers in your industry, establishing a competing business, or finding a job. On numerous occasions, my clients were asked by prospective employers if they were legally bound by any future working restrictions. Many times they were forced to provide copies of existing contracts and as a result were unable to secure employment.

If you are sued and the company seeks a temporary injunction to immediately stop you from working, your legal fees and costs to successfully defend yourself in court could be prohibitive. The problem is that many employers think they are protected when they have employees sign noncompetition clauses. Although such protection may be illusory, companies often take great pains to go to court to find out if these clauses are enforceable and to demonstrate to current employees their resolve in not allowing others to do the same thing. Thus, even if you win, you will probably get stuck with a hefty legal bill. In this country, losing parties are typically not required to pay for the prevailing party's attorney fees. Even if you think a prospective employer will foot the bill for your court fight, it's generally not wise to expose yourself to the risk of finding out.

2. AVOID SIGNING ANY COVENANT THAT CONTAINS A LIQUIDATED DAMAGES PROVISION. Such a clause may say, for example, that if you violate the agreement, you must return that portion of your compensation (e.g., extra salary or other money) you have received in consideration for signing an agreement not to compete, or you must forfeit benefits (e.g., valuable stock options) due to vest in the future. While perhaps not affecting the enforceability of the covenant itself, a forfeiture provision may represent a threat of substantial economic harm.

3. CONSULT AN EMPLOYMENT ATTORNEY IMMEDI-ATELY IF AN EX-EMPLOYER THREATENS TO SUE TO ENFORCE A RESTRICTIVE COVENANT. You may be surprised to learn that the employer will be unsuccessful in the event of a lawsuit. Courts in many states are now ruling that noncompete agreements are not enforceable (a) when they restrict a person's right to work (particularly if your trade is your only means of support), (b) when they are being used merely to guard the employer's turf, ©) when trade secrets (defined in the next section) are not involved, or (d) when you must work to support a family member with special needs (e.g., a spouse who is ill). Do not take any action detrimental to your interest, such as signing a document admitting any wrongdoing, until you have spoken with counsel. Many people are pressured by ex-employers to do things they later regret. Avoid being intimidated whenever possible.

4. DETERMINE IF THE EMPLOYER HAS BREACHED ANY OBLIGATIONS OR DUTIES OWED TO YOU. When companies are in breach of important contract terms, the law generally presumes they have "unclean hands." Sometimes in such situations restrictive covenants will not be applied against you. In one case, for example, I defended several sales employees who had gone into business in competition with their ex-employer. Earlier, these individuals had contacted me to review an employment agreement they had signed with the ex-employer. The agreement did contain a restrictive covenant, but during the consultation I had learned that the employer, to save the company money, had reduced their salaries despite their written protests. I advised my clients that since the employer was obligated to pay a predetermined salary specified by contract, the failure to do so might release them from the covenant in the agreement.

The employees were sued after commencing business operations. At the trial, the judge heard testimony regarding this unilateral unjustified cut of pay. The judge agreed that the employer had unfairly reduced their compensation without their consent and ruled that the restrictive covenant could not be enforced against them.

STRATEGY: *An employment attorney may try to get some leverage by asserting legitimate counterclaims, such as that you were victimized by sexual harassment or age or race discrimination while working. Your defense can become even stronger when you present evidence demonstrating you were treated wrongfully. If you are a salesperson, you can also gain leverage by stating your customers do not want to get involved in litigation and that you will drag them in if the case proceeds. The company may be reluctant to harm its customers in this manner and may decide that the ill will created by a lawsuit is not worth it.*

Always avoid bad-mouthing the ex-employer during litigation proceedings. It is important for a judge to view your case in a sympathetic way; the more you are viewed as the innocent party just trying to earn a living, the more likely the judge may rule that enforcing the covenant isn't fair. Also, the odds of winning your case can get better the longer the company delays in commencing action. If the employer waits several months after learning of your alleged misconduct, a judge may feel that is wasn't so important to the employer after all and deny the employer's request for injunctive relief.

5.   RETRIEVE A COPY OF ANY PERTINENT AGREEMENT YOU MAY HAVE SIGNED. When people resign or are discharged and receive a formal demand that they refrain from certain acts (usually in the form of a cease-and-desist letter), often they cannot locate the agreement containing the restrictive covenant. This places them at a disadvantage. For example, they may be unable to obtain an accurate opinion from a lawyer if he or she cannot review the contract and may be forced to spend unnecessary legal fees trying to obtain a copy from the ex-employer. Thus, request copies of all documents that you sign and store them in a safe place for later review by you and your lawyer. Plan ahead and try to obtain copies from the company before you depart or are fired because it is much easier to do this while you are still there than after you are out the door.

6.   RESEARCH THE LAW IN YOUR STATE. Restrictive covenants that are unreasonable will not be upheld. But in some states, if the court finds the covenant to be overbroad in terms of geographic scope or time limitation, it has the ability to enforce the clause merely by reducing the time frame or territory (e.g., reducing it from two years to three months), and unless the employer acted in bad faith, courts in these jurisdictions may modify covenants to the extent necessary to protect the employer's interest without imposing undue hardship on the employee.

In other "all or nothing at all" states, the covenant will be stricken in its entirety without any modification.

Each state has its own procedure and unique requirements for accepting a company's application to grant injunctive relief rather than award damages. This means that the court may issue an order (i.e., an injunction) prohibiting the individual from working for the company's competitor. If the employee fails to comply with the court's order, he or she may be held in contempt. However, in some states, during the pendency of the action, if the employee believes he is right, his attorney may request court permission to post a bond for the damages the employer may be awarded so that the employee can continue to work for the competitor. Thus, research the unique law in your state to understand your rights.

From an employer's perspective, there are a number of points to remember to increase the odds of prevailing in restrictive covenant litigation against a former employee. Reasonable, well drafted restrictive covenants can protect an employer from a disloyal ex-employee. Without a written contract containing a restrictive covenant a company cannot stop a former employee from working for a competitor except in the rare instance where it is proven that the employee has stolen and is using trade secrets (discussed in the next section). However, by inserting in a contract a restrictive covenant of reasonable geographic scope and duration, such a tactic can be pursued if someone goes over to a competitor. This is of particular significance to companies that train their own employees in a unique skill, only to lose them later to a competitor.

Companies that sue ex-employees to enforce a restrictive covenant don't always win. Since the primary focus of the court is usually the reasonableness of the covenant, it is best to limit the covenant where practical and keep it short in terms of geographic location (i.e., never prohibit the employee from calling on customers located throughout the "entire United States").

Courts respond favorably to situations where companies have paid the employee additional consideration, such as $5,000, an extra month's vacation or greater severance pay, in exchange for the employee's signing a contract containing a restrictive covenant. Better still, if the contract states that the employee will receive $X per week (i.e., one-third of his/her regular salary) while the restriction is in effect after the termination of the contract, this may constitute adequate consideration to allow the covenant to continue.

State and federal courts enable employers to pursue legal remedies when key employees depart to work for competitors. These include benefit forfeiture provisions, liquidated damages, salary continuation programs during a limited non-compete period, injunctions, and lawsuits to collect damages. But if a company fails to take action immediately after hearing the covenant has been violated, (e.g., sending a strong cease-and-desist letter to the ex-employee and her new company, and then filing a motion for a preliminary injunction in court), a case can be weakened. For example, by delaying action for six months, a skeptical judge might question just how harmful the ex-employee's move really was. And if the covenant is short to begin with (say nine months), and the employer brings an action seven months later, what is the point?

There is a greater chance of losing the right to enforce a restrictive covenant when companies require employees who are already on-the-job to sign employment contracts containing such clauses. The reason is that in many states such a request by an employer will not be viewed as conferring any additional consideration (benefit) upon the employee to make such a clause valid.

When commencing a case, employers must be able to prove in court that the person's skills are unique, special, and extraordinary. This may be a difficult hurdle to overcome. Yet in one case, a judge determined that an employee was the only "star" of the former employer, and that the business would inevitably fail if the employee left. In another case, a state trial court found that several currency traders were unique employees because of their special relationships with customers, fostered by the employer at its expense. In both cases, the court granted the employer's request for permanent injunctive relief. Note: But even when uniqueness is proved, a number of states will not allow a company to restrain a talented professional (such as a doctor), or an independent contractor sales rep, agent , or broker from working for a competitor after the contract expired or was terminated.

The successful enforcement of a restrictive covenant or forfeiture provision is based on a case's unique facts and the laws of the state where the parties work. If a company proceeds with litigation, it must not have "unclean hands," especially after receiving a written demand. The chances of enforcing restrictive covenants are slim when employers intentionally breach important financial obligations to departing ex-employees.

TRADE SECRETS AND CONFIDENTIAL INFORMATION. It was once reported that Dow Chemical and General Electric reached an out-of-court settlement over employee poaching. Dow had accused GE of systematically recruiting an engineer with no supervisory responsibility who worked with automakers in projects involving high-tech plastics. In another case, after General Motors accused Volkswagen of stealing secrets when it recruited Jose Ignacio Lopez and seven of his GM associates, it was reported that GM received $1.1 billion to settle the matter.

Experts suggest that more companies and employees are willing to steal trade secrets, especially in high-tech industries, because many workers do not feel much loyalty in this era of corporate downsizing. Often ex-employees take valuable customer lists, trade secrets, and confidential information (such as prices and requirements of key customers) with them. When the company discovers this, a lawsuit may be filed to stop the ex-employee from using the information. Whether the employer will prevail will depend on many factors, including, (often most importantly), whether trade secrets are involved.

A trade secret may consist of any formula, pattern, device, or compilation of information used in business that gives a company an opportunity to obtain an advantage over competitors that do not know or use it. Although an exact definition is impossible, trade secrets are usually involved when:

■ An employer takes precautions to guard the secrecy of the information

■ An employer has expended significant money and effort in developing the information

■ It is difficult to acquire the information outside the company (i.e., it isn't generally known to outsiders)

■ Employees are warned that trade secrets are involved and that they are obligated to act in a confidential manner

Employees are tied to restrictive covenants in written agreements that bar or limit them from revealing to others such information, especially to new or potential employers competing with the company.

Clients consult the author to determine whether a particular procedure or operating process constitutes a trade secret. Unfortunately, the answer is not always clear cut. Generally, all or most of the preceding elements have to be present to establish that a given process or procedure is a trade secret and to determine whether it has been illegally conveyed when an employee is discharged or departs. Lawsuits and injunctions brought by companies in this area are often quite complicated and costly to defend, even for victorious ex-employees, because each case must be analyzed and decided on its own particular facts and circumstances. Additionally, courts generally do not like to punish smart workers who learn on the job and try to better themselves thereafter by using their acquired knowledge on a new job. Only when an employer will be clearly damaged and lose its competitive advantage is it likely to be victorious in a lawsuit. And this is only after it demonstrates that a trade secret or confidential information has been or will be conveyed.

In one case an employer lost an injunction action brought in an attempt to stop a competitor from using its customer lists. The situation arose when a former employee who had worked as a truck driver and occasional mechanic began working for a major competitor to the company's detriment. The court noted that at least three copies of its customer list were on open display at different locations of the company's premises, and it was obvious that anyone could see the list.

Even though a trade secret can be learned by outsiders through legitimate channels such as trade publications and scientific reports, this does not mean it loses its character as a secret. If the idea is taken by an outsider or appropriated by an ex-employee, a company may be able to bar its use. The defense that the secret could have been obtained legitimately may not matter; if the employee got it improperly, he or she may not be able to use it. For example, an ex-employee's failure to show any independent research or experimentation may make it difficult to prove he or she did not resort to stealing the secrets learned on the job.

An employee who leaves one job for another generally has the right to take with him all the skill and knowledge he has acquired as long as nothing he takes is the property of the employer. Courts distinguish between skills acquired by an employee in his or her work and the trade secrets, if any, of the employer. The former may be used by the employee in subsequent jobs, the latter may not.

An employee's experience in executing a number of steps to produce a desired end is often not a trade secret. When sales employees become friendly with customers in the course of their employment, they are allowed to call on these customers for new employers. But in some instances, they may be prohibited from using their knowledge of unique customer buying habits, requirements or other special information when soliciting their former employer's accounts. For example, if a salesperson knows that a particular customer will be in short supply of a special product at a certain time, he may not be able to use that confidential information acquired while working for the former employer.

Perhaps the most frequently disputed issue concerning trade secrets involves customer lists. A "secret" list is not a list of companies or individuals that can be compiled from a telephone directory or other readily available source. A list becomes confidential when the names of customers can be learned by someone only through his or her employment, for example, when the salesperson secretly copies a list of customers that the company spent considerable time, effort, and money and kept under lock and key.

An employee cannot make deals with customers in which he or she promises to perform favors in return for secret kickbacks involving money or other benefits (such as vacations). If you engage in such conduct without the company's knowledge and consent, the employer can terminate your employment and sue you for damages. Employers typically must consider all the aspects of a potential case before bringing suit, and they have the burden of proving that trade secrets are involved. The next hurdle in any lawsuit often is proving that trade secrets were stolen or misappropriated. When bringing a lawsuit based on misappropriation of trade secrets, typically an employee will argue that the information acquired was common public knowledge obtained by going through directories, trade journals, books, and catalogs. Many times, the question before a court is not how the ex-employee could have obtained the knowledge, but how they did.

When an employer has made a special effort to remind employees of their obligation to protect the company's trade secrets, they may be held to a higher standard. For example, if posters are displayed in prominent areas reminding workers of their obligation to protect company secrets and this is published on a continuing basis in company journals, work rules, policy manuals, and memos, and if you are requested to sign periodic or yearly trade secret and confidentiality agreements similar to the one beginning on page 426, this may reduce the argument that you didn't know it was wrong to convey confidential information to a competitor.

As previously mentioned, preliminary injunction actions are often commenced by employers in the attempt to deny future employment to high-level executives and employees who possess confidential business information or trade secrets and are likely to reveal such information to a new employer. The decision whether to grant such relief generally turns on weighing the benefit of protecting proprietary business information with strong public policy against limiting competition and an individual's ability to earn a living. Generally, to win a preliminary injunction action, the party asserting it must establish the likelihood of irreparable injury in the absence of an injunction and ultimate success on the merits of the claim at trial. The risk of irreparable injury must be actual and imminent, not remote or speculative. Successful employers seeking a preliminary injunction must have concrete evidence of the harm it will suffer if an injunction is not awarded.

The following suggestions may be helpful in this area.

1. AVOID SIGNING CONTRACTS CONTAINING TRADE SECRET PROHIBITIONS. Any contract you sign that contains a trade secret policy will be slanted against you and increase the company's rights in this area. Employers commonly require employees to sign confidentiality agreements. Although the permissible scope of these agreements varies from state to state, they may be valid and can be used to convince a court that certain information is confidential and should be protected.

If you are asked to sign such an agreement before being hired, you may have no choice if you want the job. The problem becomes more difficult after you have begun working. Many cases have been decided in favor of the company in this area. If you are asked to sign such a document while working and refuse, you can probably be fired legally for insubordination. Always consult an experienced employment attorney for advice or to review any proposed trade secret agreement before you sign it.

2.   BE AWARE THAT THE TRANSFER OR RECEIPT OF CON-FIDENTIAL INFORMATION, ESPECIALLY BY WRONGFUL ACCESS TO AN EMPLOYER'S COMPUTERS, SERVERS AND/OR E-MAIL ACCOUNTS, IS ILLEGAL. Employers can assert many state and federal laws for protection in this area. In addition to traditional common law claims of breach of fiduciary duty of loyalty, misappropriation of trade secrets, unfair competition and conversion, a number of states have passed laws making theft of trade secrets a criminal offense. For example, New York declares it a felony for anyone to steal property consisting of scientific material. In the federal system, crimes involving misappropriation of intellectual property have been prosecuted under the National Stolen Property Act (NSPA) and mail and wire fraud statutes. A criminal RICO action may also be asserted.

Another law to be aware of includes the Computer Fraud and Abuse Act (CFAA). This federal law provides civil penalties when someone knowingly with fraudulent intent accesses a protected computer without authorization or exceeds authorized access, causing damage or loss to a computer network. Whether the law can be successfully applied against data thieves depends on the unique facts of each case.

Pursuant to the National Stolen Property Act, if valuable material is stolen and transported to another state, the Federal Bureau of Investigation and the Justice Department can assist employers in apprehending workers because it is a federal crime to sell or receive stolen property worth more than $5,000 that has been transported across state lines.

The Economic Espionage Act, which makes trade secret theft a federal crime, specifically addresses theft perpetrated via the Internet. Section 1832 states it is a federal criminal act for any person to convert a trade secret to his or her own benefit or the benefit of others intending or knowing that the offense will injure any owner of the trade secret. The conversion of a trade secret is defined broadly to cover most acts of misappropriation, and you can also be prosecuted for receiving or possessing trade secret information when you know it was given to you without the owner's authorization.

Penalties for violating this statute are steep. A person who commits an offense can be imprisoned up to ten years and fined up to $500,000. A corporation can be fined up to $5 million. The significance of this law is that those engaged in trade secret misappropriation can no longer be assured that liability will be limited to civil remedies and damages due to criminal penalties for transgressors.

Additionally, the Uniform Trade Secrets Act (UTSA) has been adopted by approximately 45 states. This law is used to protect employers against disloyal employees and ex-employees who improperly acquire a trade secret, even if the person acquiring the information does not use it for competitive advantage. The law is quite complex. Thus, speak to a knowledgeable employment attorney for further information where warranted.

The law is constantly changing as a result of numerous case decisions interpreting these laws, and statutory amendments by Congress and state legislatures. This is especially so due to the emergence of new technologies requiring legal protection from disloyal employees and ex-employees. Thus, research pertinent federal and state laws to know your rights in this area where applicable. Speak to a knowledgeable attorney for advice and guidance before doing anything you may later regret. Above all, always avoid the temptation of misappropriating data in computers, e-mail, and company servers. The penalties, costs, and legal fees required to mount a defense to civil and criminal charges is probably not worth it.

3. TAKE YOUR FILES HOME BEFORE BEING FIRED IF YOU CAN DO SO. You are generally not allowed to take any materials that were developed while working for the company, including Rolodexes and business-generated reports, letters, diagrams, photographs, and all copies of such valuable materials that are necessary for the company's continued operations. You may retrieve personal information, but it may be scrutinized by a company official before you depart from the premises. To minimize the possibility of being sued, anticipate ahead and take non-confidential materials away from the office before your official departure. You may thus avoid the possibility of being searched and of not being able to remove such items at the time of your resignation or discharge.

4.   LIMIT WHAT YOU SAY AT THE EXIT INTERVIEW. Many employers attempt to elicit information about what knowledge you've gained while working and how you intend to use it, especially when you are resigning from a job. At many companies, especially technology-intensive ones, there is a formal termination interview at which the question of confidentiality is discussed. Avoid providing the employer with specifics at an exit interview because the less the employer knows of your plans, the better off you'll be. Be especially careful not to confirm that you possess trade secrets or that you have a continuing obligation to protect the company's secrets and agree not to disclose them to others. If the employer identifies exactly what information it considers to be confidential and tells you that you are required not to use such information to its detriment, you may diplomatically object to such comments or state that you do not agree with the company's position.

5.   NEVER SIGN A LETTER OR AGREEMENT STATING THAT YOU HAVE NOT TAKEN CONFIDENTIAL INFOR-MATION. However, if the employer offers you a significant increase in severance or other financial benefits, it may be worth signing such a document and avoiding a lawsuit after you confer with legal counsel.

6.   CONTACT A LAWYER IMMEDIATELY. A competent lawyer can help you retrieve items that the employer does not want to release and aid you in many other important ways. Do this immediately when you are accused of stealing or misappropriating confidential information of a company's trade secrets. Never admit fault without speaking to a lawyer; defend such charges promptly and aggressively. For example, your lawyer can immediately contact the company and state that the failure to resolve the issue amicably will give rise to a claim of defamation against the company because it is unfairly ruining your business reputation. (Note: Defamation lawsuits involving employees will be discussed in the next section.)

Since it is often unclear whether trade secrets are involved, and since the employer has the burden of proving that misappropriation occurred, do not agree to settle any matter without an employment attorney's assistance. You may find, for example, that you can solicit your former employer's customers and use information in the customer lists and shipping histories if such information was easily obtainable by the general public. Although each case is decided on its unique factors and circumstances, many employers lose claims that they have a protectable interest sufficient to support enforcement of a contract's non-solicitation and non-competition provisions. Just proclaiming that it has lost a trade secret might get the court's attention but may not help the company prevail without more specific evidence. Thus, know your rights and act accordingly in this area.

When companies distribute memos, usually on an annual basis, reminding key employees of their continuing obligation to protect company trade secrets and requesting their written acknowledgment their chances of prevailing in litigation increase. The signed document should then be saved in each person's personnel file. A signed statement serves several purposes; it defines what constitutes a trade secret from the company's point of view and creates a climate of confidentiality when people are hired. Furthermore, it advises employees of the seriousness of the problem, warns employees that the company may take strong legal action if trade secrets or confidential information are conveyed to others during or after the employment relationship, and documents the employee's consent. If the employee refuses to sign such a document, a company may be able to legally terminate the person and even fight his or her claim to unemployment compensation. The Sample Statement on Trade Secrets, beginning below, illustrates these issues.

A critical element in proving a trade secret is establishing that reasonable efforts were undertaken to protect the information. The more precautions the owner of the information took to maintain the secrecy of the information, the lower the odds that the accused obtained them properly.

Thus, most employers often seek to establish policies dealing with trade secrets, confidential information, and other rules of employee conduct to protect their assets, advise employees of the seriousness of the problem, and create a climate of confidentiality.

Sample Statement on Trade Secrets

The business of our Company involves valuable, confidential and proprietary data and information of various kinds. Such data and information, called "Trade Secrets," concern:

- The names of Company customers and the nature of the Company's relationships (e.g., types and amounts of products acquired from the Company) with such customers;
- The Company's various computer systems and programs;
- Techniques, developments, improvements, inventions and processes that are, or may be, produced in the course of the Company's operations; and
- Any other information not generally known concerning the Company or its operations, products, suppliers, markets, sales, costs, profits, customer needs and lists, or other information acquired, disclosed, or made known to Employees or agents while in the employ of the Company, which, if used or disclosed, could adversely affect the Company's business or give competitors an advantage.

Since it would harm our Company if any of our Trade Secrets were known to our competitors, it is the Company's policy that:

1.   No Employee should, during or after his/her employment with the Company, use any Trade Secrets for his/her benefit, or disclose to

any person, business, or corporation any Trade Secrets without the prior written consent of the Company.

2. Every Employee shall render exclusive and full-time services and devote his/her best efforts toward the performance of assigned duties and responsibilities (which may be changed at any time).

3. Every Employee should refrain from engaging directly or indirectly in any activity that may compete with, or result in a conflict of interest with the Company or that is not likely to be in the Company's best interests.

4. Every Employee should fully and completely disclose to the Company any inventions, ideas, works of authorship, and other Trade Secrets made, developed, and/or conceived by him/her alone or jointly with others, arising out of, or relating to, employment at the Company. All such inventions, ideas, works of authorship, copyrights, and other Trade Secrets shall be the sole property of the Company. The Employee agrees to execute and deliver to the Company such assignments, documents, agreements, or instruments which the Company may require from time to time to evidence its ownership of the results and proceeds of the Employee's services and creations.

5. The Employee understands that he/she owes the highest duty of loyalty with respect to his/her duties. This means that he/she will, among other things, maintain a constant vigil over Company property, never make secret profits at the Company's expense (e.g., service customers of the Company but bill them for personal benefit, or receive kickbacks or special favors from customers, etc.), dress in a proper fashion, not use drugs or alcohol while on the job, and maintain a personal or Company automobile in good condition together with a valid driver's license.

6. Every Employee shall avoid discussing any matter of a confidential nature, or which constitutes a Trade Secret, with any competitor or its employees. This includes discussions regarding customers, pricing, and policies. The Employee is reminded that any such discussions may cause the Company and the Employee personally to have violated anti-trust laws, including the Sherman and Clayton Acts. Sanctions of up to three (3) years imprisonment and fines up to $100,000 have been imposed on those who violate such laws.

7. Upon termination of employment, or at any time the Company may request, every Employee shall promptly return to the Company all memoranda, notes, records, reports, technical manuals, and other

documents (and all copies thereof) in his/her possession, custody, or control relating to Trade Secrets, all of which written materials, and other things shall be grounds for immediate dismissal. In addition, the Company shall not be obligated in any way to pay any severance upon termination to any Employee who fails to comply with the provisions of this paragraph specifically, and this memo generally.

8.   Every Employee agrees to comply with the rules, regulations, policies, and procedures of the Company faithfully and to the best of his/her abilities. The Employee understands that the breach of any covenant contained herein may constitute substantial and irreparable harm to the Company, and the Company may seek injunctive relief and other relief which it deems necessary and appropriate under the circumstances to protect its rights and the Employee shall pay all reasonable attorney fees, costs, and expenses incurred by the Company in the enforcement of any such action.

I [Name of Employee] have received and read a copy of this Trade Secrets and Confidential Information Policy statement, understand all of its terms and agree to be bound by the provisions contained therein.

| [Printed Name] | [Signature] | [Date] |

STRATEGY: *When employers sit on their rights and not act quickly when a problem is uncovered, the chances of success at the injunction or trial may decrease. Smart companies quarantine a worker's computer immediately after learning that an employee has resigned from a job and left the premises and review the worker's e-mail on the network server to discover if trade secrets were downloaded to others or important documents stolen. If wrongdoing is discovered a company can then sue the employee for breach of contract, misappropriation of trade secret, and fraud.*

GAG ORDERS AND CONFIDENTIALITY AGREEMENTS.

Confidentiality and non-disparagement clauses, commonly known as gag orders, are provisions in agreements or stand-alone agreements that prohibit departing employees from revealing the terms of a settlement or saying anything negative about the company to others who may also have been injured or to the press. Additionally, companies sometimes insert clauses into such agreements prohibiting ex-employees from seeking reemployment with the company, participating as a party or witness in any legal action or proceeding, or soliciting others to file suits against it. To ensure compliance, it is not uncommon for employers to insert penalties with such clauses, which state that if any material statement about the settlement is revealed to others, all monies previously given to the ex-employee must be returned and additional damages paid.

The following clauses were taken from actual agreements and illustrate these points:

> *Employee acknowledges and agrees to keep the terms of this Agreement strictly confidential. Employee will not disclose any term of this Agreement, including but not limited to the salary and severance pay provided to Employee by Employer, to any person or entity whatsoever with the exception of Employee's spouse, accountant, and attorney, unless ordered by a court of competent jurisdiction. Employee understands that this provision is of material importance to the Employer, and that damages for the breach hereof will be actual, but difficult to calculate. Accordingly, if Employee violates this provision in any manner, Employee will pay to Employer, as agreed upon liquidated damages, the amount Employee has received or would receive form Employer as severance pay, and an additional amount equal to three (3) times the amount of severance pay. Employee acknowledges and agrees that the extra severance pay to be given is made in consideration for this promise and that this amount of liquidated damages is a fair estimate of the damages that the parties presently anticipate Employer will suffer in the event of a breach of this provision by Employee.*

> *You agree that you will not participate, directly or indirectly, as a party, witness or otherwise against the Company unless compelled by a judicial subpoena.*

> *You will not issue any communication, written or otherwise, that disparages, criticizes, or otherwise reflects adversely or encourages any adverse action against the Company except if testifying truthfully under oath pursuant to subpoena or otherwise.*

> *You agree never to apply for or otherwise seek reemployment with Employer at any time in the future.*

Most employers prepare such clauses with the expectation they are enforceable due to the extra payments given to the ex-employee for settlement purposes. They do so to keep other employees from learning about the terms of a lucrative severance package and acting on this information. Believing that the terms of a settlement will remain confidential often encourages employers to settle formal charges of discrimination or other litigation that could affect hundreds of other unsuspecting employees.

When judges are asked to determine whether such clauses are valid, they typically weigh general policy which favors the private voluntary settlement of employment disputes versus the public's need to obtain valid information. While such provisions have generally been enforced in the past, the answer is not always clear-cut, depending on the unique facts of each case.

For example, in areas where public safety is involved, employer claims that such confidentiality clauses are legal may not be upheld. In one case, a foreman who worked at a nuclear power plant was fired and then contacted the Nuclear Regulatory Commission to complain about numerous safety violations at the plant. He also filed a lawsuit against the company claiming that he was illegally terminated for whistle-blowing. The company proposed a settlement that contained numerous gag orders. These clauses would have restricted his ability to provide regulatory agencies with specific information and would not have allowed him to appear voluntarily as a witness in any judicial or administrative proceeding in which the company was a party. The proposed settlement also stated that if he was compelled to testify at any proceeding, he would use all reasonable steps to fight such a subpoena.

After the man's attorney rejected this proposal, his case continued. He then filed a lawsuit with the U.S. Department of Labor alleging that the proposed gag order violated his rights under the Energy Reorganization Act (ERA) by restricting free speech and his ability to testify about safety violations. He also claimed he was retaliated against by bringing this action.

The U.S. Department of Labor ruled in his favor. It found that the gag order proposal was an adverse employment action under the ERA and represented a serious threat to ensuring clear lines of communication between employees and regulatory agencies on matters of public health and safety.

Other rulings have allowed individuals to reveal discriminatory acts they observed or suffered to the EEOC even after signing separation agreements with gag orders.

To protect yourself in this area, remember the following.

1. **KNOW YOUR RIGHTS.** There is a general presumption that gag orders and similar provisions will be valid, especially when you receive extra consideration (e.g., three more months' severance pay) as inducement to sign an agreement and the clause is clearly drafted. Thus, avoid signing any agreement if you do not want to be restrained from discussing the terms of the settlement with others or from suing the company at a later date (unless you are satisfied with the financial terms of the settlement).

2. **CONSULT AN EMPLOYMENT ATTORNEY FOR ADVICE.** Always seek counsel when presented with a comprehensive settlement agreement that requires you to waive rights of free speech and other protections. You may learn, for example, that it is illegal for a company to force you to sign such a document. If you previously signed an agreement with similar restrictions, you may learn from the lawyer that it is not valid when fraud, duress, or mistake was involved. For example, before signing any such agreement, you must be given ample time (generally at least 21 days) to review the document and consult an attorney of your choosing. Not being given this opportunity might vitiate the entire agreement.

In one case, an African-American woman was terminated for no apparent reason after working seven years for a real estate company. The woman was required to sign a simple general release in order to receive seven weeks severance pay. The release did not contain

432   *The Employee Rights Handbook*

language indicating that she had a period of time to consider the offer or consult with a lawyer.

After reluctantly signing the document and receiving the money, the woman learned that other white males at the company who were fired received, on the average, three weeks of severance for every year worked. Angered by such alleged disparate treatment, she retained me to protect her rights. As her lawyer, I negotiated for the company to pay her an additional ten weeks' severance pay, despite the fact she had signed a waiver of her claims.

This case is instructive because it demonstrates that, under certain conditions, settlement agreements, waivers, and releases can be invalidated. In the case, I argued that my client had signed the waiver under duress (just so that she could collect the initial seven weeks of severance pay). Apparently, the company did not want to face the expense and consequences of a potential lawsuit based on gender and race discrimination as well as fraud, and decided to negotiate an amicable settlement.

3. BE AWARE THAT NOT ALL LIQUIDATED DAMAGES CLAUSES ARE ENFORCEABLE. Liquidated damages are an amount of money agreed on in advance by an employer and an employee in a written contract to be paid in the event of a breach or a dispute. If it is not possible to compute the amount of the loss, a judge may uphold the amount specified. However, in most circumstances, when the amount specified has no actual basis in fact (e.g., a clause that in the event the employee reveals the terms of the settlement, he or she is liable to pay back the amount of severance previously received plus an additional amount equal to three times the amount), a judge may disregard it, viewing the amount merely as a penalty.

Sometimes, if an employee cannot discuss the terms of the settlement with anyone (including a spouse, attorney, and accountant), judges in some states may rule that the clause is unconscionable and therefore unenforceable.

4. KEEP YOUR LIPS SEALED. By signing an agreement with a gag order, you are promising not to reveal the terms of the settlement to others. Thus, avoid the temptation of speaking about the settlement with anyone. That way, if you are sued for allegedly breaking your promise, you may eventually prevail in court based on the facts.

STRATEGY: *If you previously told someone about the terms of a potential settlement, tell your lawyer about this. The lawyer may be able to modify the language in the final draft of the settlement agreement that prohibits you from talking to others only after the document is signed. This can protect you if it is discovered that you discussed the pending settlement before you were aware that the company would insist on your continued obligation to secrecy (which was confirmed in the written agreement).*

Defamation Lawsuits

Employers across the country are facing a new kind of potential liability from employees: defamation actions, as fired employees are increasingly suing former employers for libel and slander. It is estimated that more than 5,000 claims are filed yearly, with the average winning verdict in the six figures. Furthermore, defending such actions can take years and typically costs employers hundreds of thousands of dollars per case.

In the employment context, defamation is defined as any false statement about an employee communicated by an employer to a third party that harms that employee's reputation or deters others from dealing with him or her in a business setting. A statement can be defamatory if it holds an individual up to scorn or ridicule, accuses an individual of committing a criminal offense or having a communicable disease that is shunned by society (e.g., AIDS), or even questions an individual's honesty or competence in certain cases. In essence, it is the invasion of the interest in a reputation and good name.

Most defamation lawsuits arise from the termination of employees. They are the result of the employer giving poor references, making false statements about fired employees, or giving false information to employees about why an individual was terminated. But the ability to sue for defamation doesn't only arise after a firing. It can also occur when false, damaging statements are revealed to nonessential third parties. In one case for example, it was reported that a salesman who claimed that he was slandered by his fellow employees was awarded $1,027,500, including $775,500 in economic and $250,000 in noneconomic damages, by a jury in Ventura County, CA. The medical laser salesman claimed that several employees slandered him to his customers to improve their own sales within his territory, causing a disruption in his business. He resigned and sued for breach of contract, breach of fiduciary duty and accounting and intentional interference (via slander) with client relations.

The author once represented a man who was falsely accused of drinking excessively at lunch. He obtained a copy of a memo confirming this, which had been read by several coworkers. After the accusation was shown to be true, the client recovered $25,000 in an out-of-court settlement.

Even more significant is that some courts have begun awarding damages to individuals suffering from negative impressions that arise from an employer's silence or inaction. For example, one worker successfully won a lawsuit against his former employer after claiming that his discharge, following the administration of a lie detector test, gave fellow employees the false impression that he had been fired for participating in a wrongful activity. After his lawyer proved that the test results had been improperly evaluated by an unqualified and unlicensed polygraph examiner and that he was not guilty of any wrongdoing, the South Carolina Supreme Court agreed that this false impression amounted to defamation and awarded him $150,000. Another court agreed that a defamation occurred by the method in which an employer packed and removed documents from a discharged employee's office. When asked by coworkers what was going on, the employer responded, "You don't want to know."

In today's technology age, be aware that defamatory actions are also occurring in e-mails and blogs, such as inflammatory comments made by an employee on a competitor's Website, chat site, public discussion group or bulletin board.

Courts are also allowing lawsuits to proceed by people who suffer damage to their reputations from statements in warning letters, office petitions, personnel files, and performance evaluations that contain false information or are used to deny a promotion. The same is true for false statements made at management or employee meetings or even when defamatory graffiti about an employee is written on company grounds and no attempt is made to remove it. If a supervisor writes a memo stating that he lost confidence in an employee's work and charges the employee with incompetence, untruthfulness, and poor attitude, the employee may have a valid defamation claim if the memo is circulated around the office and read by nonessential third parties, especially when damaging information is disseminated and the employer did not take adequate precautions to determine whether the derogatory information was accurate. For example, in one case a terminated employee sued his former boss for defamation when letters describing his poor performance were distributed and read by several executives. The employee was awarded $90,000 after proving that the information contained in the letters was false and deliberately disseminated to cause him harm.

Harshly criticizing an employee can make an employer vulnerable in a defamation lawsuit. Thus, if you are accused of stealing company property in front of others and slanderous remarks are made (e.g., "You are a crook"), your employer may be guilty of defamation if the remarks are proved false.

Protection can also extend to physical acts. One employee working for an automobile manufacturer was suspected of theft when leaving the premises. Hundreds of workers observed him being forcibly searched and interrogated. After proving the charges were unfounded, the man sued the company. He argued that the rough treatment observed by other workers held him up to ridicule and scorn, since the treatment implied he was guilty of theft; he was awarded $25,000 by a jury.

The following legal causes of action fall under the larger heading of defamation.

> **Slander** arises when an unfair and untrue oral statement is communicated to a third party that damages an individual's reputation. The spoken words must pertain to a person's poor moral character, unreliability, dishonesty, or financial instability (e.g., a statement that the person is filing for bankruptcy, is always being sued, or fails to live up to contractual obligations or business responsibilities when this is false.)
>
> **Libel** arises when an unfair and untrue statement is made about a person in writing (i.e., in a letter or memo). The statement becomes actionable when it is read by a third party and damages the person's business or personal reputation.

To win a defamation case it is generally necessary for your lawyer to prove the following elements in court:

1. A defamatory statement of fact;
2. The statement is false;
3. The statement is "published" (communicated) to a third party;
4. The statement concerns the complaining party;
5. The speaker made the statement with the required level of fault;
6. The statement caused damage, such as the loss of money or professional reputation; and
7. The statement is not protected by privilege.

Mere statements that an employee was discharged from employment and truthful statements about the employee's work habits are not defamatory because truth is a total defense against claims of libel or slander. Charging a worker with bad manners, being careless or being a troublemaker, not having sufficient skills, or not adequately performing a job will not typically qualify as defamation. However, statements that the individual was discharged for cause or unsatisfactory performance, incompetence, or insubordination, coupled with the employer's refusal to give a recommendation, may be potentially damaging and actionable as defamation.

Many states have enacted laws granting employers a qualified privilege when discussing an ex-employee's job performance with a prospective employer. This means that the employer may be excused for disseminating information about an individual that later turns out to be false if the person responsible for disseminating the information did so in the course of his or her normal duties (e.g., a personnel supervisor who writes performance appraisals about individuals). However, a qualified privilege can be lost or abused and an employer can be liable if an executive or personnel supervisor knowingly makes false defamatory comments about a former employee out of reckless disregard for the truth, ill will, or spite.

The first thing to remember in any defamation lawsuit is that you must prove that false statements were made to third parties. This is often difficult to do. For example, if you are told by an employment recruiter that he heard slanderous comments from your ex-employer, the recruiter would have to testify in court in order for you to prevail, and many people are reluctant to do this. Moreover, if your ex-employer disseminates harmful information that is true, or you are fired for a legitimate reason that is properly documented and can be proved by the company, you may lose your case. (But if the company treats you harshly in front of others after the discharge, such as escorting you out of the building with a police officer, your case may be strengthened.)

But even if an employment attorney determines that commencing a lawsuit in this area is not in your best interest, the lawyer may be able to compel an employer to stop talking negatively about you to others under the threat of litigation. Sometimes all it takes is for the lawyer to write a strong cease-and-desist letter to the ex-employer demanding that all offensive conduct stop. That is why it is critical to consult an employment attorney immediately to analyze your situation.

Companies typically defend themselves in defamation actions by arguing that the statements communicated about the employee were true, or they had a qualified privilege to say such things, thereby insulating it from prosecution. For example, a supervisor writes a memo stating that he lost confidence in a particular employee's work and charging the worker with unsatisfactory performance and poor attitude. The worker is then fired, and sues the company for libel. The company may prevail if it can prove that the contents of the memo are the supervisor's honest opinion.

Companies must carefully guard comments made by upper management regarding an employee. When untrue statements are made which cause someone a great deal of embarrassment, humiliation and stress, damages for loss of reputation are available in an action for libel or slander because the loss of reputation is a foreseeable consequence of the publication of defamatory statements.

Employers should establish policies regarding the disclosure of information. Potentially damaging communications in performance appraisals and comments made to prospective employers should be reviewed by a supervisor before dissemination and the contents should be disclosed to essential third parties only.

Supervisory personnel should be instructed to avoid making excited and emotional remarks to employees, particularly those they are in the process of dismissing. Poor references can lead to expensive lawsuits so the best rule for employers is to play it safe, whenever possible, by avoiding disparaging comments.

Writing derogatory letters concerning ex-employees are fraught with danger. Imputations that an employee is lacking in competence, sobriety, honesty, financial integrity, or chastity are especially danger-ous because they are defamatory per se, which means that the plaintiff does not have to prove actual harm to successfully recover a verdict. Money can be recovered against a company simply because the statement is untrue, especially when defamatory per se statements are made and interpreted as impairing the reputation of an individual or business (such as that the employee is a crook, is filing for bankruptcy, is dishonest, of poor moral character, unreliable or dishonest).

Strategies to Increase the Chances of Winning a Defamation Lawsuit

1.   **AVOID SIGNING A RELEASE.** When you sign a release form allowing an employer to investigate and/or discuss your background with others, the law generally allows the employer to be absolved from liability for providing negative information about you to a prospective employer even when the comments are made maliciously. Avoid signing any such waiver prior to or after taking a job or being fired if you can help it.

2.   **REVIEW THE COMPANY'S REFERENCE POLICIES.** These are sometimes contained in an employee handbook or a personnel policy statement or memo. If your employer has disseminated policies in writing, such as that no references of any kind will be given after a firing or that the company will favorably assist departing employees in pursuing and finding new employment, and the company fails to act in accordance with such policies, you may have the right to sue and allege breach of an implied or express contract.

3.   **NEGOTIATE TO RECEIVE A FAVORABLE REFERENCE AFTER A FIRING.**

4.   **TAKE ACTION IF YOU ARE GIVEN A NEGATIVE REFERENCE IN RETALIATION FOR MAKING OR FILING A DISCRIMINATION COMPLAINT.** Some employers will provide negative references to prospective employers out of spite after an employee files a gender, age, or race discrimination lawsuit. Employment attorneys increasingly confront the issue of retaliation, which stems from the way employers handle workers who have reported on-the-job discrimination or harassment under anti-bias laws. Many lawyers

believe there is always retaliation after a person files a complaint or charge. Although retaliation claims are sometimes difficult to prove, they can be identified by the negative consequences an employee suffers when the timing of the firing is clear. The reason that asserting a retaliation claim can be helpful is that even if no defamation is proved and the employee eventually loses his or her discrimination case, a retaliation claim is a separate legal cause of action and can proceed to trial. For example, one woman who lost a sexual harassment and defamation case was nevertheless awarded $73,400 by a federal jury that believed she suffered compensable retaliation after her charge was filed with the EEOC.

5. ACT PROMPTLY IF YOU DISCOVER THAT AN EX-EMPLOYER IS MAKING DEFAMATORY REMARKS THAT INHIBIT YOUR CHANCES OF OBTAINING NEW EMPLOY-MENT. By sending a letter certified mail, return receipt requested, similar to the one on page 442, you are taking an important step to protect your rights. The letter should document what you have learned and put the employer on notice that you will take prompt legal action if the problem persists. Such a letter may serve as proof that defamation occurred and help your lawsuit if you decide to proceed in court.

6. RESEARCH YOUR STATE'S LAWS AND TAKE IMMEDIATE ACTION IF YOU BELIEVE YOU ARE BEING BLACKLISTED OR WILLFULLY PREVENTED FROM OBTAINING NEW EMPLOYMENT. Many states treat untruthful job references as a crime and punish employers for maliciously attempting to prevent former employees from finding work. Additionally, some states require employers to give a terminated worker a written statement regarding the true cause of his or her dismissal. Once such an explanation has been received by the worker, the employer cannot furnish prospective employers with any reason that deviates from those given in the service letter. In order to receive the benefit of such "service-letter" laws, it is necessary to send a written request because oral requests are generally not sufficient. The sample letter on page 443 is a good illustration of the kind of letter to send. If you do not receive an answer to the letter within a reasonable period of time (e.g., 30 days), or if the employer furnishes you with reasons that are untrue, your state's service-letter statute may have been violated and you can commence a lawsuit.

While some experts believe damages awarded for defamation are more difficult to obtain in arbitration, don't hesitate to proceed if the facts warrant such action. For example, in one case it was reported that a major bank was ordered to pay a total of $3.4 million to a former senior stock trader when an arbitration panel found he was defamed after being fired without cause. The panel included $1 million of punitive damages as part of the award.

Since the laws in each state vary, it is best to do your research and get an accurate opinion from an employment lawyer before commencing litigation or arbitration. The bottom line is that employers frequently face greater exposure and potential damages in lawsuits from leaking harmful or confidential information after a firing than from the firing itself. Thus, always know your rights and enforce them as quickly as possible.

Sample Letter Protesting Inaccurate Job References

Your Name
Address
Telephone Number
Date

Name of Officer of Employer
Title
Name of Employer
Address

Dear (Name of Officer),

On (date), I applied for a job with (name of potential employer). At the interview, I learned that you had submitted an inaccurate, unfavorable reference about me.

You supposedly said the reason I was fired was that I was excessively late on the job. We both know that this is incorrect. I had the opportunity to review the entire contents of my personnel file after I was dismissed. Not one reference was made anywhere in the file to lateness.

Kindly cease and desist from making any such unfavorable remarks about my job performance, particularly to potential employers. If I learn that you disregard this request, be assured that my lawyer will take immediate legal action to protect my rights.

Thank you for your prompt cooperation in this matter.

Very truly yours,
Your Name

cc: Potential Employer

Sent certified mail, return receipt requested.

Sample Letter Demanding Written Explanation for Discharge

Your Name
Address
Telephone Number
Date

Name of Officer of Employer
Title
Name of Employer
Address

Dear (Name of Officer),

On (date) I was fired suddenly by your company without notice, warning, or cause. All that I was told by (name of person) was that my services were no longer required and that my termination was effective immediately.

To date, I have not received any explanation documenting the reason(s) for my discharge. In accordance with the laws of this state I hereby demand such information immediately.

Thank you for your prompt cooperation in this matter.

Very truly yours,
Your Name

Sent certified mail, return receipt requested.

Rights of Departing Employees

Courts generally impose a duty of loyalty and good faith on employees in all industries. This duty exists throughout the worker's employment and is also present when the employee changes jobs and joins a new company.

The crackdown on so-called white-collar crimes has produced many mail fraud and related indictments against executives and employees who use their positions for personal gain at the expense of coworkers. An executive owes a duty of undivided loyalty to the company. Any activity that creates a possible conflict of interest must be brought to the attention of the company's president or board of directors for approval before the individual proceeds with a possibly conflicting or harmful action. This even includes situations where an executive secretly promotes a product his company previously rejected.

In one case, an executive had an undisclosed interest in a competing business while employed by another company. The court noted that he contributed substantial financial support to this business and aided in the development of the competing product.

Time and time again, courts have ruled against the self-serving employee who acts for private gain. Even though his employer decides not to use a particular product, an employee does not have the right to lend assistance of any kind to a potentially competing business.

A salesperson or employee can inform her customers that she intends to leave her job and work for a competitor. However, an employee cannot work for a competitor while still employed at her present company (especially if she is supposed to work full-time and is not an independent contractor).

In one case, a salesperson told customers that he intended to leave his company to work for a competitor. Although this was perfectly legal, he overstepped his authority by distributing the competitor's catalogs to these customers while still employed with the old firm. This, the court ruled, was improper; when he was terminated by his former company and sued, the individual was required to pay a considerable amount of money in damages for his disloyal actions, including repayment of wages and commissions received during the period in question.

Generally speaking, employees are under no obligation other than their duty to give loyal and conscientious service to an employer while in its employ. In most states, salespersons have the right to advise customers or clients that they are going to quit and work for a competitor even while still working for their present employer. In preparation for quitting a job, employees can look for another job without advising their employers; advise customers, clients, and friends of the intention to leave and compete (hopefully in the absence of a written covenant); and even take minor steps to organize a new company while still working, such as print stationary, set up telephones and faxes, and begin the process of forming a corporation. What they cannot do is solicit business while on the employer's payroll, talk against their present employer and hurt its reputation, or lie down on the job by not taking orders or working as diligently as before.

Generally, one company has the right to persuade another company's employees to join its ranks when the employees are not bound by a contract or restrictive covenant. A defecting employee or executive can, however, be successfully sued for luring away key employees.

In one Massachusetts case, a manager was offered a lucrative post with equity in a competing business. Before resigning his job, the manager secretly solicited four key employees to join him in defecting. After the four left, the company sued for damages caused by the manager's disloyalty.

At the trial, the company stated that the defendant had been one of its major officers, bearing the title of vice-president and general manager. While still performing these important functions, he enticed four key employees to leave with him. Their departure had a devastating impact on the company's productivity and sales. The manager responded that since he had never signed a covenant not to compete, he was free to leave the company and go to work for whomever he wished. Furthermore, since none of the other employees had signed covenants, he should not be held responsible for their acts, since what he did was not illegal.

The court concluded that the defendant had violated his duty of loyalty and he and the new employer were required to pay damages. The Massachusetts Judicial Supreme Court reacted strongly, saying, "The defendants are liable for the breach of the manager's duty of loyalty by not protecting the plaintiff against the loss of key employees. As Vice-President and General Manager, defendant was responsible for staffing and hiring necessary replacements and his duty to maintain adequate managerial personnel forbade him from seeking to draw key managers away to a competitor."

Be aware that in most states you may not, before termination or resignation of employment, solicit employees to work with a competitor. This general rule is most clearly applicable if the supervisor-manager, as a corporate "Pied Piper," leads his company's employees away, thus destroying the employer's business. In addition to suing an individual on the basis of breach of the fiduciary duty of loyalty and good faith, some lawyers commence lawsuits against the new employer based on a legal theory called tortious interference with contractual relations, when they induce a valued employee to break a contract and go to work for them.

Generally, if the key employee is under contract with a definite term (e.g., one year) and the employee breaks the contract before the expiration of the contract period, a lawsuit may be successful. However, when no formal contract exists, and the employee is merely hired at will (i.e., capable of being terminated or leaving at any time), such suits have less chance of success.

STRATEGY: *To avoid problems, avoid signing employment contracts with clauses that prohibit you from soliciting or utilizing the services of any other employee of the company after you depart. You may not be so constrained in the absence of such a contractual provision.*

Be discreet about your future plans; do not reveal that you plan to work for a new employer while you are still on the payroll. Serving two masters or making significant preparations for the new employer while being paid by the current company can get you in trouble. In most states, you can be ordered to return all salary, bonus monies and other compensation you received during the disloyal period. The employer can also seek the imposition of a constructive trust to collect any profits derived from wrongful conduct and injunctive relief forbidding you from working for a competitor, especially if you misappropriated the employer's personal property or proprietary information such as confidential customer lists.

Corporate officers are held to a higher duty of loyalty standard than regular employees. Liability often ensues when officers use corporate assets for personal gain without first notifying or compensating the corporation, use office space to benefit another company, take advantage of a corporate opportunity without first disclosing it, or solicit employees to a rival without the employer's knowledge or consent.

Confer with counsel before making preparations to leave an important job, especially if you are an executive, manager, or officer of the company. Ask a lawyer to tell you what you can and cannot do while working for the present company. For example, while it is probably permissible to merely begin the process of forming a separate corporation on your own, you cannot spend time negotiating a lease, hiring employees, and ordering supplies while on company time. Certainly, you should not take valuable company information and confidential materials with you.

PART IV
Collecting Your Due

This section of the book might be the most important of all. Recognizing your rights is nothing without enforcing your rights and collecting what you are legally due as a result of an employer's wrongful acts. Although it is unlikely that you will succeed in getting your job back after a firing, information in this section will help you enforce your rights with or without a lawyer's assistance.

Discussion in Chapter 9 helps you learn the steps to take when a satisfactory settlement is not achieved through informal means and it is necessary to commence litigation. Included in the chapter are valuable tried-and-true strategies to help you become a better witness at depositions and trials, the best way to pick a jury, assist and work with your trial lawyer, and other important lawsuit and trial techniques. If you are victimized but cannot afford a lawyer, you will learn how to effectively represent yourself as a pro-se litigant and where to obtain assistance through various federal, state and local agencies. In addition, you will discover ways to collect evidence and strengthen a claim before a lawyer is hired. Included in the chapter are sample demand letters to send to collect earned wages, commissions, severance, vacation pay and other benefits. Information about how to maximize a claim in arbitration, mediation and small claims court is also included for your protection.

Information in Chapter 10 tells you how to hire and work effectively with your employment attorney. The chapter covers all of the pertinent issues clients must be aware of, including how to find the right lawyer, what to bring and say at the initial interview, and other items to clarify at the interview. It contains material that explains problems sometimes encountered after a lawyer is hired and steps to take if such problems arise. All of this information will make you a better and wiser client, help you achieve your legal goals, and increase your lawyer's effectiveness, no matter what type of employment case you have.

Finally, the book ends with a simple conclusion which expresses the author's approach to representing clients, achieving justice, and utilizing the material in the book to accomplish your goals.

■   ■   ■   ■   ■   ■   ■   ■   ■

9

Employment Litigation and Alternatives

After you have left your job, willingly or otherwise, how do you collect what your employer owes you if it has not been paid to you freely and promptly? Much depends on why you left the job, and under what conditions. If you left voluntarily with prior notice and under favorable circumstances from a reputable employer, you should have no problem. But what if you were fired? What if you were fired on charges of misconduct or poor performance? What are your defenses?

If you have a discrimination claim under Title VII of the Civil Rights Act of 1964, you have recourse in federal or state court with the Equal Employment Opportunity Commission or a state human rights agency.

State statutes vary widely, but in general they tell when back wages must be paid following job termination. Many states provide for penalties and payment of attorney fees if you are not paid in a timely fashion. The definition of back wages normally includes everything of dollar value owed to you, including bonuses, deferred compensation, accrued vacation, sick leave, and pension rights. Note that most courts will consider only wages due to you up to the time of the court award, not projected or future losses.

In any event, when seeking back wages, you can enforce your rights either by suing directly or through the assistance of your state labor department. (Note, however, that you are not protected by the federal Fair Labor Standards Act or state wages statutes if you are a nonemployee independent contractor.) You should always consider and follow through on your options as quickly as possible when seeking back wages and other benefits. Tens of thousands of employment-related lawsuits are filed in state and federal courts annually. Common lawsuits are for discrimination complaints and breach of contract actions to collect wages, commissions, and benefits. This chapter will provide you with an explanation of the various legal forums you may be exposed to when asserting your rights. Strategies will be provided to help win a case in court, after an appeal, through arbitration, and through small-claims court, and how to settle a matter out of court through mediation.

Litigation

The party commencing a lawsuit (called the plaintiff) must have proper subject matter and personal jurisdiction to avoid having the case initially dismissed. Having subject matter jurisdiction means filing the action in an appropriate court. For example, an ERISA benefits claim must be filed in a federal district court; a case involving significant wages cannot be filed in small-claims court. Before starting a lawsuit, speak to a lawyer to be sure you are filing your case in the proper court.

It is also necessary to demonstrate personal (in personam) jurisdiction. Typically, if the person or business being sued (called the defendant) lives or works in the state where the action is filed, or has close ties with that state (e.g., ships goods into or travels to that state to conduct business), then personal jurisdiction may be determined to exist by a judge. It will also be necessary to select the correct venue (the proper county) where the lawsuit should be filed. For example, in a wrongful discharge lawsuit, the proper venue is the county where the plaintiff or defendant resides. Since venue laws vary from state to state, ask your lawyer where the suit should be brought, to avoid having the case dismissed.

Court

A court is a place where trials are held and/or the law is applied. Depending upon one's choice and other factors, a trial may be conducted and decided by a judge only or by a judge and jury. In some appellate courts and the United States Supreme Court, only judges are present to hear arguments and make decisions.

A court can only preside over matters to which it has jurisdiction. Courts of original jurisdiction are the first courts to preside over a matter. A court of appellate jurisdiction is a higher court that reviews cases removed by appeal from a lower court.

Each state has its own court system, which operates separately from the federal court system. There are basically two levels of state courts: trial courts and appellate courts. General trial courts are typically divided into two separate, distinct courts, one to hear criminal matters and one to adjudicate civil matters. Civil trial courts may be further divided depending upon the amount of money or the subject matter at issue.

The federal court system is divided into 12 districts or circuits and has jurisdiction over the following:

- When a federal law is at issue, such as bankruptcy, copyright and patents, maritime, and postal matters
- When one state is suing another state
- When a person or entity (i.e., a corporation) is suing a person or entity residing in another state and the amount in controversy exceeds $75,000

Within the federal system are separate limited jurisdiction courts that hear matters exclusively pertaining to bankruptcy (U.S. Bankruptcy Court), tax issues (U.S. Tax Court), suits against the federal government (U.S. Court of Claims), and disputes concerning tariffs and customs (U.S. Court of International Trade).

The United States Supreme Court is the country's highest court. It considers cases from the highest courts of each state, decisions of the U.S. Court of Appeals (the highest federal appeals court), and cases where the constitutionality of federal laws comes into play.

The vast majority of lawsuits, including unemployment and workers' compensation hearings, originate in state courts. If you are thinking of filing a lawsuit, speak to an employment attorney or visit the clerk of any local court to determine where the correct place is to start. Each state has its own unique filing, procedural, and jurisdictional requirements, which must be correctly followed so the case will not be dismissed. It is essential to get proper advice from a lawyer before starting any legal process.

STRATEGY: *Where applicable, ask your lawyer about the advantages and disadvantages of commencing the lawsuit in either state or federal court. Some experts believe that federal court judges are generally more highly regarded for their legal skills than state judges and that litigants are often able to obtain a trial quicker in federal court. However, if a dispute is with an employer located within your state, you may not be able to file a lawsuit in federal court unless you are asserting a discrimination charge or other matter dealing with federal laws (such as a wage and hour or overtime violation). Conversely, if you are being sued, it may be advantageous to keep the case in a state court to "slow down" its progress.*

Among the tactical considerations of initially filing or later removing a case from state to federal court are differences in procedural rules, rules of evidence, and rules governing expert witnesses; the possibility that the parties' right to a jury trial may be broader or narrower in one court, and a difference in jury selection, verdict ranges and jury pools. For example, most state courts allow a jury to reach a verdict by a majority vote while a unanimous decision of the jurors is required in federal court.

There are other differences as well. Federal courts require plaintiffs to specify if they want a jury trial simultaneously when the initial summons and complaint is filed with the court. This differs from many state courts where you don't have to make a demand for a jury until several months later in the process.

Only a defendant may remove a case to federal court once it is filed. The original purpose of removal jurisdiction was to protect nonresident defendants from local prejudice they might encounter in state courts, as well as to assure that federal claims were properly adjudicated before federal judges. However, the fear of local prejudice and incompetent state judges are no longer the typical reasons for removal. In modern practice, defendants more often invoke removal jurisdiction based on the perceived practical and strategies advantages of litigating and defending a claim in federal court.

There are many other considerations to ponder before filing a lawsuit. For example, does your lawyer think the case has merit? If so, why? Does the defendant have a strong defense? What is your downside? Can you lose more than you'll gain if the defendant successfully asserts a valid counterclaim against you?

Other considerations include: Will you be able to prove your case? Do you have strong witnesses who will testify on your behalf? Do you currently possess important documents to prove your case or must you rely on the defendant to turn them over to you during the discovery phase of the lawsuit and face the possibility they don't exist or will be missing? Will the defendant be interested in settling the matter before protracted and expensive litigation begins? Are you emotionally up to the often long and grueling challenges of litigation? How much money can you expect to win in damages? Will the costs of litigation and attorney fees be more than your ultimate recovery?

If you're looking for an apology instead of money, filing a lawsuit is probably a mistake because parties often become insulted and more inclined to fight after they are sued. Perhaps alternative dispute resolution (ADR) such as mediation is the better way to go to resolve your problem. Explore this option with your lawyer. Have you considered having the lawyer send an initial demand letter to get the other side's attention? Such letters often get the ball rolling and expedite settlement discussions aimed at resolving a matter out of court.

Discuss legal fees and costs with your attorney upfront before filing. Information on how to work effectively with your lawyer and reduce misunderstandings is contained in Chapter 10. You and your lawyer need to decide ahead of filing the lawsuit what remedies you are seeking and what amount of money you will accept as a successful outcome of the case. Also, analyze whether the defendant has sufficient assets (such as money in the bank and property). After going through lengthy litigation and expense if the matter is not settled out of court, you don't want to win the case but be unable to collect the award.

There are investigative companies who, for a fee, can advise you about the defendant's asset picture. Your lawyer can tell you where such companies are located. You may also find them listed on the Internet or in the telephone yellow pages. Always discuss these concerns with your lawyer before the decision to litigate is made.

Discuss whether an insurance company or third party with deep pockets, such as a guarantor or bank, will be on the hook to pay the defendant's judgment if you prevail. Conversely, you need to assess whether the defendant will declare bankruptcy before the end of the trial or after you've spent large sums in legal fees and costs. In many situations, bankruptcy can either eliminate the entire judgment or cause any payments to be stretched over a long period of time. Suing someone makes no sense if the person is broke, bankrupt, or intends to file bankruptcy during or after the litigation.

Filing for bankruptcy is not always a free lunch. In most states, for example, delinquent alimony and child support payments cannot be discharged (forgiven) in bankruptcy. The same is true for taxes, student loans, judgments or debts arising from damages caused while driving intoxicated causing injury or death, and certain fraud claims. Ask your lawyer to advise you of any of the kinds of debts that may be wiped out in bankruptcy and whether this possibility serves as a deterrent to filing a lawsuit.

Be aware of statute of limitations issues. A civil lawsuit must be commenced (i.e., filed) within a certain period of time after the dispute occurred to avoid dismissal on the basis of being untimely. So if the facts which gave rise to your claim occurred more than a few years ago, your case may be unenforceable due to the statute of limitations. For example, in many states, you must file a state discrimination lawsuit within two years of when the last harmful act occurred. In certain limited exceptions the limit may be extended where the injured party was not able to promptly discover the injury, or the defendant concealed the injury.

Each federal and state court has its own rules concerning the maximum amount of time you can wait before a lawsuit must be filed and it is crucial to know how much time you have before contemplating litigation. In many states, the general statute of limitation is four to six years for breach of contract claims and two years for tort claims. However, there may be a unique statute of limitation that covers your particular situation (some require action within 30 – 180 days) so speak to a lawyer for advice. The same is true if you want to join others in one suit (called a class action). Always attempt to contact the law firm representing the class within the required period of time so you'll be included in the lawsuit.

STRATEGY: *If your lawyer procrastinates and unnecessarily delays filing your lawsuit causing the statute of limitation to expire, this is grounds for a malpractice lawsuit against the attorney, providing you can prove that the lawsuit was a valid one with a high probability of success.*

Damages

Damages are compensation or relief awarded to the prevailing party in a lawsuit. Damages can be in the form of money or a directive by the court for the losing party to perform or refrain from performing a certain action. The following briefly describes various forms of damages:

COMPENSATORY DAMAGES. This is a sum of money awarded to a party that represents the actual harm suffered or loss incurred. Since damages cannot be presumed, one must prove what the actual out-of-pocket losses are. For example, projections of future lost profits will not be awarded unless they are definite and certain.

INCIDENTAL DAMAGES. Incidental damages are traditionally direct out-of-pocket expenses for filing a lawsuit and related court costs (such as process server fees). These direct costs of litigation are sometimes awarded to the prevailing party in a litigation as part of the party's loss.

LIQUIDATED DAMAGES. This is an amount of money agreed on in advance by parties to a written contract to be paid in the event of a breach or dispute. If it is not possible to compute the amount of the loss, a judge may uphold the amount specified. However, in many circumstances, when the amount specified has no actual basis in fact, a judge may disregard it, viewing the amount merely as a penalty.

NOMINAL DAMAGES. This is a small amount of money (e.g., $1.00) awarded by the court. Sometimes a party may win the lawsuit but not have proved suffering or any actual damages.

PUNITIVE DAMAGES. Also called exemplary damages, punitive damages represent money awarded as punishment for a party's wrongful acts beyond any actual losses. When punitive damages are awarded, a judge is often sending a signal to the community that similar outrageous, malicious, or oppressive conduct will not be tolerated. Under the laws of many states, punitive damages can be awarded only in certain types of lawsuits, such as personal injury and product liability actions, and not lawsuits to enforce employment contracts or business agreements.

SPECIFIC PERFORMANCE. This is a directive by the court for the party being sued (i.e., the defendant) to perform a certain action such as sell a business or not work for a competitor pursuant to a clause in an employment contract. Specific performance is typically not awarded if monetary damages can make the party seeking the relief whole.

INJUNCTION. This is a court order restraining one party from performing or refusing to perform an action or contract.

MITIGATION OF DAMAGES. This is a legal principle that requires a party seeking damages to make reasonable efforts to reduce damages as much as possible; for example, to secure comparable employment or file for unemployment benefits if a job cannot be obtained in the short term.

Sometimes an employer is interested not only in obtaining damages but in seeking to stop you from establishing a competing business or working for a competitor. An action can be commenced called a preliminary or temporary injunction. The employer (as the moving party) will request a hearing immediately after the lawsuit is filed. A request for an immediate hearing is called an order to show cause. If a judge rules in favor of the motion, the injunction will be granted. If a judge decides in favor of the defendant, the injunction will be denied, but, depending on the circumstances, the case may be allowed to proceed like any other lawsuit to ascertain damages.

Starting an Action

A civil lawsuit must be commenced (i.e., filed) within a certain period of time after the dispute arose to avoid dismissal on the basis of being untimely (called the statute of limitations). Each state and federal court has its own rules concerning the maximum amount of time you can wait before a lawsuit must be filed; it is crucial to know how much time you have before contemplating litigation.

A lawsuit is started by preparing and filing a summons and complaint with the court. A summons is a single piece of paper typically accompanied by the complaint that, when served on the defendant (e.g., an employer), notifies the defendant of a lawsuit. A complaint is a legal document that starts the lawsuit. It alleges pertinent facts and legal causes of action that the plaintiff will rely on in the attempt to collect damages. For a lawsuit to proceed, it is necessary that the summons and complaint be served on the defendant either in person (typically with the help of a process server or sheriff) or by certified mail, return receipt requested, in states that permit mail service. If the defendant is not notified of the existence of the lawsuit or if the complaint is not drafted accurately and fails to state a legally recognized cause of action, the case may be dismissed. If a lawsuit is dismissed without prejudice, it may be started over; lawsuits dismissed with prejudice are considered final, and may never be brought again.

The summons and complaint must be drafted artfully to avoid dismissal of your case. It should set forth your claims in simple, concise, plain English with each paragraph containing a single fact or set of circumstances. The complaint should also describe in detail the relief and remedies you seek.

STRATEGY: *Some aggressive lawyers prepare, file and serve the summons and complaint first and talk settlement later. When confronted head on with the possibility of being dragged into a lawsuit (as opposed to merely receiving a demand letter threatening litigation), some employers will instruct their lawyers to quickly settle the case. The downside is that it may cost you significant legal fees and costs for your lawyer to prepare and serve the complaint, may anger your adversary, and may expose you to significant counterclaim damages if the actual case proceeds. Discuss the merits and pitfalls of such aggressive strategy with your employment attorney where applicable.*

In some states, you can file the papers with the court before serving the defendant; in other states, it is necessary to effectuate proper service before filing the papers. At some period, the summons and complaint must be filed with the clerk of the proper court together with the payment of the initial filing fee (which can be as much as $350 in some states). Filing these documents is rather easy. At the courthouse, a clerk accepts the fee and documents, stamps the papers to indicate the date and time received, and issues a receipt. The documents then become part of a file that is stored at the court. The file is given to the presiding judge of the case when appropriate (e.g., during oral arguments, before trial and at the trial). Usually, a judge is randomly assigned to preside over every filed case. The judge will rule on various pretrial motions, move the case along to the trial, conduct the trial, and render a judgment based on the evidence when a jury is not involved.

The papers are served on the defendant(s) either in person (usually with the help of a process server or sheriff) or by certified mail, return receipt requested, in states that permit mail service. Most judges now accept electronic on-line service and filing. Sometimes the lawyer for the defendant will accept service on behalf of his client.

It is important that your lawyer know all the current rules concerning service because if the defendant is not correctly notified of the existence of the lawsuit, is not served, or is served improperly (such as by slipping the documents under the wrong apartment door), a case may eventually be dismissed after a traverse hearing, and any judgment you obtain will be unenforceable.

There are special rules governing proper service if the defendant is a corporation, partnership, or not-for-profit association. Speak to your lawyer about this. Inquire what rights you have if the defendant deliberately avoids service. Be sure you understand what documents need to be served to be accepted to the court.

People who operate or own a small business usually have the title of president, CEO and manager and must make decisions on behalf of the business. What if the business is sued by a former employee, customer, or competitor? Often the plaintiff will sue the business and the owner individually. Depending on the facts, a judge may allow a case to proceed against a business owner personally. This is called "piercing the corporate veil" and serious ramifications often ensue. If you are not immediately dismissed from the lawsuit, you may be subjected to extensive discovery into your personal life and finances. If the suit is successful your personal assets can be recovered to satisfy the judgment and a judge or jury may award punitive damages if the court finds fraudulent or egregious activity.

Consider the following strategies for protection from lawsuits if you own a small business:

1. Form a corporation when you go into business. A distinct advantage of a corporation (as opposed to a partnership, joint venture or sole proprietorship) is that it can shield individuals from personal liability provided strategies 2 through 6 are carefully followed. Consider the extra money it costs to form a corporation, retain an accountant, and file annual returns like an insurance premium if you seek to reduce your personal exposure in a lawsuit.

2. Fund the business with adequate capital so the corporation runs on its own and doesn't require constant loans and money from your pocket.

3. Issue stock, conduct regular meetings with corporate minutes, file annual returns, and keep accurate records.

4. Execute all leases, contracts, tax returns and important documents in your official capacity (e.g., as Jim Smith, President). People sometimes forget to do this and merely sign their name without their title. Avoid such a mistake.

5. Maintain a separate business account. Avoid commingling corporate funds with personal money. Don't allow the corporation to pay your personal (e.g., home telephone) bills. If your business has a satellite office, be sure the lease is in the corporate name, not your name. Ask your lawyer or accountant to assist you in properly documenting all loans and capital contributions to the corporation so you're not viewed as running a personal "candy store."

6. Never personally guarantee a business commitment or debt. Doing this is the easiest way to allowing a plaintiff to pierce the corporate veil and hold you personally liable when the corporation defaults on an obligation.

7. Seek legal advice immediately when you are personally sued in any business lawsuit. Tell the lawyer to file a motion seeking to remove you from the lawsuit as soon as possible. While this may be expensive, it is usually worth the effort because the consequences of remaining in a lawsuit as an individual defendant can be devastating.

Once you have filed and served the complaint and filed proof of proper service with the court, you have done all you need to do to get the lawsuit rolling. The ball is now in the defendant's court. After being served with the summons and complaint, the defendant has a period of time (usually no more than 30 days) to submit an answer. The answer is the defendant's reply to the plaintiff's charges in a civil lawsuit. Properly drafted answers typically deny most of the plaintiff's charges, list a number of legal reasons called affirmative defenses why the case should not proceed (e.g., it is time-barred due to the statute of limitations, there is no personal or subject matter jurisdiction, there is improper service or venue, there is no legal cause of action, etc.) The answer may also contain a counterclaim. A counterclaim is a claim asserted by the defendant in a lawsuit. Sometimes the plaintiff loses his or her case and the defendant wins the case through his or her counterclaim.

Each case is decided by its unique facts. The fact that someone is the plaintiff only means that he or she filed the lawsuit first; it does not guarantee success of the matter in any way. But if the defendant fails to respond to the lawsuit by filing an answer, he or she may lose the case by default. Thus, if you are a defendant, calmly review the summons and complaint with a lawyer after receiving it. Don't ignore taking action once you're served. Some people put the papers in a drawer and refuse to deal with it. But failing to file a timely answer will only compound your problems. A good lawyer can settle a matter for a defendant or even postpone a poor result for several years in litigation. Never lose your cool when you're served because it's not the end of the world.

In addition to a counterclaim against the plaintiff, a defendant can file a cross-claim against any other defendant when that cross-claim arises out of the same transaction or occurrence as the plaintiff's suit against you. Similar to counterclaims, cross-claims are in effect separate lawsuits among the defendants which are merged with the main case. And when you have claims against others that arise out of the same facts as the claims in the main case, you can join them in the lawsuit. For example, those who may be liable with the plaintiff on your counterclaim can become additional counter-defendants.

Discovery

The discovery phase of the case begins after the answer is received from the defendant. Several pretrial devices, including interrogatories, depositions, request for admissions and productions of documents, and motions, are used by lawyers to elicit information from the opposing side, gather evidence, and prepare for the trial. The discovery phase often lasts several years in a complicated employment case and can be very expensive in terms of attorney fees and the costs of taking depositions, procuring documents, and paying for postage and related expenses.

As a party in a lawsuit, you're entitled to find out all of the factual basis for the opponent's claims or defenses, and the other party may do the same with you. By the discovery cutoff date (a date established by the court after which no more discovery will be allowed), both sides will have had the opportunity to learn the facts, witnesses and documents of the other side. But discovery is not just getting facts. It's also learning about your opponents' lawyers and their witnesses. For a trial lawyer, the purpose of discovery is to help get a case ready for a trial that you are determined to win.

Interrogatories are written questions sent to an opponent to be answered under oath. When skillfully used, interrogatories can help you obtain information and documents at a significant savings in cost and time. A problem though is that while the responses are signed by the client, the opposing party's attorney usually drafts them to minimize the dissemination of damaging statements. Often the responses are evasive and unclear. This requires your lawyer to follow up or seek the court's assistance in getting proper and complete answers to interrogatory questions.

Lawyers often submit excessively long documents with questions having no bearing to the issues or facts of the case. To avoid having the other party successfully ask the court to grant a motion to strike and not be required to answer your interrogatories, custom-tailor the document to suit the particular case. A careful editing is the very first step to a successful interrogatory. Request documents wherever possible. A tax return or a contract will tell you far more than pages of the most intricate questions.

STRATEGY: *Depending on local or federal court rules where the case is filed, you have a certain period of time to answer or object to interrogatory questions after you receive them. If you fail to respond to the questions by the deadline, you may be subject to a motion to compel you to answer the questions and may face a court imposed fine (called a sanction). Speak to your employment attorney about this where applicable.*

A deposition is a pretrial proceeding in which one party is questioned under oath by a lawyer. Depositions often lasting several days are taken by both sides. A stenographer is present to record all statements and preserve the testimony. Depositions are used to collect information and facts about the case, narrow the issues to be proven at trial, preserve the testimony of individuals who may die or be out of the jurisdiction at the time of trial or establish a record that can be used to discredit (impeach) the testimony of witnesses at trial.

Your lawyer must properly prepare all witnesses before their depositions are taken for maximum success. Many cases have been lost due to unprepared responses elicited from a witness at a deposition. If a witness's testimony at the trial is materially different (inconsistent) from statements the witness gave at the deposition, his or her credibility may be seriously undermined; if the witness gives a totally different statement about something at the trial, that side's chances of winning the case can be dramatically reduced. Also, incorrect answers at the deposition may give the opposing attorney grounds to file a motion for summary judgment to dismiss the case in its entirety or throw out certain causes of action. A motion to dismiss, sometimes called a demurrer, states that even if the plaintiff's allegations are true and there is no genuine issue as to important facts, no legal basis exists for finding the defendant liable.

Pre-trial depositions are also useful because they help you and your lawyer assess the merits of the opponent's positions and get a pre-trial look at the style and tactics of opposing counsel and the demeanor and presence of the parties and witnesses. You can learn what makes a witness angry or impatient, and the ability to handle tough questions on cross-examination. When deposing your opponent's expert witnesses, you will learn what the witness was shown, told and did in preparation for the deposition and the basis behind the rendering of his or her professional opinions. Using interrogatories to give you simple facts, dates, names, etc., the deposition gives you the opportunity to get answers to more intricate follow-up questions. If you want to learn the opponent's theory of the case, get a sense of how well the expert can present it, and help to avoid surprises at the trial, ask the right questions at the deposition.

STRATEGY: *After a hostile witness's deposition is over, write down notes on his or her strengths and weaknesses while they are still fresh in your mind. For example, does this witness seem pleasant and helpful, or condescending and rude? Is she competent and prepared or does she give the impression of shooting from the hip?*

If a witness tries to dodge a question by claiming he or she doesn't remember, your lawyer should refuse to take "I don't know" or "I don't recall" for an answer. Ask the witness the following questions: Who does know? Who might know? What documents might have the information? Were any records or memoranda made? Who made them? Who has them? What could you do to find out where the information might be? Who might know where to find the answer to the question? Did you once know the answer? Who did you tell? What might bring back your memory, that is, refresh you recollection?

Disagreements occasionally arise between attorneys as to whether a witness is or is not required to answer certain questions posed during the deposition. Courts sometimes become involved in these disputes. When that happens, the attorneys at the place of deposition initiate a conference call to chambers seeking one or more rulings on the propriety of questions. Such efforts are subject to the availability of the judge or law secretary. Or, the attorney whose questions were not answered may file and serve a motion seeking an order compelling a witness to answer the questions at another future deposition. A judge will weigh a party's need to receive information material and necessary to the prosecution or defense of an action against refusing to allow answers to improper questions which are grossly irrelevant or burdensome. Other areas where witnesses are permitted not to answer questions include the right against self-incrimination, recognized privileged communications between spouses, attorney-client, doctor-patient, and penitent-clergy.

STRATEGY: *Be sure you are properly advised by your lawyer about these exceptions so you are not unnecessarily "punished" by refusing to answer questions at a deposition. When in doubt, listen if your lawyer objects to a question before answering it. You also have the right to confer with your lawyer before answering any question at deposition, so take your time and ask your lawyer for advice if a question is confusing, misleading, or prejudicial.*

After the opposing lawyer finishes asking a question, count to three in your head before responding. Be careful. Never say things you don't mean because you're nervous or uninformed. Answer the question as simply and directly as possible. Don't embellish an answer and don't volunteer extra information. It is not necessary to explain an answer unless the question requires it. If you must explain, keep it as short and simple as possible. Make the lawyer work for everything she gets. Look out for questions that paraphrase your answer because they might be traps, especially questions that ask for absolutes (e.g., questions with words like "never," always" and "whenever" in them).

It is essential that your lawyer properly prepare and advise you before your deposition is taken. Many cases have been lost due to unprepared responses elicited from a witness at a deposition. If your testimony is materially different (inconsistent) at the trial from statements you gave at the deposition, your credibility may be seriously undermined; giving a totally different statement about something at the trial could dramatically reduce the chances of success. Incorrect answers at the deposition might also give the opposing attorney grounds to file a motion to dismiss the case in its entirety or throw out various causes of action. A motion to dismiss asserts that even if the plaintiff's allegations are true and there is no genuine issue as to important facts, no legal basis exists for finding the defendant liable.

Instruct your lawyer not to engage in abusive discovery tactics unless absolutely necessary (e.g., to stall for time). Some lawyers believe the primary goal in discovery is to inflict pain on opposing counsel. They file unnecessary protective orders to keep important information from being turned over to the other side. Fortunately, judges are aware of discovery abuses and are fining lawyers who engage in such conduct.

Keep close track of all documents that come in after your discovery requests are made. Never falsely assume that what the other side gave you is all they have. Be thorough in taking the deposition of everybody connected with the case. You must pursue every document that ought to be there and try to find out what happened to it.

Usually your lawyer will submit with your interrogatories a request that your opponent produce for your review all documents that relate to the case, including writings, contracts, memos, photographs, financial documents, floor plans, computer records, and any other information stored in electronic devices. Prepare a thorough list of the specific documents or categories of documents that you want to look at. Be sure you're thorough because you don't want to be surprised at trial by a key document you didn't ask for. The key is to get all of your opponent's documents from third parties that will help you win the case. If the opposing lawyer hides important documents or refuses to turn them over to your lawyer, ask your lawyer to prepare a motion requiring the court to order the production and inspection of those key documents. Such a motion may delay the progress of the case for months until a judge renders a decision (i.c., denies or grants the motion) and can be quite costly, so you need to carefully evaluate the advantages and disadvantages where applicable before proceeding.

Requests for Admissions are written requests that your opponent admit the truth of certain facts or the application of law to facts. If opposing counsel will admit to certain facts, such as confirm that his client did indeed sign the contract in question, the case could be streamlined and proceed quicker. Conversely, requests for admission can be used against you if you admit something damaging and the other side uses your admission to get your case thrown out in a summary judgment motion. Be sure you understand the consequences of any potential admission before agreeing to it.

At the beginning of a case, a judge will coordinate a discovery schedule with the attorneys for both sides. If one party needs more time to complete discovery, this may or may not be allowed. Generally, after a conference with the parties, a judge will be inclined to extend the discovery period up to another six months. Ultimately, however, the cut-off date will expire and no further discovery will be permitted prior to the trial.

Once the discovery phase of the case is completed, the judge will order a pretrial conference. Both attorneys are asked to appear and discuss the case and the possibility of settlement. Some judges make quite active attempts to settle cases at these conferences. If the conference is successful and the case is settled, the parties will prepare a written stipulation that describes the terms of the settlement. Typically, the judge will review and approve all settlements before they are implemented.

At this time the attorneys will also decide whether to file pretrial motions. The most common motion is called a Motion for Summary Judgment. The party bringing the motion tries to prove that there are no disputed issues of fact, and that the case should be dismissed as a matter of law.

A full-blown trial may be forestalled by a successful motion for "summary judgment." Summary judgment may be appropriate if the facts in the case are clear and the only question is how the law should be applied to those facts. In such cases there is no need for a jury or judge to hear witnesses or view the evidence regarding what happened. All that is left for the court to do is apply the law to the known facts, which can be done without a trial.

In considering whether to grant a party's motion for summary judgment, the trial judge will review the parties' affidavits (written statements under oath), exhibits, documents and other discovery materials to determine whether (viewed in the light most favorable to the opponent to the motion) there is no genuine dispute regarding an important fact. If the court is uncertain whether the case contains a genuine issue of material facts, it will deny the summary judgment motion and the case will proceed to trial. If the court is convinced that there is no such factual dispute, it will consider the parties' written arguments on the legal issues and then grant the motion for summary judgment, disposing the case.

Summary judgment motions are typically rejected since litigants are entitled to their day in court. As with motions to dismiss, many judges are reluctant to grant summary judgment except in cut and dry cases such as non-payment of a loan.

STRATEGY: *Unless you have a clear, winning argument with no material facts in dispute, summary judgment may not be worth the cost of preparing the motion, regardless of what your lawyer tells you. If your case is dismissed as a result of an unfavorable ruling, your lawyer can appeal the decision to a higher court. This too can be quite expensive, so always get an honest, comprehensive evaluation of your rights (and possibly a second opinion from another independent* *lawyer) before making any move in this area. Also, parties can stipulate to the existence of certain facts and thereby forgo the need to introduce evidence at trial to prove those facts. The jury must accept these facts and cannot decide the case contrary to them. By reducing the facts in dispute, a stipulation can shorten the trial. Discuss this option with your lawyer where applicable.*

Pretrial motions are quite lengthy and take many hours for your lawyer to draft. Summary judgment motions are fact-intensive and contain many exhibits and references to pages of deposition testimony. Before filing your papers, you and your lawyer should check for errors in your exhibits. Your papers should be bound so they do not fall apart when someone turns the pages. Each exhibit should have a tab for easy reference.

Hopefully, the lawyers representing the plaintiff and defendant in your case will not be deliberately evasive and dilatory and increase the expense of litigation in money, time, trouble and feeling. It is also hoped that the judge handling the case will not allow either party unnecessary delay in discovery or permit a party to file unnecessary motions. Effective judges do not extend discovery indefinitely at pretrial conferences. They also impose sanctions and penalties on lawyers who fail to comply with court orders. Being assigned a no-nonsense judge to your case (often just the luck of the draw) can be a big step in your favor.

Should you settle the case? Judges usually order the parties to attend a final conference after all pretrial motions have been decided. As previously mentioned, some judges will push the parties to settle a case. Think carefully before accepting or rejecting any settlement. Most civil actions take up to five years to be tried. By accepting a fair settlement early on or just before trial, you'll be able to invest the settlement money to earn more money. You may also eliminate large legal fees, court costs, and the possibility of eventually losing the case after a trial. However, if you have a good employment case, it may pay to wait before discussing and accepting a settlement. Most trial attorneys believe that large settlements are obtained for their clients by waiting until the case reaches the courthouse steps. It often appears that companies do not negotiate in earnest until the moment before a case is to be tried. Time is on the side of the defendants and their insurance carriers. It often benefits them to wait and see if the case is valid (i.e., that it is properly prepared, that strong testimony from witnesses is available, and that the evidence will prove your claim). In large cases, insurance companies continue to make money on settlement funds by keeping them invested until the very last minute.

The decision on whether to accept a settlement should always be made jointly with your attorney. An experienced employment attorney knows the merits, pitfalls, and true value of the case better than you do. But don't allow your attorney to pressure you into accepting a smaller settlement than you think you deserve. Some attorneys seek smaller settlements out of laziness or because they are not inclined to try your case (or aren't very good at it), and the settlement represents money in the bank to them.

STRATEGY: *Instruct your lawyer to provide you with a detailed written explanation of the pros and cons of settling your case. Tell her that the final decision to settle or not to settle is yours. Do not let your lawyer push you around. Your lawyer cannot settle the case without your approval. If he does, he can be sued for malpractice.*

If you are not satisfied with your lawyer's advice or conduct, consult another attorney for a second opinion before settling the matter. Do this before taking action. Once you sign the settlement papers and accept the money you will not be able to change your mind and continue with the case, since releases contained in such documents prohibit you from doing so.

When in doubt, ask to speak directly with the judge during final settlement discussions. Many lawyers settle cases with a judge in the absence of their client. Litigants are unaware they can speak to the judge and this is a good idea. Some judges are agreeable to this and often shed significant insight on why a particular settlement is in the client's best interest. A judge's comments can be very instructive, especially when he or she takes the time to explain the pros and cons of your case and how much money you could potentially gain or lose at the upcoming trial. Ask your lawyer for permission to speak to the judge where applicable. Be suspicious if your lawyer refuses to honor your request or tells you the judge is unavailable. Demand to speak with the judge or his law clerk directly if the lawyer won't honor your request.

A final word about settlements: Lawyers often say a good settlement is made when both sides leave feeling unhappy. When one side believes he paid too much and the other side feels that he accepted too little, chances are a fair settlement of a dispute was reached.

If a matter cannot be settled, the judge will discuss with both attorneys how the case will proceed. The identity and order of witnesses and exhibits to be submitted at the trial will be agreed to before the trial begins. In many types of labor cases, either party can request that a jury decide the case rather than a judge. A jury trial usually involves 12 people, although some states allow as few as six. Some states permit a civil jury's decision to be less than unanimous. If a jury trial was requested by one of the parties, arrangements will be made for the lawyers to chose a jury from the available pool of applicants before the trial actually begins.

Getting a jury trial in most states is not automatic; you must request one, typically at the start of the case. You may be required to deposit money with the court ahead of time, so speak to your lawyer or court clerk to learn how much money is needed and when it must be paid. Be sure to do this because you don't want to forfeit the right to a jury trial as a result of a simple mistake.

Jury Selection

Once a jury is requested by either party, your lawyer and opponent's lawyer must select the people who will compose the jury. The process is called voir dire. Prospective jurors are questioned to see if they are qualified to sit on the panel. Lawyers ask different kinds of questions in an attempt to learn if the person has an open mind and is not biased against you or your claim.

For instance, if you are suing an ex-employer in a discrimination case, your lawyer prefers to exclude corporate executives who may be inclined not to award damages to former employees.

To save time and taxpayer money, most federal District Court judges no longer let trial lawyers ask potential jurors questions; they do it themselves. Many state courts are disallowing lawyer participation in jury selections. In other instances, trial lawyers are limited to a small amount of time (e.g., a half-hour to two hours per side), making it essential that your lawyer handle the voir dire process properly and effectively.

Bench trial are quicker and less expensive than jury trials. With a jury trial, your attorney will spend a great amount of time drafting jury instructions and selecting the jury. Depending on the fee arrangement, you may be required to pay the lawyer for his or her time while the jury is deliberating (which could take days). You may also have to wait much longer (e.g., six months) before starting a jury trial since a judge may not be available to supervise this lengthy process. But the wait can be worth it if the jury awards a large monetary settlement, including punitive damages, out of passion, which a judge in a bench trial is not as likely to do.

Speak with your lawyer to understand the pros and cons of having a jury trial and whether the added expense and effort is worth it. Deciding whether it is in your best interest to proceed with a jury trial or a bench trial is not easy. Your decision will depend on many factors including:

- Whether the remedy of your case is limited to money damages. For example, if you are seeking other forms of relief a jury would not have the power to issue this kind of (injunction) ruling.

- Whether the contract or agreement you signed prohibits jury trials. Many employment contracts, loan documents and insurance policies expressly forbid jury trials and such clauses are usually enforceable. Always read any document carefully before signing to understand your rights.

■ Whether the judge selected to preside over the case is competent, caring, and will render a fair verdict.

Some judges are political appointees with questionable legal skills. Or, a judge's mindset may not be disposed to granting you a favorable ruling. Experienced trial lawyers know how each judge tends to rule, their courtroom style, attitude towards expert witnesses, and whether they are fairer to plaintiffs or defendants. Even personal characteristics can play a role in a judge's decision-making, such as their religious beliefs, where they went to school, hobbies or affiliations with community organizations. Discuss this with your lawyer. Hopefully your lawyer will be able to predict with reasonable accuracy how the judge will act to provide you with realistic expectations and an appreciation for the risks at trial. If your lawyer decides that it is not advantageous to rely on the judge assigned to your case, you may want to have the matter decided by six or 12 minds instead of one.

STRATEGY: *Experienced trial lawyers often comment that if the facts of your case are poor, but you have strong legal defenses, use a judge. If your facts are good, but you have weak legal defenses, pick a jury. Consider choosing a jury if you are a plaintiff with an emotional claim, such as being the victim of sexual harassment. And it is generally best to opt for a jury if you are the more sympathetic party seeking money damages only.*

When your lawyer finds people she wants to exclude from the trial, she makes a peremptory challenge. You have a number of peremptory challenges that allow you to exclude a juror for any reason, even for a bad look. Most states limit the amount of peremptory challenges your lawyer can make, so these must always be exercised carefully. Conversely, your lawyer can make an unlimited number of challenges for cause. For example, if a juror once did business with the other side or was a client of your lawyer that person can be dismissed. Since you have unlimited cause challenges, the more jurors you remove for cause the better so you don't waste precious peremptory challenges.

Voir dire offers the plaintiff's attorney a chance to counter this belief and awaken jurors' sense of fair play. When handled properly, voir dire provides an opportunity to help jurors recognize their preexisting biases so they can approach your case fairly. If a lawyer fails to slay the litigation crisis myth during voir dire, this "fantasy dragon" can emerge later to damage a plaintiff's case.

Experienced trial lawyers ask questions during voir dire to eliminate this problem where applicable. How do the prospective jurors feel about employees who file lawsuits seeking huge damages for emotional injuries? How do they feel about serving on this panel? If prospective jurors reply with hostility, your lawyer should thank them for their honesty. They should then be asked if their feelings about frivolous lawsuits even apply to cases with merit. Does the juror have an unfavorable attitude before knowing what your case is about? This line of questioning may cause hostile jurors to reconsider whether their beliefs and values apply to your case and may also impress on other jurors the unfairness of carrying general negative beliefs over to a specific lawsuit.

If you are the plaintiff, one of your goals during voir dire is that when the defense falls back on a favorite theme — that you're just looking for someone to sue — is to make jurors want to keep their promise to the court and not make up their mind until they hear the evidence. Through plain talk, effective plaintiff's trial counsel has an opportunity during voir dire to remove jurors of their prejudices and encourage them to reserve judgment until all the evidence is heard.

STRATEGY: *Studies show that juries usually reach verdicts that are consistent with their early impressions of a case. In fact, the majority of juries reach a verdict at the end of voir dire before any evidence is heard! To facilitate effective voir dire, your lawyer should put prospective jurors at ease. Assure them that voir dire is not a test, that there are no right or wrong answers, and that a truthful answer is always correct. Your lawyer must never be guilty of irritating or boring the jurors.*

Be sure you understand what type of juror your lawyer is choosing and the reasons why. Select people who can identify with you and your case. Depending on the case, look for people with compassion, a streak of independence and some indication of warmth. During a well executed voir dire, your trial attorney will use his or her presentation skills to discover as much information as possible from prospective jurors while planting the seeds of your case in the jurors' minds. The lawyer must also be able to identify which jurors are biased for or against you. Be present with your lawyer during voir dire, make your instincts known during the process, and question how the lawyer arrived at his or her decision.

The best way to pick a jury is following your gut instincts. But always consider using various forms of jury research for a large case. Effective jury research can probe the attitudes of potential jurors about the kind of claim or defense you have, test their reactions to some of the potential landmines that may be lurking in your case, tell your lawyer what they think about you and the other side, and help your lawyer identify problem jurors during voir dire. While jury research often tells you what you already know, sometimes you will be alerted to problems you didn't know and suggest solutions to overcome these difficulties.

The following is a brief description of the kinds of jury research your lawyer can conduct:

1. **Jury profilers:** Are specialists who typically put together a picture of "ideal" jurors as well as those you should exclude before voir dire begins.

2. **Jury selection consultants:** Are generally present during voir dire to listen to your lawyer's questions and give timely advice on the selection process as it unfolds.

3. **Shadow juries:** Consist of a group of people who hear everything real juries hear while the actual trial unfolds and nothing more. They give daily feedback to the shadow jury coordinator telling how they feel about the case, what they understood, what they missed, who they liked and

witnesses they didn't like. Shadow juries can give your lawyer an accurate sense of what the actual jury is thinking and feeling while the trial is proceeding and can help your lawyer correct the course of the trial as it progresses.

4. **Mock trial:** This is basically a practice run where your lawyer presents the entire case, including the introduction of witnesses, exhibits, and opening and closing arguments to a group of people pretending to be jurors. Often the trial lawyer will have a jury consultant present during the mock trial (even if it runs for a week) so the consultant can develop a strong understanding of the case and help the lawyer prepare for the voir dire and the actual trial. Experts say of all the forms of research your lawyer can conduct, mock trials are usually the most effective dollar-wise.

Jury research specialists understand jury dynamics and demographics, but are very expensive. The decision to use a jury consultant inevitably depends upon your financial resources and the size and complexity of your case.

STRATEGY: *If you can't afford to pay jury consultants, tell your lawyer to put together a focus group consisting of friends, neighbors and acquaintances to try out trial themes and theories. Get people to volunteer a few hours to listen to your lawyer's opening and closing argument and examine key evidence. Solicit their informal comments and reactions. Effective trial lawyers develop persuasive themes and theories at the onset of the trial. How did the focus group react to your theories of the case? Using a focus group during a practice run will give you a better idea of what will work at the trial. Since your goal is to select jurors who will buy into your theme of the case, an effective focus group can help you establish a profile ahead of time to determine what kind of jurors you want.*

If you decide to use a consultant or a focus group, be sure to get answers to these questions:

- How likely is it that damages will be awarded?
- What amount of damages is likely to be awarded?
- What type of juror is most (or least) likely to award high-damages?
- How accurate should the results of jury research be?
- How many jury subjects are enough?

Voir dire is the first time the jury sees you. First impressions are important, so be sure you get off on the right foot. Your lawyer should be able to clearly define and communicate the key issues and facts of the case with potential jurors. It is important for your lawyer to make you likeable. Jurors are more willing to award fair compensation to claimants who are likable. They also tend to want to help people who are trying to help themselves. For example, if you are a plaintiff, your chances of receiving compensation will be enhanced if you have returned or are trying to return to work after being unfairly fired. Likewise, if you are a defendant, will the jury understand your actions and agree that you acted appropriately under the circumstances?

In some states judges only permit a maximum of ten to 15 minutes per potential juror, so your lawyer has to quickly grasp which people might be favorably disposed to your case. He should ask broad, non-threatening, general questions to get them talking and to put jurors at ease. Let the jurors talk and answer questions fully to properly evaluate them. Don't break the flow of dialogue with the jurors by trying to write down their responses because your lawyer is supposed to be asking more questions. Your lawyer should read from notes (but never from a script) and avoid using complicated legal words when speaking to the jury. Effective lawyers also know when to stop asking questions to favorable jurors. Counsel should never argue the case during voir dire. Rather, he or she should be attempting to gain insights into how a prospective juror thinks.

Be sure your lawyer shows respect during the process and does not talk down to potential jurors. Your lawyer should act casually and friendly. The goal is to empathize with jurors and demonstrate that your lawyer cares about them. All conduct should be calculated to gain the juror's trust. For instance, by telling them that everyone appreciates their taking time off from work or their families, and even by pointing to the courtroom clock to demonstrate to the judge he's ready to proceed and doesn't want to waste the jurors' valuable time, counsel can gain sympathy and score points right off the bat.

Jurors tend to identify your lawyer with you. If you are a plaintiff, you want the jury to give you substantial amounts of money. If you are a defendant, you want the jury to understand you, what you did and why. You hope they will conclude they would have done exactly the same thing. By asking the right questions, your lawyer will get to know the jurors better, perhaps learning which jurors have experiences similar to yours.

It is wise to review biographical information on each prospective juror before asking questions whenever possible. Watch closely how the jurors are responding to your lawyer and the theme of your case. How are they responding to your opponent and your opponent's theme of the case? How do they feel about the issues of your case? Some lawyers believe it is best to disclose weaknesses of a case during voir dire to avoid surprises later. Experienced trial lawyers may even ask jurors if there is anything about the case or you that offends them because you need to know about any preconceived agendas. Your lawyer should share your concerns about the most important and dangerous aspects of your case. If such questions are asked, look into the juror's eyes. Try to get a sense if they can be fair. Ask if they are capable of awarding extra damages for your injuries. If you are a defendant, ask the jurors if they will look at the case fairly and not award damages just because the plaintiff is requesting them.

Pay special attention to what the jurors say and how they react to questions. You can often learn a lot from a person's body language, how they carry themselves, what they wear, their accessories, hair styles, and what they read.

Select jurors with interests common to yours. Ask jurors questions about things they can relate to in their own lives and weave bits and pieces from your case into the theme of your case. Proper jury selection is a critical step to winning or losing a case. Spend a significant amount of effort in understanding the voir dire process to maximize your lawyer's effectiveness in front of a jury.

STRATEGY: *If you are unsure about the voir dire process, or seek additional valuable strategies, talk to the Commissioner of Jurors at your local court. Such an individual possesses a wealth of information about the jury pool and selection process and may be helpful.*

Opening Arguments

After a bench trial or jury is selected, the plaintiff's lawyer begins the trial with an opening statement. This is a speech designed to explain the nature of the case, what the plaintiff intends to prove from the facts and what damages are sought. The defendant's attorney then gives an opening statement which explains how the defendant's version of the facts differs from the plaintiff's case, why there is no liability, and what the defendant's theme of the case is. If the defendant filed a countersuit (called a counterclaim), the defendant's lawyer will state why damages are due and how the defendant intends to prove its case for damages.

During opening statement your lawyer must establish a rapport with the jurors, earn their trust, and plant the seeds that will later yield a victory. The opening argument is essentially a road map of what jurors will hear during trial. Your lawyer will discuss what the case is about and explain what will happen as the trial unfolds. The parties will be introduced. Your lawyer will identify the issues in dispute and describe how the parties differ. His narrative should outline all of the important evidence the judge or jury will hear. It should be in a clear, simple message emphasizing your theme of the case. Key witnesses will be mentioned and your lawyer will say what they will testify to at the trial.

In thinking about the most effective way to ask for damages (if you are the plaintiff), experts say the direct approach works best. Jurors try to do the right thing. The amount of money a jury will award often depends on how the jurors feel about the wrongdoing they perceive.

When they are angered by or gain a negative impression about the defendant at trial because of his or her bad conduct, the defense attorney's mistreatment of the plaintiff, the overuse of defense objections, or the defendant's attempt to hide evidence, such negative feelings may be considered when deciding on a damages award. If your lawyer gets the jurors to understand your suffering and sympathize with your plight, the amount of damages to be awarded will be enhanced.

Your lawyer should state what your case is worth during opening argument. She should speak sincerely and always look each juror or the judge directly in the eye when doing so. Your lawyer should avoid asking for a far greater sum (e.g., triple) than you deserve in the expectation you will get less. Asking too much can result in getting nothing since the best way not to be perceived as greedy is not to be greedy. By initially requesting a realistic number a judge or jury will appreciate your lawyer's honesty.

It is often more effective to keep the opening argument short so you don't put the jurors or judge to sleep. Experts suggest that if your lawyer can't compress what has to be said into 45 minutes, he or she is not doing a good job.

It is also important to know your judge. What will the judge allow on opening? How much time will you have? Judges in many state and federal courts are exercising direct control over the substance of opening remarks and issuing pretrial orders barring lawyers from raising certain issues. Effective trial lawyers don't read opening statements; rather, they refer to an outline or notes. Their delivery is spontaneous, sincere and direct. They talk from the heart to make you more believable since it is important for the jury to know and understand you as a person, not as a litigant. Your lawyer should avoid referring to you as the "defendant" or a "party to this lawsuit." Using your real name can add a touch of humanity.

Your lawyer must try to make a good appearance and not hide behind a lectern. He or she should avoid a stiff wooden stance as well as any distracting physical or verbal mannerisms.

Discuss the use of visual aids during opening argument. We all know a picture is worth a thousand words. If you have a good quote from a deposition or a document that ties into the theme of your case, displaying it visually can be an effective way to drive the point home. Helping jurors visualize important facts via the use of charts, diagrams, models, photographs and other aids is quite effective.

To win the jurors' trust during opening argument, your lawyer should be careful not to make promises he or she cannot keep during the trial. It is an error for counsel to discuss evidence that will not be eventually introduced at the trial. Unkept promises of what the "evidence will show" can dash your hopes of a successful verdict. Nor is it acceptable to mention evidence which is inadmissible. Your lawyer must be candid. Competent lawyers avoid hiding the weaknesses of a case. They often mention problems during voir dire and opening argument. If your lawyer knows of any bad evidence which is admissible and will be introduced by your opponent's lawyer during the trial, it is probably best to tell the jury now. This is because you want to prepare the jury or judge to conclude that bad facts are insignificant in the context of your case as a whole. Never assume that if your lawyer omits problems in your case, opposing counsel will also. Opposing counsel will point out every negative aspect and this will hurt your case more if he or she tells the jury first. Thus, your lawyer should acknowledge problems during opening argument and explain them so the judge or jury understands that a problem is not what the case is about. Accentuate the positive.

A key objective of effective opening argument is to win the jurors' trust. If jurors believe your lawyer is trustworthy and has integrity (as opposed to a slick lawyer who hides information), winning your case will be easier. Experienced trial lawyers pay strict attention to an opponent's opening statement. If an adversary overstates the case, your lawyer in closing argument can remind the jury of these broken promises to your advantage.

Competent trial lawyers speak in plain language during opening arguments. They establish direct eye contact with the court. They communicate will all members of the jury and do not concentrate their stares on one individual. Effective opening statements are sincere, short, easy to understand, create a theme, avoid exaggeration, cut to the core of the controversy, and are believable. Select themes that relate to the jurors' life experiences. Your lawyer should use impact words such as tragedy, wrong, and justice, especially if you are the plaintiff. A good opening paints a picture that is vivid, clear, or detailed and involves the jurors emotionally. Lawyers who ramble, ridicule the judge or opposing counsel, use complicated language or exaggerate often fail to win the confidence of the judge or jury.

If your opponent's lawyer objects during your lawyer's opening statement, say nothing. Likewise, do not visibly react to opposing counsel's opening statement. Grimaces and head-shaking indicate nervousness and disrespect (which is a turn-off) so always be careful of your own body language.

Hopefully your lawyer will create a strong first impression during your opening statement. The final few sentences should conclude with a restatement of your theme and a request for an award people will remember. To be effective, your lawyer must conclude the opening statement with powerful and direct language that creates a positive lasting impression with the judge or jury.

Trying the Case

The trial begins after lawyers for both sides give their opening statement. Witnesses are called by the plaintiff's lawyer and give testimony under oath. The testimony of a witness is called "direct testimony." Other forms of evidence, such as documents, exhibits, and the testimony of expert witnesses (where required) are submitted during this process. After a witness finishes giving direct testimony, opposing counsel will typically cross-examine the witness to establish a lack of credibility, bias, loss of memory, or other faults with his or her testimony. This process continues until all of the plaintiff's witnesses have been called and testify. After cross-examination of a witness has ended, the lawyer first calling the witness may ask additional questions to explain answers given by the witness during cross-examination. This is called re-direct testimony.

After the plaintiff's case is concluded, the defendant presents its case. Witnesses are questioned and cross-examined by the plaintiff's lawyer. Rebuttal testimony of key witnesses by the plaintiff may also occur. This is the presentation of additional evidence by the plaintiff in response to the defendant's evidence.

Closing arguments are made after the defendant concludes its case. These are speeches by lawyers for both sides which summarize the evidence presented during the trial and each side's version of the significance of such testimony and evidence.

In a civil case, the plaintiff has the burden of proving its case by a legal standard called preponderance of evidence ("more likely than not") through witnesses, charts, documents, photographs, and other forms of physical evidence. In a criminal case, the prosecution must prove a person's guilt beyond a reasonable doubt. This is a more difficult standard to achieve.

Each side tries to get certain evidence admitted into the court record for consideration by a judge or jury during the trial. The other party, through his or her lawyer, will seek to exclude such evidence through objections by stating that the evidence is irrelevant or inadmissible. A judge will either deny the objection and allow the evidence to be admitted or sustain the objection and exclude the evidence. The introduction of evidence in any case depends on an attorney's arguments and the judge's interpretation of court rules in your state or federal court rules. Certain types of evidence, such as hearsay evidence (i.e., a witness's testimony about what someone else said outside the courtroom) must be excluded, sometimes in advance of trial.

The key to the successful direct examination of a witness is to make the judge or jury like and respect the witness because he or she is believable. This is not an easy task. It takes careful pre-trial training and preparation from your lawyer. Some lawyers don't train their clients to be effective witnesses at trial. To be an effective participant and achieve your ultimate goals, you must first understand how the system works, the theme of your case, your opponent's positions, and what must be proved at trial. Depending on the nature and complexity of the case, it is best to be prepared by your lawyer in stages. A comprehensive planning meeting should be scheduled with your lawyer approximately 30 days prior to the start of the trial, followed by a dress rehearsal a week before the trial begins. A final warm up session should be conducted the day before the trial. (Note: Avoid having the final meeting run into the wee hours of the morning because you'll need a good night's rest.)

It is unethical for a lawyer to knowingly assist in offering false or perjured testimony. A lawyer's coaching cannot change the substance of your testimony, only the style of the presentation. It should be a discussion of what you know and how you'll answer questions at trial. This includes being told the actual questions you'll be asked at trial from your lawyer and the kinds of questions to expect from opposing counsel during your cross-examination.

Effective preparation with your lawyer should include discussing your role at trial; effective courtroom demeanor; your recollection and probable testimony; other testimony or evidence that will be presented and asking you to consider your recollection of events in that light; the applicability of the law to the events at issue; reviewing the factual context into which your observations or opinions will fit; reviewing the documents or other physical evidence that may be introduced; and possible lines of hostile cross-examination that you may encounter and how to effectively handle such tough questions. Your lawyer can suggest words to use to make your points clear, but he or she cannot assist you in testifying falsely as to material facts. Your lawyer should use the preparation process to enhance your recollection of events, not materially alter them.

Believable witnesses do not get rattled, confused or intimidated. While rehearsing what you will say can enhance your presentation and help you relax, don't memorize your response. You don't want your answers to appear rehearsed and phony. Look at the lawyer when questions are being asked but face the jurors or judge when answering. Make brief eye contact with each juror to establish rapport. Keep your voice steady; this will cause listeners to believe you are confident, intelligent and knowledgeable. Witnesses who avert their eyes, act nervous, or squirm in their seats are often perceived as liars. Be yourself and avoid speaking in an arrogant or patronizing tone.

STRATEGY: *If possible, visit the courtroom where you will testify to familiarize yourself with the surroundings. It is also a good idea to video rehearsals with your lawyer to improve your appearance and mannerisms. For example, if you display a nervous laugh when asked difficult questions, you may be able to eliminate this trait before the trial.*

STRATEGY: *There are other tips to enhance your credibility and effectiveness. For example, it is essential to dress appropriately. Your goal is to look dignified and conservative; avoid flashy or gaudy clothing, accessories and hairstyles. Dress as you would for church or a job interview. Male witnesses should wear a conservative business suit.*

Be sure you know where the courthouse is located, including easy parking arrangements. Make arrangements to meet your lawyer at his or her office on the first day of trial to avoid getting separated or be unable to find each other (adding to your anxiety). Practice what you'll say once again if time permits and ask your lawyer to review anticipated trouble spots, including testimony given at a prior deposition which may not have been accurate.

Effective lawyers ease witnesses into their testimony. Simple answers should first be elicited detailing your background, education, current employment, special training and ties to the community. Let jurors hear you are held in high regard by your employer or members of the community. If you are married and have children, mention this because most jurors consider that positively. Answering easy questions first will put you at ease before launching into the events that gave rise to the lawsuit. You then should be asked what happened before, during and after the lawsuit was filed to provide a comprehensive chronology of key events. Your lawyer should make sure the direct testimony flows logically so the jury will remember important details. Thus, you should be asked questions to keep the story in logical sequence.

If you remember an important incident because it was a departure from your normal routine, this can impress a judge or jury why your recollection is so good after all these years.

Your lawyer should give you encouragement, support and confidence. He or she can put you at ease by saying, "I know you're nervous, but I would like to ask you some questions." Don't be afraid to correct answers you realize may be inaccurate. Be familiar with important documents and the substance of previous statements so you won't be surprised by questions from opposing counsel.

If you are the plaintiff and suffered physical injuries, you should describe them in detail and recount the medical treatment received in an emergency room and immediately thereafter. Where appropriate you should describe to the court your continuing medical treatment. You should also discuss the on-going pain and physical limitations you face and economic damages you suffer and will continue to suffer.

No matter what type of damages you are seeking, jurors need to know you did not try to bilk the justice system. You should be asked questions to show that upon being injured you did not think "Great, a chance to make a lot of money." You should be asked when the lawsuit was filed so the judge or jury knows it was not filed within days of the injury-producing event. You might even be asked when a lawyer was first consulted and why.

Never be afraid to say so if you are being paid expenses to give testimony in court. Get this out in the open as soon as possible so the jury will not believe your testimony is tainted. Note: most states prohibit fees for testifying but allow payment for expenses. Speak to your lawyer for information concerning where this is relevant.

Final words about effective direct testimony strategies: Experts say your lawyer should begin the trial with the strongest witness because jurors tend to make up their minds early in the case. This person should be a strong fact witness and difficult for the defense to cross-examine. Follow your strongest witness with your second strongest witness and so forth. For maximum effect, your lawyer should use simple language and keep questions short. Short questions make it easy for the jury and witness to follow and reduce the chances that opposing counsel will object to the form of the question to divert the jury's attention.

CROSS EXAMINATION. Testimony elicited on cross-examination can be more memorable to jurors and carry more weight than direct testimony. If your lawyer can prove facts critical to the case by cross-examining the opponent's witness, do so. The basic purpose of cross-examination is to show the witness agrees with certain elements of your case, respects the opinion, qualifications, or training of your witnesses or expert witnesses, and/or agrees with your theory of the case. It may also be used to show that the witness has lied, changed his or her story, or testified differently in the past. Effective cross-examination can help establish a witness's bias or prejudice, often due to a financial interest in the outcome, and show his or her testimony is contradictory, unreliable, or wrong.

Successful cross-examination of a hostile witness is not an easy thing to do. Competent trial lawyers have a thorough working knowledge of the laws of evidence and civil procedure in your jurisdiction together with good advocacy skills. The most important element is preparation. Your lawyer should read and re-read the witnesses' deposition testimony to know what the witness will say on the stand. This will enable him or her to establish that the witness is neither trustworthy nor credible, especially when trial testimony is inconsistent with previous deposition testimony.

Effective cross-examination is often brief; once an answer is given that is favorable to your case, it may be wise for your lawyer to stop asking more questions. Your lawyer should be courteous at all times because the jury is watching the interchange carefully. As a general rule, jurors dislike lawyers who pick on witnesses.

Unlike direct examination, cross-examination is optional. The first thing your lawyer must decide is whether to cross-examine the witness at all. If the witness has not hurt your case on direct and knows of no helpful facts, a wise attorney may elect to forego cross. Most of the time, you already know what the witness will say from deposition testimony. Armed with that knowledge you can make an intelligent decision about whether to cross-examine the witness based on trial preparation and the witness's courtroom testimony and demeanor. During cross-examination your lawyer should explore any bias the witness has against you or your claim, such as whether the person has a pecuniary interest in the outcome of the case.

STRATEGY: *If the witness has demonstrated he or she was untruthful in the past, such as lying on an application for a job, the witness may be questioned about this on cross to discredit his or her current testimony. Discuss this strategy with your lawyer where applicable.*

Your lawyer should be prepared to repeat a question if the witness does not answer. This technique requires your lawyer to repeat the question until the witness is responsive or until the jury sees the witness is being evasive. Most importantly, your lawyer should ask questions only if he or she knows the answer. Many lawyers have been burned by asking questions they didn't know the answer to.

Some lawyers agree it is best to find out from the witness where and how your adversary found him, what relations he has to the parties, attorneys, or other witnesses in the case, what documents he has seen, and how many meetings or contact he has had with opposing counsel or the client. All of this can help undermine his or her credibility.

By asking the witness to explain how he acquired the alleged knowledge set forth in his direct testimony and testing his memory and opportunities to observe what he claims to know, you can reduce his or her believability. Finally, experts suggest it is best to ask cross-examination questions out of sequence. By not following a predictable sequence in the questioning, the witness may be less likely to become comfortable with the examination.

EXPERT WITNESSES. Many cases require the service of an expert to prove a claim. An expert witness is an individual with specialized knowledge or experience whose expertise and testimony can help a judge or jury understand a complicated matter, such as a medical malpractice case. In such a lawsuit the testimony of a medical doctor expert would be required to explain to the judge and jury whether or not a doctor's acts constituted negligence.

Expert testimony adds a unique facet to the trial. It permits witnesses who are retained by one side to offer information and educate the jury on issues which are beyond the scope of an ordinary juror's knowledge. The outcome of complex cases often hinges on conflicting expert testimony since the jury is asked to resolve a case where the subject matter is unfamiliar to them. In doing so, they must accept one expert's version and reject another's. The impression an expert witness leaves with regard to his qualifications and honesty may carry the day. Juries typically give more weight to experts who testify and communicate their opinions in a convincing way.

Effective experts present dynamic, riveting testimony to impress the trier of fact. They are pleasant (and sometimes charming), intuitively know when to be quiet, and have a multitude of degrees, honors, awards and authoritative publications that address the main issues of your case. They also have considerable hands-on knowledge of the people, places and things at issue.

Experts are often found by referrals from other lawyers, by listings in prestigious associations, or through their publications. They testify about many things, such as the value of a family business in a divorce case, or the nature or severity of injuries sustained in a pregnancy discrimination matter. While your lawyer will make the ultimate decision whether to hire a particular person as your expert, you the client should play an active role with your lawyer in selecting a competent, reliable and cost-effective individual.

STRATEGY: *Good experts are generally well-known to trial lawyers. Some have been observed in court before and their credibility has been assessed. Look for a courtroom veteran. Investigate his or her qualifications. Interview the prospective expert to form your own impression. Does the individual possess strong communication skills? Is the subject matter appropriate for this expert?*

Beware of the arrogant expert who bristles when his or her opinion is questioned. Avoid experts that advertise extensively. Don't use experts who have testified so many times they're looked upon as "hired guns."

Is the witness willing to testify for a reasonable fee? Steer clear of experts with outrageous fee demands. Confirm all fee arrangement in a written retainer agreement to minimize misunderstandings.

Experts perform a variety of functions; these can be limited or extensive depending on the case and your needs. Initially you want the expert to educate your lawyer about the problems presented by your case. In a difficult or novel case, the expert can teach you and your lawyer what you don't know and what questions to ask. The expert can also hone your discovery requests and help you answer those of your opponent.

Be sure your lawyer is aware of your state's discovery rules before going too far with early-on assistance because the expert's written reports are discoverable (i.e., reviewable) by the other side. So too are letters and notes provided by the expert. Thus, where possible, avoid having your expert communicate to you in writing because your opponent may be able to review this information.

How long ahead of time must your lawyer inform the adversary of the existence of your expert? Local civil practice rules determine this. But the key is to have your expert help develop your theory of the case and evolving trial strategy as early as possible.

Make sure the expert provides the services you hired him or her to do. For example, some experts have assistants read pertinent exhibits and depositions and summarize the testimony for them. There is no way the expert can be knowledgeable with the facts of your case if she only relies on a summary prepared by someone else. Also, always keep close tabs on your costs. Learn what information the expert needs to address the issues and provide all information that minimizes your review cost.

Investigate their backgrounds with your lawyer once the other side's expert witnesses are named. If they will play an important role at the trial, obtain copies of depositions and trial testimonies from court litigation files in other cases to learn about their style and how they testify. Read articles or books they may have authored that relate to your case. Compare copies of their prior resumes with current ones to see if any damaging information in your case was intentionally omitted.

Note: In one case where the author was retained as an expert witness, opposing counsel purchased several of my books and tapes of television appearances and brought them to the deposition. I was methodically questioned about my comments in those publications in an effort to identify inconsistencies with facts of the present case. Fortunately, no negative information was discovered, but this experience created a lasting impression in the steps opposing counsel may and should employ (depending on cost and other factors, including time constraints) when researching the qualifications and background of an opposing expert witness. At the trial your lawyer must successfully challenge the expert's opinions. Merely showing that the witness is mistaken is not enough. The trick is to demonstrate that the expert does not know pertinent facts or knows them but does not want to say. Then the jury will have reason to disbelieve the expert and reject his opinions. While a plaintiff can score points with an impressive, forthright expert, effective cross-examination of a defendant's expert, showing he is deceitful or dishonest will anger a jury and provide lasting memories at the trial.

Since the opposing side's expert witness can destroy your case, it's up to your lawyer to inflict as much damage as possible to the opposing witness on cross-examination. This is done by attacking the substance of the expert's opinion or the witness himself. You accomplish this objective by convincing a judge or jury that the witness is not qualified to give her expert opinion or that her testimony should not be believed.

At trial, no matter how experienced, your expert will need considerable preparation in terms of the issues that must be addressed, the manner of presentation of those issues, and the anticipated opposition to the testimony. The standard of qualifying your expert varies from state to state. Your lawyer should be prepared with precedent to support your position if you expect your expert's qualifications to be challenged or if you intend to challenge the qualifications of an opposing expert. Tough attacks on the witness's education, training, or experience may not result in disqualification, but raising these questions may seriously dilute the effectiveness and the weight given to the expert's testimony by the trier of fact.

While all expert witnesses generally work for pay, prepare your expert for the inevitable question regarding remuneration. Usually there is nothing damaging about the expert admitting to previously testifying for your lawyer in another case where a successful verdict was obtained, having discussed his or her testimony with you before taking the stand, or acknowledging being paid. Just try not to make a big deal out of it.

Encourage your witness to look and act helpful. The expert who pontificates, is arrogant or condescending, or expresses annoyance with questions from the lawyers or the judge will not help your case. Neither will the expert who speaks in complicated jargon.

If your witness prepared a written report, be sure he or she remembers what was written and why. Make sure your expert has not testified previously to a position contrary to what he or she is taking in your case. If all the above guidelines are followed, you should be in a stronger position of receiving positive results from your hired expert witness.

Closing Arguments

When both sides are finished presenting their case, each attorney gives a summation. This is a review of the facts and testimony and other evidence. In many ways the closing argument is the plaintiff lawyer's crowning achievement. By the time the closing is delivered, your case's foundation has already been laid. Hopefully, the judge or jury's trust has already been earned. But the final words spoken can cement the case. During closing argument, effective trial lawyers restate evidence that was adduced during the trial and argue the merits of their case based upon the proof that was offered.

Experienced lawyers discuss the case with the jurors. They don't complicate the case or dwell on only one part of it. They also don't oversell the case to the jury.

A good way to score points during closing argument is through the use of rhetorical questions. Jurors are often persuaded by being told what the opposing party could have done at trial but didn't. For example, why was the witness not called to testify? Why didn't opposing counsel discuss them during the trial?

Your lawyer can destroy an opponent's position and credibility through the use of carefully planned rhetorical questions that focus on the other party's failure to act in a manner consistent with its side of the case.

Inexperienced lawyers give a summation and not a final argument during the closing. Effective lawyers tell stories and describe analogies that jurors can relate to and that emphasize your theme of the case. These techniques often cause the jury to think and understand your case through their own personal experiences. Juries also look favorably on lawyers who display a friendly and compassionate attitude towards their clients. They like when lawyers refer to their clients by name, not as the impersonal "plaintiff" or the "defendant."

Your lawyer should keep the closing simple, short, direct and to the point (similar to the opening statement), and avoid using notes. The lawyer should try not to cover too much, but emphasize the highlights. Besides talking up the positive, your lawyer should discuss your case's weaknesses.

Finally, after concluding closing argument, your lawyer should graciously thank the judge or jury for their time, act courteous, smile, and sit down.

After both sides have finished closing arguments (and there are no post-trial motions), the judge will render a decision if no jury is involved. Typically both parties have to wait a period of time (sometimes up to 60 days) before receiving the judge's written decision. If a jury is involved, the judge instructs its members as to what law is applicable to the facts and statements they heard. The jury then leaves the courtroom and returns later with its determination.

In rare cases a judge may disregard the jury's findings and grant a motion for judgment notwithstanding the verdict (called a JNOV) when he or she believes there was insufficient evidence to support a jury's conclusion.

After the judgment is made, either party can appeal the decision by filing a written document called a brief. Information about appeals is discussed in the next section. It is also important to take proper steps to collect the judgment if the losing party doesn't pay. This may involve placing a lien on real estate property owned by the losing party or attaching such property to prevent the transfer, assignment, or sale without your consent. Speak to your attorney for more information about how this can be accomplished.

STRATEGY: *Litigation is complicated, time-consuming, and subject to many hazards. Unless absolutely necessary, or unless the case involves a small amount of money that can be handled by yourself in small-claims court, do not attempt to file papers and represent yourself (pro se) in a lawsuit without an attorney.*

STRATEGY: *Because the success or failure of a case often depends on the type of evidence introduced and admitted (or excluded) from* *the record at a trial, it is important to hire an employment lawyer who is very knowledgeable about the rules of evidence. For maximum success, hire an employment lawyer who possesses competent trial skills.*

Appeals

The vast majority of lawsuits never go to trial; they are either discontinued or settled. However, every case that is tried has a loser, and the losing party must decide whether to appeal the unfavorable decision. An appeal is a request that a higher court review the decision of a lower court. The losing party challenging a trial court decision, called the appellant, first brings the appeal to the initial appeals court. The party opposing the appeal is called the appellee or respondent. In the federal court system, the losing party brings the appeal to the court of appeals in the appropriate circuit. For serious criminal cases (such as felonies) the right to an appeal is mandatory. In civil cases, an appeals court has discretion not to consider the appeal. Or, if it reverses the trial court's decision, it may remand the case back to the trial court to hear more evidence.

Your case can be further reviewed if a higher appeals court decides to review the decision of the lower appeals court. In most cases requests for further consideration by the higher appeals court are denied. If the higher appeals court agrees (i.e., affirms) the lower appeals court decision, only a review of the case by the U.S. Supreme court can get the decision overturned. In the federal system, after the appeal is decided by the U.S. Court of Appeals, the Supreme Court of the United States has the power to review and rule on the history of the case and the most recent appeal. Both of these instances rarely occur.

Appeals are also allowed from rulings made by administrative agencies and after arbitration awards in limited situations involving arbitrator misconduct, bias or dishonesty. It is extremely difficult to overturn administrative rulings, especially if a ruling is supported by substantial evidence. Penalties imposed by administrative agencies are subject to the review of the courts only when they are grossly excessive. An appeals court does not generally have the power to modify an administrative agency's award even if it is excessive; rather, the matter must be sent back to the agency to amend the award.

Appeals judges read the transcript of the trial together with legal documents called briefs to determine if the trial judge or jury erred in their decision. Appeals courts typically concern themselves with issues of law as opposed to facts. It is rare that an appellate court will overturn a jury's factual decision. Rather, a verdict can be reversed if the wrong law was applied, incorrect jury instructions were given by the judge, or significant mistakes occurred during the trial, such as a judge making grossly erroneous rulings or excluding crucial trial evidence.

Less than 20 percent of all criminal cases and 30 percent of all civil cases are reversed on appeal. Most decisions do not get reversed, but if a person or business has spent years and tens of thousands of dollars pursuing or defending a valid claim, the additional money spent on an appeal can be worth it, particularly if the delay caused by the appeals process works to an appellant's advantage.

While appeals are usually filed by a defendant who loses and wants to get the judgment reversed, a plaintiff who lost the case or didn't win everything as expected can appeal to have the award reconsidered. It's also possible for both sides to appeal different aspects of the same case.

Parties to a lawsuit may attempt to settle the matter after the initial ruling by the judge or jury. This sometimes occurs before the filing of post-trial motions and appeals. It makes sense when the judge hints he or she will order a new trial. For example, if you are the plaintiff who won $4 million in an age discrimination lawsuit and are informed the defendant will file an appeal claiming the award was grossly excessive, you may decide to accept $2.5 million now to avoid waiting several years before receiving the money, spending thousands of dollars fighting the appeal, and possibly losing in the end.

There are a number of pre-appeal motions your lawyer can immediately file after a judgment is rendered and you lose a case. One motion asks a judge to reconsider his ruling if there was a bench trial.

Another motion requests a new trial with a new jury when you disagree with the jury's finding.

Parties may also file a JNOV motion. This requests the judge to enter a verdict different from what was decided while not selecting a new jury or trial.

STRATEGY: *You can also file a motion to modify the size of the award if your lawyer believes the award doesn't conform to the evidence heard at the trial. Discuss the merits of filing post-trial motions with your lawyer where applicable. Also, post-trial and pre-appeal motions must be made quickly after the trial verdict to preserve your rights; in most jurisdictions, the time frame is within ten days of the award.*

Since trial judges rarely grant new trials or reconsider their rulings, the best way to overturn a trial decision is through an appeal. Appeals seek the review of questions of law, questions of fact, exercises of discretion or a combination of each. The broadest standard of review is de novo, which means that an appeals court is free to decide an issue differently without considering the trial court's ruling, such as interpreting unambiguous written documents.

Since appeals courts recognize that trial courts are in a better position to assess witness credibility they generally give deference to the resolution of factual issues at the trial level. However, appeals courts sometimes rule that the trial court did not resolve important factual issues correctly or that a judge abused his discretion, causing injustice to one of the parties. In such cases, a reversal will ensue.

Unlike a criminal case, you have only a small chance of winning an appeal in a civil case on the basis of evidentiary mistakes by the trial judge. Few trials are free from error so the relevant inquiry for an appellate court is not whether errors occurred but whether the trial was free from substantial errors prejudicing a party's case. This only occurs when the excluded evidence (such as expert testimony) together with all the other evidence presented at trial would have resulted in a contrary verdict. Conversely, if erroneous evidence is admitted on the record, a reversal will only occur if a contrary verdict would have been reached without the introduction of such evidence.

Issues raised for the first time on appeal will not be grounds to reverse an order or judgment if your lawyer failed to object to the introduction of evidence by opposing counsel during the trial. If your lawyer disagrees with any aspect of how a trial is proceeding, he or she must clearly object on the spot to preserve your rights on appeal. This is called "protecting the record" during a trial. Additionally, because appeals courts look more favorably on errors, stress this in your brief to increase the chances of a successful appeal. Errors of law include a judge approving the wrong verdict form or not properly applying the correct law in the case.

Not every prejudicial error requires a new trial. Prejudicial errors bearing on the issue of damages only warrant a new trial to properly compute damages. In cases involving jury misconduct, such as learning that jurors reached a verdict by flipping a coin, a new trial may be ordered, but this is not always so. Jurors as a rule are allowed to decide the case as they please. But where it is proved that outside influences interfered with the process, such as the bribing of a witness, a jury's verdict will be set aside.

Appeals take many months. The court reporter must prepare a transcript of the testimony. The appellant must review the evidence and write a brief. The appellee responds with his or her own written brief, and attempts to persuade the appeals court that the result reached at trial was correct and should not be reversed. The appellant has the right to reply to such responses. Judges on the appeals court read the briefs, review the evidence, and allow the parties to orally argue their position in open court. The court will render its decision in writing after all the briefs have been submitted and oral arguments heard. The process can take years before you receive a final decision.

But it may not be over yet. A party who is dissatisfied with the appeal court's decision in some cases may seek to have the court reconsider its ruling by filing a motion for rehearing. The opposing party may respond after such a motion is filed. More briefs and oral argument will be permitted if the motion is filed.

Each state has its own procedures governing appellate practice which must be precisely followed. The rules govern the contents of the record, appendix and briefs, and the number of pages contained in a brief. Be sure your lawyer knows these rules. Appellants must assemble a proper record. This includes the complete court transcript, exhibits introduced at the trial, and legal memorandum. Do this in a timely fashion. After filing a notice of intent to appeal the award (referred to as a Notice of Appeal) usually within 30 days after entry of a judgment, you generally have up to nine months to submit your brief. This is called "perfecting the appeal." Failure to comply with your state's requirements will result in a dismissal of your appeal.

Extensive research of applicable case law is required in well-written briefs. Be sure your lawyer takes advantage of all the time available to get the job done properly. Experienced lawyers avoid the temptation of writing and submitting briefs at the last possible moment.

Request your lawyer to orally argue the case. Having worked so hard on the written appeal, don't waive the opportunity for oral argument where permitted.

Report to the courtroom in advance before the oral argument. Observe how the judge is treating other lawyers. If a comprehensive argument was planned and you see other lawyers being cut off, your lawyer may wish to reshuffle your arguments so important points are made at the beginning of the presentation rather than at the end.

Your lawyer should study all relevant cases applicable to your matter that may have been reported between the time your brief was written and oral arguments are heard. A fair amount of relevant case law may have been decided during the intervening period and such cases must be discussed during oral argument where appropriate.

Because your lawyer may have only 15 minutes to argue your appeal, spending hours of preparation is the key to success. There is no short cut to the preparation process of reading and rereading the briefs and legal authorities cited therein and familiarizing oneself with the record on appeal. By the time your lawyer appears in court, she should know the facts cold and where they're found in the record (with page references) to answer any questions about the decision below, the facts, or any particular bit of testimony or documentary evidence. If your lawyer doesn't know the answer to a question, or didn't give that aspect of the case any thought, she shouldn't be afraid to say so since oral argument is not a time for improvisation.

Is there a faster way to obtain the decision? Sometimes it takes months before the ruling is reported in a local bar journal or sent to your lawyer by mail. Find out if the wait can be shortened by a telephone call to the judge's law secretary.

Can you attend the hearing and assist your lawyer during oral argument? Perhaps you should take notes of the arguments and specific points raised by opposing counsel and questions asked by the judges. You may even assist your lawyer by organizing and retrieving documents, exhibits, and other exhibits during oral argument.

When the losing party fails to win the final appeal it's time to collect your money if you are a plaintiff. Your lawyer should take proper initial steps after the award (but often before the appeal) to insure the collection of the judgment if the losing party doesn't voluntarily pay. This may involve placing a lien on real estate property owned by your opponent, attaching such property to prevent its transfer, assignment, or sale without your consent, or garnishing the person's wages and salary, among other remedies. Speak to your lawyer for more information about how this can be accomplished if you are the prevailing party to a lawsuit.

Many states require the losing party to post a bond for the judgment amount if you want the appeal to be processed. This is very costly since you are required to post cash or collateral generally equal to several times the judgment. Also, interest on the award continues to accrue during the appeal and the losing party is often ordered by the court to pay the winning party's appeal costs

Speak to a lawyer immediately if you receive an unfavorable trial verdict. There is a limited period of time (often 30 days) in which to file a notice that you intend to appeal. This must be done without delay to preserve your rights. To evaluate the chances of a successful appeal, it is necessary to objectively reconstruct the reasons the case was lost. Consider whether to hire a specialist in appeals matters. Although your current attorney is familiar with the case, there are distinct advantages to hiring an attorney who makes a living writing briefs and arguing oral appeals (it is an art), and a new attorney is more likely to discover mistakes made by the original lawyer. Trial lawyers are a distinct breed and their legal strengths differ from appellate experts. Don't assume your trial lawyer has the requisite skill-set to achieve success at the appeals level. Appellate experts may not be able to argue a case persuasively before a jury, but they are usually more adept at writing and researching briefs, arguing complicated issues of law, and engaging in sophisticated legal analysis.

Be certain you know how much the appeal will cost. Always sign a retainer agreement similar to the example shown on page 504 that clearly spells out attorney fees, costs, and disbursements. No matter which lawyer handles the appeal, it is costly, time-consuming, and frequently does not produce anticipated results.

STRATEGY: *A major reason appeals are expensive is that your lawyer must spend an enormous amount of time studying the court record and witness testimony at the trial and during pre-trial depositions. This is before she begins researching and writing your brief and preparing for oral argument. Your legal bill can be staggering when you're paying a lawyer and his staff by the hour. By negotiating a flat fee arrangement with your lawyer, you may know the maximum amount of money you will spend for legal work during the appeal process.*

If you have any questions concerning appeals, particularly if you don't have a lawyer and are representing yourself pro se, contact the clerk's office of the appellate court in your jurisdiction for advice. Personnel in appellate courts may take the time to answer your questions. Often they are quite helpful.

Sample Retainer Agreement With Attorney for Appeal

Date

Name of Client
Address

Dear (Name of Client):

This letter confirms that you have retained me as your attorney to represent you in the prosecution of an appeal of a judgment granted against you by Justice (specify name) on (specify date) in the (specify trial court) and entered on (specify date) in the Office of the Clerk. The appeal will be taken to (specify court).

You have agreed to pay me promptly a flat fee of (specify $) for all legal services to be rendered in this matter. The fee shall be paid as follows: (specify how much up front and how much later upon the happening of certain events). In addition to my fee, you also agree to pay for all costs and disbursements upon my request. Disbursements include, but are not limited to, the cost of the transcript of the trial (which the court reporter has estimated at about $XXX), the cost of the appellate printer to print the record on appeal and the briefs we submit, and to cover the costs for serving the papers on appeal. All of these costs and disbursements are estimated to be approximately (specify $) but the actual disbursements may vary from the estimates, which are only approximate.

I promise to keep you informed of all developments as they occur and to send you copies of all incoming and outgoing correspondence immediately after it is generated/received.

I will personally handle the drafting of your brief and the arguing of any motions or the appeal in court if necessary.

I look forward to working with you on this matter. Kindly indicate your understanding and acceptance of the above terms by signing this letter below where indicated.

Very truly yours,

Name of Attorney

I, (name of client), have read and understand the above letter, have received a copy and accept all of its terms:

_____
Name of Client

Strategies to Help Your Lawyer Win the Case Before and During the Trial

Lawyers often do not train their clients to be effective participants before and during the trial. This is a mistake. Effective clients have a strong knowledge of how the legal and court system works, the theme of the case, the opponent's position, and what must be proved at trial. Detailed preparation will dramatically increase your chance of success. You and your lawyer must have total command of the facts of the case, including how and when exhibits, documents and other forms of evidence will be used at trial.

Clients should be involved in the case right after the lawyer is retained. Request that copies of all pleadings and correspondence be forwarded to you for review, analysis, and suggestions. Ask your lawyer to advise you when important hearings will be held in your case so you can attend. Ask if you can assist your lawyer in developing evidence in support of your case. Keep a notebook available to record any thoughts, points, or suggestions regarding the case as they occur to you and convey these thoughts to your lawyer in a timely fashion. Also, keep your lawyer informed of any travel plans and where you can be reached at all times.

Take the time and effort to inquire what your lawyer is doing to prepare for the trial several months before it is time to begin. If your lawyer is busy with other trials and doesn't have time to meet with you or answer your questions, speak regularly to his or her assistants. Have all the charts, pictures, videos, photographs, models and re-creations to be used at the trial been timely reproduced? Inquire if all key witnesses have been prepped and are ready to testify at the trial. Have they been prepared as to what tough cross-examination questions they will face?

Effective clients help their lawyers gather and organize exhibits. You should be instructed to review all of your interrogatories, transcripts from prior proceedings, and depositions for inconsistencies. With proper instructions, a capable client can save time and legal fees by handling administrative and clerical tasks necessary to prepare and organize exhibits.

During jury selection, you may have suggestions as to particular questions which may be asked to prospective jurors to determine the likelihood they will not be fair and impartial. If there are numerous documents, you may be in a position of assisting your lawyer organize and produce them on the spot. As the trial unfolds, you may also suggest additional questions to ask important witnesses. Take notes of important testimony during the trial and help your lawyer spot inconsistent statements of witnesses.

Be aware that everything you do or say in the courtroom sends a message. Assume that the jury sees and hears everything that happens. If you grimace or display anger when your opponent questions your behavior, the jury will see it. If you whisper nervously in your lawyer's ear, or frantically scribble notes, this may convey a poor impression. Always display a calm demeanor at the trial.

Final Words on the Subject of Litigation

Litigation is complicated, time-consuming, and subject to many hazards. Unless absolutely necessary, or if you have a small case that you can handle by yourself in small-claims court, do not attempt to file papers and represent or defend yourself in a lawsuit without a lawyer. The following is a summary of key strategies to follow in any lawsuit, whether you are the plaintiff or the defendant.

1. Hire a lawyer skilled in conducting trials.

2. Play an active role in all phases of the case. Request that your attorney routinely send you copies of all incoming and outgoing correspondence on a regular basis. This will help you monitor and question the progress of your case.

3. Never ignore a summons and complaint if you are served. Ignoring a summons and complaint can result in the imposition of a default judgment with huge damages, penalties, and interest assessed against you without your

filing a defense. Speak to a lawyer immediately to protect your rights. Insist that the lawyer file a notice of appearance and/or answer on your behalf immediately. The answer should also contain counterclaims and affirmative defenses where appropriate.

4. Never ignore a subpoena if you are summoned to court to appear as a witness. A subpoena is an order requiring your presence to testify. It differs from a summons, which is a document served on a defendant in a lawsuit notifying him or her of a pending lawsuit. If for some reason you cannot be present on the date specified, speak to the clerk of the court for advice and guidance. Ignoring a subpoena can result in a fine, imprisonment, or both. Speak to a lawyer about possible grounds to "quash" or void a subpoena.

5. Be prepared at all times. Competent attorneys work with their clients in anticipation of the upcoming deposition and trial. There should be no surprises in what you will testify to and what the opposing lawyer will ask you. Your lawyer should advise you how to react if you do not understand a question or do not want to answer.

6. Consider alternative methods to settle your dispute. These include arbitration and mediation. Ask your lawyer to actively seek and encourage a settlement where warranted.

7. Determine if the opposing party has sufficient assets to pay a successful verdict before starting any action.

8. Assess the chances of winning or losing and how much a lawsuit will cost to commence or defend before getting in too deep.

Pro Se Representation

It is possible to represent yourself in a legal proceeding if you don't hire a lawyer. This is called pro se or self-representation. Think twice before doing this, since even lawyers hire other lawyers in complicated lawsuits or proceedings. Unfortunately, the well-known expression "he who represents himself has a fool for a client" is generally true.

There are occasions where you may be unable to retain a lawyer at the last minute and must proceed in court alone as a plaintiff or defendant. Or, you may not have sufficient money to pay for competent legal representation and don't qualify for legal aid. In such circumstances, you may be forced to appear without a lawyer. The fact you appear pro se doesn't necessarily mean you'll lose the case. What is the best way to win as a pro se litigant? This section will explain how.

Plan ahead if you decide to represent yourself and wish to sue. It is essential to understand the substantive law and procedural rules of the court where you are appearing. Start by speaking with the clerk of the court. Clerks are generally prohibited from giving legal advice, but you may be lucky and receive important tips and strategies, especially if you are polite. Many federal and state courts have pro se offices to help indigent litigants process their cases. Review the yellow pages or Internet to determine if such an office is located near you.

Many courts publish rules for lawyers and litigants to follow; ask for a copy to familiarize yourself with the legal system. Show the clerk the papers if you have been sued. Ask him or her to explain their significance and how to reply. If you are the plaintiff, ask what documents must be filed with the court to get the case started. In most states, individuals are forbidden from initiating or defending an action on behalf of a corporation or partnership and must hire a lawyer to do so.

Some courts have printed instructions and/or manuals to help pro se litigants understand their rights. These often include copies of the actual papers you need to file and process your case, such as the summons and complaint, answer, motions, notice of appeal, motions for reconsideration after judgment, forms to apply for a waiver of the required filing fee based on demonstrated financial need, and copies of applicable federal and state laws. Are such materials available to the general public? If so, can they be obtained or purchased? Hopefully, you can get copies of important documents free of charge.

While speaking to the clerk, get answers to the following questions if you are a pro se plaintiff:

- What are the procedures to file your papers with the court? How much does it cost to file an action? Can the filing fee be waived based on financial hardship? If so, what forms must be submitted?

- Are you in the proper court? If not, where should the lawsuit be brought?

- How many months or years will it take for the lawsuit to be heard at trial?

- Do you have proper subject matter jurisdiction, personal jurisdiction and venue over the defendant(s)?

- What applicable federal or state laws, ordinances, regulations, recent case decisions, and rules of evidence govern the case? Where can you review such laws and cases? Where is the nearest law library open to the general public?

- Is the lawsuit timely or is it barred by the statute of limitations? How should you draft the summons and complaint? What is the most effective way to describe the facts and remedy sought? Are there form complaints available for your use? Where can you purchase computer software or pre-printed legal forms for assistance?

- Are there agencies or pro bono lawyers you can call for free advice? If so, where? Do any law schools provide law students as mentors or coaches? If so, where can you find them? How can you obtain a legal aid lawyer?

- If you are seeking injunctive relief rather than money damages, what procedures must be followed?

- Have you named the proper defendants in the complaint?

- What are the procedures to serve your pleadings on the defendant(s)? Do you need a sheriff or process server to do this? If so, what is the cost and how do you contact them?

- Should you ask for a jury trial? How do you go about doing this? How long do you have before losing your right to a jury trial?

- When will your case be assigned a docket number?

- What is the name of the judge presiding over your matter? Will he or she handle the case from start to finish?

- Is the judge assigned to your case fair? Does he or she assist pro se litigants in the presentation of their case? Does the judge communicate in short clear sentences, avoid legalese and keep questions simple?

- What important rules does the judge follow? What should you do if you cannot meet scheduling guidelines?

- What motions are available before trial, during trial and after trial? How do you prepare a motion? How do you deal with a defendant's motion to dismiss or motion for summary judgment? When is the return date for a motion? How do you properly oppose a motion? Will the judge hear oral argument, or will the motion be decided only upon submission of briefs and other papers?

- What is an order to show cause and how do you obtain one?

- How do you gather evidence via discovery? What is the correct form for written interrogatories, requests for admission, requests for production of documents and depositions? What should you do if an opponent doesn't cooperate or attend a scheduled deposition? What do you do if an opponent makes abusive or oppressive discovery requests?

- Should you agree to mediation to resolve the matter voluntarily? If so, how does the process work?

- What is a good settlement based on the facts of your case? Should you attempt to settle the case? If so, how?

- How can you compel witnesses to testify via a subpoena who do not wish to appear?

- What are the rules governing jury selection, opening statements, direct and cross-examination of witnesses and closing arguments?

- How long will it take to receive a judge's or jury's decision?

- If you obtain a default judgment, how do you enter it? How do you enforce a default judgment?

- How do you appeal an adverse decision? What are the chances of winning an appeal based on the facts of your case?

Ask the following if you are a pro se defendant:

- What steps can you take to dismiss the case early on?

- How do you draft and submit the answer, counterclaims and affirmative defenses?

- What is the best way to contest improper service?

- How do you vacate a default judgment?

When filing papers in court, sign your name on documents in all the places a lawyer would sign. Below your name, always add "attorney pro se." This alerts the court that you intend to represent yourself and lets the clerk and the other party know that all documents and communications that would normally go to your lawyer should go to you. If you do not receive proper notification, you could unknowingly fail to file important paperwork or miss a court appearance.

STRATEGY: *If you don't know how to draft legal papers and the clerk won't provide you with samples, ask to review case files of similar lawsuits. This will help you understand and copy the format used by lawyers in such cases. Inquire how to locate the files at the courthouse or office where your case, arbitration or administrative hearing is being conducted.*

Since the outcome of a pro se case often rests on the assigned judge, try to attend a hearing of a similar proceeding in front of the same judge before you try a case. Familiarize yourself with the judge's style, preferences and dislikes. Make a list of the facts, what you are seeking in damages or relief, and how you will prove your case. Understand your opponent's position, strengths and defenses. How will you overcome them? Identify your opponent, and if additional parties or individuals might be responsible, add these defendants to your case. Do they have assets to satisfy a judgment if you prevail? Organize your proof. Compile as much evidence as possible. Prepare a list of witnesses. Know what each will testify to. Get sworn affidavits where possible.

Research the laws, cases, and regulations that govern your proceeding. Bring them to the hearing to support your position.

Understand the rules of evidence and the best way to submit evidence. Prepare a chart that states your claim, each fact that led to it, each piece of evidence that supports it and each legal principal that confirms it. Practice what you'll say at the hearing and hope for the best. For a modest fee, some lawyers may give their input and how to improve your case. Some are amenable to act as an informal mentor or coach. If so, inquire if they are available for several meetings on an on-going basis as the case unfolds. A legal mentor can:

1. Tell if you have a valid claim in the early stages of the dispute.

2. Help you prepare subpoenas, documents, forms and motions.

3. Review your pleadings and responses.

4. Help you outline the points to raise at a hearing or mediation.

5. Review your evidence, testimony and outline the case.

6. Review the settlement or mediation agreement before you sign it.

7. Advise when the case has become too difficult to handle pro se and recommend a lawyer if he or she is not willing to formally represent you.

8. Advise when it makes sense to appeal an adverse decision and how to perfect the appeal.

Consider using a legal advisor as a mentor or coach whenever possible, especially if the price is right.

When appearing in court pro se, dress appropriately. Have your documents organized and easily retrievable. Show respect to the judge. If he or she rules that you failed to take proper steps or did not supply necessary information, request a continuance or short recess to regroup.

An over-zealous pro se litigant can present a unique problem for the courts and opposing counsel, but while judges sometimes excuse or tolerate improper behavior, you don't have greater rights than any other litigant and will not be allowed to abuse the judicial system. Commencing a frivolous claim, making erroneous objections in court, demanding improper discovery, and failing to introduce required expert testimony at trial will not be tolerated, even if you are inexperienced. Thus, always consider receiving assistance or legal representation before attempting to prosecute or defend a complicated or expensive case pro se.

Whether you proceed pro se or work with a lawyer, the key to winning a case often depends on how well you documented the claim. Maintain a diary of key events that happened. Include as much detail as possible, specifically what was said, who said it, and when. Write letters of protest when you are dissatisfied with the conduct of another party. Save copies to create a paper trail and produce them when necessary. Always remember that proper documentation is key to successful litigation.

Representing yourself pro se in a complicated employment case such as a discrimination proceeding is never a good idea. However, you can succeed by understanding the legal system, following the rules, drafting and filing papers properly, gathering evidence, preparing witnesses and competently representing yourself at a trial or hearing. If you are prepared to invest a significant amount of time and effort in this pursuit, you may be surprised by the results.

Class Action Lawsuits

Class action suits are lawsuits filed by one or a few individual plaintiffs in state or federal court on behalf of themselves and many other people with similar claims. They are typically used when individual suits are too numerous or expensive to try separately and affect a large number of people. For example, hundreds of people who suffer alleged employment discrimination, including sexual harassment and wage and hour violations are now pursuing their job rights through class action lawsuits. Class action lawsuits are also available to challenge a policy or interpretation of a statute or regulation, such as in a Medicaid case.

Cases are commenced by individuals called class representatives (also called named plaintiffs) who retain lawyers to represent them and the class. These lawyers are usually paid a contingency fee ranging from five to 30 percent of the settlement amount when a settlement or judgment is obtained. Attorney fees are approved by the judge presiding over the class action and the remaining funds are divided up among the class members.

Not all cases are allowed to proceed as class actions. After the lawsuit is commenced, a judge will decide whether to approve the case as a class action. Generally, to be allowed to proceed as a class action lawsuit:

1. The class of people must be a clearly definable group.

2. People in the class must have suffered similar harm.

3. Most members must be identified and be able to be contacted.

4. Members of the class must receive the same fair treatment they would get if they brought individual lawsuits.

When these factors are present, a judge may give the group legal status to conduct their suit as a class action. Such a ruling is usually a victory for the plaintiff's lawyer because class action cases are a very efficient way for lawyers with limited resources to obtain relief for a large number of clients or potential clients.

Also, class action lawsuits save the court and the parties valuable time and money because most members of the class usually share common questions of fact or law so interrogatories, depositions, and other pretrial discovery devices for each individual party is not required.

From the defendant's perspective, class actions are expensive to defend. One way to try to knock one off at a low cost is to seek summary judgment before the suit is certified as a class action. However, many judges will not dismiss the class action at an early stage to avoid prejudicing the interests of the putative class members.

After a class action lawsuit is approved, the presiding judge will determine the most effective way to notify similarly situated individuals about the existence of the lawsuit and how they can join the action. This often involves sending a letter to thousands of potential litigants or posting details about the case in local, regional or national newspapers and magazines. The judge will attempt to ensure that the best interests of all the members of the class have been adequately represented by the parties who filed the suit and their lawyers. The plaintiff's lawyer may also seek a summary judgment ruling after certification of the class, which, if successful, will spare the plaintiffs the trial expense while obtaining class wide remedies. Such a motion is aggressively contested by the defendant's lawyer.

If the motion is not granted (which is generally the case), the discovery phase of the lawsuit begins. After it is completed (usually several years later), the judge may approve a settlement and oversee the distribution of the money to all registered members of the class and those who can be found. The same process occurs if money is awarded by a judge or jury after a trial. Courts look with favor on the voluntary resolution of class action litigation through settlement. No case brought and certified as a class action may be settled or compromised without court approval.

The approval process generally involves several steps: preliminary approval of the proposed settlement and plan of distribution to the class members; approval of the form of notice and dissemination of the notice of the proposed settlement to all class members; and a fairness hearing at which class members may be heard regarding the adequacy of the settlement amount, the method of distribution, and the amount of attorney fees. It is the judge's responsibility to approve the terms of the settlement and contents of the notice so members of the class who receive it can understand their rights, options and obligations.

The benefit of a class action lawsuit is that claims may be asserted on behalf of absent parties. After you receive notice of the class action (sometimes long after the case is filed) you can join or opt out. If you join, your claims are treated like those of everyone else in the class, and any judgment or release in the lawsuit binds you. Once you elect to stay in, you simply wait until the case is resolved to get what everyone else gets. If, on the other hand, you want to pursue your claim on your own you can opt out of the class, receive none of the benefits of the class action, and are not bound by any decision.

While class action procedures differ in state and federal courts, the reality is that they often provide the only means for hundreds of claimants to effectively litigate their overtime or discrimination claims by providing for pooled litigation resources and greater settlement leverage. If you have a small claim, the time and expense of litigation is often not worth the trouble, so a class action may be the best way to receive payment for your injuries or financial damages. It is also effective if a defendant is obligated to set aside money to pay claims while it is still financially solvent and you believe it may file for bankruptcy or have no assets to pay a private judgment later on.

But if you incurred significant damages which the defendant has the financial means to pay, or aren't offered an adequate financial recovery, think twice before agreeing to join the class or accept the settlement offer as a class member. Speak to a lawyer to evaluate whether to participate in or opt out of a class action lawsuit. Always obtain sound legal advice because you may be entitled to far more money by opting out of the class. In addition to notification problems and not understanding the terms or ramifications of the settlement, common criticisms of class action settlements arise over excessive legal fees, insufficient payouts to claimants, and settlements that sharply limit recovery for future claims. Be aware of this and act accordingly.

STRATEGY: *If you receive a notice in the mail describing a class action that might affect you, or if you see an advertisement in a magazine concerning a suit, follow the directions in the notice and investigate the matter. Usually an e-mail address or telephone number is listed. At some point you will be asked to submit proof of your claim, and a court will review it. If you fit into the certified class and the group bringing the lawsuit wins, you should receive a portion of the amount awarded or benefit in some way from its success.*

If you belong to a class and the lawsuit or settlement is successful, read the notice carefully. Contact the judge's law clerk for more information if you're unsure what you will receive. Question ambiguous language you don't understand. Get legal advice if you don't wish to accept the settlement or desire to opt out of the class and file your own lawsuit.

Administrative Agency Hearings

Administrative agencies are created by Congress or your state's legislature. They include local, state, and federal boards, bureaus, commissions, and departments. Federal agencies include the Immigration and Naturalization Service, Social Security Administration, and the Internal Revenue Service. State agencies include the Department of Motor Vehicles, Unemployment Insurance, and Workers' Compensation Boards. Agency rulings involve property tax and zoning assessments, housing code violations, disability and Medicare claims, and obtaining a gun permit or liquor license. At every level, government enacts legislation creating programs, benefits and policies. Administrative agencies write and enforce ordinances and regulations telling people how to obtain benefits, participate in programs, defend against charges of violating rules, and seek approval to participate in certain activities. Sometime in their lives, most people find themselves seeking monetary benefits or objecting to an agency's decision to deny, limit or terminate benefits or a license or permit at a hearing before an administrative law judge.

There are procedures to follow to request a hearing when an agency makes a decision you disagree with. An agency administrator will review your case, make a determination about whether the agency decision was correct or fair in your circumstances, and approve any compensation. Since it is difficult to successfully appeal the decision made at a hearing unless you can prove you were denied due process, the agency's regulation was not constitutional, or the decision was not supported by the facts or evidence, it is important to present your case effectively the first time because you usually only get one good bite out of the apple.

Administrative hearings are handled differently from court cases. Usually, the administrative law judge meets with representatives from the agency and the claimant or applicant seeking benefits. You may choose to be represented by an attorney, paralegal, or law student. Each side presents its evidence and elicits testimony from witnesses. The hearing is often tape recorded, instead of being transcribed by a stenographer. Strict formal rules of evidence are not usually followed, and the administrative law judge then renders a written decision called an administrative order, which may be reviewed by either a higher level within the agency or by a court.

Consider the following strategies to improve the chances of winning a hearing:

1. Take action immediately. Don't delay when you receive a notice of a decision you desire to fight because you typically have only a few weeks to request an administrative hearing.

2. **Understand the rules.** Study the agency's regulations that apply to your case. Understanding the procedures will help you learn whether subpoenas are issued, the kinds of penalties that are imposed, how to apply for or extend the term of a benefit, steps to take if a permit is denied, and how administrative orders are reviewed or appealed.

3. **Retain a knowledgeable lawyer.** Consult an experienced practitioner who has handled matters before the particular agency. Such a person will be able to discuss the agency's rules and procedures, how to file for benefits, steps to take to prepare for the hearing, and how to obtain important documents and forms. A lawyer's political clout and personal relationship with a regulator may come in handy. Thus, even though you can represent yourself, it's best to hire an experienced lawyer to guide you through an agency's complex procedures. If applicable, ask people at the agency for the names of experienced lawyers who frequently handle similar cases at reasonable rates. This is a good way of locating practitioners who are respected by your adversary.

4. **Gather evidence.** Present documents and other materials demonstrating why the agency did not apply its rules properly in your case.

5. **Learn how the hearing is conducted.** View an administrative hearing to understand how it is run.

6. **Present your case.**

7. **Defend yourself or your business if you are accused of unlawful practice.** If so, it will be necessary for you and your counsel to meet with representatives of a regulatory agency to persuade them to reduce or eliminate the penalty. Review the particular regulation or statute you are accused of violating. Present witnesses to explain why the incident occurred. Bring copies of all important docu-

ments, such as letters sent to the agency, to demonstrate good faith efforts to follow the statute or regulation.

STRATEGY: *Know your appeal rights and the steps to take to appeal an unfavorable administrative agency decision. The extent to which the courts are permitted to control agency discretion depends on the particular action taken. Although it may be difficult to win an appeal, speak to your attorney about contesting an adverse ruling if you believe the agency ruled on an important matter incorrectly given the facts of a case and the evidence introduced at the hearing. Agencies sometimes exercise power they don't possess or exercise their discretion in a manner that is arbitrary. Do this in a timely fashion to avoid having the appeal dismissed.*

Interpretations of law by administrative agencies are generally subject to independent judicial review. Thus, a federal court may hold unlawful a finding not based on substantial evidence. Be aware of federal laws that protect private rights and regulate activities of administrative agencies in the public interest. For example, pursuant to the Freedom of Information Act, you have the right to receive privileged and confidential information possessed by an agency. A request under the Freedom of Information Act has to be written in a manner that targets the particular document wanted so your request is not viewed as a fishing expedition. If you require such material to help defend or win your case, speak to a lawyer for more information on how to properly obtain it. Thus, try to obtain under the Freedom of Information Act all of the relevant documents that formed the basis of the agency's decision and use the compliance procedures in the Administrative Procedures Act as a discovery tool to determine the basis for a proposed agency action.

Mediation

Mediation is an alternative to resolving employment disputes via formal litigation or arbitration. A neutral intermediary (the mediator) defines the conflicting interests of the parties, explains the legal implications, and attempts to help the parties reach and prepare a fair settlement. When settlements are achieved, they are typically reached more quickly and cheaply than litigation because opposing parties have not hired opposing counsel to fight it out in court. More and more employment-related cases are now being resolved this way. For example:

- When an employer alleges it was justified in firing an executive for cause prior to the expiration of the stated term in an employment agreement

- When an employer is confronted with a breach of contract or wrongful discharge case

- When a worker threatens to file a lawsuit alleging sexual harassment

- When there is a significant dispute over the terms of an important clause in an employment contract

The parties may prefer to work out their problems in the privacy of a business suite instead of a crowded public courtroom and negotiate the terms of a settlement based on their best mutual interests. If a mediator (usually a trained lawyer, businessperson, or retired judge) is hired to assist in the process, he or she will not make decisions for the parties but will help them reach an agreement within the realistic limits of their budget.

Resolving a dispute by mediation requires that both parties agree to mediate the dispute. It also requires a good-faith effort by the parties to resolve the dispute, not to determine who is right and who is wrong. Nonbinding mediation may not work when one party strongly believes he or she is entitled to punitive or extra damages that can be awarded only via litigation.

Various community associations, private enterprises, and the American Arbitration Association (AAA) offer mediation services. The AAA is often selected to assist parties in the mediation process. It is a public service nonprofit organization that offers dispute settlement services to business executives, employers, trade associations, unions, and all levels of government. Services are available through AAA's national office in New York City and through many regional offices in major cities throughout the United States.

Once both parties agree to try to solve their differences through mediation, a joint request for mediation is usually made through an AAA regional office. The request identifies the parties involved in the dispute, gives their current addresses and phone numbers, and briefly describes the controversy and the issues involved. The employee and the company should include whatever information is helpful to appoint a mediator.

The AAA assigns a mediator from its master list. The parties are then given information about the mediator. Typically, the mediator has no past or present relationship with the parties. A mediator is free to refuse the appointment or resign at any time. Likewise, the parties are free to stop the mediation or ask for the services of a different mediator. If a mediator is unwilling or unable to serve, or if one of the parties requests that the mediator resign from the case, the parties may ask the AAA to recommend another mediator. The mediator is compensated on either an hourly or a daily basis. Both parties are informed of potential mediator fees and are sometimes requested to sign a document evidencing approval of the compensation arrangement and an agreement to share fees.

Before choosing a mediator, inquire if the mediator's approach is suited to your needs. Ask the following questions at the initial interview:

- How does the mediator operate?
- How much experience and training does the mediator have?
- What is the mediator's background?
- How many sessions are required?
- How much will mediation cost?

After the initial interview takes place and the mediator is found to be acceptable, he or she will arrange the time and place for each conference with the parties. At the first conference the parties will be asked to produce information required for the mediator to understand the issues. The mediator may require either party to supplement such information. The mediator will explain what the parties should expect. Good mediators explain that the process is entirely voluntary, that they are not judges and have no power to dictate solutions, and that the parties are free to terminate the mediation process at any time.

A mediator does not have authority to impose a settlement but will attempt to help the parties reach a satisfactory resolution of their dispute. Although usually trained in law, the mediator is not supposed to give legal advice. While parties do not have to be represented by counsel at the mediation sessions, most claimants and employers retain attorneys in employment and business disputes.

Conferences are private. The mediator will meet with both parties, and then sometimes with each privately. Other persons, including witnesses, may attend only with the permission of the parties and at the invitation of the mediator.

The mediator is hired as a consultant, jointly retained, to help the parties work their way through their problems to resolution. At some point the mediator may make a recommendation or proposal. Both parties can agree or disagree or come to a compromise of their own. The mediator will draft a report confirming the agreement. The report is then submitted to the parties for submission to their attorneys for incorporation into a formal document, such as a settlement agreement.

If the parties fail to agree, or do not agree with the mediator's recommendation, they can break off the mediation, consult another mediator, give up, settle their dispute without a mediator, or go to court. The following is a typical mediation scenario from start to finish:

1. The mediator and parties meet at the initial conference. The mediator's role is explained and the responsibilities and rights of the parties are set forth.

2. The mediator designs a schedule for the sessions.

3. The parties sign a formal retainer agreement with the mediator.

4. A method is adopted for obtaining whatever information is required to understand the parties' problems.

5. The mediator identifies the various areas of agreement, defines the issues to be resolved, and assists the parties in their negotiations.

6. A final settlement may be proposed.

7. The mediator arranges for the terms of the settlement to be transmitted to the attorneys of the parties for filing in court, if necessary.

Some mediators do not possess sufficient skills or training to be effective. Others have been criticized for not ending the process when the interests of each party are not receiving balanced treatment. If the mediator is a lawyer, he or she often has to make an adjustment in attitude. Unlike the lawyer, who tells the client what to do, a mediator must allow the parties enough freedom to structure their own unique solutions to problems. Mediation by attorneys has raised the concern of whether one lawyer can adequately advise two parties with opposing interests and whether a mediator can invoke the attorney-client privilege in any future litigation. For example, if lawyers are present with the parties at mediation sessions and incriminating or damaging statements are made by a client, a lawyer may seek to prevent a judge or jury from hearing such statements in court when the mediation fails. A judge may not allow such oral testimony to be admitted in court depending on a number of facts, such as whether the parties formally agreed beforehand that such statements were confidential and could not be introduced in subsequent court hearings.

STRATEGY: *To avoid problems, interview the mediator carefully; be sure to hire the mediator only on the basis of a written retainer agreement. If you believe the process is not working or do not feel comfortable with the person hired, terminate the relationship* *immediately and discuss further options with your attorney or other professional adviser.*

Understand that mediation will not work unless both parties are willing to cooperate and recognize the savings and other benefits to be achieved versus litigation, such as:

- Eliminating the anxicty of preparing a case before going to court
- Avoiding potential poor publicity
- Maintaining privacy
- Obtaining a quicker result
- Eliminating uncertainty as to outcome when the case is tried in court
- Maintaining a desire to continue good business relationships

If either party has a great need to even the score, mediation will probably fail. Speak to your professional adviser to determine if mediation is a proper means of resolving any employment dispute before resorting to litigation or arbitration. When involved in mediation with a company representative, inquire if that person has sufficient authority to resolve and settle the matter on the company's behalf once a resolution is imminent. Finally, since your lawyer may be able to meet and question important witnesses, the benefits of learning more about your adversary's case may make the exercise worthwhile even if a settlement is not forthcoming. (In some employment lawsuits, nonbinding court-ordered mediation is required before a trial begins. Speak to your lawyer for more details.)

Arbitration

Arbitration is a formal mechanism for resolving disputes that differs from litigation or mediation. Hearings are conducted by arbitrators rather than by judges and are not limited by strict rules of evidence. Arbitrators can consider all relevant testimony when making an award, including some forms of evidence (e.g., hearsay, questionable copies of documents) that would be excluded in a regular court. Arbitrators have the authority to hear witnesses out of order. Their decision is usually final and unappealable. Limited circumstances for appeals are mentioned later in this section.

To obtain an arbitration, the law requires both parties to agree to the arbitration process beforehand in writing to prevent claims of unfairness by the losing side. Typically in an employment contract, lease, loan agreement, or other document, the relevant clause may state some version of the following: "Any controversy or claim arising out of or relating to this agreement or the breach thereof shall be settled by binding arbitration in accordance with the rules of the American Arbitration Association, and judgment upon the award rendered by the arbitrator(s) may be entered in any court having jurisdiction thereof."

Advantages of Arbitration:

1. **Expense.** Substantial savings can be achieved through arbitration. Attorney fees are reduced because the average hearing is shorter than the average trial. Time-consuming and expensive pretrial procedures, including depositions, interrogatories, and motions, are usually eliminated. Out-of-pocket expenses are reduced because stenographic fees, transcripts, and other items are often not required.

2. **Time.** Arbitration hearings and final awards are obtained quickly; cases are usually decided in a matter of months, compared to several years in formal litigation.

3. **Privacy.** The arbitration hearing is held in a private conference room, rather than a courtroom. Unlike a trial, the hearing cannot be attended by the general public.

4. **Expertise of arbitrators.** Arbitrators usually have special training in the area of the case. In a breach of an entertainment contract dispute, for example, arbitrators serving on the panel are typically respected lawyers or other professionals with significant experience in the entertainment

industry. Their knowledge of trade customs helps them identify and understand a problem more quickly than a judge or jury.

5. **Increased odds of obtaining an award.** Some lawyers believe that arbitrators are more likely than judges to split close cases down the middle. The theory is that arbitrators bend over backward to satisfy both parties to some degree, since their rulings are final and binding. This tendency to compromise, if true, benefits claimants with weaker cases.

Disadvantages of Arbitration:

1. **Finality.** Arbitrators, unlike judges, need not give formal reasons for their decisions. They are not required to maintain a formal record of the proceedings. The arbitrator's decision is binding. This means that an appeal cannot be taken if you lose the case or disagree with the size of the award except in a few extraordinary circumstances where arbitrator misconduct, dishonesty, or bias can be proved.

2. **Arbitrator selection.** The parties sometimes agree that each will select its own arbitrator. In such cases it may be assumed that the chosen arbitrators are more sympathetic to one side than the other. However, arbitrators are usually selected from a list of neutral names supplied by the AAA. This method generally eliminates bias.

3. **Loss of sympathetic juries.** Some knowledgeable lawyers believe that juries tend to empathize more with certain kinds of people such as fired employees, destitute wives, and older individuals. Arbitrators are usually successful lawyers and businesspeople whose philosophical orientation may lean more toward companies than toward individuals.

4. **Loss of discovery devices.** Some claimants must rely upon an adversary's documents and records to prove their case. For example, sales agents, authors, patent holders, and others often depend upon their company's (or licensee's) sales figures and accurate record-keeping to determine

how much commission and royalties they are owed. The same is true for minority shareholders who seek a proper assessment of a company's profit picture.

These people may find a disadvantage in the arbitration process. Trial lawyers have ample opportunity to view the private books and records of an adversary long before the day of the trial. This is accomplished by pretrial discovery devices, which include interrogatories, depositions, and notices to produce documents for inspection and copying. However, these devices are not readily available to litigants in arbitration. In many instances records are not available for inspection until the day of the arbitration hearing. This makes it difficult to detect whether they are accurate and complete. And it is often up to the arbitrator's discretion whether to grant an adjournment for the purposes of reviewing such records. Such requests may be refused.

Sexual harassment and sex discrimination issues are currently being resolved in arbitration as well as by litigation. Often an employee prefers that her matter not be resolved through arbitration because in many states punitive and other special damages are not granted in an arbitrator's award. However, if you signed an employment agreement containing an arbitration clause, you may be forced to arbitrate your case (including claims made by a fired employee for age discrimination under the Age Discrimination in Employment Act), especially if you work in the securities industry.

STRATEGY: *Courts favor resolving cases through arbitration when agreed beforehand by the parties. Thus, it is essential to understand the ramifications of signing any employment agreement or contract containing an arbitration clause.*

Commencing the hearing is a relatively simple matter once arbitration has been selected as the method of resolving a dispute. A party or her lawyer sends a notice called a Demand for Arbitration to the adversary. See page 530 for an example of this notice. Copies of the demand are sent to the American Arbitration Association, along with the appropriate administrative fee.

The notice briefly describes the controversy. It specifies the kind of relief sought, including the amount of monetary damages requested. A response to the charges is then sent by the opposing party, usually within seven days. This may also assert a counterclaim for damages. Either party can add or change claims in writing until the arbitrator is appointed. Once this occurs, changes and additional claims can only be made with the arbitrator's consent.

After the AAA receives the Demand for Arbitration and reply, an AAA administrator usually supplies the parties with a list of potential arbitrators. The list contains the arbitrator's name, current occupation, place of employment, and appropriate background information. The parties mutually agree to nominees from this list. Potential arbitrators are obligated to notify the AAA immediately of any facts likely to affect their impartiality (e.g., prior dealings with one of the litigants), and disqualify themselves where appropriate. If the parties do not agree beforehand to the number of arbitrators, the dispute is decided by one arbitrator, unless the AAA determines that three arbitrators are appropriate.

Once the arbitrator is selected, the AAA administrator schedules a convenient hearing date and location. There is no direct communication between the parties and the arbitrator until the hearing date; all requests and inquiries are received by the administrator and relayed to the arbitrator. This avoids the appearance of impropriety. The parties are free to request a prehearing conference to exchange documents and resolve certain issues. Typically, however, the parties, administrators, lawyers, and arbitrator meet face-to-face for the first time at the actual hearing.

Most hearings are conducted in a conference room at an AAA regional office. A stenographer is present, if requested (the requesting party generally bears the cost unless the parties agree to split the cost). The arbitrator introduces the parties and typically asks each side to briefly summarize its version of the dispute and what each intends to prove at the hearing.

Sample Demand for Arbitration

American Arbitration Association
Commercial Arbitration Rules
Demand for Arbitration

                                                        Date

Name of Employer
(Name of party upon whom the demand is made)
Address
Telephone

Named claimant, a party to an arbitration agreement contained in a written contract dated (specify) providing for arbitration, hereby demands arbitration thereunder.

(Attach arbitration clause or quote hereunder, such as)

"Any controversy or claim arising out of or relating to this contract, or any breach thereof, shall be settled in accordance with the Rules of the American Arbitration Association, and judgment upon the award may be entered in any court having jurisdiction thereof."

NATURE OF DISPUTE: Breach of contract action

CLAIM OR RELIEF SOUGHT: (amount, if any) $50,000 plus attorney fees as payment of salary through the termination date of employment agreement

TYPE OF BUSINESS:

Claimant: Executive
Respondent: Financial

HEARING LOCALE REQUESTED: New York, NY

You are hereby notified that copies of our arbitration agreement and of this demand are being filed with the American Arbitration Association at its New York Regional Office, with the request that it commence the administration of the arbitration. Under Section 7 of the Commercial Arbitration Rules, you may file an answering statement within seven days after notice from the Administrator.

Signed
(May be signed by attorney)
Name of Claimant
Address
Telephone

Name of Attorney
Address
Telephone

To institute proceedings, please send three copies of this demand with the administrative fee, as provided in Section 48 of the Rules, to the AAA. Send original demand to Respondent.

The complainant's case is presented first. Witnesses are called to give testimony (usually under oath). After witnesses finish speaking, they are usually cross-examined by the opposing party's lawyer. They may also be questioned by the arbitrator. The complainant introduces all its witnesses, documents, and affidavits until it has finished presenting its side of the case.

The opposing party then introduces its witnesses and documents to defend its case and/or prove damages. After the opposition has concluded its case, both sides are usually requested to make a brief summary of the facts (i.e., what they felt was proved at the hearing). Sometimes the arbitrator may request that legal briefs be submitted that summarize the respective positions of the parties before rendering a final decision.

Sample Award of Arbitrator

In the Matter of Arbitration between
Sally Smith
and
Doe Corporation Inc. Case No.

I, the undersigned Arbitrator, having been designated in accordance with the arbitration agreement entered into by the above-named parties, and dated (specify), and having been duly sworn and having heard the proofs and allegations of the parties, AWARD as follows:

1. Within ten (10) days from the date of this AWARD, Doe Corporation Inc. ("Doe") shall pay to Sally Smith ("Smith") the sum of Twenty-Five Thousand Eighteen Dollars ($25,018.00), plus interest in the amount of Two Thousand Two Hundred Dollars ($2,200.00).

2. The counterclaim of Doe against Smith is hereby denied in its entirety.

3. The administrative fees of the American Arbitration Association totaling Eleven Hundred Dollars ($1,100.00) shall be borne equally by the parties. Therefore, Doe shall pay Smith the sum of Five Hundred Fifty Dollars ($550.00) representing one-half (50%) of the filing fees previously advanced by Smith to the AAA.

4. Each Party shall pay one-half (50%) of the Arbitrator's fee in this arbitration.

5. This AWARD is in full settlement of all claims and counterclaims submitted in this arbitration.

Signature of Arbitrator

Dated

Arbitrators are generally required to render written decisions within 30 days unless the parties agree to some other time period. The arbitrator can make any award that is equitable. She can order the losing party to pay additional costs, including AAA filing fees and arbitrator fees. Legal fees may be awarded if the arbitration clause so provides.

Arbitrators volunteer their time for hearings lasting under a full day; they are paid a per diem rate (up to $1,500) for additional hearings. If the parties settle their dispute prior to a decision, they may request that the terms of the settlement be embodied in the consent award.

Arbitrators have no contact with the parties after the hearing is concluded. The parties are notified in writing by the AAA administrator and are sent a copy of the award. The decision in a typical employment case is brief—usually no formal reasons are given to explain why a particular award was rendered or the basis on which damages were calculated.

It is practically impossible to appeal a losing case. The arbitrator has no power once the case is decided. The matter can be reviewed only by a judge, and judges cannot overturn the award on the grounds of insufficient evidence. The only ways a case can be overturned on review are:

- For arbitrator dishonesty, partiality, or bias
- When no valid agreement was entered into that authorized the arbitration process
- When an issue that the arbitrator was not authorized to decide was ruled upon

Awards are modifiable only if there was a miscalculation of figures or a mistake in the description of the person, property, or thing referred to in the award.

How to Increase the Chances of Success in Arbitration

Since the arbitrator's award is final and binding, it is essential to prepare and present a case properly the first time around, because you won't get a second chance. The following strategies may help increase the chances of success.

1. HIRE A LAWYER. People have the right to appear themselves (pro se), but it's best to have a lawyer represent you at the hearing, particularly if the dispute involves a large amount of money or complicated legal questions. The familiar expression "He who represents himself has a fool for a client" is certainly applicable in arbitrations. Seek the services of an experienced lawyer who is familiar with the intricacies of the arbitration process. Ask your prospective lawyer how many times he or she has represented clients in arbitration within the past several years. If the answer is "never" or "only a few times," look elsewhere for representation.

2. PREPARE FOR THE HEARING. It is important that both you and your lawyer submit evidence to prove the case, so:

- Organize the facts. Gather and label all documents needed at the hearing so they can be produced in an orderly fashion.
- Prepare a checklist of documents and exhibits so nothing will be forgotten during the presentation.
- Make copies of all documents for the arbitrator and adversary.
- If some of the documents needed are in the possession of the other party, ask that they be brought to the hearing or subpoenaed.
- Interview witnesses.
- Be sure that friendly witnesses will attend and testify; if there is a possibility that additional witnesses may have to appear, alert them to be available on call without delay.
- Select witnesses who are believable, who understand the case and the importance of their testimony, and who will not say things at the hearing to surprise you.
- Coordinate the witnesses' testimony so your case will seem consistent and credible.
- Prepare witnesses for the rigors of cross-examination.
- If a translator is required, make arrangements in advance.

- Prepare a written summary of what you hope each witness will prove and refer to it at the hearing.

- Anticipate what the opponent will say to defeat your claim, and be prepared to refute such evidence.

- Practice your story to put you at ease and help organize the facts.

- Prepare a list of questions your lawyer should ask the opponent at the hearing,

- Dress appropriately by wearing conservative business clothes.

- Act professionally and show respect for the arbitrator.

- Listen to the arbitrator's questions and instructions; never argue with the arbitrator.

- If a question is posed while you are speaking, stop talking immediately.

- Answer all questions honestly and directly.

- Avoid arguing with your opponent at the hearing; interrupt his presentation only where absolutely necessary.

Most losing parties voluntarily comply with the terms of an unfavorable award. However, if your opponent decides not to pay, you can enforce the judgment in a regular court. Speak to a lawyer for more details.

Small-Claims Court

Before considering filing a lawsuit in small-claims court, attempt to resolve your dispute in a reasonable fashion. It is often best to write a demand letter to your employer or ex-employer and send it certified mail, return receipt requested. In addition to documenting your claim, the letter will advise the company that the matter must be corrected to your immediate satisfaction or you will take additional action. If there is no response to your letter, send a follow-up letter reporting that your initial letter has not been answered. The letter should also state what your next step will be if this letter is ignored.

If you cannot get satisfaction in an employment, financial, or business dispute by personal negotiations, you might consider suing in small-claims court. Small-claims courts, which help you collect wages, commissions, and money in an inexpensive manner without hiring a lawyer, hear over 1 million cases a year in the United States. They can be used in many situations. For example, you may wish to sue for money damages when your employer fails to pay you or someone damages your property and refuses to pay for repairs. Many small-claims courts have night sessions, and matters are resolved quickly, sometimes within a month from the time an action is filed. The maximum amount of money you can recover varies from state to state. It is usually up to $5,000.

The following guidelines describe the procedures of a typical small-claims court. However, the rules vary in each city and state. Before you contemplate starting a lawsuit, call the clerk of that court and ask for a written explanation of the specific procedural rules to be followed.

Small-claims court can be used to sue any person, business, partnership, corporation, or government body owing you money. If you sue in small-claims court and recover a judgment, you are precluded from suing again to recover any additional money owed to you. Thus, if your claim greatly exceeds the maximum amount of money that might be awarded in small-claims court, consider hiring a lawyer and instituting suit in a higher court.

In order to be successful, you must have a valid claim. This means that you must:

- Identify the person or business that damaged or caused you harm.
- Calculate the amount of damages you suffered.
- Show that there is some basis in law to have a court award you damages.

■ Be sure that you were not the main cause of your own harm, that you haven't waited too long to start the action (statute of limitations), and that you did not sign a written release.

Call your local bar association, city hall, or the county courthouse to discover where the nearest small-claims court is located. (In some states small-claims court is called justice court, district court, municipal court, or justice of the peace court.) In most states suit must be brought in the county in which the person or business you are suing lives or does business. Confirm this with the small-claims court clerk and ask what days and hours the court is in session. Ascertain the maximum amount of money you can sue for, what documents are needed to file a complaint, the filing fee, and whether this can be paid by cash, check, or money order.

You can sue only to collect money. Thus, before you begin to sue in small-claims court, estimate the amount of money you wish to collect. When calculating the amount of your claim, include all incurred expenses, including gasoline bills, tolls, telephone costs, losses due to time missed from work, sales tax, and interest, if applicable. Save all your receipts for this purpose.

STRATEGY: *In certain states an employer's willful failure to pay earned vacation money, wages, or other accrued compensation or promised benefits may cause it to be liable for extra statutory damages (such as an additional 25 percent) plus legal costs and expenses. Check your state's law to ascertain whether this applies in your case.*

You begin the lawsuit by paying a small fee (about $25) and either going to the court in person or mailing in a complaint that states the following information:

■ Your name and address
■ The complete name and address of the person, business, or company you are suing (the defendant)
■ The amount of money you believe you are owed

■ The facts of your case

■ The reasons you (the plaintiff) are seeking redress

If you are filing a claim on behalf of an individually owned business, you must list the name of the owner in addition to the name of the business. If you are filing a claim on behalf of a partnership, you must list the name of the partnership as the plaintiff. (Some states do not allow a corporation to sue someone in small-claims court.)

Be sure to write the accurate and complete name and address of the defendant on the complaint. Write the corporation's formal name rather than its "doing business as" (d/b/a/) name. Thus, if you are suing a corporation, contact the county clerk's office in the county where the corporation does business to obtain its proper name and address. Better still, call the department of corporations in your state to obtain such information.

At this time you may also be required to prepare another form called a summons, which notifies your opponent of the lawsuit. Sometimes the clerk will do this. Ask the clerk whether the court will mail the summons by registered or first-class mail, personally serve the defendant on your behalf, or whether you must hire a professional process server. If a professional process server is required, ask what is necessary to prove that service was accomplished. You may have to pay the process server an additional fee (between $20 and $50). However, if you win your case, you can ask the judge to include the process server's fee in the award. When the clerk gives you a hearing date, be sure that it is convenient and you have no other commitments.

Some states require that you send a "30-day demand letter" before filing a small-claims action. The letter should briefly describe your money loss and what you want the employer to do to remedy the situation. Add that you are giving the employer 30 days to make a good-faith response. Otherwise, you will begin legal action. Send the letter certified mail, return receipt requested, and consider sending copies to your state attorney general's office and your attorney. If the letter is answered and the ex-employer refuses to pay, you may learn what position it intends to take at the trial. If your letter is ignored, that is evidence in court.

When the person or company you are suing receives the summons, the defendant or his or her attorney can:

- Deny your claim by mailing a written denial to the court
- Deny your claim by personally appearing in court on the day of the hearing
- Sue you for money you supposedly owe (this is called a counterclaim)
- Contact you to settle the matter out of court

If an offer of payment is made, ask to be reimbursed for all filing and service costs. Notify the court that you are dismissing the action only after you receive payment. (If you are paid by check, wait until the check clears.) Do not postpone the case. Tell your opponent that unless you are paid before the day of the trial, you are prepared to go to court and either commence with the trial or stipulate the offer of settlement to the judge.

If a written denial is mailed to the court, ask the clerk to read it to you over the phone or go to the court and read it yourself. This is your right and may help you prepare for your opponent's defense. The following is an example of a simple denial in an answer: "I deny each and every allegation in the face of the complaint." Now you must prove your allegations in court to recover your claim.

It is up to you to follow the progress of your case. Call the clerk and refer to the docket number to discover whether the defendant received the complaint and whether it was answered. If you discover that the defendant did not receive the complaint by the day of the trial, request that the clerk issue a new complaint to be served by a sheriff or process server. Go to court that day anyway to be sure that the case is not dismissed because of your failure to appear.

If the complaint is personally served and your employer does not appear at the trial, he will be in default and you may be awarded a judgment automatically. In some states you still have to prove your case in order to be successful. Defendants sometimes file motions (legal affidavits) requesting the court to remove the default judgment on the grounds that there was a valid reason for not attending the hearing. If this motion is granted, your trial will be rescheduled.

If you are unable to come to court on the day of the trial, send a certified letter, return receipt requested, to the clerk asking for a continuance. The letter should specify the reasons you will be unable to appear and include future dates when you will be able to come to court. Send a copy of this letter to your opponent. When you receive a new date, send your opponent a certified letter, return receipt requested, informing the employer of the revised date. Requests for continuances are sometimes not honored. Call the clerk on the day of the original trial date to be sure that your request has been granted. Be prepared to send a friend or relative to court to ask for a continuance on your behalf if a continuance has not been obtained by the day of the trial.

You have several weeks to prepare for trial. Use the time wisely. First, be sure that your friendly witnesses, if any, will attend the trial and testify on your behalf. Select witnesses who are believable and who will not say things that will surprise you. In some states you can present the judge with signed affidavits or statements of witnesses who are unable to appear at the trial. Some states also permit judges to hear testimony via conference telephones.

If necessary, the clerk can issue a subpoena to ensure the attendance of important witnesses who you believe may refuse to attend and testify. A subpoena is a document that orders a person to testify or produce books, papers, and other physical objects on a specified date. If the subpoena is issued and the person refuses to appear, a judge can direct a sheriff to bring the witness into court or even impose a jail sentence for a willful violation of the order.

When you come to court for the trial, check to see if the clerk has received any subpoenaed documents. If such records are crucial to your case and have not been received, you can ask for a continuance. If you have subpoenaed an individual and do not know what he or she looks like, ask the clerk to call out the name to determine if he or she is present so you can proceed with the trial.

To maximize your chances of success, organize your case before the trial. Gather and label all your evidence so that you can produce the documents easily. You may also wish to speak with a lawyer or call a lawyer's referral service for legal advice. Many communities have such advisory organizations, and they are willing to inform you, without charge, about relevant cases and statutes. This may help you know what damages you are legally entitled to. You may cite these laws, if applicable, at the hearing.

Arrive early, locate the correct courtroom, find the name of your case on the court calendar, and check in with the clerk. You should be properly attired, preferably in business clothes. Come prepared with all relevant documents. Examples are:

- Receipts and canceled checks
- Correspondence
- Contracts
- Letters of protest demanding unpaid wages
- Unpaid invoices
- Contemporaneous memos of promises and statements made to you
- Signed affidavits or statements from friends and witnesses unable to appear at the hearing
- An accountant's statement of lost wages
- Prior years' tax returns
- Diagrams or charts
- Copies of applicable statutes, cases, and regulations

When your case is called, you and your opponent will be sworn. The judge or court-appointed arbitrator will conduct the hearing and ask you questions. Be relaxed. Keep your presentation brief and to the point. Tell why you are suing the defendant and what monetary damages you are seeking. Show your evidence. Bring along a short written summary of the case. You can refer to it during the trial, and if the judge does not come to an immediate decision, he or she can use your outline for reference. Talk directly to the judge and respond to his or her questions. Show respect. Always refer to him or her as "Your Honor" or "Judge." Listen to the judge's instructions and never argue. If the judge asks you a question while you are speaking, stop immediately. Then answer the question honestly and to the point. Be diplomatic rather than emotional. Avoid arguing with your opponent in court and never interrupt his or her presentation.

After both sides finish speaking, you will have the opportunity to refute what your opponent has told the judge. Do not be intimidated if he or she is accompanied by a lawyer. Simply inform the judge that you are not represented by counsel and are not familiar with small-claims court procedures. Ask the judge to intercede on your behalf if you feel that your opponent's attorney is treating you unfairly. Most judges will be sympathetic, since small-claims courts are specially designed for you to present your case without an attorney.

Follow the same procedures as the plaintiff: prepare your testimony; contact your witnesses to be sure that they will appear at the trial and testify on your behalf; collect your exhibits and documents; arrive early on the day of the trial and check in with the clerk. If you have any doubts about your case, try to settle with the plaintiff before the judge hears the case. Request that the case be dismissed if your opponent fails to appear. Your opponent will speak first if he or she appears. Wait until he or she is finished speaking before telling your side of the story. Point out any inconsistencies or flaws in your opponent's story. Conclude your remarks by highlighting the important aspects of the case.

Some small-claims court judges render oral decisions on the spot. Others issue a decision in writing several days after the hearing. This gives them time to weigh the testimony and exhibits. If your opponent failed to attend the hearing, judges usually render a judgment of default immediately after your presentation.

If you win the case, make sure you know how and when payment will be made. Check to see that all your disbursements, including court costs, filing fees, service of process, and applicable witness fees, are added to the amount of your judgment. Send a copy of the decision by certified mail, return receipt requested, to your opponent, together with a letter requesting payment. Some states require that payment be made to the court; others allow payment to be made directly to you.

Do not hesitate to act if you do not receive the money. First, contact the clerk and file a Petition for Notice to Show Cause. This will be sent to the defendant, ordering the employer to come into court and explain why no payment has been made. You should also file an Order of Execution with the sheriff's, constable's, or clerk's office in the county where the defendant is located or owns a business. This will enable you to discover where the defendant has assets. The sheriff or other enforcement agent has the power to go out and collect the judgment by seizing personal property, freezing the defendant's bank accounts, placing a lien on any real estate, or even garnisheeing an individual's salary where appropriate. The clerk of your small-claims court should tell you exactly what to do to collect your judgment.

By bringing suit in small-claims court, you usually waive your right to a trial by jury. However, the defendant can surprise you. Some states allow defendants to move a small-claims court case to a higher court and/or obtain a trial by jury. If this occurs, you will need a lawyer to represent you, and his or her services could cost as much as your claim in the dispute.

Some states do not allow losing plaintiffs to appeal, but if you can and do appeal, be aware that an appeals court will overturn the decision of a small-claims court judge only if there is strong proof that the judge was biased or dishonest. This may be difficult to prove.

Benefits-Related Lawsuits

A job is like a romance. Companies woo applicants with promises of security, fulfillment, and riches. Then, when the honeymoon is over, even qualified people often find themselves being treated unfairly. Many employees are fired for no justifiable reason in breach of contract. Still others fail to receive anticipated, promised or earned benefits.

Claims arise because exploited workers fail to receive earned and expected compensation including wages, overtime pay, accrued vacation pay, bonus monies, promised raises, commissions, expenses and stock options. Lawsuits are also asserted for pension and profit sharing monies, workers' compensation, disability, and social security benefits when monies have been unlawfully withheld.

Breach of Contract Litigation

Lawsuits for employee benefits and compensation are often asserted as breach of contract claims. The best way to avoid such lawsuits is to carefully discuss and clarify all key terms, conditions and responsibilities of the job before accepting it (e.g., while you are an applicant). Breach of contract litigation increases when the compensation arrangement and benefits package are not agreed on before a hiring since the law will not generally impute such rights and you cannot force an employer to give valuable benefits which weren't promised or offered.

Request a written employment contract spelling out your rights and duties before commencing employment to reduce potential misunderstandings. Read the document carefully to be sure it is clearly and properly drafted. If you fail to receive a written agreement, you may still be entitled to promised benefits by proving an oral contract or a contract implied by the actions or intentions of the parties (although this is more difficult).

It is necessary to prove the following for a valid contract to exist:

1. The parties entering into the contract were of sound mind and had the required legal capacity and mental ability. For example, in many states, minors under eighteen are legally incapable of making a binding contract.

2. There was mutual acceptance of the agreed-upon terms. All contracts require an offer and an acceptance. An offer is

the presentment of terms, which, when accepted, may lead to the formation of a contract. The terms offered have to be definite and clearly understood by the person receiving the offer. The offer must be certain and not an invitation to bargain or negotiate. The acceptance must be clearly made for the same thing offered in the manner specified by the offer. For example, if the offer says a response must be in writing by mail, a verbal acceptance may not be legally sufficient.

3. Consideration was given. Consideration is an essential element of an enforceable contract; it is something of value given or promised by one party in exchange for an act or promise of another. The amount of consideration paid in money is typically not important in determining whether the contract is valid (e.g., $1 could be sufficient as consideration).

4. The subject matter was legal.

Contracts can be express, implied by conduct, or implied by law. An express contract is either an oral or written agreement whose terms are manifested by clear and definite language. An implied contract is an agreement inferred from the conduct of the parties. This occurs where the employer and employee may not have precisely agreed on all key terms, but the contract was performed anyway. An implied-in-law contract (also called a quasi contract) is created by operation of law to avoid unjust enrichment of one party at the expense of another. In a quasi contract there has been no agreement or meeting of the minds; one party has conferred a benefit on another under such circumstances that fairness and equity require compensation. This may occur, for example, when a salesperson solicits and procures a major customer who purchases a large amount of product. Since successful effort was provided by the salesperson with the expectation of being paid, the employer may be required to pay a reasonable commission to the salesperson after its goods are shipped and payment is received from the customer.

Although an employment contract can be oral and still enforceable, it must be in writing if you are hired for more than a year to satisfy a legal principal called the statute of frauds. Additionally, when a legal dispute arises concerning the terms of an oral contract, a court will resolve the problem by examining all the evidence both parties offer and weighing their testimony to determine whose claims should be upheld. A problem with oral contracts is that the same words discussed and agreed upon by both parties (assuming what was said can be proved) often have different interpretations.

STRATEGY: *Insist on a written document that clarifies and confirms the terms of any employment arrangement that has been agreed upon. Ask the employer to provide you with a contract defining compensation, benefits, job security, notice of termination and other considerations. If you don't receive a written agreement, send a letter spelling out all important terms you have reached with the employer. Often a letter can act in lieu of a written contract provided it states that if any of the terms are incorrect or incomplete, an immediate reply is necessary. Write the letter with precision, since ambiguous or unclear language will work against you. Keep a copy of the letter for your records. Send it certified mail, return receipt requested, to prove delivery. If an employer does not respond to the letter or does not raise objections to the stated understanding, a written contract may be deemed by a judge to exist. That is how you can protect yourself and turn an oral handshake into a legally enforceable written contract in certain situations.*

When a contract is formed, all parties must live up to the promises set forth in the agreement. Breach of contract is the unjustified failure of a party to perform a duty or obligation specified in a contract. If a contract is impossible to perform because of force majeure (i.e., a flood, strike or other event making performance impossible), this may be a defense. Other defenses typically raised to defeat the validity or enforceability of a contract are: important terms were intentionally misrepresented; the contract was entered into under duress or coercion; the parties were unclear about key points of the deal; or important terms in the contract were ambiguous.

When a contract is deemed to be breached, damages are awarded to the innocent party as compensation for financial loss or injury. In order to recover damages, it is necessary to prove that a contract existed, that there was a breach, and that you were injured or damaged as a result. If damages are nominal, a small amount of money may be recovered. If damages are significant, the injured party will be compensated by a sum of money to make him or her whole (e.g., payment for owed bonus or commissions due). If the breach is minor, a party can treat the contract as continuing and seek reimbursement for damages. Typically, in the event of a material (i.e., major) breach, the contract is treated as being unjustifiably terminated, relieving the non-breaching party of obligations and allowing that party to seek compensation.

The law does not allow people to recover money in excess of their damages as the result of breach of contract. Parties to a contract are required to make reasonable efforts to reduce losses ("mitigate damages") as much as possible. Thus if you found a new job after being unjustifiably fired prior to the expiration of a contract with a definite term (i.e., a year), your damages would probably be reduced by the amount of earnings received from the new position.

Some employment contracts contain written clauses that stipulate what damages are to be paid in the event the contract is breached. For instance, an employer may insist that in the event the employee decides to resign and work for a competitor, fifty thousand dollars will be paid to the employer. These are referred to as liquidated damages. If a judge or jury is unable to calculate the actual damages sustained, a liquidated damages clause may be enforceable. In many situations, however, liquidated damages clauses are not honored by the courts because they are deemed to be a penalty and not representative of actual losses incurred by the breach.

In some situations, parties considered by a judge to be in breach may be ordered to continue performing terms of the contract. This is referred to as specific performance. For example, if an actor refuses to continue to perform in a Broadway show because he wants to star in a motion picture, a judge may order him not to shoot the film until his contractual Broadway performance obligations are completed.

Gathering Evidence

Before you file a formal breach of contract lawsuit or contact an agency such as the Department of Labor to enforce your rights, it is crucial to bolster a claim. You are nowhere legally, without evidence proving the existence of a contract and what you are owed. Since you may be fired after filing a grievance, collect as many documents as you can while working prior to commencing litigation. Gather all relevant and non-confidential documents you can so that you have a copy of all such documents, including contracts, correspondence, e-mails, performance reviews, and kudos letters.

Act Promptly to Protect Your Rights

If you are owed earned and accrued benefits, it is strongly recommended that you send a letter or series of letters to the ex-employer immediately after being fired. You should do this before you decide to consult with or hire a lawyer, and you should do it promptly in order to document a claim. The letter(s) will help prove that a claim was made and that monies are due. If you still have trouble receiving the money, you can then contact a lawyer or a regional office of your state's Department of Labor for assistance. Examples of such letters, called demand letters, begin below. These valuable letters can be used by anyone without the expense of hiring a lawyer. Simply fill in the blanks with the appropriate information, draft it neatly (preferably in type), and send the letter by certified mail, return receipt requested, to prove delivery. Always make and save a copy of the letter and the return receipt for your records.

Often such a letter will do the trick because the employer will know you are serious about protecting your rights and that you are knowledgeable concerning the law.

Sample Demand Letter for ERISA Retirement Benefits

Your Name
Address
Telephone Number
Date

Name of Officer or Employer
Title
Name of Employer
Address

Re: My ERISA Retirement Benefits

Dear (Name of Officer):

As you know, I was terminated (or resigned) on (specify date). However, I have not received a written description of all my retirement benefits under federal ERISA law. (Or, if applicable, state: I have not received the correct computation of all benefits due me. Or, I believe I was fired shortly [i.e., two months] before the vesting of a pension, in violation of my ERISA rights)

Your company has a legal obligation to provide me with accurate information concerning all applicable profit-sharing, pension, employee welfare, benefit, and other plans. Therefore I would like you to send me (specify what you want, such as to receive a copy of the employer's formal pension and/or profit sharing plans, re-compute your benefits, or offer you a pension, if applicable).

It is imperative that I receive a response to my request immediately in writing to avoid having me take prompt legal action to enforce my rights.

Hopefully, this will not be necessary, and I thank you for your prompt attention in this matter. If you wish to discuss this matter with me, feel free to contact me immediately.

Very truly yours,

Your Name

Sent certified mail, return receipt requested

Under federal ERISA law, if you request materials from a plan and do not receive them within 30 days, you may file suit in federal or state court. Contact the plan administrator for the company immediately in writing if your claim is denied or if you do not receive an adequate response shortly after a firing. If no adequate response is received, seek assistance from the US. Department of Labor to protect your rights.

Sample Demand Letter for COBRA Medical Benefits

Your Name
Address
Telephone Number
Date

Name of Officer or Employer
Title
Name of Employer
Address

Re: My COBRA Medical Benefits

Dear (Name of Officer):

As you know, I was terminated on (specify date) due to a job elimination (or specify, such as business reorganization). However, more than 30 days has elapsed from the date of my discharge and I have not yet received official notification from either your company or your medical carrier that my medical benefits have been maintained and/or extended under federal COBRA law.

It is imperative that I receive such notification immediately in writing, specifying my cost at the group rate for such coverage.

I trust that such information will be forthcoming immediately so that I am not required to take prompt legal action to enforce my rights.

Hopefully, such additional legal action will not be necessary, and I thank you for your prompt attention to this apparent oversight.

If you wish to discuss this matter with me, feel free to contact me immediately.

Very truly yours,

Your Name

Sent certified mail, return receipt requested

Federal COBRA law requires that most employers offer continuation of coverage for an additional 18 months to former employees who were discharged as a result of a voluntary or involuntary termination (with the exception of gross misconduct); all terminated employees have the option to continue medical plan benefits at their cost. You must be notified within 60 days of your right to continue such coverage. Send a similar letter whenever you do not receive such a notification shortly after a firing. A well-drafted letter should spur the company into action and protect your rights.

Sample Demand Letter for Earned Commissions

Your Name
Address
Telephone Number
Date

Name of Officer or Employer
Title
Name of Employer
Address

Re: My Commissions

Dear (Name of Officer):

It has been (specify) days from the effective termination date of our agreement. Despite our discussions and your earlier promises that all commissions presently owed would be paid immediately, I still have not received my money.

Please be advised that under this state's law, unless I am provided a final, accurate accounting together with copies of all invoices reflecting shipment of my orders (or state if you require anything else) and payment of commissions in the amount of (specify $X if you know), within (specify, such as five days) from your receipt of this letter, your company will be liable for additional damages, attorney fees, costs, and interest upon my institution of a lawsuit to collect same.

Hopefully, such action will not be necessary, and I thank you for your prompt attention to this apparent oversight. If you wish to discuss this matter with me, feel free to contact me immediately at the above phone number.

Very truly yours,

Your name

Sent certified mail, return receipt requested

Always send a detailed written demand for unpaid commissions. This should be done by certified mail, return receipt requested, to document your claim and prove delivery. Such a demand will "start the clock" for the purpose of determining the numbers of days that commissions remain unpaid and put the employer on notice that additional damages and penalties may be owed if money is not received immediately. A written demand is essential in enforcing your rights and may get the employer to contact you and resolve the matter amicably.

Sample Demand Letter for Earned Bonus

Your Name
Address
Telephone Number
Date

Name of Officer or Employer
Title
Name of Employer
Address

Re: My Bonus

Dear (Name of Officer):

Please be advised that I am currently owed a bonus of (specify $X if you know). I was fired on (specify date, such as January 15) suddenly for no valid reason and not as a result of any negative or detrimental conduct on my part. Prior to my termination, I complied with all company directives and was expecting to receive a bonus for the work I rendered in the preceding year.

This expectation was in accordance with our previous understandings and practices since I have regularly received bonuses for the past (specify) years ranging from (specify dollar amounts).

Therefore, to avoid further legal action, I request prompt payment of my earned bonus. Hopefully, additional legal action will not be necessary, and I thank you for your prompt attention to this apparent oversight.

If you wish to discuss this matter with me, feel free to contact me immediately.

Very truly yours,

Your Name

Sent certified mail, return receipt requested

Some employers fire workers right before they are scheduled to receive a bonus and deny such bonuses by stating a worker must be employed on the day bonus checks are issued as a condition of payment. If this happens to you, or you are denied a bonus for any reason, send a letter similar to the one above to protect your rights. Argue that you would have received the bonus but for the firing. Demand that you are entitled to receive a pro rata share of the bonus if you are fired close to but before the end of the year. For example, if you are fired on December 1, negotiate to receive eleven-twelfths of the bonus you were expecting.

Sample Demand Letter for Accrued Vacation Pay

Your Name
Address
Telephone Number
Date

Name of Officer or Employer
Title
Name of Employer
Address

Re: My Earned Vacation Pay

Dear (Name of Officer):

Please be advised that I am currently owed vacation pay totaling (specify number of days or weeks due or $X if you know). As you know, I resigned (or was fired) on (specify date). According to your company's policy specified in (state, such as a handbook or manual), I am entitled to (specify) weeks per year.

To avoid having me take legal action, including my contacting this state's Department of Labor and requesting a formal investigation, I expect to receive my earned, accrued vacation pay immediately.

Hopefully, additional legal action will not be necessary, and I thank you for your prompt attention to this apparent oversight. If you wish to discuss this matter with me, feel free to contact me immediately.

Very truly yours,

Your Name

Sent certified mail, return receipt requested

Most states require employers to pay accrued vacation pay in all circumstances, even after resignations by employees or terminations for cause. Although each company is free to implement its own rules governing vacation pay, employers must apply such policies consistently to avoid charges of discrimination and breach of contract. To reduce problems, be sure you understand how long you must first work to qualify, whether vacation days must be taken in a given year, whether they can be carried over to the next year, and whether you can be paid in cash for unused, earned vacation days. Also, how much notice is required before being allowed to take vacation time? If the ex-employer fails to respond to your initial letter and even a second, final request, contact your state's Department of Labor for assistance.

Sample Demand Letter
for Accrued Overtime Pay

Your Name
Address
Telephone Number
Date

Name of Officer or Employer
Title
Name of Employer
Address

Re: My Earned Overtime Pay

Dear (Name of Officer):

Please be advised that I am currently owed (specify hours) of overtime pay totaling (specify $X). (Or I did not keep records of the overtime hours, but I know that I worked substantial overtime, and I estimate the such overtime, on average, was about [specify hours] hours per week, which means that the company owes me overtime pay totaling [specify $X]). As you know, I resigned (or was fired) on (specify date). Under federal law, since I was an hourly worker for your company, overtime at one and one half times my regular pay rate must be paid for hours worked in excess of 40 hours per workweek.

To avoid having me take prompt legal action, including my contacting this state's Department of Labor, and requesting a formal investigation into your company's violation of the Fair Labor Standards Act, I expect to receive my earned, overtime pay immediately, with accrued interest.

Hopefully, additional legal action will not be necessary, and I thank you for your prompt attention to this matter.

If you wish to discuss this matter with me, feel free to contact me immediately.

Very truly yours,

Your Name

Sent certified mail, return receipt requested

Sample Demand Letter for Earned Salary

Your Name
Address
Telephone Number
Date

Name of Officer or Employer
Title
Name of Employer
Address

   Re: Earned Salary

Dear (Name of Officer):

   It has been (specify) days from my termination (or resignation). However, I have not received all salary due me totaling (specify $X) per our agreement.

   Please be advised that under this state's laws, all earned salary must be paid within (specify) days of an employee's termination (or resignation).

   To avoid legal action, including my contacting the state's Department of Labor and having the agency commence an investigation leading to the imposition of additional penalties, costs and interest, I request payment in the aforesaid amount immediately.

   Hopefully, such action will not be necessary, and I thank you for your prompt attention to this apparent oversight. If you wish to discuss the matter with me, feel free to contact me immediately at the above telephone number.

Very truly yours,

Your Name
Sent certified mail, return receipt requested.

Sample Letter Filing a Charge for Earned Benefits With the Department of Labor

Your Name
Address
Telephone Number
Date

Name of Investigator
Title
Department of Labor
Address

Re: Earned Salary (or other Benefits)

Dear (Name of Investigator):

Per our telephone discussion, it has been (specify) days from my termination (or resignation) from (Name of Employer, address, telephone number, etc.). However, I have not received all salary due me totaling (specify $X) per our agreement. Despite my requests for payment, including telephone calls and letters to (specify), the president (or other officer) of Employer, my requests have been ignored. For your edification, I am enclosing copies of several letters I sent certified mail, return receipt requested, with proof of delivery. I am also enclosing copies of pertinent evidence, including (specify, such as the parties' contract or letter agreement, employee handbook specifying salary and severance policies, etc.) confirming my entitlement to these monies. If you need the originals for a hearing, please advise.

I hereby authorize you to commence an investigation on my behalf to collect my earned and due salary (or other benefits). Please keep me promptly apprised of the progress of the case.

If you need further information or wish to speak to me, feel free to contact me anytime at the above telephone number.

I appreciate your efforts on my behalf.

Very truly yours,

Your Name

Sent certified mail, return receipt requested.

10
Hiring a Lawyer to Protect Your Rights

F ew legal problems disappear at a lawyer's touch, and lawyers cannot significantly reduce the time you must wait before receiving your day in court. What a lawyer can and should do is zealously protect your interests. He or she should represent you competently, keep you informed, and bill reasonably for services. The good lawyer fights for you and protects you.

Lawyer-client disputes sometimes arise because:

- Fee arrangements are not spelled out
- Clients are not consulted regarding settlement negotiations
- Phone calls are not promptly returned
- Work on legal matters is put off
- Potential conflicts of interest are not fully disclosed
- Client funds are used improperly

Do you know how to get the most out of your employment attorney and how to work effectively with one? This chapter will tell you how to avoid potential misunderstandings involving lawyer billing, what to include in retainer agreements, and how to recognize when your problem is not being handled competently or in a timely fashion. You will learn what to bring to the initial interview and what to say, how to negotiate a fair fee arrangement, and how to stay informed and keep your lawyer working on your case.

When You Need a Lawyer

Labor laws and regulations are unduly complicated, and people often need attorneys to guide them properly. The time to determine whether you need an employment lawyer is before legal action is considered. Common situations that might call for legal help are:

- Deciding to resign from a lucrative job
- Considering filing a discrimination case with the EEOC or a state agency, or filing a private lawsuit in federal or state court
- Before commencing or threatening to file a lawsuit for breach of contract, commissions, wages, bonuses, benefits, or other monies due
- Negotiating severance and other benefits resulting from a firing
- Defending a charge of violating a restrictive covenant or confidentiality agreement
- Reviewing a proposed independent contractor or employment agreement

The best time to determine whether a lawyer is needed is before legal action is contemplated or necessary, and the best way to decide if a lawyer is needed is to speak to one. Hopefully, you won't be charged for brief information given over the telephone.

How to Find a Lawyer

Select a lawyer with care. The right choice can mean recovery of thousands of dollars or satisfactory resolution of a conflict or other problem and peace of mind. The wrong choice can cost money and aggravation.

Your first step is to speak to an experienced attorney to determine if your problem warrants assistance. If it does, then a consultation should be scheduled so your problem can be reviewed in greater detail.

The place to start is to call a lawyer you have dealt with in the past and ask for the name of an employment law specialist. You should also inquire if your matter warrants a consultation. If the lawyer you speak to is willing to conduct the consultation, ask if he or she has sufficient expertise to provide you with competent advice. This is important. Most lawyers who represent clients in other fields are not qualified to represent people in employment matters because the law has become quite specialized. Just as you would not consult a heart surgeon about a skin problem, you should not consult a lawyer who does not regularly handle labor matters (i.e., does not devote at least 50 percent of his or her working time to representing individuals with employment-related disputes). If the lawyer tells you that she does not commonly handle your type of problem, ask for the names of other lawyers she is willing to recommend. Clients often receive excellent assistance through lawyer referrals.

STRATEGY: *Recognize that many attorneys who competently represent clients in one area (e.g., criminal law) are not qualified to represent the same client in an employment matter because most lawyers become familiar with certain types of cases, which they handle promptly, efficiently, and profitably. When lawyers accept matters outside the realm of their daily practice, the chances of making mistakes or not handling matters promptly increase. Ask the attorney what proportion of his working time is spent dealing in the field of law related to your problem. Finally, be wary of recommendations from people whose advice may be self-motivated.*

If you don't deal regularly with a lawyer, you may have to ask friends and relatives for referrals. However, this may not be wise unless the person tells you about a lawyer who handled a labor matter (not a house closing or divorce) satisfactorily. You may also wish to call your local bar association and ask for the names of employment lawyers. Some associations maintain legal referral services and lists of labor lawyers who will not charge you more than $35 for a half-hour consultation. Bar association personnel who handle incoming telephone requests are generally unbiased when referring names of lawyers. However, inquire whether the names supplied are experienced practitioners or inexperienced neophytes; be sure to ask for the names of experienced lawyers only.

Be wary of attorney advertising. Some lawyers have misled the public with their advertising. One common method is to run an advertisement stating that a particular matter costs only $X. When a potential client meets the attorney, she learns that court costs and filing fees are that amount, but attorney fees are extra. Also beware of advertisements that proclaim the lawyer is a "specialist." Most state bar associations have not adopted specialist certification programs.

If you have attempted to negotiate your severance package but are not satisfied that you adequately discussed your options and benefits, if the company refuses to deal with you in good faith, or if you feel you lack the aggressiveness, inclination, knowledge, or stamina to initially negotiate the package on your own, you must decide whether to accept the company's offer or retain a lawyer in the attempt to obtain additional compensation. When there is a large amount of money at stake or the employer is acting unfairly or pressuring you, it may be a good idea to hire an employment attorney. It is also advisable to consult a lawyer when you are told that you must sign a release and waive potentially viable claims before receiving any severance pay.

Always consider hiring an employment attorney to negotiate your package when you believe the employer has violated the law. This is especially true if you believe you were fired for any of the following reasons: to be denied accrued benefits; due to a legitimate illness or absence; as a result of whistle-blowing; for complaining about a health or safety violation; for serving in the military; in a manner inconsistent with a company handbook, manual, or disciplinary rule; as a result of discrimination; after asserting a sexual harassment claim or in retaliation for filing a discrimination complaint; as part of a large layoff without receiving adequate notification; when the company acts inconsistent with a verbal promise; when the company is in breach of a contract right or provision in your written employment agreement; or for a host of many other illegal acts cited in this book.

Before deciding to hire a lawyer as your negotiating agent, answer some of the following questions:

- Are you prepared to lose the offer currently on the table in the remote possibility that the company will revoke it when your lawyer gets involved?

- What are the chances you will receive a better package?

- Is the additional amount to be gained worth the price of hiring the lawyer in the first place? Will you be satisfied if you don't get more money but receive more benefits and perks?

- Is it worth it to hire a lawyer merely to get the company to agree that it will not contest your employment benefits or that it will give you a favorable reference or outplacement assistance? What is the minimum amount of money and perks you will accept going into the negotiations?

- What is the minimum amount of money you will accept to sign a release and thereby be precluded from ever suing the company in the future?

- Is it advantageous for you to hire a lawyer as a coach to give you behind-the-scenes advice while you negotiate the package on your own? This can save you legal fees if you are successful.

- Can you effectively handle the negotiation yourself given the maxim "He who represents himself has a fool for a client"?

- If you can, is the lawyer agreeable to initially serving you in an advisory capacity and under what terms? At what stage should the lawyer get involved if you fail? Will your failed efforts impair the lawyer's chances of success?

- Who is the most sympathetic person you or your lawyer should initially contact in the attempt to get the best results?

- What are the strongest reasons why you are entitled to a better package?

- Are you aware of better deals other people got from the employer in the past?

■ Will the company respond negatively or positively when you bring in a lawyer to negotiate? Does the company regularly back off from confrontations, or does it have a history of sticking to its guns and fighting it out in court regardless of the cost?

■ If the employer is litigation-prone, is it more advantageous for you to first deal with it directly without a lawyer so you do not jeopardize a positive relationship?

All these questions should be discussed with a lawyer before retaining him or her so that you know where each party stands in the attempt to obtain favorable results.

Before retaining a lawyer, be sure that you feel comfortable with him or her and that the lawyer will be able to render competent services on your behalf.

The Initial Interview

Arrange an interview after you find a lawyer who will discuss the case. The interview will help you obtain a sound evaluation about your legal problem and decide if the lawyer you met should be hired. This is also the time to discuss important working details, such as the fee arrangement. Bring all pertinent written information to the initial interview including copies of contracts, checks, letters, bills of sale, and photographs. Tell the lawyer everything related to the matter. Communicate relevant information without inhibition because the discussion is privileged and confidential and it will facilitate the lawyer's work and time.

Once the lawyer receives all of the pertinent facts, she should be in a position of advising if the matter has any legal validity or consequences depending on state and/or federal law. You should also be advised whether the matter can be resolved through legal assistance. If so, inquire how quickly the lawyer believes the matter can be resolved, what must be done, and how much the lawyer intends to charge for the contemplated services.

For example, after meeting with the author at an initial comprehensive consultation, a recently terminated employee is advised about whether the employer has violated the law and the chances of obtaining more money in a negotiated out-of-court settlement. The potential client will learn the steps I intend to take after being retained, such as what the initial demand letter will say, when it will be received by the employer, and why such steps are to be taken. I try to give precise odds based on my experience in handling similar matters in the past. For example, a potential client may be told there is a 75 percent chance of receiving an extra $5,000 in a settlement but only a 25 percent chance of receiving an extra $50,000.

If a lawsuit is considered, or if you have been sued and need the lawyer to assist in defense of the case, the lawyer will then:

- Decide whether the case has a fair probability of success after considering the law in the state where the suit will be brought.
- Give an estimate as to how long the lawsuit will last.
- Make a determination of the approximate legal fees and disbursements.
- Explain what legal papers will be filed, when and what their purposes are.
- Discuss the defenses an opponent will probably raise, and how to deal with them.

If the lawyer sees weaknesses in the case and believes that litigation will be unduly expensive, she may advise to compromise and settle the claim without resorting to litigation. In any event, the chosen course of action should be instituted without delay to be able to receive remuneration as quickly as possible and insure that the requisite time period to start the action (i.e., the statute of limitations) will not have expired.

For all matters, the lawyer should advise what legal work needs to be done, how long it will take, and how much it will cost. Some lawyers neglect to give honest appraisals. Clients are then misled and spend large sums of money on losing causes. Be wary if the lawyer states, "You have nothing to worry about." Prudent attorneys tell clients that "airtight" cases do not exist, and that the possibility of unforeseen circumstances and developments is always present.

Recovery is never guaranteed because no matter what the lawyer tells you, and no matter how strong a case may seem, there are always pitfalls. Cautious attorneys avoid specificity when discussing recovery awards at the initial interview. When a client asks a lawyer, "What is my case worth?" and the lawyer gives a specific answer, she may be raising unreasonable expectations. Clients remember and will blame the lawyer if what is promised is not delivered. Experienced trial lawyers know it is impossible to ascertain your injuries and damages during the initial interview without further investigation.

STRATEGY: *Discuss recent legal trends in cases similar to yours. Ask if the lawyer is familiar with the judge or court in which you'll appear. Does the attorney remain current with recent developments in the law relating to your case? If so, how? What percentage of cases are actually tried in court as opposed to being settled? Does the lawyer enjoy court battles? How many court cases did she try in the past three years? What were the results? Seek answers to these questions. Tell the lawyer you want to attend her current or next trial. This is an excellent way to observe first-hand if the attorney is a competent trial specialist. Trials are conducted in open courtrooms and the general public can attend. Since "the proof is in the pudding," visit the next hearing or trial to observe your prospective attorney in action.*

If applicable, request an opinion letter that spells out the pros and cons of the matter and how much money may be spent to accomplish your objectives. Even if you are charged for the time it takes to draft it, an opinion letter can minimize future misunderstandings between you and your attorney and help you decide whether or not to proceed with a lawsuit. (Note: If you're the defendant, however, you probably have no choice but to fight the case to the end or until it is settled once you're served with legal papers.)

It is important to leave the interview feeling that the attorney is open and responsive to your needs, is genuinely interested in helping you, will return your telephone calls promptly, and will prepare and handle your case properly. Are the attorney's answers comforting? Did she discuss how the legal system works? Did he familiarize you with the rules of civil procedure, legal maneuvering, and obstacles that must be overcome before the case can be resolved? Were you told that most cases do not reach trial for up to three years after a suit has been filed? Can you work closely with this individual?

Although it is difficult to predict how well an attorney will perform, there are certain clues to look for during the interview.

1. Does the attorney present an outward appearance of neatness and good grooming?

2. Are you received at the appointed hour or kept waiting? Some attorneys believe that if clients are kept waiting they will think the attorney is busy and therefore good. Keeping you waiting is merely a sign that the attorney is not organized or is inconsiderate.

3. Does the attorney leave the room frequently during the interview or permit telephone calls to intrude? You deserve his complete attention.

4. Does he demonstrate boredom or lack of interest by yawning or finger tapping?

5. Is he a clock watcher?

6. Does the attorney try to impress you by narrating other cases he handled? Good attorneys do not have to boast to obtain clients.

7. Does he fail to discuss the fee arrangement up front? Some attorneys have a tendency to wait until all work is done before submitting large bills. The failure to discuss fee arrangements at the initial interview may be a sign the attorney operates this way.

Successful litigators win cases and make money for their clients. Don't be fooled by appearances. Plush offices, fancy cars, and expensive clothes may signal you'll pay exorbitant fees for routine work. Unless you're involved in a complex lawsuit, such as a complicated anti-trust or securities violations case, don't be impressed by the school where the attorney graduated. Most law schools do not give their graduates practical litigation experience, and many less prestigious "local" law schools offer superior training in trial practice, which is what you are paying for.

Be sure the attorney of your choice will be working on the matter. People often go to large prestigious firms, expecting their matter to be handled by a partner. They pay large fees and sometimes wind up being represented by a second-year associate. Be sure your retainer agreement states that the matter will be handled by attorney X (the attorney of your choice). Ask to be introduced to the trial lawyer's supporting staff at the initial interview. Some work on your case will be performed by associates, paralegals, secretaries, bookkeeping staff, and others at a lower billing rate. The key is to get the right person with the right billing rate for the right job.

STRATEGY: *The major factor in determining whether a particular attorney should be hired is the amount of experience and expertise he or she has in handling similar litigation cases. Use an attorney who devotes at least 50 percent of his practice to such cases. Avoid inexperienced attorneys if possible. Novices charge less, but often require more time to handle a problem. If you are being charged on an hourly basis, you may pay the same amount of money and not obtain the experience of a pro.*

Although anyone with a law license is qualified to try a case, it takes years of practice to be good at it. If your case involves a substantial amount of money or complicated legal issue, never retain a neophyte to represent you.

Hire an attorney to whom you can relate, who will work diligently for you, and who will pursue the lawful means necessary to present or defend your case. Ask the attorney about his outside activities and professional associations. Inquire if you may speak to any of his previous clients; references can help you learn more about the attorney. If you speak to former clients, question them in detail about their cases and the lawyer's performance. Compare the facts and law of their cases to yours. Was the lawyer prepared for depositions and court? Did she ask clear questions and make persuasive arguments? Did she write well? Were the bills fair?

If you do not feel comfortable with the first attorney you meet, schedule appointments with others. For best results, make a list of candidates, question them on the phone, weed out some of them, prepare more questions, and interview at least two lawyers face-to-face. Then review your options. Never hire the first lawyer you talk with and never hire an attorney who acts like you can't win. When you have all your questions answered, thank the attorney for his time, offer to pay the initial consultation fee by check, and tell him when you expect to make your selection. Then go see the next attorney.

USING A LEGAL AID OR COURT APPOINTED LAWYER. If you lack sufficient financial resources and are unable to represent yourself pro se, you may be able to receive legal advice and representation from a legal aid or court appointed lawyer. Virtually all states provide assigned counsel to indigent people in criminal cases and for minor children in abuse, neglect, and custody cases through a law guardian.

Each state has its own rules for determining eligibility, how much lawyers can charge by the hour, and who pays their bills. Many of these lawyers are overworked and underpaid compared to lawyers in private practice. If you need court-appointed representation, you may not receive the same amount of care and attention you would receive by hiring a private lawyer (especially in a civil case), because of the lawyer's low hourly rates.

If you are sued, or wish to pursue a complicated case or matter as a plaintiff and cannot afford to hire a lawyer, inquire with the clerk of the particular court if you qualify for free or low-cost legal representation.

Consult the yellow pages or Internet for the addresses of inexpensive legal advice clinics which may exist in your town. Some law schools also provide a similar service. Ask a court clerk if you qualify for assistance and what forms you must complete to prove eligibility (i.e., lack of assets or funds).

Finally, understand the difference between being provided free counsel and private lawyers who charge less than regular rates. There is a distinction between public defenders, court appointed counsel, and legal aid lawyers depending on your state. Hopefully, you'll be able to utilize the best lawyer at the lowest cost if expense is an issue.

Confirming the Arrangement

After you decide to retain an attorney, it is necessary to discuss a variety of points concerning fees to eliminate potential misunderstandings. This includes clarifying the fee. Most attorneys charge a modest fee for the first visit to the office. Fees should be charged only when actual time is spent working on a matter. Charges are based on the amount of time and work involved, the dollar amount of the case, the result, the urgency of the problem (e.g., an order to show cause the lawyer must draft and argue in court a day after being retained costs more than routine work), and the attorney's expertise and reputation in handling your type of lawsuit. Operating expenses and office overhead are elements that may also affect the fee arrangement.

Frequently, an attorney cannot state exactly how much will be charged because he is unable to determine the amount of time the lawsuit will entail. If so, ask for an estimate of the minimum and maximum fee you can expect to pay. Question this if it seems high. If necessary, tell the attorney that you intend to speak to other attorneys about fees.

The fee arrangement is composed of several elements which you must clearly understand. Costs are expenses that the attorney incurs while preparing a case (e.g., photocopying, telephone, mailing, expert witness fees, and fees paid to the court for filing documents). Be certain the fee arrangement specifically mentions in writing which of these costs you must pay. If you don't have the money to pay for expert witness fees, stenographer fees, travel, and other large costs, inquire if the lawyer will front these costs for you. In some states, lawyers are permitted to advance the client the money to cover litigation costs provided you remain ultimately liable for the full amount. Other states do not permit this so research the law in your state where applicable and avoid arrangements where you must reimburse the lawyer for such costs if you ultimately lose the case.

Attorneys use different forms of fee arrangements. In a flat-fee arrangement, the attorney is paid a specified sum to handle the case. It is rare that a flat-fee arrangement is used in civil litigation matters. Most attorneys prefer to use an hourly-rate arrangement, with the rate ranging from $300-$750 an hour for a senior partner, $155-$400 for an associate, and $70-$150 for a paralegal. Under this arrangement, you will be charged on a fixed hourly rate for all work done. If you are billed by the hour, ask if phone calls between you and the attorney are included. If so, ask that you be charged only for calls exceeding a certain number per month. This can be justified by arguing that you should not be charged when the attorney fails to clarify a point, provide additional information, or discuss news regarding the progress of your case.

In a contingency-fee arrangement, the attorney receives a specified percentage of any money recovered via a lawsuit or settlement. Many plaintiffs favor contingency-fee arrangements because they are not required to pay legal fees if their case is unsuccessful. However, contingency fees are not permitted in certain kinds of actions. For example, an attorney cannot agree to structure the size of his fee based on the type of verdict obtained for a client in a criminal proceeding. Contingency fees are also looked upon unfavorably by courts and disciplinary boards in matrimonial actions because they are viewed as encouraging divorces. So, too, are contingency fees in personal injury suits that exceed maximum allowable percentages (typically 40 percent). If an attorney proposes contingency fees in these areas, never hire him. (Note: Defendants to lawsuits will not be offered the option of a contingency-fee arrangement unless they have large, valid counterclaims.)

Another commonly used form of fee arrangement in litigation cases is the "hybrid" or blended fee arrangement. Lawyers who handle cases which are complex, expensive to litigate, or where success is unpredictable often request a fee which combines an hourly rate and a contingency fee. These hybrid or blended fee arrangements are designed to share the risk of the outcome between the attorney and the client.

Always spell out contingency arrangements or hybrid fee arrangements in writing to prevent problems. This is now required in many states. The agreement should state who is responsible for costs in the event you are unsuccessful. All provisions should be explained so they are clearly understood; be sure to save a copy for your records. (The sample contingency fee arrangements on pages 572 and 574 illustrate many of these points.)

There are distinct advantages and disadvantages in using different fee arrangements. For example, in a flat-fee arrangement, you know how much you will be charged but not how much care and attention will be spent on the matter. The hourly rate may be the way to go, but some dishonest attorneys "pad" time sheets to increase their fees. In addition, as stated earlier, although contingency-fee arrangements are beneficial to clients with weak cases, they sometimes encourage lazy attorneys to settle "winner" cases for less money rather than go to court. This is why, no matter what type of fee is agreed upon, it is essential to hire an attorney who is honest and has your best interests in mind at all times.

Ask for a receipt if you pay the initial consultation or retainer in cash. If a retainer is required, inquire whether the retainer will become part of the entire fee and whether it is refundable. The retainer guarantees the availability of the attorney to represent you and is an advance paid to demonstrate your desire to resolve a problem via litigation. Ask if the retainer and other fees can be paid by credit card. Will interest be added if you are late in paying fees? If so, how much?

Request that all fees be billed periodically (e.g., monthly) so there are no surprises. Insist that billing statements be supported by detailed and complete time records that include the number of hours (or partial hours) worked, a report of the people contacted, the services rendered, and the amount of work done by other associates and staff at the firm at reduced rates. Some attorneys may be reluctant to do this, but by receiving these documents and statements on a regular basis, you can question inconsistencies and errors before they get out of hand, be aware of the amount of the bill as it accrues, and pay for it over time. (The sample monthly billing statement of page 577 is the kind of bill I prepare for my clients who are charged on an hourly basis. Insist on nothing less.)

To avoid problems and reduce misunderstandings, always insist on receiving a written retainer agreement before hiring the lawyer. The following are actual examples of retainer agreements given to my clients in various employment-related matters. The first letter is sent whenever a client retains my office to engage in settlement negotiations after a firing; the second letter is sent when negotiations are unsuccessful and litigation may be necessary.

Sample Retainer Agreement With Attorney (Version 1)

Law Office of Steven Mitchell Sack
110 East 59th Street, 19th Floor
New York, NY 10022
Telephone (917) 371-8000 or (212) 702-8843
Fax (516) 623-9115
E-Mail Address: stevensackatty@hotmail.com

Date

Name of Client
Address

Re: Termination of Employment by (Name of Employer)

Dear Jordan,

This letter will confirm the terms of my engagement as your attorney regarding the above.

I met with you, reviewed your file, and conducted preliminary research to learn the pertinent facts with respect to your current problems and drafted a letter of protest for you to protect your rights. For those and additional services to be rendered, you have paid me a retainer of Five Hundred Dollars ($500.00).

I will now contact the above in the attempt to negotiate a favorable settlement to collect salary, severance pay, and commissions allegedly owed for an additional period of time beyond the company's unilateral decision to pay you only until (date). For my efforts, it is agreed that I shall be paid a contingency fee of One Third (33%) of all gross monies collected on your behalf exceeding the company's prior offer, less the $500.00 previously paid, if a settlement can be effectuated.

All settlements will require your approval before I conclude same. Additionally, the aforementioned contingency-fee arrangement is for legal work performed in negotiations only and does not cover work rendered in connection with a lawsuit. In the event you desire this office to assist you in formal litigation, both of us will discuss and agree upon a suitable fee arrangement in writing at a later date. Finally, you are aware of the hazards of negotiations and that, despite my efforts on your behalf, there is no assurance or guarantee of the success or outcome of this matter.

Finally, I have advised you and you are aware of the hazards of litigation and that, despite my efforts on your behalf, there is no assurance or guarantee of the outcome of this matter, particularly with respect to your claim for reorders through the end of the selling season (since there was no written agreement confirming your right to receive such post-termination compensation). Also, you have assured me that there is no counterclaim exposure and no detrimental acts were committed on (name of employer), such as slander or breach of your fiduciary duty of loyalty or good faith while representing the line, and I have only agreed to represent you in this matter based on those assurances.

In the remote event there is a substantive fee dispute regarding payment of legal fees, you will, in all likelihood, have the right to choose between having the matter arbitrated or litigated. The text of the arbitration rules entitled Part 137. Fee Dispute Resolution Program is available online and if you would like a hard copy of the rules, please notify me and I will be happy to furnish them. Additionally, if any dispute arises under this Agreement, it shall, consistent with the rules governing fee dispute resolution, be resolved by a tribunal located in the City and State of New York, without regard to conflicts.

Kindly indicate your understanding and acceptance of the above by signing this letter below where indicated and returning the signed original to this office, keeping the copy for your files.

As always, I look forward to serving you and will keep you posted with all developments as they occur.

Very truly yours,
Steven Mitchell Sack

I, (name of client), have read the above letter, understand and agree with all of its terms, and have received a copy:

Name of Client: _____   Date: _____

SMS/nc
Enc.

Sample Retainer Agreement With Attorney (Version 2)

Law Office of Steven Mitchell Sack
110 East 59th Street, 19th Floor
New York, NY 10022
Telephone (917) 371-8000 or (212) 702-8843
Fax (516) 623-9115
E-Mail Address: stevensackatty@hotmail.com

Date

Name of Client
Address

Re: Commission Owed by (Name of Employer)

Dear Susan,

This will confirm our agreement whereby you have retained this office to represent your rep firm in a lawsuit in the Supreme Court, New York County, to collect commissions allegedly earned and due from the above conceivably worth in excess of One Hundred Thirty Thousand Dollars ($130,000.00).

In that regard, you have forwarded a retainer of Three Thousand Five Hundred Dollars ($3,500.00). This retainer shall be applied against, and deducted from, a contingency fee of Thirty-Three Percent (33%) of all money collected in settlement, judgment, or otherwise. In the event your matter proceeds to trial and an actual trial occurs, you also agree to pay an additional trial fee of One Thousand Dollars ($1,000.00) per day or any part of a day thereof, which will be a separate fee and not deducted from the above contingency-fee arrangement.

All settlements will require your approval before I conclude same. Additionally, the above fee arrangement only covers work rendered in connection with this lawsuit and does not cover any work in appellate courts, other actions or proceedings, or out-of-pocket disbursements. Out-of-pocket disbursements include, but are not limited to, costs of filing papers, court fees, process servers' fees, witness fees, court reporters' stenographic fees, and out-of-state travel and lodging expenses, which disbursements shall be paid for or reimbursed to me immediately upon my request. It is noted that you have forwarded the sum of Five Hundred Dollars ($500.00) for me to hold in my escrow account for such initial costs and disbursements.

Finally, I have advised you and you are aware of the hazards of litigation and that, despite my efforts on your behalf, there is no assurance or guarantee of the outcome of this matter, particularly with respect to your claim for reorders through the end of the selling season (since there was no written agreement confirming your right to receive such post-termination compensation). Also, you have assured me that there is no counterclaim exposure and no detrimental acts were committed on (name of employer), such as slander or breach of your fiduciary duty of loyalty or good faith while representing the line, and I have only agreed to represent you in this matter based on those assurances.

In the remote event there is a substantive fee dispute regarding payment of legal fees, you will, in all likelihood, have the right to choose between having the matter arbitrated or litigated. The text of the arbitration rules entitled Part 137. Fee Dispute Resolution Program is available online and if you would like a hard copy of the rules, please notify me and I will be happy to furnish them. Additionally, if any dispute arises under this Agreement, it shall, consistent with the rules governing fee dispute resolution, be resolved by a tribunal located in the City and State of New York, without regard to conflicts.

Kindly indicate your understanding and acceptance of the above by signing this letter below where indicated and returning the signed original to this office, keeping the copy for your files.

As always, I look forward to serving you.

Very truly yours,
Steven Mitchell Sack

I, (name of client), have read the above letter, understand and agree with all of its terms, and have received a copy:

Name of Client: _____   Date: _____

SMS/nc
Enc.

It is wise to ask for a monthly statement of services rendered, particularly if you are being charged by the hour. Request that billing statements be supported by detailed and complete time records including the date service was rendered, the time, type of service provided, and names of people contacted. Some lawyers are reluctant to do this, but by receiving these statements on a regular basis, you will be able to question inconsistencies and errors before they get out of hand and keep billing mistakes to a minimum.

The following is an example of an hourly billing statement sent by my office to a client. Note that the client is only billed for a five-minute telephone call where warranted. Some lawyers bill in minimum increments of 15 minutes. Avoid this arrangement, because if the lawyer is charging a high hourly rate (i.e., more than $300 per hour), the additional ten minutes can be very expensive.

Sample Monthly Billing Statement

Date

Name of Client
Company
Address

Re: Current statement for all services rendered in the matter of the contract negotiation between (name of client) and (name of employer) at the rate of $450.00 per hour per agreement:

I.	1/05/2011	Tel. conv. with Employer's Attorney 9:40-9:45 a.m.	5 min.
		Tel. conv. with Client 9:15-9:20 a.m.	5 min.
		Tel. conv. with Client 12:10-12:15 p.m.	5 min.
2.	1/04/2011	Draft of revised Agreement and tel. conv. with Client 6:50 a.m.-8:05 a.m.	75 min.
3.	1/03/2011	Meeting with Client 1:40-2:50 p.m.	70 min.
4.	12/19/2010	Review of initial proposed Agreement 7:30 a.m.-7:55 a.m.	25 min.
		Tel. conv. with Client 9:35-9:40 a.m.; 3:40-3:45 p.m.	10 min.

Total time spent on Matter from December 19, 2010 through January 5, 2011 at standard rate of $450.00 per hour: 195 min. or 3.25 hours

Amount earned: $1,462.50

Wrongful billing practices have occurred in which lawyers were sent to jail by criminal authorities and/or disbarred by disciplinary authorities. Examples include billing for hours that were never actually worked and seeking reimbursement for expenses that were not actually incurred in connection with representing a client. Less extreme wrongdoing occurs when charges to more than one client for the same work or same hours are demanded, or when charges beyond reasonable costs for in-house services like photocopying (e.g., more than 25 cents per page) or office supplies are billed.

Insist on receiving contemporaneous records, copies of paid receipts, and detailed itemized bills to avoid such problems. Question all legal research billed to your case. Before hiring a trial attorney, ask if legal research is required. If so, discuss and agree how much money you will be charged for legal research before it is incurred. While it is unethical for a lawyer to conduct unnecessary legal research, some firms do this to pad a bill. Also, request the attorney to send you copies of all law review articles, cases, and statutes researched to determine if it was thorough.

At the initial interview, insist that any fee dispute be resolved by mediation or binding arbitration. Some states now require this. Include this clause in your retainer agreement for added protection. Doing so may increase the odds that any dispute with your lawyer over fees will be resolved quickly and more efficiently.

In New York, for instance, a fee dispute program was initiated by the Office of Court Administration. It calls for mandatory arbitration, at the client's request, of all attorney-client fee disputes where the amount in controversy ranges from $1,000 to $50,000 and where representation of the client by counsel commenced on or after January 1, 2002. If there is no retainer agreement requiring fee disputes to be settled via arbitration, counsel must inform clients of the existence of such a program. However, unlike typical arbitration (where decisions are final and binding), if a party is dissatisfied with the arbitrator's ruling, either person may renounce the verdict and obtain a trial.

Other states have voluntary mediation programs to resolve client-attorney fee disputes. Studies show most mediated matters result in amicable settlements. Learn the procedures in your state regarding fee disputes with a lawyer and how to resolve them.

Understand what legal fees are tax-deductible. Legal fees are tax-deductible provided they are ordinary and necessary business expenses. This means that the cost of legal fees paid or incurred for the "collection, maintenance, or conservation of income" or property used in producing income can be deducted. For instance, attorney fees for services tending to increase or protect taxable business income is deductible. Ask the attorney whether fees paid are deductible. Structure the fee arrangement to maximize tax deductions. Ask for a written statement that justifies the bill on the basis of time spent or some other allocation to support the claim. Keep the statement in a safe place until tax time and show it to your tax preparer. Accountants and other professionals sometimes clip copies of the statements directly to the return so the IRS won't question the deduction.

There are many other items to clarify during the initial interview such as:

WILL THE LAWYER YOU ARE SPEAKING TO HANDLE THE MATTER? When dealing with law firms, clients may think they are hiring one lawyer but their case is then assigned to another. To avoid this problem, specify in writing which lawyer will handle your case.

WILL THE ATTORNEY BE AVAILABLE? Complaints often arise because of poor communication. In fact, the most frequent complaint clients have is that the attorney kept them in the dark. At the initial interview, ask what the attorney's normal office hours are. Advise the attorney that availability is very important to you since you are paying for this service. Request that he return calls within 24 hours. Insist that his secretary or associate return phone calls if he will be unavailable for extended periods of time, but make it clear you will not call him unnecessarily. Discuss case priorities. Your lawyer should explain that on certain days, depending on the status of the case, your case will have priority over others and vice versa.

WILL THE ATTORNEY WORK ON THE MATTER IMMEDI-ATELY? The legal system is often a slow process. Don't stall it further by hiring a procrastinating lawyer. Insist that the attorney begin working on the matter as quickly as possible. If you are the plaintiff, insist that the summons and complaint be drafted and filed within two weeks after hiring the lawyer. Include this in the retainer agreement for protection. The agreement should state you have the right to withdraw as a client and receive a full refund of your retainer if the summons and complaint are not filed and served on the defendant within the specified date.

ARE THERE HIDDEN CONFLICTS OF INTEREST? Attorneys must avoid even the appearance of impropriety. For example, when an attorney represents both a husband and wife in a divorce, there is an inherent conflict that limits his ability to zealously promote the interests of each of them. Ask the attorney up front if he perceives any potential conflict of interest (e.g., is he related to or was he or anyone at his firm ever employed by the company you are suing?). An attorney must decline representing a client when his professional judgment is likely to be affected by other business, financial, or personal interests. If an attorney is disqualified, his associates and partners are also forbidden to serve you.

HOW WILL FUNDS BE HANDLED? Attorneys are obligated to keep client funds in separate accounts. This includes unearned retainer fees. The rules of professional conduct state that an attorney cannot comingle client funds with his own and that bank accounts for client funds must be clearly marked as "Client Trust Accounts" or "Escrow Accounts."

An attorney must notify the client immediately when settlement or judgment funds from a lawsuit are received. You must also receive an accurate accounting of these funds. This consists of a complete explanation of the amount of money held by the attorney, its origin, and the reason for any deductions. Be sure you receive this. Ask for a copy of all checks received before the attorney deposits funds into his trust or escrow account. Demand that all settlement checks be issued jointly in both of your names. Doing this will require your endorsement before the check can be deposited, and you will be able to make a copy before signing. Tell the attorney to place your funds in an interest-bearing escrow account. Later on, when the funds are remitted, be sure the interest is included in the amount returned to you.

WILL THE ATTORNEY TALK YOU INTO A POSITION OR ACTION YOUR CONSCIENCE WOULD NOT ALLOW? As long as you control the checkbook, you're the boss. Don't let your lawyer treat you in a patronizing manner. Agree on what the game plan is and what you both are willing to accept as a successful result. Before proceeding, there should be a clear understanding of exactly what you want and how the lawyer will get it for you. As a client you have the right to make final decisions regarding your legal matter. Your attorney must discuss the negotiation process with you and agree to a settlement offer only if you have approved it.

INQUIRE HOW MUCH MALPRACTICE INSURANCE THE ATTORNEY MAINTAINS. Who is the carrier? Ask if the lawyer has ever been sued for malpractice. Contact your state's lawyer's disciplinary board to determine if he or she is telling the truth.

WHILE COMMUNICATIONS WITH YOUR ATTORNEY ARE CONFIDENTIAL, ASK YOUR LAWYER TO EXPLAIN AHEAD OF TIME WHEN THE STATEMENTS YOU MAKE OR SECRETS YOU REVEAL ABOUT YOUR CASE CANNOT BE KEPT CONFIDENTIAL. Understand that by filing a lawsuit or being sued, privacy rights concerning your medical, financial, and family data may be diminished. While your lawyer may try to protect your privacy, a lawsuit won't help you in this regard because it's often necessary to obtain records of past medical conditions, wages, and financial data from tax returns. This information may be revealed to your adversary.

Resolving Problems After the Lawyer Is Hired

The best way to reduce problems with your lawyer once he or she is hired is to stay on top of the progress of your case. Attend all court conferences and hearings. Insist on receiving copies of all incoming and outgoing correspondence. If the lawyer is not devoting sufficient time or effort to your case, or several months have gone by and you haven't heard a word, call your lawyer to find out what's happening. If you're not satisfied with the lawyer's response or can't get him on the phone, write a letter. Letters usually get lawyers' attention because they know you may be building a case against them. Save a copy for your records. If the matter is not resolved or you do not receive an adequate response to the letter, write another letter, speak with the head of the litigation department if the lawyer works for a large firm, or discuss the matter with his law partner. If you are part of a prepaid legal plan, take your complaint to the plan administrator.

Scrutinize all billing statements when they are received. Discuss ways to keep costs as low as possible.

Laws in most states make it difficult for lawyers to resign from a litigation case. For instance, a lawyer cannot drop your case just because he grows tired of the matter, it's taking longer than expected, the case is not as financially rewarding as it once appeared, or the lawyer wants to free up time to take more lucrative cases. A lawyer is generally obligated to stay in your case through thick and thin once representation has been accepted. Withdrawal is only permitted after a motion is filed in court, a hearing is conducted, and approval is obtained from the trial judge. As previously mentioned, failing to pay your bill may not be a valid reason for withdrawal. Usually, the lawyer can only quit upon a showing that the client wants him to do something illegal or unethical, the client lied, the lawyer discovers a conflict of interest, or the client is making it unreasonably difficult for the lawyer to represent him or her by failing to return phone calls, appear in court, depositions or at motions, or not furnishing the lawyer with sufficient information to process the lawsuit. If your lawyer seeks to remove herself from your case, get a second opinion from another lawyer about the pros and cons of consenting to or contesting the request.

Never date your lawyer while he or she is still representing you. In many states, it is improper for a lawyer to begin an intimate relationship with a client in a case before the matter is over. Having an intimate relationship can make the lawyer less effective as your advocate and lose the attorney-client privilege. Never agree to submit to sexual favors in exchange for legal work.

You have the right to change attorneys at any time if there is a valid reason. Valid reasons include improper or unethical conduct, conflicts of interest, and malpractice by the attorney. If you are dissatisfied with your attorney's conduct or the way the lawsuit is progressing, consult another attorney for an opinion. Do this before taking action, because you need a professional opinion on whether your attorney acted correctly or incorrectly.

Never fire your attorney until you hire a replacement because you may be unrepresented and your case could be prejudiced or dismissed by the court. If you fire your attorney, you may be required to pay for the value of work rendered. You may also have to go to court to settle the issue of legal fees and the return of your papers, since some attorneys assert a lien on the file. If you have a fee dispute with your lawyer, he or she may be able to institute a claim against your money or property by asserting either a retaining lien or a charging lien. A retaining lien gives the lawyer the right to hold onto your money or property (such as a deed) until you pay the bill. The attorney does not have to go to court to institute the lien. He or she just keeps the property until you pay or go to court asking a judge to order a release. The judge would probably hold a hearing to determine whether the lawyer had good reason to keep your possessions.

A charging lien entitles a lawyer who has sued someone on your behalf the right to be paid the proceeds of the lawsuit, if there are any, before you receive those proceeds. The lawyer is entitled to payment for the amount of services rendered, even if you fired the lawyer other than for cause. Some states allow lawyers to collect on both forms of liens.

If you're upset with the lawyer's work, talk to him or her about correcting such problems. Approach changing attorneys in midstream with caution, as this maneuver can greatly increase your expenses. However, added expenses should never impede you from taking action if warranted.

The following generally summarizes the kinds of claims you can make against your lawyer:

1. **Financial misconduct.** This is where your attorney mishandled funds that you entrusted to him or her or intentionally overbilled you.

2. **Malpractice.** This is where your attorney negligently handled your case.

3. **Ineffective assistance of counsel.** This is where your attorney did not effectively represent you.

4. **Breach of contract.** This is where your attorney did not follow the terms of your agreement for his or her services.

5. **Conflict of interest.** This is where your case was harmed by your attorney having personal interests that conflicted with your interests.

If you have evidence that your attorney misused finds for personal gain or committed fraud, you may file a complaint with the state grievance committee or local bar association. Don't be afraid to do this. All complaints are confidential. You cannot be sued for filing a complaint if it is later determined that the attorney did nothing wrong.

Many states have enacted programs to reimburse clients from lawyer thefts by establishing special funds. Voluntary or mandatory contributions from all the practicing lawyers in a particular state are collected and pooled. In New York, for example, each lawyer must contribute $100 every two years. When a client can prove that his or her lawyer stole money, such as the settlement proceeds in a court case, the client is entitled to recover his or her actual damages up to $200,000.

Critics contend that while these funds are helpful (since the average claim the fund reimburses is $15,000), the amount of money a person can receive may not cover the full extent of the loss. For example, while some states reimburse clients up to $250,000, other states only earmark $50,000 per claimant. You should also recognize that in most cases you cannot recover money given to a lawyer for an investment gone sour. It typically applies only to legal work performed by your lawyer.

Other safeguards to protect clients against a lawyer's wrongful acts have also been implemented. For example, some states have enacted "bounced check" rules. These rules require banks to notify the client protection fund whenever they dishonor a check written on a lawyer's trust or escrow account for insufficient funds. The fund then forwards the notice to the local grievance committee for investigation. According to recent reports, bounced check notices have led to the apprehension of dozens of lawyers for theft of client funds.

Legal malpractice arises when an attorney fails to use "such skill or prudence as attorneys of ordinary skill commonly possess and exercise in the performance of tasks they undertake." This doesn't mean you can sue if your attorney gets beaten by a better attorney. You can only sue if he renders work or assistance of minimal competence and you are damaged as a result. You can also sue for malpractice when there is a breach of ethics (e.g., the failure to remit funds belonging to a client), in addition to suing for breach of contract and/or civil fraud.

The following are examples of attorney malpractice:

- Settling a case without your consent.
- Procrastinating work on a matter (e.g., neglecting to file an answer after being retained which causes a default).

- Failing to file a claim within the requisite time period (statute of limitations).

- Failing to competently represent a defendant in a criminal matter.

- Charging grossly improper fees.

If you believe a lawyer has mishandled your case, attempt to first discuss the matter directly with the lawyer. You may learn that your suspicions are unfounded. If you are not satisfied with the lawyer's explanation, or she doesn't respond to your questions, get a second opinion from another lawyer. If you are not sure you have a valid complaint, go to the state bar association's attorney disciplinary committee with questions. If you think the lawyer's fees are higher than they should be, consult a fee arbitration committee of your local or state bar association. If the problem is more than a dispute over fees, for example, if a lawyer has stolen money from you or defrauded you, contact the bar associations' client security trust fund and file a complaint to obtain reimbursement for your losses. You should also notify the district attorney or the police. If you suspect your lawyer has acted unethically, go to the attorney disciplinary board. If his conduct violates state standards, file a complaint. Your lawyer may then be disciplined, possibly losing the right to practice law, temporarily or permanently. Finally, you can sue your lawyer for malpractice and seek reimbursement if he has acted negligently and your rights have been damaged. Consult a lawyer who handles professional liability cases for guidance.

Some critics say a major problem with the disciplinary process is that hearings are conducted behind closed doors, away from public scrutiny. To combat the impression that secrecy engenders distrust, many states are proposing to increase public access while attempting to safeguard the reputations of unfairly accused attorneys. This is a justifiable concern since the vast majority of lawyer disciplinary charges are unfounded. The best way to utilize the disciplinary process effectively is to speak with a representative at your state's grievance committee, thoroughly understand all the roles and procedures, and discuss your case with an experienced lawyer.

Complaints to grievance committees about attorney conduct have escalated and neglect has been one of the most common complaints. Neglect can be described as indifference and a consistent failure to carry out obligations involving more than a single act or omission; negligence may arise from a solitary significant error in judgment. To determine whether neglect has occurred, the trier of fact must analyze the length of the delay, the urgency of the legal matter, the complexity of the legal matter, the harm of the client, and the harm to the profession.

The best way a lawyer can avoid a neglect complaint is to be punctual to a client's legal matters. Once retained, the attorney should keep you informed of all developments and send copies of all correspondences and pleadings in a timely fashion. If nothing has transpired for a substantial period of time, the lawyer should write you a letter explaining why.

Consult another attorney before embarking on any course of action to learn if you have a valid malpractice action, negligence lawsuit or claim of neglect against the lawyer. An honest and unbiased attorney can tell you what steps should be taken to protect your rights. You should also speak to a representative from your state's lawyer's disciplinary committee for more information; each state has its own rules to file a charge and successfully proceed against a wrongdoing lawyer.

Anytime you go before the court, allow enough time with your lawyer ahead of the scheduled court appointment to privately review the objectives and options of the appearance. If your lawyer is not prepared to go into court, don't go. If your lawyer isn't prepared more than once, dismiss him and find a new attorney.

Another form of lawyer misconduct involves improper witness preparation. Preparing witnesses before they testify in a deposition or trial is a practical necessity. It is also an aspect of competent, zealous advocacy. If your lawyer is not devoting a sufficient amount of his time in this area, or is attempting to distort your testimony, consider discharging the lawyer.

Finally, when the case is over, ask the lawyer to send you a letter explaining that his or her representation has ended to eliminate the belief you have a lifetime retainer. Important documents in the file should also be returned to you.

Summary of Steps to Take to Use an Attorney Effectively

1. Speak to an attorney before action is contemplated to determine if one is needed.

2. Schedule an interview if necessary; inquire if you will be charged for it.

3. Bring relevant documents to the interview.

4. Do not be overly impressed by plush surroundings.

5. Be sure the lawyer of your choice will be handling the matter.

6. Hire an experienced practitioner who devotes at least 50 percent of his working time to litigating your type of problem.

7. Look for honesty and integrity in a lawyer.

8. Insist on signing a retainer agreement to reduce misunderstandings.

9. Have the agreement read and explained to you before signing, and save a copy for your files.

10. If the lawyer cannot state exactly how much you will be charged, get minimum and maximum estimates. Include this in the agreement.

11. Be certain you understand how additional costs are calculated and who will pay for them.

12. If an hourly rate is agreed on, negotiate that you will not be charged for a few telephone calls to your lawyer.

13. Inquire if you can pay the bill by credit card.

14. Structure the fee arrangement to maximize tax deductions and savings.

15. Insist on receiving copies of incoming and outgoing correspondence and monthly, detailed time records.

16. Be sure the lawyer will be available, will immediately commence work on your matter, and has no potential conflicts of interest.

17. Demand to be informed if for any reason your case cannot be resolved in a timely fashion.

18. Demand to be told if other lawyers will be involved in your representation.

19. Insist that communications with your attorney be confidential. Insist that your lawyer explain to you ahead of time when the statements you make or secrets you reveal about your case cannot be kept confidential.

20. Seek your attorney's advice before discussing any information relating to your legal matter with others.

21. Be on time for all court hearings and appointments with your attorney and let him or her know in advance if you cannot be on time.

22. Complete the tasks requested by your attorney in a timely fashion or let your attorney know when you cannot.

23. Insist that all funds received by the attorney be deposited into an interest-bearing escrow account. Don't forget to ask for the interest later on. If legal fees will be applied against a settlement, be sure your attorney provides you with a final statement after the matter is concluded

detailing what costs and expenses are being applied against your settlement and the amount you will receive.

24. Never allow the attorney to pressure you into settling a case or making a rushed, uninformed decision. Discuss your expectations about what you want to accomplish in your lawsuit with your attorney before and during his or her representation. Talk to your lawyer when your expectations are not being met.

25. Consult another attorney before deciding to fire the present one, file a complaint with the grievance committee, or commence a malpractice lawsuit. You have the right to change attorneys if you are dissatisfied with the representation you are receiving. However, under certain circumstances you will need the court's permission. It is also important for you to know that your attorney may decide to stop representing you. This may be due to you not meeting your financial obligations or for some other reason. This too may require court permission.

26. Don't sign a substitution of attorney form without first getting your file back.

27. Do not expect miracles.

Sample Statement of Client's Rights
(As adopted by the Administrative Board of the Court)

1. You are entitled to be treated with courtesy and consideration at all times by your lawyer and the other lawyers and personnel in your lawyer's office.

2. You are entitled to an attorney capable of handling your legal matter competently and diligently, in accordance with the highest standards of the profession. If you are not satisfied with how your matter is being handled, you have the right to withdraw from the attorney-client relationship at any time (court approval may be required in some matters and your attorney may have a claim against you for the value of services rendered to you up to the point of discharge).

3. You are entitled to your lawyer's independent professional judgment and undivided loyalty uncompromised by conflicts of interest.

4. You are entitled to be charged a reasonable fee and to have your lawyer explain at the outset how the fee will be computed and the manner and frequency of billing. You are entitled to request and receive a written itemized bill from your attorney at reasonable intervals. You may refuse to enter into any fee arrangement that you find unsatisfactory. In the event of a fee dispute, you may have the right to seek arbitration; your attorney will provide you with the necessary information regarding arbitration in the event of a fee dispute, or upon your request.

5. You are entitled to have your questions and concerns addressed in a prompt manner and to have your telephone calls returned promptly.

6. You are entitled to be kept informed as to the status of your matter and to request and receive copies of papers.

You are entitled to sufficient information to allow you to participate meaningfully in the development of your matter.

7. You are entitled to have your legitimate objectives respected by your attorney, including whether or not to settle your matter (court approval of a settlement is required in some matters).

8. You have the right to privacy in your dealings with your lawyer and to have your secrets and confidences preserved to the extent permitted by law.

9. You are entitled to have your attorney conduct himself or herself ethically in accordance with the Code of Professional Responsibility.

10. You may not be refused representation on the basis of race, creed, color, age, religion, sex, sexual orientation, national origin or disability.

**Prepared and presented by the
NEW YORK STATE BAR ASSOCIATION**

Sample Statement of Client's Responsibilities

Reciprocal trust, courtesy and respect are the hallmarks of the attorney-client relationship. Within that relationship, the client looks to the attorney for expertise, education, sound judgment, protection, advocacy and representation. These expectations can be achieved only if the client fulfills the following responsibilities:

1. The client is expected to treat the lawyer and the lawyer's staff with courtesy and consideration.

2. The client's relationship with the lawyer must be one of complete candor and the lawyer must be apprised of all facts or circumstances of the matter being handled by the lawyer even if the client believes that those facts may be detrimental to the client's cause or unflattering to the client.

3. The client must honor the fee arrangement as agreed to with the lawyer, in accordance with law.

4. All bills for services rendered which are tendered to the client pursuant to the agreed upon fee arrangement should be paid promptly.

5. The client may withdraw from the attorney-client relationship, subject to financial commitments under the agreed to fee arrangement, and, in certain circumstances, subject to court approval.

6. Although the client should expect that his or her correspondence, telephone calls and other communications will be answered within a reasonable time frame, the client should recognize that the lawyer has other clients equally demanding of the lawyer's time and attention.

7. The client should maintain contact with the lawyer, promptly notify the lawyer of any change in telephone number or address and respond promptly to a request by the lawyer for information and cooperation.

8. The client must realize that the lawyer need respect only legitimate objectives of the client and that the lawyer will not advocate or propose positions which are unprofessional or contrary to law or the Lawyer's Code of Professional Responsibility.

9. The lawyer may be unable to accept a case if the lawyer has previous professional commitments which will result in inadequate time being available for proper representation of a new client.

10. A lawyer is under no obligation to accept a client if the lawyer determines that the cause of the client is without merit, a conflict of interest would exist or that a suitable working relationship with the client is not likely.

**Prepared and presented by the
NEW YORK STATE BAR ASSOCIATION**

Conclusion

■ ■ ■ ■ ■ ■ ■ ■ ■

If you have read this book carefully and thoughtfully, you now have a hands-on guide to avoiding many of the employment problems you may face, and for those you cannot avoid, you have a guide on how to detect employer improprieties to protect your rights. Many of the items discussed in these pages encompass simple rules of common sense and reason.

The body of employment law has been created to further fairness and justice. It is there to protect you, but it will not help you unless you participate in your own defense. Before you make a major move, reread the appropriate portions of this book. Know the law. Discuss your situation with an attorney who specializes in labor and employment law. And, above all, good luck.

Steven Mitchell Sack, Esq.

Glossary of Terms

Abuse of process: A cause of action that arises when one party misuses the legal process to injure another.

Accord and satisfaction: An agreement between two parties, such as the employee and his or her company, to compromise disputes concerning outstanding debts, compensation, or terms of employment. Satisfaction occurs when the terms of the compromise are fully performed.

Action in accounting: A cause of action in which one party seeks a determination of the amount of money owed by another.

Admissible: Capable of being introduced in court as evidence.

Advance: A sum of money that is applied against money to be earned. Sometimes referred to as draw.

Affidavit: A written statement signed under oath.

Allegations: Written statements of a party to a lawsuit that charge the other party with wrongdoing. In order to be successful, allegations must be proved.

Answer: The defendant's reply to the plaintiff's allegations in a complaint.

Anticipatory breach: A breach of contract that occurs when one party, e.g., the employee, states in advance of performance that he or she will definitely not perform under the terms of his or her contract.

Appeal: A proceeding whereby the losing party to a lawsuit requests that a higher court determine the correctness of the decision.

Arbitration: A proceeding whereby both sides to a lawsuit agree to submit their dispute to arbitrators, rather than judges. The arbitration proceeding is expeditious and is legally binding on all parties.

Assignment: The transfer of a right or interest by one party to another.

Attorney in fact: A person appointed by another to transact business on his or her behalf; the person does not have to be a lawyer.

At-will employment: *See* Employment at will.

Award: A decision made by a judicial body to compensate the winning party in a lawsuit.

Bill of particulars: A document used in a lawsuit that specifically details the loss alleged by the plaintiff.

Breach of contract: A legal cause of action for the unjustified failure to perform a duty or obligation specified in an agreement.

Brief: A concise statement of the main contents of a lawsuit.

Burden of proof: The responsibility of a party to a lawsuit to provide sufficient evidence to prove or disprove a claim.

Business deduction: A legitimate expense that can be used to decrease the amount of income subject to tax.

Business slander: A legal wrong committed when a party orally makes false statements that impugn the business reputation of another (e.g., imply that the person is dishonest, incompetent, or financially unreliable).

Calendar: A list of cases to be heard each day in court.

Cause of action: The legal theory on which a plaintiff seeks to recover damages.

Caveat emptor: A Latin expression frequently applied to consumer transactions; translated as "Let the buyer beware."

Cease and desist letter: A letter, usually sent by lawyer, that notifies an individual to stop engaging in a particular type of activity, behavior, or conduct that infringes on the rights of another.

Check: A negotiable instrument; the depositor's written order requesting his or her bank to pay a definite sum of money to a named individual, entity, or to the bearer.

Civil court: Generally, any court that presides over noncriminal matters.

Claims court: A particular court that hears tax disputes.

Clerk of the court: A person who determines whether court papers are properly filed and court procedures followed.

Collateral estoppel: *See* Estoppel. Collateral estoppel happens when a prior but different legal action is conclusive in a way to bring about estoppel in a current legal action.

Common law: Law that evolves from reported case decisions that are relied on for their precedential value.

Compensatory damages: A sum of money, awarded to a party, that represents the actual harm suffered or loss incurred.

Complaint: A legal document that commences a lawsuit; it alleges facts and causes of action that a plaintiff relies on to collect damages.

Conflict of interest: The ethical inability of a lawyer to represent a client because of competing loyalties, e.g., representing both employer and employee in a labor dispute.

Consideration: An essential element of an enforceable contract; something of value given or promised by one party in exchange for an act or promise of another.

Contempt: A legal sanction imposed when a rule or order of a judicial body is disobeyed.

Contingency fee: A type of fee arrangement whereby a lawyer is paid a percentage of the money recovered. If unsuccessful, the client is responsible only for costs already paid by the lawyer.

Continuance: The postponement of a legal proceeding to another date.

Contract: An enforceable agreement, either written, oral, or implied by the actions or intentions of the parties.

Contract modification: The alteration of contract terms.

Counterclaim: A claim asserted by a defendant in a lawsuit.

Covenant: A promise.

Credibility: The believability of a witness as perceived by a judge or jury.

Creditor: The party to whom money is owed.

Cross-examination: The questioning of a witness by the opposing lawyer.

Damage: An award, usually money, given to the winning party in a lawsuit as compensation for the wrongful acts of another.

Debtor: The party who owes money.

Decision: The determination of a case or matter by a judicial body.

Deductible: The unrecoverable portion of insurance proceeds.

Defamation: An oral or written statement communicated to a third party that impugns a person's reputation in the community.

Default judgment: An award rendered after one party fails to appear in a lawsuit.

Defendant: The person or entity who is sued in a lawsuit.

Defense: The defendant's justification for relieving himself or herself of fault.

Definite term of employment: Employment of a fixed period of time.

Deposition: A pretrial proceeding in which one party is questioned, usually under oath, by the opposing party's lawyer.

Disclaimer: A clause in a sales, service, or other contract that attempts to limit or exonerate one party from liability in the event of a lawsuit.

Discovery: A general term used to describe several pretrial devices (e.g., depositions and interrogatories) that enable lawyers to elicit information from the opposing side.

Dual capacity: A legal theory, used to circumvent workers' compensation laws, that allows an injured employee to sue his or her employer directly in court.

Due process: Constitutional protections that guarantee that a person's life, liberty, or property cannot be taken away without the opportunity to be heard in a judicial proceeding.

Duress: Unlawful threats, pressure, or force that induces a person to act contrary to his or her intentions; if proved, it allows a party to disavow a contract.

Employee: A person who works and is subject to an employer's scope, direction, and control.

Employment at will: Employment by which an employee has no job security.

Employment discrimination: Conduct directed at employees and job applicants that is prohibited by law.

Equity: Fairness; usually applied when a judicial body awards a suitable remedy other than money to a party (e.g., an injunction).

Escrow account: A separate fund where lawyers or others are obligated to deposit money received from or on behalf of a client.

Estoppel: A legal bar to prevent a party from asserting a fact or claim inconsistent with that party's prior position that has been relied on or acted on by another party.

Evidence: Information in the form of oral testimony, exhibits, affidavits, etc., used to prove a party's claim.

Examination before trial: A pretrial legal device; also called a deposition.

Exhibit: Tangible evidence used to prove a party's claim.

Exit agreement: An agreement sometimes signed between an employer and an employee on resignation or termination of an employee's services.

Express contract: An agreement whose terms are manifested by clear and definite language, as distinguished from agreements inferred from conduct.

False imprisonment: The unlawful detention of a person who is held against his or her will without authority or justification.

Filing fee: Money paid to start a lawsuit.

Final decree: A court order or directive of a permanent nature.

Financial statement: A document, usually prepared by an accountant, that reflects a business's (or individual's) assets, liabilities, and financial condition.

Flat fee: A sum of money paid to a lawyer as compensation for services.

Flat fee plus time: A form of payment in which a lawyer receives one sum for services and also receives additional money calculated on an hourly basis.

Fraud: A false statement that is relied on and causes damages to the defrauded party.

General denial: A reply contained in the defendant's answer.

Ground: The basis for an action or an argument.

Guaranty: A contract in which one party agrees to answer for or satisfy the debt of another.

Hearsay evidence: Unsubstantiated evidence that is often excluded by a court.

Hourly fee: Money paid to a lawyer for services, computed on an hourly basis.

Implied contract: An agreement that is tacit rather than expressed in clear and definite language; an agreement inferred from the conduct of the parties.

Indemnification: Protection or reimbursement against damage or loss. The indemnified party is protected against liabilities or penalties from that party's actions; the indemnifying party provides the protection or reimbursement.

Infliction of emotional distress: A legal cause of action in which one party seeks to recover damages for mental pain and suffering caused by another.

Injunction: A court order restraining one party from doing or refusing to do an act.

Integration: The act of making a contract whole by integrating its elements into a coherent single entity. An agreement is considered integrated when the parties involved accept the final version as a complete expression of their agreement.

Interrogatories: A pretrial device used to elicit information; written questions are sent to an opponent to be answered under oath.

Invasion of privacy: The violation of a person's constitutionally protected right to privacy.

Judgment: A verdict rendered by a judicial body; if money is awarded, the winning party is the "judgment creditor" and the losing party is the "judgment debtor."

Jurisdiction: The authority of a court to hear a particular matter.

Legal duty: The responsibility of a party to perform a certain act.

Letter of agreement: An enforceable contract in the form of a letter.

Letter of protest: A letter sent to document a party's dissatisfaction.

Liable: Legally in the wrong or legally responsible for.

Lien: A claim made against the property of another in order to satisfy a judgment.

Lifetime contract: An employment agreement of infinite duration that is often unenforceable.

Liquidated damages: An amount of money agreed on in advance by parties to a contract to be paid in the event of a breach or dispute.

Malicious interference with contractual rights: A legal cause of action in which one party seeks to recover damages against an individual who has induced or caused another party to terminate a valid contract.

Malicious prosecution: A legal cause of action in which one party seeks to recover damages after another party instigates or institutes a frivolous judicial proceeding (usually criminal) that is dismissed.

Mediation: A voluntary dispute resolution process in which both sides attempt to settle their differences without resorting to formal litigation.

Misappropriation: A legal cause of action that arises when one party makes untrue statements of fact that induce another party to act and be damaged as a result.

Mitigation of damages: A legal principle that requires a party seeking damages to make reasonable efforts to reduce damages as much as possible, e.g., to seek new employment after being unfairly discharged.

Motion: A written request made to a court by one party during a lawsuit.

Negligence: A party's failure to exercise a sufficient degree of care owed to another by law.

Nominal damages: A small sum of money awarded by a court.

Noncompetition clause: A restrictive provision in a contract that limits an employee's right to work in that particular industry after he or she ceases to be associated with his or her present employer.

Notary public: A person authorized under state law to administer an oath or verify a signature.

Notice to show cause: A written document in a lawsuit asking a court to expeditiously rule on a matter.

Objection: A formal protest made by a lawyer in a lawsuit.

Offer: The presentment of terms, which, if accepted, may lead to the formation of a contract.

Opinion letter: A written analysis of a client's case, prepared by a lawyer.

Option: An agreement giving one party the right to choose a certain course of action.

Oral contract: An enforceable verbal agreement.

Parol evidence: Oral evidence introduced at a trial to alter or explain the terms of a written agreement.

Partnership: A voluntary association between two or more competent persons engaged in a business as co-owners for profit.

Party: A plaintiff or defendant in a lawsuit.

Perjury: Committing false testimony while under oath.

Petition: A request filed in court by one party.

Plaintiff: The party who commences a lawsuit.

Pleading: A written document that states the facts or arguments put forth by a party in a lawsuit.

Power of attorney: A document executed by one party allowing another to act on his or her behalf in specified situations.

Pretrial discovery: A legal procedure used to gather information from an opponent before the trial.

Process server: An individual who delivers the summons and/or complaint to the defendant.

Promissory note: A written acknowledgment of a debt whereby one party agrees to pay a specified sum on a specified date.

Proof: Evidence presented at a trial and used by a judge or jury to fashion an award.

Punitive damages: Money awarded as punishment for a party's wrongful acts.

Quantum meruit: A legal principle whereby a court awards reasonable compensation to a party who performs work, labor, or services at another party's request.

Rebuttal: The opportunity for a lawyer at a trial to ask a client or witness additional questions to clarify points elicited by the opposing lawyer during cross-examination.

Release: A written document that, when signed, relinquishes a party's rights to enforce a claim against another.

Remedy: The means by which a right is enforced or protected.

Reply: A written document in a lawsuit conveying the contentions of a party in response to a motion.

Restrictive covenant: A provision in a contract that forbids one party from doing a certain act, e.g., working for another, soliciting customers.

Retainer: A sum of money paid to a lawyer for services to be rendered.

Service letter statutes: Laws in some states that require an employer to furnish an employee with written reasons for his or her discharge.

Sexual harassment: Prohibited conduct of a sexual nature that occurs in the workplace.

Shop rights: The rights of an employer to use within the employer's facility a device or method developed by an employee.

Slander: Oral defamation of a party's reputation.

Small-claims court: A particular court that presides over small disputes (e.g., those involving sums of less than $3,500).

Sole proprietorship: An unincorporated business.

Statement of fact: Remarks or comments of a specific nature that have a legal effect.

Statute: A law created by a legislative body.

Statute of frauds: A legal principle requiring that certain contracts be in writing in order to be enforceable.

Statute of limitations: A legal principle requiring a party to commence a lawsuit within a certain period of time.

Stipulation: An agreement between the parties.

Submission agreement: A signed agreement whereby both parties agree to submit a present dispute to binding arbitration.

Subpoena: A written order requiring a party or witness to appear at a legal proceeding; a *subpoena duces tecum* is a written order requiring a party to bring books and records to the legal proceeding.

Summation: The last part of the trial wherein both lawyers recap the respective positions of their clients.

Summons: A written document served on a defendant giving notification of a lawsuit.

Temporary decree: A court order or directive of a temporary nature, capable of being modified or changed.

Testimony: Oral evidence presented by a witness under oath.

"Time is of the essence": A legal expression often included in agreements to specify the requirements of timeliness.

Tort: A civil wrong.

Unfair and deceptive practice: Illegal business and trade acts prohibited by various federal and state laws.

Unfair discharge: An employee's termination without legal justification.

Verdict: The decision of a judge or jury.

Verification: A written statement signed under oath.

Waiver: A written document that, when signed, relinquishes a party's rights.

Whistle-blowing: Protected conduct where one party complains about the illegal acts of another.

Witness: A person who testifies at a judicial proceeding.

Workers' compensation: A process in which an employee receives compensation for injuries sustained in the course of employment.

Index

Pro se representation, 286, 508-514
Public Health Service, 299
Punitive damages, 458, 474

Q

Quid pro quo sexual harassment,
212

R

Racial discrimination, 260-265
    affirmative action plans,
        264-265
    in hiring, 265
    in hiring interview, 261
Racketeer Influenced and Corrupt
    Organizations Act (RICO), 28,
    422
Raises, 46
Rastafari beliefs, 268
Rebuttal statements, 114, 325, 328
References, 372-373
Religious discrimination, 265-269
Relocation expenses, 46-47
Resignations, 338, 372, 401-408
    sample letter of resignation,
        407-408
Rest room visits, 157-158
Restrictive covenants, 50-53, 324,
    408-417
Retaliation discrimination, 88, 105,
    277-281, 439-440
Retiree medical benefits, 95-96,
    321-322
Retirement plans and forced
    retirement, 242-247. See also
    Pensions and profit-sharing plans

Ricci v. DeStefano, 264-265
Rights of due process, 140-150
Rights of privacy, 109-150
    of employees, 117-120
    of gays and lesbians, 219
    of job applicants, 19
Right to sue letter, 284, 286, 288

S

Safety in the workplace, 158-161
Salary, 555
Sarbanes-Oxley Act (SOX),
    301-305
Searches, 117-120
Securities and Exchange
    Commission (SEC), 302-303
Severance letter laws, 440-441
Severance pay, 47, 349-357
Sex discrimination, 202-233
    abortions, 229
    equal pay, 206-210
    federal statutes, 203
    hiring interviews, 222
    hostile intimidating
        environment, 213
    in benefits, 221-222
    independent contractors, 222
    office romances, 156
    pregnancy, 223-233
    sample letter protesting sexual
        harassment, 218
    sexual harassment, 127,
        210-219
Shop right concept, 191
Slander, 120, 131, 136, 436

About the Author

■ ■ ■ ■ ■ ■ ■

STEVEN MITCHELL SACK maintains a private law practice in New York City where he handles severance negotiations of terminated workers and executives, discrimination lawsuits, representation of salespeople and employees in breach of contract and commission disputes, wage and hour violations, and general labor law. He is a Phi Beta Kappa graduate of the State University of New York at Stony Brook and graduated from Boston College Law School with a Juris Doctor degree in 1979.

Mr. Sack is the author of many legal books for the American public, including *The Lifetime Legal Guide*, *The Working Woman's Legal Survival Guide,* and *Getting Fired*. His views on employment law have been reported in *The Wall Street Journal, The New York Times*, *Fortune*, *BusinessWeek*, and other well-known publications and magazines. He has appeared on *The Oprah Winfrey Show*, *Jenny Jones, The Sally Jesse Raphael Show*, *CNN*, *Smart Money* and *Steals and Deals* on CNBC. He also hosted a weekly radio talk show called "Steven Sack, The Employee's Lawyer" for five years through the i.e. america radio network.

Mr. Sack is the president of Legal Strategies Inc., a publishing firm. He is a member of the American Bar Association Labor and Employment Sections and is admitted to practice before the U. S. Tax Court. He has worked as a commercial and labor arbitrator for the American Arbitration Association, conducts seminars on employment issues for both employee and employer groups, and for more than two decades serves on the employment panel of the New York City Legal Referral Service. He has also been engaged by law firms throughout the United States to strategize cases and testify as an expert witness.

Mr. Sack is married and has two sons. He enjoys boating and sports in his spare time. To learn more about Steven Mitchell Sack, visit his home page at www.TheEmployeesLawyer.com.

Additional copies of
The Employee Rights Handbook
are available through your favorite
book dealer or from the publisher:

Legal Strategies Publications
1795 Harvard Avenue
Merrick, NY 11566
Telephone: (917) 371-8000
Fax: (516) 623-9115
E-mail: LegalStrategies@hotmail.com
Website: www.TheEmployeesLawyer.com

The Employee Rights Handbook
(ISBN: 978-0-9636306-7-4)
is $39.95 for hardbound edition, plus
$5.50 shipping for first copy
($2.00 each additional copy)
and sales tax for NY and OH orders.

If you wish to contact Steven Mitchell Sack, his
E-mail address is stevensackatty@hotmail.com
and phone number is (917) 371-8000 or
(212) 702-8843